THE
INCREDIBLE
IVAR KREUGER

The Incredible Ivar Kreuger

BY ALLEN CHURCHILL

RINEHART & COMPANY, INC.

New York
Toronto

Published simultaneously in Canada by
Clarke, Irwin & Company, Ltd., Toronto

© 1957 by Allen Churchill
Printed in the United States of America
Library of Congress Catalog Card Number: 57-5057

ACKNOWLEDGMENTS

Grateful acknowledgment is made to the following for permission to reprint material from their publications:

The Auxiliary Council to the Association for the Advancement of Psychoanalysis, New York, N.Y., and Dr. Ralph Slater, for permission to reprint excerpts from his pamphlet, "Narcissism Versus Self-Love."

Peter Davies, Ltd., London, England, for permission to reprint excerpts from THE FINANCIER: The Life of Ivar Kreuger, by George Soloveytchik.

The New York Times, for permission to reprint excerpts from the column of Jules Sauerwein which appeared in *The New York Times* of April 22, 1932.

CONTENTS

THE
INCREDIBLE
IVAR KREUGER

End and Beginning

At approximately 11 A.M. on the morning of March 12, 1932, a man with a sallow, puffy, immobile face stretched himself out on a bed in an expensively furnished third-floor apartment on the Avenue Victor Emmanuel, in Paris.

Lying flat on his back, he pushed back the coat and vest of his conservative suit to expose his white shirt. Then he lifted up a heavy revolver until it pointed directly at the left side of his chest. With a skill typical of most of his earthly acts, he pulled the trigger and fired a bullet into the exact center of his heart—a feat which, Paris police later declared, occurs only once in ten thousand such suicides.

The man who ended his life with such unerring dispatch was Ivar Kreuger, the Match King, and to those who would shortly be composing his obituaries, he was a fascinating figure. One would call him: "An all-omniscient ghost, stealing silently among men, arranging vast deals imperturbably, achieving all he wished with satanic adroitness."

Others would stress that in life he had been content to immerse himself in high finance, deriving his satisfaction from the accumulation of power, rather than from the softer pleasures money can bring. More than any other man alive, the solitary, Swedish-born Kreuger had represented the lone wolf among contemporary titans of finance. He was a remote, mysterious man whose towering and nearly accomplished dream it had been to control every match manufactured and sold on the face of the earth. A lifelong bachelor, he had made himself into a man far too preoccupied with power to care how much he ate or slept, or even how he dressed. He had been a man much too busy to enjoy society or the company of women. And, of course, such a man was far above having a sex life.

In the hours immediately following his death, all the power the Match King had accumulated in life seemed to remain with him. Acting on orders from high in the French government, Paris police kept his suicide a secret for five long hours. This was done because March twelfth fell on a Saturday, a day the New York Stock Exchange closed at noon. When Kreuger killed himself it was shortly after 7 A.M., New York time. In the high echelons of finance it was deemed best to keep the news of his death a secret until the Wall Street Exchange had closed.

But shortly after 5 P.M. in Paris the news was permitted to break, and all over the 1932 world its impact was enormous. In New York, newspapers shoved the eleven-day-old Lindbergh kidnaping, already rated the Crime of the Century, off front pages to headline: KREUGER, MATCH KING, A SUICIDE. Kreuger was a world figure because hundreds of thousands of people, especially in the United States, owned Kreuger stocks and securities, or regarded as extremely fortunate anyone who did. Since October, 1929, when the financial structure toppled, the world had been undergoing a period of deepest Depression. Alone among contemporary investments, the Kreuger companies—International Match, Kreuger & Toll, Swedish Match—had continued to pay dividends of a pre-1929 variety. But there was more. Among contemporary financiers and statesmen, Ivar Kreuger alone had appeared able to retain faith in a speedy recovery for a depression-ridden world and in the over-all financial future. As practically the only optimist remaining in high places, Kreuger's views had often been sought by heads of governments, and his frequent conferences with President Hoover in Washington were said to act as a tonic on the mind of that much-beset man. Kreuger's opinions were equally popular with the journalists of the world, and only a few weeks before his death he had been searchingly interviewed as the basis for an article in *The Saturday Evening Post*. Altogether, the figure of the Match King had so caught the imagination of the world that when news of the inscrutable man's death flashed over the wires the *London Daily Express* reported the sky seeming to darken and "the same thoughts came to men as when Caesar died."

Not unnaturally, the news hit hardest in Kreuger's native Sweden—and in Nice, where the tennis-playing King Gustav of Sweden, enjoying a winter vacation, was sitting down to dinner when word was brought to him. In Stockholm the Regent, Prince Gustavus Adolphus, was attending the Masonic induction of his oldest son when an aide suddenly appeared to whisper in his ear. The Prince jumped to his feet and hurried to the Royal Palace, where he instructed that all Cabinet members be summoned to an emergency meeting. The Cabinet meeting had hardly got underway when word came that King Gustav had boarded a plane and was flying home to be with his people in their hour of sorrow.

As the news seeped through Stockholm, crowds gathered on street corners to discuss the national tragedy in sorrowful whispers. For in Sweden Kreuger had been a person of the utmost importance, perhaps even outranking the King. In a period when the country had withdrawn from an active part in world affairs, he had brought it back to prominence in world finance, at least. It made him a hero to the Swedish nation, and especially to citizens of Stockholm who often saw him being driven through the streets in his glistening

Rolls Royce limousine, or occasionally afoot, a tall, prim, bankerish figure, who always seemed to carry with him an air of intense preoccupation, a neat dispatch case, and a cane. Practically to a man, the people of Stockholm felt numb, as if on their peaceful city some enemy had suddenly and inexplicably dropped a bomb.

On Sunday, at midnight, the first moment the Sabbath would permit, the Swedish Parliament met in hasty session. But all the repercussions from the Match King's suicide were not confined to his native country. In Basle, Switzerland, the Bank for International Settlements, which owed its existence largely to Kreuger, called members to a Monday meeting. In Paris, Premier Tardieu swept his calendar clear to allow for a lengthy conference with the Swedish Ambassador, while in Estonia, in seeming emulation of his departed chief, the head of the Kreuger-controlled State match monopoly locked a door behind him and killed himself with a pistol shot.

On Wall Street, the highly respected firm of Lee, Higginson & Company, which for ten years had sponsored Kreuger stocks on the American market, had been the first to learn of his suicide. Immediately after the close of the Exchange on Saturday noon, it issued a reassuring statement declaring that the Match King's sudden death could have no possible effect on the soundness of his world-girdling affairs.

Yet on Monday the New York Stock Exchange—as well as others the world over—opened to turmoil. Kreuger stocks were dumped so fast that the ticker could not keep up. One transaction involved 673,000 shares, the largest yet known on the Exchange. Nothing like this had been seen since the actual days of the 1929 Crash, and it made one harried broker call out to a passing *New York Times* reporter, "Everybody's unloading but the cannibals in Africa."

Still, such activity, hysterical though it might be, was

only natural in the event of the death of an important financier. One of the vital props had suddenly been removed from the shaky international structure. As days went by, with Lee, Higginson issuing further statements of reassurance, sanity seemed to return to the New York Exchange. It was reasoned that someone else would be appointed to step into the shoes of the awesome Swede, taking over his gigantic holdings and perhaps handling them as well as the Match King himself. Gradually, most of those who had unloaded so frantically began to wish they had not. Many even began buying Kreuger stocks again.

So in the days between Kreuger's suicide on March twelfth and his funeral in Stockholm on March twenty-second, the international financial balance slowly righted itself, and Kreuger was mourned by the people of the world as a martyr whose life had been cut short at the age of fifty-two by the upset financial times.

But in Stockholm, the hub of the Kreuger universe, a curious development could be observed. Many of the men of international money who had journeyed to attend the Match King's funeral seemed unable to leave the city. As if restrained by an invisible hand, or held by a premonition of coming events, they retained their suites in the Grand Hotel and sat in the lobby waiting, accepting calmly, as if inevitable, such surprising developments as the appointment by the Swedish government of an Investigating Committee to examine Kreuger books, and the swooping down by Stockholm police on Kreuger's ornamental Match Palace headquarters where all memos and even the contents of wastebaskets had been officially impounded.

But the most important development was one few were aware of. Waiting until the hours just before dawn so that he could board a plane unseen, Sweden's Foreign Minister

Hellner flew to Rome, where on landing he was taken immediately to the presence of Benito Mussolini. After making sure that he and the Italian Dictator were alone, Hellner inquired whether several years before Kreuger had loaned Italy a huge sum of money in return for a monopoly on match manufacture and sale within the country. Mussolini shook his head in an emphatic negative. "Signor Kreuger and I discussed such a loan twice," he stated. "Once was in 1927 and again in 1930. We were never able to come to terms."

"But," the elderly Hellner protested, "shortly after Herr Kreuger's recent suicide we found in his private safety vaults two series of Italian notes. The first consisted of forty-two Bonds, each worth £500,000 sterling and signed by the Director General of the Italian Government Monopolies, Giovanni Boselli. These were also guaranteed by the Kingdom of Italy and signed by Finance Minister Antonio Mosconi. The second series consisted of five notes, each worth £1,533,700 sterling, also issued by the Italian Government Monopolies through Signor Boselli."

With which, he extracted from his dispatch case the $143,342,500 in notes, and placed them on Mussolini's desk. The Dictator lifted one and examined it carefully, his eyes pausing at the signature of his Finance Minister, Mosconi. Then he dropped that Bond to pick up one of the other series, studying the signatures of both Mosconi and Boselli. Suddenly he flung the Bond on his desk and leaped to his feet. "Those signatures are forged!" he shouted in tones of outrage.

It may have been what Foreign Minister Hellner feared he would say, but still it was a shock. "Forged?" he gasped.

"Forged," Mussolini repeated with the greatest finality. "It is so evident you can see for yourself."

Taking a genuine State document from his desk, he

showed Hellner the signatures of both Mosconi and Boselli. Mosconi's true signature did not include the first initial A., though all the signatures on the Bonds had that letter. Also there was considerable difference in the formation of the letter M, nor did the forgeries end with the comma Mosconi always placed after his signed name. As for Boselli's name, it was not even spelled correctly in the forgeries.

Hellner slumped back in his chair. The best he could do was request Mussolini to summon Mosconi and Boselli. If they too called the signatures forgeries, he would need a statement to that effect to carry back to Stockholm. "I would like a joint statement by Mosconi and Boselli, with your signature to attest it," he requested weakly.

The two ministers arrived and promptly denied ever having seen, much less signed, the Bonds. Mussolini dictated a statement which the three men signed. Hellner put it with the forgeries into his dispatch case and began the unhappy trip back to Stockholm.

Now the rumors began. Fanning out from Stockholm to other world capitals, they whispered not only of the forged Italian Bonds, but quoted one member of the newly formed Investigating Committee as saying that what was being found in the Kreuger books was "beyond belief." Another member supposedly had described the ledgers as being in a state of chaotic confusion. It was true, he said, that some entries in them led to transactions that were legitimate and aboveboard. But far more disappeared into a labyrinthine maze of swindle and deceit. The investigators were unearthing private Kreuger banks all over Europe, but they were banks existing on paper only, to safeguard nonexistent assets. There were holding companies and sub-holding companies, all of which seemed in fact to hold nothing. There were secret, unsuspected companies dealing with secret, unsuspected funds. There were faked balance sheets, false bookkeeping entries, properties mortgaged again and again, assets created out of thin air, securities boldly faked, and signatures clumsily forged.

Now the Stock Exchanges really tottered, while a wave of suicides swept over Sweden, the country that had been so proud of its Match King. In Vatican City the Pope heard and sadly began pondering an Encyclical to be titled Money Is the Root of All Evil. For if the stories coming from Stockholm were true, they pointed incontrovertibly to one hand. It was the hand of a criminal, a shadowy, two-faced figure who, as the sums linked to his name rose from millions to hundred millions to billions, could no longer be called an ordinary criminal. He was a master criminal—an archcriminal—if all this was to be believed, the greatest swindler the world had ever known.

It was to be believed. In Stockholm, verification was contained in the preliminary report of the Investigating Committee. In the United States, it came with the abrupt bankruptcy of the International Match Corporation, which had always operated from Wall Street. And now around the world people turned from the still-unsolved Lindbergh case to watch as another story of titanic crime unfolded. It was shocking, but with it there seemed to go strangely little bitterness. Instead, the reaction seemed to be awe, a kind of grudging wonder, with perhaps a slight feeling of excitement at having been alive in the same period as one of the greatest criminals of all time. It was a feeling expressed by a financial writer who, temporarily setting aside facts and figures, declared, "If he was a crook, he must have been a crook of an exceedingly attractive kind."

But how had he done it? Kreuger had not been an ordinary man. He had moved among the most admired figures of his time, the bankers, the financiers, the capitalists, the super-men of Wall Street. If he had deceived the world, he had deceived these men first, for it was their confidence in him which gave the Match King his first claim to the respect of the great world public. But since the end of the American Civil War it had been a truism that these hardheaded, ruth-less, mighty men of money could not be fooled.

Yet he *had* fooled them. True, he had been an undoubted business genius, but he had used this genius chiefly to create a purposely tangled maze of international corporations. Into them with one hand he had poured hundreds of millions in legitimate profits, while with the other hand he had whisked the money away without leaving a trace. His millions had been shifted from nation to nation, corporation to corpora-tion, without being moved from his desk. A cable to Wall Street, a telephone call to Amsterdam, a wire to Zurich, and trusting bookkeepers would enter the sum in their different books. Or perhaps it would simply be debited, in Stockholm, to Kreuger himself. Investigators were discovering hundreds of entries where the magician of money had apparently wearied of his endless financial legerdemain and merely charged the vast amounts off to himself. To only one of his apparently countless companies, he owed the sum of $107 million—which is to say the money had completely disap-peared.

Of this new, emerging Kreuger, a writer now stated: "Financial genius or gifted rogue, superman or impostor, sane or mad, he cannot readily be reduced to human dimen-sions." It was true, for the paradoxes only increased. . . . The archcriminal had been born with advantages in brains and breeding. . . . He had been able to make millions legitimately, seemingly enough for any man. . . . With all his wealth and power, he had lived a hidden, shadowlike existence. . . . He had looked down on his fellow man, and his fellow man had responded by looking up to him.

Certainly an incredible man—and slowly the question of how he had done it ceased to be the vital one. In a world just becoming conscious of the true depths of human motives, his contemporaries began asking another question. Joining the *how* of Ivar Kreuger was the *why*. Why as well as how had Kreuger done it?

The answers—if answers they be—must begin in a quiet, historic locality. . . .

Chapter 2

A Scoundrel Is Born

The town of Kalmar, in Sweden, is a pleasant place. Lying some 250 miles south-southwest of Stockholm, it is one of the most picturesque towns in all Scandinavia, with quaint, slant-roofed houses built along winding streets, nearly all of which find their way to the crystal-blue Baltic, only partially shut off by the large island of Oland, which Kalmar faces.

"The pace of life is slow and measured there," a guidebook says of Kalmar, and there is a reason. Only a third of the town lies on the mainland, while the rest covers two closely adjacent islands. On one island looms a constant reminder to Kalmarites of the limitlessness of time and the fickleness of fortune. This reminder is a gigantic medieval castle, gabled, turreted, warlike, "with deep-echoing chambers and immense round bastions pitted with embrasures and loopholes," recalling to all who pass by land or sea the days when Sweden was a world power, standing shoulder to warlike shoulder with Russia, France and England.

This mighty pile is Kalmarnahus—Castle Kalmar—and it has always made a visit to Kalmar akin to entering a bygone century. Architecturally, Kalmarnahus ranks with the two other great castles of Sweden, Gripsholm and Vadstena, all three powerfully expressing, in their strong proportions and vast dimensions, the rugged manliness of the Viking builders.

Castle Kalmar as seen today is largely a reconstruction of the noble fortress begun in the twelfth century and completed in the sixteenth and seventeenth. Through medieval years of battles, feuds, massacres, attacks, victories and defeats, it was known as the Key to Sweden, since its strategic position allowed it to face the east and ominous Russia. Yet it is an odd fact that in history, Kalmarnahus is remembered for an act of peace rather than one of war. In 1397, Queen Margaret, the most formidable ruler of medieval Scandinavia, established herself in the newly constructed castle long enough to proclaim the Kalmar Union, which brought under her queenly sceptre the largest kingdom in the Europe of the day, a union of Norway, Sweden and Denmark, the most important of the three nations being Denmark.

Then for the next three hundred years the focus of history left Kalmar. Time slowly passed until, in the middle 1600's, a ship loaded with emigrants set out from the shadow of Kalmarnahus. Fittingly, it was named *Kalmar Nyckel*, and after crossing the Atlantic the rugged ship arrived on the coast of Delaware, where it set down the first Swedish colonists to reach the New World.

After that Kalmar returned to its contented picturesqueness, while the Swedish nation, oldest and purest of the so-called Aryan bloods, slowly retired from the turmoil of European politics to become a nation and a people dedicated less to war than to physical fitness, spiritual poise and a tempered life.

Winters in Kalmar were, of course, long and during them the town took on a Christmas-card beauty. White, piled winter snows, contrasting blue sea, looming castle, low houses, all combined to make it seem like a medieval painting. For nearly eight months of the year it was hemmed in by heavy mountains of snow. Through those months the only sounds to disturb the hushed stillness would come from the tinkling of sleigh bells and the happy shouts of children as they threw snowballs at each other. Or as, with bright stocking caps streaming behind, they hurtled on skis down the slopes leading to the town.

In summer, life in Kalmar changed. By May the days began to lengthen—ever an alarming phenomenon to strangers from other countries. Longer and longer the daylight hours grew until in mid-June it was Midsummer Night, with the sun sinking just before midnight, to rise again only fifteen minutes later. This made Sweden indeed the Land of the Midnight Sun, and after it came other seemingly endless days when in seaside towns like Kalmar swimming, boating and all-night picnics under the twilight glow of the Midnight Sun took the place of winter sport.

But again the stream of history washed over the tranquil little town when in our time Kalmar produced a strange and enigmatic figure, a man who—no less than Queen Margaret of medieval times, who conquered her world—tried to conquer his. Unlike Margaret, he did not use force of arms. Instead, he tried intellect, well bolstered by a conviction that, for him alone among men, achievement of ends sublimely justified any means. He made himself one of the most honored and respected men alive, achieving for a Swede a world-fame comparable to that of Emperor-King Charles XII who, with his Swedish armies, ranged far enough afield to engage the Turk. He rubbed elbows with kings, prime ministers, presidents, titans of finance. He even dictated to heads of state. But in him the gratification of one great ambition merely led to the creation of another. Never once in life did he seem satisfied. Always he seemed impelled to push on to greater conquests. This Swede who again brought the tide of history to Kalmar seemed to be living out the words of

Goethe's Faust: *"Zwei Seelen wohnen, ach, in meiner Brust*
—Two souls, alas, are living in my breast."

Such a man was Ivar Kreuger and, to add to his strange-
ness, his beginnings in Kalmar were commonplace. He was
born a stone's throw from the looming Kalmarnahus on
March 2, 1880, of stock which would seem to be of the
soundest Sweden could offer. On his father's side there was
Teutonic blood, for in 1710 a German baker named Johann
Kröger herded his family into a small boat and sailed from
the politically dependent province of Pommern, or Wismar,
across the Baltic to Sweden. He settled in Kalmar, where he
landed, and shortly his sons were marrying Swedish girls and
his daughters finding Swedish men. Johann Kröger set up
new ovens in Kalmar and continued life as a baker. His oldest son succeeded him at the family trade, but his oldest
grandson, Peter, broke away from tradition to become a shop-
keeper. It was he who changed his name to the more
Swedish Kreuger, and after him no member of the family
was ever a baker. Instead, the Kreuger men became members
of the guild-craftsman class, coppersmiths and merchants. A
few adventurous family members went to sea, and one even
became an Admiral of the Swedish Navy. After the Admiral
had been honorably retired, a national poll was conducted
to select the most honest man in all Sweden, to be entrusted
with a diplomatic mission of the utmost responsibility. Admiral Kreuger was voted Sweden's Most Honest Man. He
handled the important mission successfully, and returned to
live out a life of still more honorable retirement. Years later,
when Ivar Kreuger was congratulated on having such a noble
ancestor, he always seemed to turn his face aside.

By 1830, Johann Kröger's descendants had ceased to
think of themselves as possessing German blood. They were
now indubitably Swedes, the more so because in that year

Peter's grandson, Anders Lorentz Kreuger, achieved the status of highly respected businessman. He became senior partner in the Kalmar shipping firm of Kreuger & Jennings, and soon added to this eminence by also representing Russian interests in Kalmar—for in those days foreign countries did not appoint consuls to seaport towns, but utilized outstanding local businessmen instead. As Russia's representative, Anders was entitled to be called Consul Kreuger, but this did not confine his dealings with the outside world to his employer country. From 1860–65, Kreuger & Jennings did a lively trade, despite the wartime blockade, with America's Confederate States.

Anders's oldest son, Pehr Edvard Kreuger, further advanced the family fortunes by marrying Sophia Amelia von Sydow, daughter of the wealthiest man in Kalmar. Prosperous Pehr Edvard begat three sons, the oldest Ernst August. In time, Ernst started his working life as manager of a match factory in nearby Fredricksdahl. For an ambitious young man in Kalmar—as Ernst August was—choice of the match business was far from unusual. Kalmar lay in the province of Småland, the chief match-producing region in Sweden. To say this also meant the entire world, for immediately after the invention of matches in Germany—probably by the chemist-revolutionary Ludwig Kammerer in 1832—Sweden attained match-making supremacy by Janne Lundström's invention of the safety match. Lundström shrewdly switched the phosphorous from the matchhead to the striking surface on the box, thereby rendering the dangerous innovation nearly one hundred per cent harmless. His apt phrase summing up his formula—"Will Only Light on the Box"—made Swedish matches known around the world.

When Ivar Kreuger was born in 1880, Ernst August was already the father of two daughters. The year signalized another step forward for the young father. Only two days after Ivar's birth, the local newspaper carried this item: "The firm of Kreuger & Jennings are selling phosphorus matches of the Fredricksdahl brand." With help from his prosperous family, Ernst August had bought the small match factory he had managed. Shortly he bought another. Ten years later he acquired a third, in nearby Möntserås.

During those years three more children had been born to him—two more daughters and a boy, four years younger than Ivar, named Torsten. With six children to provide for Ernst August looked around for supplemental income, and found it by becoming local representative of the Swedish firm Skandia. Next he followed through the family tradition by winning the post of Russian representative. Now he too was entitled to the resounding title of Consul.

So, industrious, ambitious, solid, stood Ernst August Kreuger, Ivar's father. There seem to be none of the later complexities of the Match King to be found in Ernst August. Indeed, if such are anywhere in Ivar's heritage it is in the background of Jenny Forssman, his mother.

All things considered, there is little enough color there, but compared to the Kreuger lineage there is some. One of Jenny's mother's seven brothers was insane. Another brother, becoming paralyzed, examined the possibilities of the life stretching ahead of him. Then, as so many Swedes seem able to do, he calmly killed himself.

Any real color in Ivar's background must have come from Jenny's father. Though Kalmar people always seemed content to remain in Kalmar, the elder Forssman possessed an itching foot plus a lively imagination. A surveyor and civil engineer, he began hearing tales of the opening of the great continent of Africa. Shortly he gathered up his wife and made the long journey there, to settle at Pretoria, in the

Transvaal, Dutch South Africa. Almost immediately Herr
Forssman was appointed Surveyor General for the Dutch
South African Government, and Jenny was born while he
held that responsible post. But if the Surveyor General was
happy in the rugged African environment, his wife apparently
was not. When Jenny was five, mother and daughter came
back to Kalmar, never to return to Africa. Nor did the husband and father ever rejoin them. After finishing his job
as Surveyor General, he went into business for himself, remaining happily industrious in the Transvaal until his death
in Pretoria in 1874.

It could be that the exotic—for Kalmar—background
of Jenny Forssman made Ivar Kreuger into a strange man.
Or that his birth in quiet Kalmar was one of the tricks played
by nature in an antic mood. Or that a strange destiny set
him down in the midst of this family, this town, this country.

For Ivar's parents were traditional Scandinavian types,
large, blond, big-boned. His four sisters and his brother all
gave signs of future sturdiness. Indeed, his younger brother
Torsten had hardly been born before he gave signs of becoming the fat boy of song and story.

Yet Ivar was frail, slight, delicate-looking. He did not
seize the world and use it for his pleasure, as most Swedish
children do. He regarded it out of cool, calculating eyes,
which, as years went by, became faintly mocking. He had a
sharp nose, set in a pale solemn face. His hair was not Nordic
blond, but a nondescript brown. He was always fairly tall,
but it was a stooped, unimpressive tallness. His voice was
soft and gentle, with a quality that made it oddly pleasant
and persuasive, but it was never raised with the shrill enthusiasms of childhood. Everything about Ivar suggested
a subdued indoorishness, rather than the outdoor sturdiness of the traditional Swedish boy. Rather than Scandi-

navian, there was something almost Oriental about a boy with such sallow skin, such self-preoccupation, and such lack of enthusiasm in one so young.

But if to others Ivar seemed a hybrid, the elder Kreugers appear not to have been bothered. "He was so easy to bring up," his mother recalled later. In more detail, she remembered that almost from the moment of birth, Ivar had been content with three meals a day, consuming these at approximately the same time as his elders. As a child he never cried, just as in later life he was noted for a poker-faced lack of emotion. Further, from infancy he showed an uncanny ability to amuse himself. With five other children in the house, it is to be presumed that Fru Kreuger was pleased to have such an undemanding child and left him largely to his own devices. "He was an angel," she repeated later. "I could always leave him alone while I took care of the others." But among those who later explored Kreuger's beginnings was Dr. Poul Bjerre, the noted Swedish psychoanalyst. He saw things somewhat differently. "Ivar was spoiled," he believes. "I do not mean in the sense that he was lavished with gifts, but rather that there were no barriers put around his activities. He was allowed to do anything, provided he kept quiet and did not bother anyone. In the household he became a law unto himself, operating only by rules he himself devised."

In the Kreuger home there was neither luxury nor poverty. Despite the Consul's manifold business activities, he did not make enough to rise financially far above the demands of his large family. The Kreugers lived in a "spacious flat on the upper floor of the noble mansion on the corner of Kaggans and Storgatan. There was a large drawing room and also an enormous ballroom which was used for children's parties, dancing lessons, and the occasional balls given by Consul and Mrs. Kreuger."

But long before the age of dancing lessons, the parents must have realized that in Ivar they had a child unusual in other ways than looks. If they were able to view as normal his self-sufficiency, his silence, and the preternatural calm with which he accepted the world, they could not help being surprised when, as a child of six, he accompanied his parents to church, then returned home to recite almost word for word the lengthy sermon delivered by the minister. It was a feat the awestruck parents could not help boasting about, and the following Sunday the Kreuger neighbors gathered to hear the phenomenal child duplicate his trick.

But with Ivar's precocity seemed to go a redeeming shyness and sensitivity, as in later life his personality was never sharp black or sharp white, but always a shadowy gray, sometimes quite pleasant. As a boy he could "blush like a maiden when praised," and now surrounded by the inquisitive neighbors, he refused to repeat the sermon to an audience other than his close family. One of his aunts insisted, however, and since she was a relative he had to give in. Once the neighbors had left he delivered the sermon especially for her. But he made her stand behind him, where she could not be seen.

The atmosphere of the Kreuger apartment on Storgatan apparently was healthy and normal, but somehow not right for Ivar. Though seemingly surrounded by love and affection, he still was growing up in an alien world. At home, this was bad enough. Outside, among the other citizens of Kalmar, it was increased. Physically, Ivar was like some member of a weakling race born into a world of giants, where inhabitants strapped knapsacks around broad shoulders and strode off across the countryside. Or perhaps they traveled on skis or snowshoes, returning after dark to polish off mountainous meals of *smorgasbord* and *snaps*.

Like all sensitive children, Ivar early found a way to defend himself against the pressures of unsympathetic surroundings. He did it by beginning to sharpen his mind, and he found there a most willing tool. For as he grew up, the boy discovered that with almost no effort he could remember whole pages of books. Continuing the sharpening process, he found himself able to retain chapters, bringing them almost verbatim to his lips days later, as he had done with the sermon. He had, in short, a truly remarkable faculty for retaining what he read, whether he wanted to remember it or not. But always with him this remained a feat of memory. One of his teachers later declared Ivar never really absorbed what went into his blotting-paper mind. Instead, he merely stored it emptily away until the day it was needed.

In every way, the sedentary-looking Ivar followed through on his appearance. He despised outdoorishness, vastly preferring to spend his free time at home, sprawled atop the down-filled bed in the room he shared with Torsten, reading books or day dreaming. One summer, he discovered another diversion. This was walking in the silver-birch woods, studying wild flowers. "Solitary botanizing," he himself dubbed it, and when he became a millionaire, able to afford the most exotic flowers, he still retained this early love for wild flowers. It was such a conspicuous trait that one writer, after trying hard to analyze his baffling character, concluded hopelessly, "Only one thing can be stated with certainty—that this man is passionately fond of lilies of the valley."

In those days Swedish children entered school at the age of seven. When pale-faced Ivar appeared for his first grade, the schoolmaster found to his surprise that the boy could already add, subtract, multiply and divide. Also, he could read. Accordingly, he was promoted to the second grade. This was an unusual occurrence in Swedish schools and may have given Ivar his first inkling that he was a bright and precocious student.

But though he was always beyond his age in studies, school did not satisfy his odd mind. Schoolmasters in the 1800's did not believe in encouraging precocious children, and possibly Ivar's efforts to obtain information really interesting to him were squelched by a stern schoolmaster, whose position in town was second only to that of the Mayor. Possibly this in turn drove the boy deeper into himself, making him suspicious of the help he might expect from the outside world. But it is not likely that a single factor could have stifled Ivar's healthy mental growth, turning his mind into different channels. Instead, it was probably a combination of all the pressures that made him an alien in Kalmar. These inevitably drove him into a pleasanter world of illusion, or daydreams. Most unhappy children do this, and later spend complicated years trying to reconcile dreams with reality. But occasionally a child is gifted with a mind so exceptional that he can all but make the daydreams come true. This, perhaps, is genius—and so it remained throughout the life of Ivar Kreuger.

At the same time it brought him, even as a child, an almost total absorption in himself, *his* plans, *his* feelings, *his* desires. Combined with a toughness and steadiness inherited from Viking ancestors, this developed a will-to-succeed that was almost hypertrophic. It pushed him into contests in which he contrived to sharpen his already sharp mind. Thus at the tender age of eight or nine he is found sitting in a class which has been given half an hour to commit the Lord's Prayer to memory. In only a few minutes Ivar's hand shot up. While the others sat still, he rose and began,

"*Fader Var,*" continuing perfectly to the end. Then, instead of sitting down in triumph, he announced, "I can also recite it backward." Without awaiting permission, he spouted a bewildering but accurate jumble of words beginning, "*Amen evighet . . .*"

In school, Ivar made no effort to hide from other pupils the fact that he never bothered to study. Indeed, he boasted of it. "Just as the boy with outstanding physical development must flaunt his muscles, no less must the boy of superior mind want the whole world to know it," is a truism of human behavior. But it put Ivar in a strange position with classmates, for by using his retentive memory he could, when he desired, get the top marks in his class, while making less effort than anyone.

It galled some. In the schoolyard one day an older boy walked up to young Kreuger and hit him hard across the mouth. This was a shock that crumbled Ivar's almost mature composure. "What did you do that for?" he gasped out. "Because you never *do* anything," the older boy snapped, and strode away.

Such harsh episodes are the kind that every growing child must rationalize in his own way. Ivar shortly arrived at his rationalization, at the same time establishing a pattern of conduct that lasted a lifetime. "People can never understand superiority," he decided. "They always try to destroy it."

Chapter 3

The Cancer of Cleverness

But if some schoolfellows found the presence of Ivar in their midst an irritation, there was one Kalmar group which did not. This was the mothers of other children. In their eyes, Ivar could do no wrong. "Ah, that little Kreuger, such an angel child," was a statement young Ivar must have often overheard applied to himself. In truth, the pale child with the precociously grave countenance did have something of an angelic look. For as he grew his face took on the expression of innocent sweetness which has always appealed to women in the children of others. His quiet, reserved, utterly self-sufficient behavior made him seem more the model child. Added to it all was his brilliance in school. "You have to forgive him where you can't forgive others," the mothers would fondly say.

As the years passed Ivar's dislike of outdoor sport increased. His reading was channeled almost exclusively to the lives of great men, and after several chapters his book might fall to his chest so that he could associate in intoxicating daydreams with the titans he had been reading about. All of which took him far from slow Kalmar. In time, his favorite dream refuge became the life of Napoleon, to whom, largely because of his pallid skin, he believed he bore a resemblance. "If I grow up to be like Emperor Napoleon," he earnestly informed his family one day, "you won't find me winding up on St. Helena."

Yet the annoying thing to schoolmates was that the delicate, introverted boy possessed a steely nerve, a seeming absence of fear, a skill at sports that contrasted completely with his sallow appearance. Though no one ever saw him practice, he could ski when he had to. In summer, he could swim as far as anyone. Without a quiver of fear he had gone through the usual Swedish baptism to the water, with his father taking him out to sea in a boat and tossing him in. Calmly he stroked his way back to the boat and climbed in.

But though he could, if he liked, excel in games, he considered them dull and pointless. "Most of what other boys did seemed childish to Ivar," a contemporary has recalled. "Though still a boy himself, he disliked our cheerful noisiness, our thoughtless shouts, the whole happy play with which we worked off animal spirits." One of his teachers recalls, "Self-restraint and self-discipline were the striking characteristics of Ivar." Kreuger himself later put it this way: "I was not quite like other boys," he said once. "I thought things through for myself."

What he called "thinking-through" put him in a peculiar position with contemporaries. Though he would not join in animal-spirited games, he was because of his clear mind much in demand as a referee in sporting contests and an arbitrator in disputes. He performed so well in such tests of judgment "that through them he never made an enemy."

Why he failed to make enemies is indeed a question. Young Ivar would seem to have been the superior, condescending type traditionally disliked by other boys. In the United States, he would have been branded a sissy and left strictly alone. Yet this is one of the numerous paradoxes in Kreuger. All through life he held himself apart from others. Even so, nearly everyone who came in contact with the man seemed to like him. A possible explanation is charm. "He was a charmer, and he knew it," one of his associates has said. Another added: "He had an *attractive* way of doing things." Kreuger became a man able to intrigue multitudes, and just as easily cast a spell over individuals or small groups. It was the same in childhood, with the preternaturally serious boy performing deeds which one classmate calls, "clever, daring and resourceful." It would seem, however, that the charm and cleverness were more like insolence; the daring and resourcefulness, sheer gall. For as a boy Ivar seemed to be training—or testing—his will power no less than he was training his mind. Far more than his husky contemporaries he could be fearless, even devilish. It was he, the studious-looking boy, who dared rugged classmates—not they him— to think up dangerous stunts for him to do. Then coolly, apparently without a single inner qualm, he would perform the rash act, his attitude expressing contempt for both the stunt and the boys stupid enough to dream it up. Which should have made him an object of dislike. But there always seemed to be the close-quarter charm. As much as he would permit, it all seems to have made him friends.

Another contemporary pictures Ivar studying his teachers harder than he studied books. By ferreting out the weaknesses and eccentricities of each, he knew exactly how much he could get away with in class. He further proved his superiority over both teachers and other classmates by becoming expert at the naïve, red-herring question. Called upon to answer a question, he would skillfully insert a question of his own. It set the teacher rambling off on a tangent, and unobtrusively Ivar sat down. "He loved to test how far things he set in motion would develop, and it was priceless to contemplate the expression of concentrated innocence on Ivar's face when he had just played some trick or other, such as when he poured all the acids in the laboratory into one receptacle so that the teacher could not get his experiment to work. But despite such things Ivar was never in real trouble with schoolmasters. He was too clever, and the closer he got to final exams the better his marks got. He was like a runner who saves all his strength for the final sprint."

At first Ivar's schoolmasters were delighted to find before them a boy with a rare mind. The good men naturally expected an extra-intelligent youth to display a hunger for learning, perhaps even aspire to be a schoolmaster himself someday. But the boy with the mocking eyes had other plans. His attitude toward subjects under study was cold or apathetic. In later years he would work incredibly hard, but now he lacked both the interest and the sense of duty which might have caused him to make even token efforts at studying.

All of which left a gulf between the boy and his teachers, as well as between him and classmates. It was an ever-widening gulf, since some drive deep in young Ivar's personality appeared determined to have it that way. By his own testimony, he already felt "different" from the rest of Kalmar, and impulses in him apparently worked tirelessly to increase the difference. It was a drive which in no sense could be called healthy. For by the time he achieved high school, the boy who had early resolved to make himself superior decided that he had succeeded in becoming so. He consequently turned his efforts to becoming what might be called superior-*plus*. The *plus* meant that not only would he achieve superiority, but he would get it by means of some extra trick of wits, some short cut or cutting of corners which would only make his superiority the more delicious to him. In his decision to be superior-*plus*, Ivar may be said to have concluded that honesty was the best policy—for everyone else. But perhaps it is best summed up by one word—*cleverness*. He now determined to make it a life work to be cleverer than the rest of the world, and the writer Max Lerner has pointed out the terrible dangers inherent in this. "The trouble with cleverness," Lerner writes, "is the trouble with cancer. Clever people let their cunning run away with them, cell of cleverness spawning cell of cleverness, until they end by being over-clever and destroying themselves."

One of the first steps in Ivar's cleverness campaign is to be seen in a famous anecdote about him—one he himself in later years modestly told about his boyhood.

In high school Ivar called the smartest boys in his class together. He was already aware of an ability to put an almost hypnotic quality into his gentle, sibilant voice, and now he used this persuasiveness to the utmost. "You, Krister, excel in math. You, Karl, are best in history. You, Sven, lead in science. Now each of you needs study only his best subject. Then every morning before school we meet and pool our knowledge."

The boys agreed. Ivar, who decided that a necessary step in the climb to superiority-*plus* was to learn to use the minds of others, studied nothing. He merely sat and listened to all.

Equally indicative of Ivar's character was the way he cheated in school. No one can deny that cheating among schoolboys is common. It was even so in Sweden during the last century. But in all the comments by classmates special mention is invariably made of the inspired way Ivar could cheat. "He was a past master in the art," one recalls. "When questioned he would have one book closed on the desk, another open on his knee. We all tried to follow his lead in this, but we always got caught. He never did." Another states it more succinctly: "It isn't that he cheated more than any of us, he just did it better."

Through Ivar's school life runs a chain of such admir-

ing tributes. So does a recurring remark, "Ivar always succeeds." In truth, he appeared to, for the audacious boy never
seemed to get caught. With each new success he worked
ever harder to achieve the next by skating over thinner ice.
Where at first it had been a challenge to wait until the last
possible moment before preparing for exams, it now became
an even greater one not to prepare at all—and still get passing
grades.

He did this once in a way immortalized in another of
the anecdotes Kreuger later told as proof of his boyhood
superiority. In high school, having failed completely to study
for an important exam, he mounted his bicycle to ride to
school with no idea what he would do, only a sublime faith
that something brilliant would occur to him.

It did. Pedaling along the main street he saw the Mayor
of Kalmar and his Council in the midst of a sidewalk conference. Unhesitatingly Ivar sharply twisted the handle bars
so that the bicycle shot out from under him, sending him
skidding along the ground to a skin-scraping halt at the
Mayor's feet.

The good man knelt down. "My boy, my boy," he
clucked, "you're hurt."

Young Ivar acted stunned. *Hjärskakning*, a concussion,
the Mayor decided. Still, the boy seemed able to talk.

"I have an important examination at school," he muttered. "I've got to get there."

The Mayor himself assisted him up and walked with
him to the classroom. There he whispered to the schoolmaster, "This boy is hurt, but he is such a brave one. Go
easy on him today, make sure he passes."

The schoolmaster, knowing Ivar only too well, started
to speak, but thought better of it. After all, this man was
the Mayor, the dispenser of jobs. He looked at Ivar's blood-

scraped countenance, out of which two knowing eyes regarded him levelly. Then he must have known he was beaten and given a hopeless shrug.

The gradual change in Kreuger's youthful character can also be traced in his boyhood nicknames.

In all countries children use nicknames for each other, but in Scandinavia, where grown men are addressed elaborately by occupation, boys go in for it more seriously. Thus young Ivar, because of his reserved nature, his solitary botanizing, and his refusal to join the games of others, was early dubbed "the Quiet One." Sometimes he was called "the Solitary One."

These were suitable nicknames until Ivar reached his early teens. Then a different one appeared. "The Solitary One" and "the Quiet One" were forgotten in favor of "the Sneak," a name which Kreuger in his mature years fought hard to obliterate. But the Swedes are a realistic people and when journalists got through Kreuger's guard to visit Kalmar and ask about him, they were told by contemporaries, "All the stories about him say we called him 'the Solitary One' in school. But most of the time it was 'the Sneak.' "

With such facts of Kreuger's youth before him, Dr. Bjerre concludes that early in life Ivar Kreuger developed into—or, by other schools of thought, was born—an amoral person. This means that in his personality some part of the moral sense was lacking. He would not respond to the standards of civilization as a normal, morally healthy person should. The wrongs in antisocial, unjust, destructive—or too-clever—acts would not be apparent to him.

Dr. Bjerre and other psychoanalysts do not take a totally defeatist view of amorality. An amoral person can go through life without appreciably injuring himself or the rest of humanity. He may even grow in moral stature, with the help of "desire, clear intellect, and constructive energy." Yet, the amoral person is always poised on what might be called a personality-tightrope. He may just as easily give in to opposite pressures which turn him into an unmoral person. And for unmoral—in most cases—it is usually necessary, eventually, to substitute the word *criminal*.

In his study of Kreuger, Dr. Bjerre states that numerous interviews with surviving classmates convinced him that during school days, Ivar got hold of a key to the headmaster's desk. At night he would slip through the window of the school office, open the desk, scan the questions destined for examination papers, and repeat them to favored classmates.

Since he did not need to break into the school office—for why should a boy who could pass any exam by committing to memory the contents of a few books do that?—Dr. Bjerre thinks that the act of rounding up boys he liked and telling them to wait outside while he made his night foray into the principal's office brought satisfying feelings of power and superiority.

Other on-the-spot probers into Kreuger's beginnings also report that he honed his superiority by charging twenty-five ore (about six cents) for the examination questions. Having done this, he waited until the exam was over and made another trip through the principal's window to learn the grades each pupil had received. Here his plans hit a snag. He found pupils who had been eager to pay ore for the questions reluctant to shell out for grades they would soon learn anyway. So the canny youth applied his cleverness to the problem, and next term refused to sell the questions until his friends had signed up for the grades also.

Investigators also claim that Kreuger as a youth was the only pupil in the school considered "capable" of forging a parent's name on a report card. Yet there is no sign that he ever actually did this. What seems to be important is that he conveyed the impression of willingness to deceive to that extent. This highlights another facet of the boy's developing character. He also had a reputation among contemporaries of being a skilled liar. Yet with all the delving into his early life, there is no record of a barefaced lie on his part. Even as a boy he had discovered the effectiveness of what he used with such mastery as a man—the elusive, misleading half-truth which cannot quite be pinned down.

There is sadness, too, in Kreuger's youth. The home of Consul and Fru Kreuger, with its six children, should have been a warm and healthy place. Yet in all the stories turned up about Kreuger none concerns his home life, or any affection and guidance it might have provided. For unfathomable reasons the Kreuger home, with all its surface solidity, seems to have been empty—for Ivar at least. And nowhere else in Kalmar did he find a helping hand that might have guided him.

This made him a boy who seemed to have no hobbies, no enthusiasms, who lived locked in a world of day dreams, inner challenges and cryptic plans.

Yet his youth was not without some periods of male companionship—though in the end they may have hurt more than helped him. When his sisters began turning into attractive young ladies, Ivar apparently attained popularity with boys who were trying to make a favorable impression on the girls, but Ivar seems to have had absolutely no sympathy for, or interest in, such puppy love. Nor did he manifest the mischievous, annoying qualities that some younger brothers adopt when sisters begin receiving beaux. Instead, he regarded it all impersonally, out of the mocking eyes.

But it may have been the influx of young men into the Kreuger home that brought him one of his close male relationships. A young man named Gosta, who first came to visit the sisters, took a liking to Ivar, possibly seeing his steely nerve as a means to facilitate his own approach to still other girls. At any rate, their friendship is chronicled in the high-school paper, a chatty publication which reported the activities of students in the manner of a metropolitan newspaper. Under the heading POLICE NEWS there appears in the school paper this item:

> Count Gosta and Mr. Ivar Kreuger were brought before the Court yesterday on a charge of impeding traffic on Storgatan [Main Street] on the evening of November 22nd. They explained that they had arranged a walking match that evening on the Storgatan pavements. Count Gosta won, completing 54 turns, while Kreuger had only 50 to his credit. In the course of their wild career they knocked over a great many young ladies and behaved in a fashion which does not bear describing in this newspaper. Sentence will be pronounced December 5th.

In succeeding items the school paper traces the further friendship of Gosta and Ivar, still beamed on the rowdy chasing of girls. Perhaps, lacking a sympathy for puppy love, Ivar found much more compatible the predatory approach of the older, handsome Gosta. Thus Gosta's attitude toward girls may have influenced Kreuger's later attitude toward women.

But there is little time to draw serious conclusions from the Gosta-Ivar friendship, for shortly—sadly—it was over. Says another supposed ad in the indefatigable school paper:

> HELP WANTED: A boy in 6R can be employed by the undersigned to take the place of the Count since the intimate relationship between us has ceased.
>
> Ivar Kreuger

Chapter 4

Disappearance of the Sneak

So Ivar lived until the age of sixteen when, still the youngest pupil in the class, he graduated from high school in Kalmar and decided to go to Stockholm for three more years' study at Tekniska Högskolen—technical high school.

In his last summer before departing for Stockholm, Ivar worked as an apprentice-trainee at his father's Kalmar match factory. Matches, indeed, had been one very definite influence in his somewhat wavering childhood. Says one writer: "The hum of the score of local factories, the talk of business problems of the industry, the romance of the Swedish safety match that was made there before his eyes and shipped off to the far ends of the earth, those things were with him from the beginning."

When Ernst August Kreuger was home there was usually talk of matches in the house. For though he was Consul to the Russians his main income-producing business remained matches. On winter nights he and his associates would gather in the Kreuger kitchen to discuss business matters, and on Saturdays he often took Ivar and Torsten on his visits to the factories.

Yet when the time came to choose a lifetime profession, Ivar seems to have been inspired less by matches than by the tales he had heard of his redoubtable grandfather—the man from stodgy Kalmar who had become Surveyor General for the Dutch in South Africa.

For now he decided to be an engineer. He enrolled at the Tekniska Högskolen in Stockholm for a two-year course in mechanical engineering. After that he planned on a year of civil engineering, in further emulation of his rugged grandfather.

Accordingly, after his summer in the match factory, he arrived in Stockholm in September, 1896. Finding a room in the home of a married relative, he made his appearance for the beginning classes at the technical school, where immediately he picked up the pattern of his school life in Kalmar.

His career at technical school only shows a deepening of all the traits begun in Kalmar. He did not speak often, but what he said went unerringly to the point. Nor did he ever seem to laugh. Instead, he expressed amusement by a mocking, quizzical half-smile, never more than a faint quirking of one corner of his mouth, that remained a characteristic all his life. But without laughing, Ivar occasionally made humorous remarks. Usually these were ironic, some pointing-out of human foibles which showed his instinctive knowledge of the recesses of human nature. "I loaned him money, and probably lost a friend," he said as a schoolboy in Stockholm.

As in Kalmar, his schoolmates at first hardly noticed Ivar, then slowly became conscious of his lightning mind and mature judgment. "He was younger than any of us," said one later, "but in nearly every way he seemed older."

Yet again Ivar—generally liked by most classmates—did nothing in a social sense to utilize the admiration others gave him. He did not make himself the center of a group, or in any way try to cement friendship. As in Kalmar, he was still the Solitary One, removing himself whenever possible from the school world. A later poll of technical-school classmates finds such words as "introspective," "reserved," "reticent," "distant," and "peculiar," applied to him.

Again, the students who were impressed by Ivar's logical mind were even more impressed by something else—his skill at cheating. Later, writing from Stockholm, the American journalist, William H. Stoneman, put it this way:

> Ivar's classmates remember him as a young man completely lacking in principle, who cheated whenever he thought he could do it without being caught. In one examination, according to a man who sat beside him, he copied his entire paper from that of a companion, transposing just enough to prevent suspicion on the part of the teacher.
>
> "He seemed to take pleasure in his mental agility and to enjoy using it for the deception of everyone with whom he came in contact," says this same classmate. "He knew his teachers were preoccupied and he took advantage of their preoccupation." It was this same feeling of superiority over other mortals and his ability to spot their weaknesses and to take advantage of them that marked Kreuger's whole career.

Ivar's cheating won special admiration because he thought of so many angles to protect himself. Once students were required to build a model steam engine. This would require the constructive type of application that Kreuger had avoided since childhood, and faced with it, Ivar inquired around, to find that each year's class was required to make a similar engine model. He approached an upperclassman and used his uncanny persuasiveness to get the fellow to give him the model he had made the year before. This would have satisfied the average cheater, but not Ivar, who always thought things through. He realized the professor might remember the model, so he persuaded two other upperclassmen to give him theirs. He broke them all up, and by liberal applications of glue used the salient parts of each to create an engine no professor had ever seen. A year later he pulled precisely the same trick with a model drawbridge.

In every way the technical school seems to have been for Kreuger an experimental field in bluffing and cheating. A factor which could have made it particularly suitable for this was the muddleheadedness of the professors under whom he studied. As in Kalmar, he seems to have analyzed each teacher to find his weaknesses, and his ability to fool the professors in Stockholm with the old tricks seems to have brought him new confidence.

Ivar's attitude toward all his classes in Tekniska Högskolen is described as superior nonchalance. He still studied less than anyone, but occasionally a real interest in engineering seems to have driven him to extra reading. Once, to inform himself, he read a just-published volume on railroads. A few days later, the luckless professor chose to lecture on that subject, and assigned students the task of writing a paper on his remarks. Kreuger's just-off-the-press information proved the professor wrong on many points, and he showed no hesitation in stating this in his paper. When the class convened next day the professor was furious. "Herr Kreuger, is this your paper?" he shouted. In leisurely, contemptuous fashion young Ivar pulled himself to his feet. "It has my name on it," he answered indifferently. Before Ivar's insolent look the professor withered. "Very well then, sit down," he muttered.

Other professors who chose to tangle with the preternatural youth also came to regret it. In any test of will, Ivar was like a superior general. He always seemed to have hidden reserves and he could produce them with rare cunning. Here his classmates comprised a group of unshakable allies. With all Ivar's lack of warmth, he seems to have charmed most of them to the point where he could lean on them whenever necessary. When one professor sought to show up the tricky Ivar by failing to give him passing marks on a term's work, Ivar indignantly took him to task. "Every one of my classmates will assure you I know as much about the subject as they do," he informed the teacher coldly.

"They will not," the professor snapped back.

An ordinary student might have subsided, but not Kreuger. "Then let's take a vote of the class on it," he suggested.

"No vote would be accurate," the professor countered. "Everyone here is your friend, and wouldn't want you to know what they really think about you."

"Then have a secret ballot," the youth persisted.

The professor gave in. In the ballot, Ivar's classmates loyally gave him a full vote of confidence. "Yet," says the classmate who passed the story along, "the suspicion remained with all of us that he had not bothered to study at all and did not know as much as we said he did."

One factor which seems to have allowed Kreuger to outsmart his professors so continually appears to lie in the fact that the men had so much to do. What the student quoted by Stoneman calls preoccupation on the part of professors could be a work-load which kept them from concentrating on the development of a brilliant pupil, and by the same token, kept them from taking time out to squelch one who got out of hand. Leaving aside the effect this might have had on Kreuger's scholarship, it seems to have planted another lifelong conception in the fertile mind of the amoral youth. It was this: That those in exalted positions could be fooled as easily, if not more easily, than the man in the street.

Certainly the most-quoted story of Kreuger's technical-school days bears this out. It concerns an examination for knowledge of minerals, in which each student was handed a tray and graded on his ability to identify the different stones piled on it. The trays were passed along the rows of students, while the professor followed along after, grading each student. When Ivar got his tray, the professor was busy entering in his book the grade made by the previous pupil. Lightning-fast, Ivar's fingers sorted through the minerals on the tray, selecting those he did not know. These he shoved into his pocket. When the professor was ready, Ivar scored nearly one hundred per cent. But the harried man never noticed that the pile of stones on the tray had dwindled perceptibly.

The faculty of getting along without others was as apparent in Stockholm as it had been in Kalmar. Students at the technical school—presumably without knowledge of his home town nicknames, the Solitary or Quiet One—began calling Ivar the Still One.

But instead of the solitary reading and botanizing he loved so much in Kalmar, Ivar now strolled through the streets of picturesque Stockholm. One charitable writer states he was studying the faces of passersby, storing up characteristics for future psychological reference. This hardly seems to fit, for Ivar's knowledge of human weaknesses, deep though it was, seems to have been born in him. What does seem likely is that when strolling the streets he was merely indulging in his Kalmar pastime of daydreaming, and that now his daydreams were grander than ever. One anecdote especially indicates this. On such a bemused stroll, Ivar bumped into a fellow student. Coming out of his daze he said offhandedly, "See that place over there, I'm going to have one like it someday." The building he had so idly indicated was the Royal Palace!

As a boy from out of town, Ivar might be expected to be lonely or homesick. He was neither. It is said that he received many invitations from students who lived in Stockholm to dine or spend Sundays at their homes. But he refused. Here he shows another trait that remained with him all his life: an ability to adjust himself immediately, wherever he happened to be. This was not a particularly constructive adjustment in the sense that he tried to make the most of a new environment, by visiting museums and theatres. Rather, it was a matter-of-fact acceptance of change. It did not seem to be in his character ever to think back to where he had been, or forward to where he might be going. Kreuger always seemed to live in the precise moment and if, as a young engineering student, he spent much time daydreaming, this did not seem to make him discontented with the present. Rather, his success as a student and manipulator of professors seemed to bring him a hard core of confidence in himself, even a basic euphoria, which made him sure that he would achieve all his daydreams. He—the Quiet, Solitary, Still One—was always quite willing to wait patiently through any present, no matter where it might be.

His letters home from Stockholm bear out this incapacity for homesickness, sentiment, or even real feeling. They are matter-of-fact, their most interesting feature, in the light of future events, being the neat way he itemizes the money he spends. Carefully he lists for Ernst August such expenditures as pennies for shoe repair and larger amounts for schoolbooks. But the total always comes out a neat, round sum. Thus one group of expenditures adds up to 200 kroner, another to 250. Never is there a loose financial end.

But there is no real feeling in any of his letters. They remain devoid of warmth, affection or even interest. At best they are perfunctory. Indeed, now as much as later, Kreuger personifies the psychopath, who, in the words of writer John Bartlow Martin, "may be of over-average intelligence. It is his emotions that are out of kilter, his moral development. He is cold, remote, unreachable. He never learns by experience. He never feels remorse or shame. He rejects society. He rejects any obligation to it."

Kreuger's lack of feeling at this particular point in life is the more telling because, at eighteen, he had reached the end of adolescence. At the threshold of maturity, new forces have broken through to mold a man, and latent characteristics have finally reached the surface. If the decent, sensitive instincts that refine a personality have not appeared by the end of adolescence, they never appear. With Kreuger, everything seems to indicate that not only had he failed to develop the finer instincts, but that this important period of transition failed to mean much to him. Nowhere in his life, now or previously, is there any indication of what might be called mental or emotional growing pains. He always seemed to remain on an even keel. It was as if he had been created clever, calculating, and unerringly shrewd. And had never really changed.

Still, somewhere in his long walks through Stockholm, he seems to have stopped his intoxicating daydreams long enough to take a penetrating look at his true qualifications for conquering the world. The result was the conclusion that his drive for superiority-*plus*, if it made him superior, was not calculated to give others much faith in his character or honesty. The impression of extra-cleverness bordering on deviousness which he had thus far given to classmates was not—he decided—one which would help him succeed in the future.

Thinking along these lines, he seems to have laid down

lifetime rules for the success of Ivar Kreuger. He decided
first that an aura of confidence in himself—total self-confidence—was essential in any climb to the top. In this direction, he had already made considerable progress. But his
second conclusion was that he must also give an impression
of absolute honesty. His inability to radiate this quality was
one obstacle the young Kreuger did not choose to walk
around, but to face. It took a great re-evaluation on his part
to realize that if he gave an impression of self-confidence
to the outer world, he did not present an honest one. For
now comes a *volte-face* in the personality of Kreuger. Never
again—until far too late—is there the slightest hint of dishonesty or unscrupulousness in any of his actions. Instead,
the façade he increasingly presents to the world is one of
complete, disarming honesty. Added to it is the total confidence, so that slowly he became a man "who *knows*, and
because he *knows* is able to make the world believe he
knows."

For the young technical student, achievement of his
ideal personality was still far away. It would require steely
concentration for years to come. But it was the new, "honest" Ivar, who after two years at technical school returned
to Kalmar for a last summer of work at the match factory.
Then there remained only one semester in Stockholm, with
emphasis on civil engineering and the study of "road-build-
ing and waterways." After that, the future.

Ivar, at nineteen, pondered two alternatives. He could
remain in Sweden, working as an engineer, or perhaps apply
his engineering knowledge to the match factories. Or, like
his grandfather, he could travel, maybe to South Africa,
where grandfather Forssman would certainly be remembered. Or he might travel to other climes.

After a serious talk on the subject with Ernst August,

he decided to go to America. So a year later, in 1899, a graduate of Tekniska Högskolen, and proud possessor of the title Engineer Kreuger, which he valued enormously all his life, he set sail for New York.

In later years, Kreuger would infuriate passengers on luxury liners by tying up the ship's wireless facilities as long as twenty-four hours while he transacted his far-flung business. But his first transatlantic crossing was different. Ernst August had been able to spare him $100, to which from other sources he added about $50 of his own—for whatever characteristic he had shown to date the unusual youth had not been a money earner.

He traveled steerage.

Chapter 5

Travel and Romance

The America of 1899–1900, where young Ivar found himself, was a sprawling country whose citizens were constantly kept aware of Big Business.

Though the average man had little hope of ever holding stock in a large corporation, as he can today, he nevertheless watched with fascinated interest while the mighty Wall Street men of money, led by Morgan, Rockefeller, and Harriman, pulled hundreds of small companies together in mergers that created giant monopolies. Even as Kreuger arrived in the United States, J. P. Morgan was putting the finishing touches on his Steel Trust, adding $700 million to the capital structure of the mills he had merged and selling the whole handsomely at $55 a share. Buy the factories other men had built, merge them, establish a monopoly, then recapitalize at a fancy figure—such was the super-capitalist formula. Already nearly 5,300 different units of industry had been merged into 318 trusts, and there was far more to come. People like Theodore Roosevelt, Lincoln Steffens and Ida Tarbell raised voices in protest over the power of such colossal trusts, but few citizens bothered to listen. If a Wall Street financier had sufficient intelligence and ruthlessness to create himself a gigantic industrial empire, the public seemed perfectly willing to let him.

In New York City there was such talk of trusts and monopolies that even a young Swedish immigrant immediately heard it. Ivar, whose interest in finance at home had been nonexistent, within a week paid a visit to the Stock Exchange. There he watched the frenzied activity from the gallery, and from that moment became so interested in American finance that a friend, endeavoring to recall Kreuger in America, finally said, "He seemed most intrigued by the subject of business organization and carefully studied the history and activity of the Rockefeller Standard Oil Trust."

But aside from his rewarding visit to the Stock Exchange, New York, which eventually became his favorite world-city, did not treat Ivar too well on this first trip. He had no success in finding an engineering job and later he would tell—at first bitterly, then ruefully—how his youthful appearance all but prevented him from getting a hearing for any kind of work. "I would have done well to grow a beard and moustache rather than get an engineering degree," he wrote home to his family. Ivar had studied English in Kalmar and Stockholm, and now the boy who learned so much faster than his schoolmates received another blow. He had thought his English was flawless, but surrounded by people who really spoke the language, he found that his *v*'s came out *w*'s and that his sentences depended too heavily on roundabout Swedish constructions, which in English sounded awkward. Altogether, Ivar, the young man who had never felt awed by anything, suddenly found himself awed by New York City. He tarried only a week, after the first rebuffs in job hunting, turning to sight-seeing and contacts with fellow Scandinavians. When one told him the Midwest was more receptive to Swedes, he spent his last dollars on the fare to Chicago.

A job was now imperative, and again local Swedes pointed the way. Ivar was told that a large real estate firm had a preference for hiring young foreigners. At the office

of this company Ivar got his first practical lesson in American methods. It indicated that, crafty and precocious as he
had been at home, he still had much to learn from business
in the United States. He was informed that after a course
in salesmanship, covering "approach, convincing the cus-
tomer, and closing the deal," he would be put to work selling lots on a commission basis. The young Swede protested
that his accent and clumsiness with the language would
make it impossible for him ever to be a salesman-spellbinder.
"That's just the point," he was told. "You'll be selling mostly
to Swedes and Germans. If you talk good English, they don't
trust you."

Despite this, Ivar did not fare well as a real estate salesman. For three weeks, living on money borrowed from local Scandinavians, he used his accent, his Swedish, and the
magic persuasiveness that had never failed him at home. He
sold nothing. Then, just as he was on the point of quitting,
came a sale that netted him fifty dollars in commission.

So far as is known, this was the first money Ivar Kreuger
ever earned, for if Ernst August paid him during the sum-
mers he worked in the match factories the fact has gone
unrecorded. The $50, then, represented a proud moment
in Kreuger's life, and he often harked back to it nostalgically.
But as with almost every important event in his life, there
are conflicting accounts of the source of this money. One
is human, flattering, complimentary. The other features the
slippery half-truths always found in Kreuger's verbal de-
ceptions. A shadowy story insists that Ivar did not earn the
$50. Instead, the room in which he lived while in Chicago
had just been vacated by a young architect. In the bureau
drawer, Ivar found a roll of semi-completed plans for a
small house. The next night a man appeared at the door
and asked for the architect. "He was planning my house,

for fifty dollars," the man explained. Kreuger's mind might still be confused by impressions of the new world, but in a crisis it was capable of summoning up his old cleverness. "He had to leave town," he improvised rapidly, "but I'm an architect and he turned the job over to me. I'll have it done tomorrow." Ivar's engineering training had given him enough architectural knowledge to polish up the plans. Next evening, so goes the story, he gratefully pocketed fifty dollars.

However it came to him, the fifty dollars brought an abrupt end to the first step of Kreuger's business career. With money to tide him over, he quit selling real estate and shortly found work as a lineman for the Illinois Central Railroad, operating some fifty miles outside Chicago. It is likely that the young man who valued his superiority of intellect so highly considered this sort of outdoor labor beneath him. At any rate, he performed prodigies of saving and soon had enough money to travel to Denver where he believed that mining operations would require surveyors and builders. However sensible this idea may have been, reality was different. Ivar could not find employment—or perhaps he did not like Denver. For only a short time later, on November 10, 1900, he is to be found in New Orleans.

Now—perhaps—comes a moment Kreuger treasured all his life. On November tenth, according to his own account, he was a passenger on an excursion boat on the Gulf of Mexico, when a girl of seven tumbled off the deck into the water. The seemingly nerveless Ivar promptly jumped in and rescued her. For this he was not only effusively thanked by the parents but—his story would indicate— rewarded by the City of New Orleans which struck off a medal in his honor. On the medal was the date and this inscription: "Only a hero would risk his life for others." But nowhere on it is Kreuger's—or anyone's—name.

Did the rescue really take place? If so, did it happen in New Orleans? Kreuger kept the medal near him for the rest of his life, and became a past master at toying with it until visitors asked what it was. Then with seeming reluctance he would allow the story of the rescue to be drawn out of him. Yet some to whom he recounted the episode got the impression it happened in Havana Harbor. Others thought South Africa. The fact that his name was nowhere on the medal raises yet another doubt—it could have been purchased in any pawnshop. But it continued to mean much to the Match King. His mother once stated that he considered it his most valuable possession.

Hero or not, Kreuger found no work in New Orleans. That drove him back to New York, where he became a wire-stringer on such projects as the Flatiron Building and the Plaza and St. Regis Hotels. His letters home make him appear quite contented at this, but they are as matter-of-fact as those he wrote home from Stockholm: full of the height of buildings, another visit to the Stock Exchange, things *outside* him, never *in*. Says Dr. Bjerre: "There is something disheartening in these letters. They are so lacking in emotional qualities. He is twenty years old, out in the big world, with no feeling of loneliness. He is not at all discontented, there is not a trace of disorientation in the New World. He is just as much at home as he had been in Stockholm."

Yet in one letter Kreuger does express emotion—and also show that he is becoming partial to the American way. Dropping his matter-of-fact description of externals, he suddenly states: "There is no point in climbing to the top step by step at home. Here there is plenty of room. The people are hard, but they give one a chance. At home everyone talks about his love affairs in his spare time. Here instead people discuss their prospects. That suits me—I can breathe here."

But from lowly wire-stringer to top of the engineering profession is still a mighty distance, even in opportunity-prone America. At the age of twenty-one—and it is interesting to note that nearly everything Kreuger did in life was accomplished at a remarkably early age—he made a move calculated to raise himself quite a few rungs upward. Like some character in a story by Jack London or Richard Harding Davis, he signed up for a job in the jungles of Mexico. With ten other engineers he was sent to supervise the building of bridge foundations in the vicinity of Vera Cruz. It was the most rugged kind of engineering work, with yellow fever and jungle perils rampant. And here also Fate, which had already endowed him so well mentally, seems to have singled out Kreuger.

In company with the others, he went to Mexico by way of Havana—where he may have rescued the child. He was the youngest, least strong and least experienced of the eleven engineers. But in the end he was the only one to return. During the months in the jungle nine of his companions died of yellow fever, while the tenth was shot in the back by a vengeful Indian. Kreuger, too, was stricken by fever, but his was a comparatively light case. Still, it incapacitated him and he returned to New York. Then he sailed for Sweden. He was still ailing on reaching Kalmar, and because of this was exempted from the military service to which every young Swede was subject. Fever left him with a slightly weakened heart that remained with him through life, causing him to return to the slight stoop of his childhood. Always he seemed to be slightly favoring his left side.

While recuperating, Kreuger worked again in his father's match factories in Kalmar and Mönsterås. But after his adventures in America, this work must have seemed tame. Shortly he moved to Stockholm, and if nothing else this second phase of his Swedish recuperation is notable for the fact that for the first and only time in his life Kreuger's name was romantically attached to that of a girl.

Dr. Bjerre thinks Kreuger remained a virgin until his return from America, despite the tutelage in girl-chasing from his Kalmar friend, Gosta. Other writers are less sure, perhaps because his later years show such considerable interest in sex. William H. Stoneman states that Kreuger's introduction to physical love came as a youth in Kalmar, "from a woman much older than himself, a friend of his mother's." During his schooldays in Stockholm, Kreuger reportedly showed slight interest in several girls, and one story has it that shortly before graduation from technical school he got one in a family way—an occurrence which could be borne out by a bizarre accusation which came later in his life. But now, as a twenty-two-year-old engineer getting over an attack of yellow fever, Ivar openly began courting a beautiful Norwegian girl.

Like many other vital personalities in the Kreuger saga, this girl remains nameless. But on the testimony of none other than Kreuger himself, she played a crucial part in the development of his character. "In my early twenties," he wrote once, "I very much loved a girl about my own age. This was my first love. This girl I wanted to marry."

But he never did—and this makes a bewildering, romantic, and slightly dubious story which is important less for the nature of the events involved than for the fact that Kreuger kept harking back to it as a milestone in his existence.

The story is this: Apparently Kreuger first met the young girl when he was a student at Tekniska Högskolen. Now, returned to Stockholm in 1902, he resumed the friendship, which proceeded to ripen into considerably more. But as a result of his bout with yellow fever, Ivar was suffering from what in letters to his family he calls an "eye-disease." It made him almost blind, and both Kreuger and his doctors took a serious view of the affliction. As a result, for what appears to be the first time in his life, Ivar went through a period of acute depression. At one point of it, he pessimistically told the girl he loved, "I would not want to bind myself to a woman when I am in danger of going blind." After these fine words, he told her she was free to sever the relationship between them.

Instantly she did, returning to her home in Norway. Kreuger, who may have expected his noble announcement to increase the girl's love, first acted stunned, then distracted, going through agonies of unrequited love and remorse. Unable—or afraid—to make a trip to Norway himself, he persuaded his sister Ingrid to act as his deputy in a mission to induce the girl to come back. Ingrid went and found that, in violation of all the canons of romance, the girl refused to return. Ivar's words had killed her love, she declared. Further, she had consulted with her father and he agreed that Ivar was no proper match for her.

Bearing these sad tidings, Ingrid journeyed back to Stockholm. There Ivar threw himself into further transports of grief which caused some acquaintances to fear for his sanity, while others thought he might kill himself. Such grief, if genuine, would indicate that Ivar was anything but the emotionally barren type he had appeared since childhood—but was it genuine? Considering Kreuger's total career, it is hard to conceive how such a thing could be. Far more likely his vast pride, or false pride, was hurt. Because of a rash statement on his part—he found he had lost control of a crucial situation. It was sharp failure, rejection—something he had never really experienced. It could have robbed him of the self-confidence on which he had labored so hard. Or, to put it another way, his image of himself had been violated.

But slowly, as men do, he mended, and the net result of his agony would seem to be the same whether the cause was true love or false pride. For the anguish he suffered seems to have made him resolve to seal off forever the love compartment in his character. From then on he worked never to let his real emotions slip from his grip. Sex, yes; love, no. It was a decision which did much in shaping the final Kreuger, a fact an associate recognized when he wrote: "Perhaps his love-life had to die away to make room for other things he had to accomplish."

Whatever its long-range effects, the love affair seems to have persuaded him to return to the United States. In February, 1903, he boarded ship again, eyesight improved and health restored. This time he actually did utilize his shipboard days to grow a moustache and possibly because of this, immediately landed a job with the Fuller Construction Company, one of the foremost builders in New York City. Ivar worked as a checking draughtsman whose main responsibility was verifying calculations for that exciting new type of building, the skyscraper. Legend has it that the draughting tables adjacent to his were occupied by the Starrett brothers from Kansas who became the greatest skyscraper builders of all. In many ways the Fuller office was a stimulating place and Kreuger felt it. "There was ferment in those offices," says one study of American architecture. "Over George Fuller's draughting boards men were conceiving the skyscraper, were dreaming of a shining, high-towered city that would be like no other city ever known." Working on these buildings, even in so minor a way, seems to have brought out the best in Ivar. For the first time he lost the superior non-chalance that had characterized his actions and became engrossed in his work—"thrilled by the adventure to be found in this new and daring type building." The young man who always enjoyed getting by with a minimum of effort suddenly began shouldering the maximum. He remained to pore over his calculations after the office was officially closed at night and—exactly as contemporary success-literature said it should —this extra industry dramatically paid off. Ivar found a flaw in one blueprint. It was a serious one, potentially dangerous, which had been skipped by other examining eyes. For a few days he was an office hero.

It also brought him a raise and a reputation for more-than-ordinary engineering know-how, even brilliance. Soon he had moved to a better job with Purdy & Henderson, then with the firm of M. N. Pott. A representative of the London firm of Waring & Gillow, engaged in construction in South Africa, also offered him a job and here Kreuger performed one of the paradoxical acts of friendliness which studded his life. In New York he had met a young Norwegian engineer named Anders Jordahl. Kreuger was not interested in working in South Africa but recommended Jordahl. Then he set to and helped the Norwegian prepare the blueprints that clinched the job. Through the next year a grateful Jordahl wrote his benefactor in New York extolling the virtues of South Africa. When again Waring & Gillow made an offer, Kreuger decided to accept. He journeyed to London, discussed the work with chief engineers there, then set off for Johannesburg to work on construction of the Carlton Hotel.

The robust land where his grandfather had once been important seems to have had an invigorating effect on the sallow, still solitary, increasingly enigmatic young man. Or perhaps it was that for the first time in his career he held a position of authority and was not confined to an office. Except for his stint in Mexico, Ivar had up to that time been engaged in sedentary work under strict supervision, which may have outraged his carefully nurtured feelings of superiority, bringing the drive that made him so restless. The Kreuger who had lived so much in magnificent daydreams was hardly one to be restricted by pedantic bosses, and his itching foot—which continued after South Africa—may have been caused by an instinctive search for the niche where once and for all he would be his own boss, with limitless opportunity ahead to carry out his own soaring schemes.

In South Africa he was a "specialist" whose responsibility it was to check and make final decisions on the construction of the hotel. But this work, difficult though it might be, seemed to require only part of the energies of the blossoming Ivar. His friend Jordahl recalls Kreuger as arriving with £300 and impatiently demanding to be told how best to invest it. Jordahl was unable to furnish this advice, so Kreuger investigated on his own, bought some gold- and diamond-mine stocks. Nor was this all. He persuaded Jordahl to join him in a most peculiar enterprise. The two men bought a Johannesburg restaurant at which they worked in after-engineering hours. Surprisingly, it flourished. For the first time Kreuger seemed to be discovering that he had real skill at making money.

He also visited the grave of his grandfather and became fascinated by Cecil Rhodes, placing the latter on a high pedestal next to Napoleon, whom Kreuger increasingly resembled facially. Of Rhodes, he liked to say, "He is my god, and my example." He enrolled in the Transvaal Militia, sported a khaki uniform and rode happily around the countryside on a fine horse, carrying a gun. But with all this bravura activity, and the increasingly honest surface of his developing personality, there were little licks of gossip in his background. The story of the building of the Carlton Hotel has been obscured by the passage of time, but in connection with it Kreuger has been accused—as he was so often later—of "availing himself of the misfortune of others." This time he is said to have given improper instructions to the contractor, causing him to fail in his part of the Carlton construction job. This allowed Kreuger to call in another contractor who had promised him kickbacks. To him he gave proper instructions.

Still, most people who encountered the energetic young Swede found themselves impressed by him. His investment in diamond and gold shares doubled, the restaurant continued successful, and his engineering skill grew. Success did not blind him. He studied the country and in conversations with citizens of Johannesburg "struck listeners with the depth and correctness of his knowledge." It was in Johannesburg, too, that the final act of the drama with his Norwegian sweetheart played out. Jordahl recalls visiting Kreuger's quarters one Saturday afternoon, to find Ivar sobbing uncontrollably on the bed. "My girl is dead," he finally told Jordahl, continuing that a letter from home had brought news of the girl's sudden demise. "He was very depressed and sad a long time after this," Jordahl goes on, which could either indicate that Kreuger really loved the girl, or that he still had hopes of salving his hurt pride by winning her back. Whichever, he never forgot her. She became the Woman in his Life. "This girl whom I wanted to marry, died," he would conclude, in telling the story of his blighted romance. "Such a thing one cannot get over easily."

The girl's death may also have made him think of home. Or South Africa may have been too small, too far removed from the world stage—or perhaps he felt an increasing determination to work for himself. Now, while everything seemed so fortuitous, Kreuger proceeded to break loose from Waring & Gillow, who had, after completion of the Carlton, set him to supervising other construction. He and Jordahl disposed of the restaurant, vowing never to tell anyone in Sweden that they had run it, "as such work seemed beneath us." He profitably sold the diamond and gold shares and with pockets well lined, set off in 1904 for Sweden, by way of India. He remained at home for several months, then traveled to Paris where he stayed from December, 1904, until June, 1905, giving as an excuse for the long stay that he was busy learning the language. Late in 1905 he was off to New York again, going by way of Canada. In Toronto he worked briefly for a construction firm, and did the same in Buffalo and Toledo. In Philadelphia, anxious to make quick money, he tried to emulate his successful South African restaurant, and failed. Finally in New York once more, he landed a job with the Consolidated Engineering Company and because of his African experience was given an important hand in the construction of the Archbold Stadium at Syracuse University. Later, in 1930, the University showed its appreciation by conferring on him the degree of Doctor of Business Administration, *honoris causa*. Sharing the honors with him on that occasion were Governor Franklin D. Roosevelt and Rabbi Stephen S. Wise.

The Archbold Stadium meant a considerable responsibility for a young man of twenty-five, and indicated a considerable rise in the world. Even so, Kreuger suddenly began entertaining doubts as to whether he should remain in the United States. The man whose life until then had been a mixture of extreme daydreams and practical reality now began to think of merging the two in a kind of future he had never visualized before. To the great surprise of his family, he wrote home: "I cannot believe that I am intended to spend my life making money for second-rate people. I quite see that I must serve my apprenticeship, but by this time I know more than the most up-to-date director of any firm in Sweden. I hate the American outlook, but I shall bring American methods back home. Wait and see—I shall do great things. I'm bursting with ideas. I am only wondering which to carry out first."

An answer to his wondering came almost immediately. In his work at Syracuse and on other jobs, he had become interested in a new commodity on the building market called reinforced concrete. As a factor in structural engineering, this concrete was comparatively new. With it building in the mass was possible. There was new impetus in it, the opportunity of doing things never done before. "The possibilities of it attracted Kreuger immediately," an engineering associate recalls.

Through his interest in the new concrete, Kreuger met Julius Kahn, inventor of a specialized iron used with the concrete. Kahn had an office in Detroit and headed a company called the Trussed Concrete Steel Company. In the trade, his product was known as "Kahn Iron." When he and Kreuger met, an instant liking sprung up between them. "Why don't you represent me in Europe?" Kahn suggested. "It will make you a big man over there."

Such a suggestion neatly paralleled Kreuger's new inner dreams. It was now 1907 and, pulling up his few American stakes, he left for London, where Kahn's firm had an office. There he was told that a Swedish engineer named Paul Toll had already requested the European agency for Kahn Iron. Arriving in Stockholm, Kreuger visited Toll, to find a man several years younger than himself, strong-jawed, enthusiastic, practical. In a few hours' talk, the two decided to go into business together as building contractors, relying heavily on Kahn Iron.

Their firm was to be called Kreuger & Toll—in time a name known around the world.

Chapter 6

A Chance to Soar

The Ivar Kreuger who, after nearly ten years of world travel, in 1908 set up a building construction firm with Paul Toll came in for considerable scrutiny on the part of the business community of Stockholm.

Swedes who departed their native land seldom returned, especially those who had accomplished as much as Kreuger apparently had. Yet here he was, a man who recognized himself as knowing "more than the most up-to-date director of any firm in Sweden," returning to set himself up in backward Sweden. It was almost unprecedented. Why had he done it?

Kreuger himself was too astute to let on that his reasons were more practical than emotional—that his tirelessly calculating mind had concluded that in Sweden he could hope to be outstanding, where in the United States he might eventually become merely successful. He was content to let others speculate about him, and speculate they did! "I always had the impression we could expect great things from him," said one of his former classmates at technical school, "and when he came back from America I felt this more than ever." Stated another, "Nobody in this country could wake up the possibilities in him, but America certainly did it." Others accused him of too much "go-ahead, push-ahead spirit," which in Swedish is called *framåtanda*. Kinder observers called this "the optimism of America," but one took a different view. He blamed the "demoralization" of Kreuger more on Africa than on America. Colonizing produces a certain lack of responsibility, he reasoned. There was a lack of morality inherent in the process, and Kreuger with his admiration for Cecil Rhodes had fully absorbed it. "Colonizing," he concluded, "encourages a superiority complex."

Those who so carefully scrutinized Kreuger also took note of his appearance and manner. For after his travel Kreuger could hardly be called a citizen of Sweden, but rather a citizen of the world. His clothes, though dull and correct, came from New York or London. He now spoke some five languages almost perfectly, and in English his v's and w's were in the proper place. Physically, he already looked amazingly like the Match King of decades to come. He was tall and big-boned, but more sedentary in appearance than robust. He still seemed younger than his age—and always did—even though at twenty-eight there were beginning signs of future semibaldness, the hairline receding from a high, back-sloping forehead. He had kept a slim, youthful figure, for travel had developed in him a most un-Scandinavian appetite for salads and other light, summery foods. His skin was large-pored and sallow. With the years his lips had become perpetually pursed, and this brought a somewhat prim look to the lower part of his face.

Around his sharp, bony nose, thick flesh was gathering, to bring a contrasting sensual, almost voluptuous, look. Here the face was broad, with mounds of pulpy flesh forming over cheekbones already high. These added to the hidden quality of his eyes, which from childhood had been deep, cryptic and oddly magnetic. Kreuger's distant, hooded eyes always seemed to be more sensed than seen. Nevertheless, they were the most striking part of his countenance, though people queried about them had to admit it was impossible really to see them—"they always seemed veiled, shaded, one might say concealed." The few who did claim to recall them correctly saw them as an icy blue-gray, regarding the world with a look of steely calculation, occasionally sending out a quizzical spark to match the quirking, half-serious, half-mocking semi-smile on his lips. One man who indubitably did see them was a news photographer who, in later years, set off a magnesium flash full in Kreuger's face. On him the Match King turned a furious glare, and the photographer never forgot the eyes which, he said, gave him a "piercing, vicious look."

But if his physical appearance was that of a man young in years, his manner was always one of responsible maturity. All through life he retained the seriousness of the boy who had never permitted himself to have fun. In the condescending way he scrutinized the world there was ever the look of the Solitary One standing on the sidelines in Kalmar, watching the others make fools of themselves at play. He was aloof, superior, unexcited, unexcitable.

To Kreuger would eventually be applied such adjectives as "inscrutable," "impassive," "quizzical" and "sphinxlike." But there was far more to his true personality than a masterfully controlled calm. Even as a young-man-before-thirty, he radiated a serene sense of destiny. His imperturbable patience, infinite self-control and impassive calm combined to bring a colorlessness to his personality which blended into the one native characteristic he seemed to possess: an air of limpid melancholy peculiar to some Swedes. This also prevented him from appearing the dynamic person he really was. Rather it made him seem shy and retiring, so that Ivar Kreuger never was a man to stand out in any crowd. But at the same time he possessed a brushed-by-destiny aura which, when noted, made him an impressive figure indeed.

Stockholm was not long in noting it. As senior partner

of the construction firm of Kreuger & Toll it was Kreuger's job, in general, to bring in contracts and figure out the most efficient way of carrying through on the construction. After which the practical Paul Toll supervised the actual building. The team's first contract was for constructing flooring in the buildings of the Electro-Chemical Stock Company. Next came a viaduct outside Stockholm, and after that a switchback railroad. Each contract was four times larger than the one before, and in May, 1908, a Stockholm newspaper saluted the successful new firm by writing:

> This firm . . . is owned by Ivar Kreuger and Paul Toll and is affiliated with the Trussed Concrete Steel Company of Detroit, in which for a year Mr. Kreuger has had a position. This company has given 75,000 kroner in order to introduce its product—iron for concrete building—into Sweden. Also Mr. Kreuger put in 30,000 kroner and gives the impression of being a hard worker and doing a job well. . . .

Though this would seem to signalize considerable progress for a new firm, the senior partner, his mind bursting with American business methods, was far from satisfied. While Stockholm businessmen watched, he proceeded to attack his competition with a vigor that smacked of ruthlessness.

Some Swedish builders had a habit—almost a tradition in the industry—of getting a building half completed, then informing the owner that the original estimate had been too low: the building could not be finished without additional funds. The owner could only yield to this polite shakedown, since to hand the job over to another contractor would mean even more money.

Kreuger first let it be known that Kreuger & Toll would

never descend to such tactics. All estimates submitted by the firm would be binding, and any losses would be borne by Kreuger & Toll. Next he sent out a brochure showing how the new company planned to operate with such up-to-date American innovations as concrete mixers and derricks, in addition to the benefits to be found in Kahn iron and reinforced concrete. This was a stunning blow to rival firms, for Victorian building methods were still in vogue in Sweden.

For his own part, Kreuger was always on time for appointments, another rarity in Sweden. Added to ever-present ability to persuade were the basic American selling techniques taught him in the land-the-customer course in Chicago. To all this Kreuger now brought a new ingredient which he used all his life—flattery. Those who watched him operate often were astonished at the fawning depths to which he would sink to influence prominent people. Straightforward Paul Toll was perhaps the first to express surprise at this. "Must you flatter people so much?" he demanded of Kreuger one day as the two men left an office after landing an important contract. "I can't stand hearing you do it." Kreuger smiled his quizzical half-smile. "Why not?" he asked. "It worked, we got the contract." He paused, then went on reflectively, "You know, it is possible to flatter so much that one is ashamed of oneself, but never so much that the person you are flattering feels ashamed."

But still progress was not fast enough for the American-minded Kreuger. He wanted the entire city of Stockholm made aware of Kreuger & Toll and realized that the best way to achieve this ambition was to build a skyscraper. This was something Sweden's largest city had yet to see, and he made contacts tirelessly, showing sets of American plans to groups of businessmen and landowners, until at last one combine offered him a contract to construct a tall building at the juncture of Kungsgaten and Norrlandsgaten, two of Stockholm's main thoroughfares. "The entire city will watch with interest as this curious new iron skeleton is being built," a newspaper stated in announcing the projected structure.

It is likely that the men who provided the backing for this venture were the first to encounter the true potentialities of Ivar Kreuger. For despite his assurances, the investors feared the traditional demand for more money when the building was half done. They insisted on inserting a clause which would penalize Kreuger & Toll 500 kroner for each day over the stipulated date of completion.

Toll started to protest this clause, but Kreuger signaled him to let it pass. Once the clause was included, he too had a request. "I have a stipulation to make myself, gentlemen," he announced with disarming gentleness, "that Kreuger & Toll get the same amount for every date we are ahead of the date agreed on."

The investors were agreeable. No one in Sweden ever finished construction on time. Without hesitation, they permitted the clause to be added.

The next day Kreuger locked himself in his office and remained all day in a state of deep concentration. By nightfall he had in his remarkable mind—so far as is known he never committed any of his monumental plans to paper—a complete blueprint for finishing the new building with record speed.

While an astounded Stockholm watched, he began using American construction methods with a vengeance. For the first time in Scandinavian history, it is said, workers labored around the clock, a night shift moving in when day men finished. Kreuger erected giant tarpaulins around the building site. It was midwinter and behind the canvas huge bonfires brought both light and heat to the laborers. A system of bonuses, another unheard-of thing, spurred the men on, with a double bonus for those who were willing to work on Sunday. Kreuger had discovered that, like his idol Napoleon, he was capable of going for long periods without sleep. Now he seemed to go without sleep altogether, though actually he took occasional cat naps in a rented room nearby. He seemed to be everywhere at once, urging the men on. Those who had known him at technical school shook their heads at his demoniac activity. "He seemed lazy to us in school, but look at him now!" one reputedly said.

Kreuger's high-powered American methods became the talk of Stockholm, but some of the city's inhabitants found them more annoying than amazing. Among those objecting were the folk who lived nearby. Not only was their neighborhood noisy all day, but the horrendous din of Kreuger's night work kept them sleepless. At first these harried individuals only wrote letters to the Stockholm papers. Then everyone in the locality signed a petition, which complained particularly of the all-night crunching of Stockholm's first cement mixer. The number of signatures carried such weight that Kreuger himself was forced to take pen in hand to write an answer. In his letter the persuasive, hypnotic voice which later accomplished so many verbal wonders can almost be heard spinning out half-truths:

> In the first place it is only a machine which is working during the night, a concrete mixer which operates very quietly and does not cause undue disturbance. The firm has done all in its power to cause the neighbors as little displeasure as possible and the police have shown that the evening calm has not been disturbed to any great extent. One ought to be able to understand that the firm does not take delight in running night shifts when it is remembered that we must pay double-time for night work.

Kreuger & Toll started laying the foundations for Stockholm's first skyscraper on November tenth. By January tenth, the skeleton structure was up, and a month later the building was nearly finished. It is to be presumed that the owners were delighted by this, but their joy may have been mitigated by the fact that the day of final completion came no less than two months ahead of the date stipulated in the contract. Thus, by the clause they had so indifferently permitted, they were obligated to pay Kreuger & Toll the neat sum of 30,-000 kroner. This feat so buoyed up the usually unemotional Kreuger that he next conceived the idea of putting on the side of another Stockholm building an electric sign spelling out the firm's name. This was another American stunt which had never been seen in Stockholm before, and the populace turned its back on brilliant displays of Northern lights to gape in wonder at the electric bulbs which spelled out KREUGER & TOLL.

It is probable that no firm ever flourished so rapidly in Scandinavia as did Kreuger & Toll. By 1910, it was incorporated at one million kroner, and a year later this sum was raised to two million. With financial success went accompanying creative achievement. The firm built the foundations for the Stockholm City Hall, still considered by many the most beautiful building in all Scandinavia. Here, too, the work was finished two months ahead of time, though it was "fraught with many technical complications." In 1912, Kreuger & Toll erected the Stockholm Stadium for the Olympic Games, "a structure with a fine, massive gateway like that of a castle, the whole combining beauty with utility." With such monuments to its skill and efficiency, the firm soon became the foremost construction company in Scandinavia and altogether it—which is to say Kreuger, with his American ideas—can be credited with making Sweden among the first, if not the first, country in Europe to possess modern office, apartment, and factory buildings.

This fact has given rise to a public portrait of Kreuger working from 1908–1913 with such intense, controlled energy and constructive passion that he became known as the most imaginative builder in Europe, a man totally absorbed by his work and because of that able to adjust to a bachelor life without the warmth of a wife and home. "There was a peculiar similarity between Kreuger's own structure and the structure of his work," one writer has opined. "He seemed to be one of the very few persons alive who could immerse his whole personality in his job."

Which is right—up to a point. Kreuger's total immersion in his work was all too true. But a close scrutiny of the work itself shows a somewhat different Kreuger. After his first success in construction, he began to lose interest in building as such. Occasionally, on projects like the Olympic Stadium or Stockholm City Hall, he slipped back into harness to use his powers of concentration and his engineering know-how to cut corners and figure ways of accomplishing the seemingly impossible.

But from 1909–1913, he increasingly left planning and construction to Paul Toll while he reached into such promotional aspects as securing contracts, raising capital and buying and selling American machinery. Finally, he launched what has been called his "foreign invasion" which meant opening branch offices of Kreuger & Toll in Germany, Finland, Russia and the Scandinavian countries. Through these outlets he not only sold the building services of Kreuger & Toll, but also Kahn iron, building equipment and various types of steel—anything, indeed, calculated to make money.

From the rapidity and vision with which Kreuger planned his foreign invasion, it is possible to conclude that expansion had been in the back of his mind all the time—that he came back from America with the goal of making himself as soon as possible into an industrialist of the Morgan-Rockefeller type. Or perhaps the idea took possession of him when at last he found himself working solely for Ivar Kreuger. This, of course, was the opportunity he had been waiting for. Suddenly he was the master of his fate, with the road to achievement stretching before him. As soon as possible he slipped away from actual building, to shift around, ever with an eye to the main chance—the opportunity to become a robber baron on the American grand pattern.

It also made a personality change in the still-young man. Like an inflated balloon which, after being secured to the ground, is suddenly let loose to soar skyward, Kreuger also began to soar. The man who for years could have been accused of feeling superior to his fellow man seemed to shift mental gears and start the journey to superman complex. Had he been under supervision in a mental clinic, this bourgeoning state might have been diagnosed as the first stages of delusions of grandeur, or megalomania. The Swedes themselves have a word for it. It is *Storhetsvansinne,* an affliction of the brain which magnifies matters, causing the victim to "think big, to see himself and the world in Napoleonic proportions."

In view of this soaring state of mind, incipient though it might be, Kreuger's sudden decision in 1913 to abandon building construction and enter the match business is perhaps easy to understand. But at the time it appeared baffling. It was considered violent and inexplicable that a prosperous and celebrated builder should quit his flourishing business to take up a post in a floundering match business.

In fact, Kreuger's 1913 move seemed such a strange one that stories about it still exist. The most widely circulated states that in 1912 there was a general building lull in Scandinavia. Several construction firms failed, and even Kreuger & Toll felt a depression. Kreuger—as sometimes happened when things beyond his control befell him—went to pieces. Holding head in hands, he mourned to Toll the ephemeral nature of business success. "A sudden vague, creeping horror began to crush him," says one version of the story. "Of what avail was all this hard work if suddenly circumstances could go against him?"

According to the story, the practical Paul Toll sought to reassure his partner. "You have to expect such things in our business, Ivar," he said soothingly. "If you want complete security, you must make something people absolutely must have."

At which Kreuger supposedly pricked up his ears, and shortly he had renounced the building business. To his family's vast surprise, he returned to Kalmar to take over the family factories, which made something people absolutely needed.

Like so many pat stories, this one has little basis in fact. Kreuger and Toll—so close that in correspondence each addressed the other as "Brother Kreuger" or "Brother Toll" —may well have discussed the general insecurity of business, and Toll may well have made his remark about absolute necessity. But Kreuger got into the match business for more practical reasons. In 1912 his father Ernst August Kreuger's match factories were not doing well. What was more natural than for the Stockholm banks financially concerned to call in Ernst's brilliant son for a consultation. This was done and—for a fee—Ivar agreed to make an analysis of his father's business. He returned this to the bank in March, 1913, and the bankers who perused it found that Ivar had not confined himself to analyzing his father's factories. He had surveyed the entire Swedish match industry and believed it threatened by ruin because of internal competition and excessive undercutting. There were far too many small factories scrambling to capture the market, he concluded, and the entire industry was badly "in need of someone with vision and organizing ability who would generally pull together the interests of the industry as a whole."

This conclusion was of small interest to the Stockholm bankers, who were concerned solely with Ernst August's three mortgaged factories. But the report so impressed them that they took the step of asking Ivar if he would consider taking over reorganization and operation of his father's factories.

It is said that, as always when facing a vital problem, Kreuger retired to his office and concentrated until he had examined every possible angle involved. This time he reached the conclusion that the match business was the right place for him. Much has been made of his farsightedness in reaching this decision. But was it so farsighted? It would seem more likely that, in his solitary concentrations, Kreuger might better have castigated himself for not thinking of matches long before.

For the man who, during the past five years, had cast around Scandinavia and eastern Europe for an opportunity to become an American-type industrialist had now found an industry which was perfect for his purposes. It needed "someone with vision and organizing ability" to pull it together, and who was better prepared for that than Ivar Kreuger?

And all the time opportunity had been on his family doorstep! It was ironic, but Kreuger, the rabid business opportunist, did not pause to let the irony sink in. He disposed of his modest Stockholm living quarters, packed his bags, and set out for Kalmar.

Chapter 7

Steps Toward a Dream

A *curious* episode took place in Kreuger's life shortly after he returned to his father's Kalmar match factories.

On the surface he seemed to be turning his back on Kreuger & Toll, but actually he carried with him control of the firm. Departing for Kalmar to enter the sprawling, disorganized match business, he retained his majority stock so that he still was, to all intents and purposes, the "boss," though reliable Paul Toll was actually in charge. Kreuger was especially anxious to retain all the Kreuger & Toll "foreign-invasion" business and, since Toll was busy with building, had picked another man with excellent business connections and proven selling ability to carry this on.

Unfortunately, the man's name is as lost to the record as that of Kreuger's Norwegian girl friend. But he is remembered as an excellent choice. In later years, Kreuger would be accused of surrounding himself with men of inferior mental ability, but not in the case of this subordinate. Here he used all his basic knowledge of human character to pick the best man possible.

If anything, the man was too good. For his feats of enterprise and selling began threatening the records set by Kreuger in his five years of effort, which until then had been considered the ultimate in accomplishment. This fact did not escape the eyes and ears of Kreuger, though supposedly he was busily immersed in making over three match factories.

To the surprise of Paul Toll and others who had worked close to him, the apparently emotionless Kreuger began manifesting what appeared to be extreme jealousy. Over the 250 miles separating Kalmar from Stockholm he began sending orders which, if carried out, would put obstacles in the path of the new man's achievements. This only seemed to spur the man to greater efforts, and Kreuger himself hurried to Stockholm to call a stockholders meeting. At this gathering, for the first time in anyone's memory, the calm man lost control of himself. He became "hysterical."

While in the grip of this unlikely emotion, Kreuger summoned his subordinate back from Finland to the Kreuger & Toll office. But before the man could arrive, Kreuger did an incredible thing. He complained to police that his representative was guilty of falsifying the records he sent into Kreuger & Toll. In other words, that the man's considerable accomplishments were false.

He insisted that police interrogate the man. This was done, and authorities quickly became convinced that no false entries had been made, a fact which seemed to drive Kreuger deeper into a vengeful fury. He started personal action against his subordinate, but in court his accusations seemed as ludicrous as they had to police. He was ordered to return the Kreuger & Toll foreign-invasion business to the man at once.

In the life of the Match King, all this contributes an odd footnote. For one thing, it shows that Kreuger, whose self-control always seemed so uncanny—he is even considered by Dr. Bjerre to have had "no inner conflicts, only outer ones"—did indeed have conflicts. But up to this point, he had been fortunate in that his genius-mind had kept his image of superiority from injury. Now it had been violated by the efforts of a mere salesman who seemed able to outdo the superman. It was more than Kreuger could take. The impassive, controlled man went to pieces like any spoiled child, putting on a temper tantrum and shouting threats of "getting even." By so doing he carried through on the belief of many that Kreuger, despite all his surface maturity, was always basically immature, perhaps living out his life on what Sigmund Freud has called the youngest, or narcissistic, emotional level.

Whether or not this is so, there can be no doubt that hidden in the fastnesses of the Ivar Kreuger personality was a very human human being. Yet this is one of the few glances the world gets at it. For Kreuger's attack of jealousy disappeared almost as fast as it came. With the subordinate back at work and out of the country, Kreuger returned to Kalmar in apparent control of his emotions. Indeed, as in the agony of his love affair, he may have been strengthened by his unseemly seizure. It was as if the belief he had nurtured from childhood—that one got nowhere by displaying human emotions—had been given practical proof. It made him colder, more determined than ever to rise above his feelings.

And to this one odd footnote on Kreuger's career can also be added another—which those who see him as a villain-from-birth have not hesitated to point out.

For in the episode of the foreign salesman, Kreuger, with the speed of reflex action, accused the man of falsifying his financial reports to make them seem better. This was a thing which, at some point in his life, Kreuger unquestionably began doing himself. His detractors say that because this type of crime leaped immediately to his mind, he had probably already begun to falsify the books of Kreuger & Toll, to make the firm's remarkable upward spiral of success the more remarkable. So if—detractors continue—he had over the years been padding Kreuger & Toll books, he was probably doing the same, or contemplating it, with match-company books.

Why else would falsification of accounts leap so readily to his mind?

But on this psychological foundation only rests the accusation of early wrongdoing. No one knows, exactly, when Kreuger began "improving" the books of his companies. In his lifetime only a few stray employees of his many enterprises ever suspected him of doing it, and certainly it was far from anyone's mind when late in 1913 the thirty-three-year-old Kreuger, with the unpleasant Stockholm incident apparently forgotten, again buckled down to work with his three match factories.

On the surface of his business operations, Kreuger began to set the pattern of his entire legitimate business career. He was bold, resourceful, tireless, inspired. His skill, accomplishments, and farsightedness as a businessman and industrialist can never be questioned or tarnished. He was indubitably Kreuger the Genius.

Yet beneath the surface another Kreuger was slowly taking hold. Whether from *Storhetsvansinne*, or legitimate ambition, he was beginning to dream of match control that went even beyond the borders of Sweden. He made no secret of his dreams. Indeed, he told everyone. Writing in *The New York Times*, journalist Harold Callender states that Kreuger first envisioned his match conquest of the world at a dinner given him in the summer of 1913 on his assumption of control of the family factories. Callender pictures Kreuger rising to his feet to make a perfunctory speech of thanks, then suddenly becoming "lyric" as he finds himself carried away by the possibilities of the match business. It was at this moment Callender believes that his "dream first took possession of him."

Several months later the dream had assumed more definite shape. Meeting his old friend Anders Jordahl on a Baltic steamer, he held his South African companion intensely by the arm and "told me with great enthusiasm that he was going to try to collect all the match factories of the world on one hand—to form a match monopoly over the whole world. He showed me that if he succeeded in this plan everybody who was interested in investing money in match factories could expect to make huge profits."

As so often happens with men who achieve great heights in their own time, Kreuger, in his dream, was assisted by the times themselves. The outbreak of World War I in August, 1914, immediately filled the Baltic and the North Sea with submarines of the combatant nations. Frontiers bristled with bayonets and impregnable barriers. The considerable export market for Swedish matches vanished at one fell swoop, and the import of new materials became exceedingly difficult.

To nearly everyone in the world, this was dreadful calamity. But to Kreuger, just getting a grip on his three Kalmar match factories, it was something of a boon. For he knew that in order to gain control of the Swedish match industry, which would be the first step in any world plan, he would have to crush the great Jönköping-Vulcan combine, the mightiest in Sweden. Jönköping was named for the beautiful old town at the southern end of the Wattersee which became the cradle of the Swedish match industry. The company stemmed straight from Janne Lundström who chose the town for his first factory, consisting of two rented rooms. There, after acquiring patent right to the rough, so-called Pach process (based on the idea of transferring the phosphorus from match head to friction surface), he perfected the safety match. After which considerable achievement Janne Lundström faded from the picture.

His brother Karl Franz took over, conceiving plans for promoting the safety match in Sweden and abroad. The smartest thing Karl Lundström did was to carry his Swedish safety matches to the Paris Exposition of 1855. There they won top honors. It was these two gold medals which focused attention on the excellent Swedish matches, creating a world-wide demand for them.

Still a third member of the Lundström Jönköping firm—Alex Lagerman—invented most of the machinery which rapidly and efficiently prepared and finished the individual Swedish match. In the decades following—and even today—the process of making safety matches to be put in wooden boxes has hardly changed. Even adapted to book matches, the basic operation is still that of Lundström's idea, plus Lagerman's invention. Few have been able to improve on the process which has been described by the Swedish author Sterner in a monograph:

> Here the matches are in readiness. They too are made chiefly of aspen wood. The tree trunks have been planed, sawn into blocks twenty to twenty-five inches long, damped, softened, barked, and cut into pieces exactly the thickness of a match. These pieces are divided into long strips by matchwood cutters. The tree has now been turned into matchsticks—the material has been reduced to the required dimensions. A machine now arranges the masses of little slips of wood and forces them on to a board with innumerable holes which receive the columns of matches, wedge them in, and press them into flat pans containing the inflammable matter. This clings firmly to their heads. Then another machine fills them into the boxes, and yet a further one wraps up and labels the finished boxes in tens.

Such a machine as Lagerman's could not long be confined to a single factory and before the end of the nineteenth century "match-making had taken Sweden by storm, and every person, it seemed, who had nothing better to do started a match factory." Most of these factories speedily failed, but enough remained so that when Kreuger entered the business, the Swedish match industry was still "debased." Practically the only firm far-seeing enough to combat this debasement was Jönköping, which in 1903 had effected a merger with a rival named Vulcan, to make eight large factories into one big concern. When Kreuger appeared on the scene, Jönköping-Vulcan was to the Swedish Match business what U. S. Steel is to the American steel industry. It was this combine —capitalized at 17 million kroner—which eventually Kreuger would have to control.

To the conservative, hidebound Jönköping—one of whose major markets was British India—the outbreak of war in 1914 was indeed a calamity. It was a situation made to order for the daring, adroit Kreuger.

As with Kreuger & Toll in Stockholm, he placed his reliance on American methods. Before the declaration of war he had with "huge, vital energy," begun importing modern machinery from America, and organizing his distribution along efficient, flexible Yankee lines. He also introduced worker-specialization in his factories—that is, each man had a single assembly-line job to do. This had never before been done in Swedish industry, where the integrity of the worker was valued highly.

With the coming of actual hostilities, Kreuger set about making a virtue of necessity, using in the process far more vision and drive than anyone at Jönköping-Vulcan seemed to possess. Were phosphorous and potash difficult to import? He built factories in Sweden equipped to produce both. Were raw materials almost impossible to get? Kreuger got all he could, hired bright young chemists whose clever formulas made up for part of the lack. Were foreign markets closed because of the war? Not at all—Kreuger, with his pre-war "foreign-invasion" of eastern Europe could still find a few outlets, and acting on his instructions men in London worked to find similar outlets in the West.

While doing all this, Kreuger used his hypnotic capabilities as persuader and charmer. Working on the owners of six nearby match factories, he soon persuaded them to sell out or combine with him. By 1915 he had ten match companies under his control. He called them the United Swedish Match Factories, or the Kalmar Trust. Against Jönköping's eight large factories Kreuger now stood arrayed with ten small but perfectly equipped ones which exported to Canada and the United States as well as supplying a large part of the domestic market.

This swift success brought Kreuger a new weapon in his fight to conquer competition. In fact, through his later business life Kreuger always had this weapon, which was awe. Rivals in business stood in awe of him not so much because of any ruthless, inhuman qualities—indeed, in person Kreuger always seemed courteous and mild—as because of his seemingly superhuman skill. The sallow, enigmatic man began to seem so diabolically clever, so totally convinced of ultimate success, that most of those who sat down to negotiate with him were beaten from the start.

This all brought great prosperity to the Kalmar Trust, which by 1917 was showing an annual profit of two million kroner, and had just opened a new wood-conversion factory. At this point of his career, Kreuger began initialing office memos with a quick I.K. Soon he became I.K.—which in English sounds like Ee-Ko—to most of his subordinates, except those of the highest echelon, who would always call him

Ivar. "I.K. will manage, I.K. can do anything," became the motto of his concerns. This was no small tribute, for one of the problems Kreuger faced in absorbing new match companies was the stubborn, old-fashioned ideas on the part of employees. "He had to fight conservatism and tradition in places where they exuded from the walls," one writer says. Kreuger—still under forty—everywhere found entrenched doggedness and obstinacy, "but by using his charm he won most over. When this was impossible he showed that he had not roamed the world and rubbed shoulders with all manner of men for nothing, he could intrigue and scheme. . . ."

Vastly strengthening the hand of the already awesome Kreuger was the fact that annual balance sheets of his Kalmar Trust showed such neat, convincing profits. So attractive were these sums that Swedish money circles began to apply to Kreuger the ancient saying, "He can make gold." Indeed, the Kalmar Trust profits were so perfect that even so partial a biographer as Dr. Bjerre wonders if the books were not doctored. "The upward swing of profits is so striking that one cannot help suspecting that the balancings of the books might have been fixed," he writes.

But again no one ever uncovered falsifications, perhaps because Kreuger seemed able to perform the miracle of fixing the books before figures were even entered.

He did this by a method soon to become familiar to his associates. At an annual meeting of stockholders he would take the floor and in his winning voice inform the assembled group that in some cases the company assets were difficult to evaluate. "Perhaps they are sound today, but not tomorrow," he would declare disarmingly. "Profits in our company should therefore be held below six million kroner and arranged so that part of this profit comes from 'free' shares from our affiliated companies. By this, profits to be taxed can be held under five per cent of company funds, and thus escape government tax."

But suppose—to further illustrate the Kreuger technique of "elusive half-truths, buttressed by elusive, sometimes wholly irrelevant facts"—one of the stockholders listening had risen to ask: "What do you mean, Herr Ingenjör? Do we really arrive at a year's profits in this prearranged way? The profit should be an honest, straightforward declaration of what a business has earned. How can our company make up a projected balance sheet which increases dividends and reduces assets in this almost illegal way?"

In answer, Kreuger would no doubt first smile in superior fashion and allow himself a few paces up and down the room, as he always did when thinking. Then, quietly and modestly he would begin: "The public wants to see its shares rise, and it wants to get as much interest as possible on its money. That is all the public wants. As far as the company is concerned, in order to do this, we must perhaps anticipate the profits of coming years, and this anticipation will always be as good for the company as for shareholders, since it gives the company an opportunity to strengthen its position in different ways. It is nothing new to treat company books this way."

Patiently, condescendingly, as if talking to a backward child, he would continue to explain how this custom of adjusting books was nothing but a necessary consequence of contemporary capitalism. He would give an overwhelming array of evidence to prove this, "putting forth impressive facts from his phenomenal memory, so that listeners thought: He certainly knows what he is talking about." He would do all this so logically and convincingly that his unfortunate questioner would get the impression that he himself was stupid not to understand and a fool for having brought the matter up in the first place.

But most important of all, he would decide never again to question the ethics of Herr Ingenjör Kreuger.

8

The Swedish Match King

The big Jönköping-Vulcan combine collapsed under pressure from Kreuger's smaller but streamlined Kalmar Trust in the winter of 1917. "It came to a short but fierce struggle between them," says one account, "but the end was never really in doubt, for at the head of the Kalmar concern was Ivar Kreuger. . . ."

Chief among Kreuger's assets was his uncanny adroitness in creating raw materials where, because of wartime blockades, none seemed to be. Largely, he outstripped his big rival by securing the available potash and phosphorus factories. In December, 1917, Jönköping found itself in the disastrous position of having a phosphorus supply sufficient for only two more months. Kreuger, the man who always looked ahead, had just bought the phosphorus firm of Hamilton & Hansell in Trollhäten, thus assuring himself an indefinite supply. He was strong, Jönköping weak.

From this position, he stepped forward to suggest a merger of the two firms, which between them now constituted the entire Swedish match industry. Jönköping offered a loose merger under which both would combine with the name of the Swedish Match Company. Kreuger agreed.

Swedish Match would be incorporated with a capital of 45 million kroner and a reserve fund of 61,740,000 kroner. With all this, it would have no factories of its own, for it was purely a holding company for the stocks of Jönköping

and the Kalmar Trust. Theoretically, because of his strangle-
hold on Jönköping, Kreuger would be top man in Swedish
Match. But at the same time Jönköping retained a measure
of independence. Jönköping-Vulcan was still larger than
Kreuger's companies and on paper its stock far overwhelmed
his. Such a situation was not one calculated to satisfy Kreuger,
who was never a man to co-operate with another company
even though—to all intents and purposes—he dominated it.
He had to attain complete control of Jönköping and he did
so by a device which has since become ordinary, but was then
somewhat rare. He got control of the votes of enough small
stockholders to command the majority block of stock. The
Swedish writer, Helmut Wickel, pictures him thinking it
through this way:

> Kreuger said to himself: I cannot get half the shares
> of Swedish Match, because the individual shareholders
> of the two match concerns have a claim to the greater
> number of these shares and will certainly not waive
> that claim. But there are plenty of individual share-
> holders who have been independent match manufac-
> turers and were not particularly clever business men. It
> is I who first put the Swedish match industry on to a
> sound basis. If I acquire enough shares to make it im-
> possible for the other shareholders to out-vote me unless
> they are all united against me, I shall certainly be able
> to carry my own ideas into effect—I can always man-
> age to get a few shareholders over on to my side. If I
> am careful, I need never fear the formation of a majority
> against me.

Before gaining full control of Swedish Match, Kreuger
took another most important step. Asserting his majority
control of Kreuger & Toll, he organized another firm called
Kreuger & Toll Building Company. Into this he pushed Paul

Toll and his still-successful building operations. Toll retained his stock in the parent company, and stayed on as a director. But from now on Kreuger & Toll was Ivar Kreuger.

Like Swedish Match, Kreuger & Toll was also purely a holding company. But after that came a vast difference. Where Swedish Match had been organized only for match-company stocks, Kreuger & Toll was to function as a holding company for anything Kreuger chose to buy with its funds. Or to credit it with. "Kreuger & Toll was from this moment a completely one-man operation," one writer states. Immediately he used Kreuger & Toll capital to purchase 120,000 shares of Swedish Match—slightly more than one quarter of the total stock. Thus he created the first of the bewildering interlocking-company deals that were to characterize his future activities. Next he issued an annual report on Kreuger & Toll. This claimed earnings of over 1 million kroner, which, Kreuger said, justified declaring a dividend of 20 per cent. Then he put Kreuger & Toll stock on the market. In 1918, a year later, he made two new capital issues, raising its share-capital to 16 million kroner and its reserves to 21 million.

Had anyone cared to look intently at Kreuger & Toll—as no one did—the results might have been interesting!

The Board of Directors consisted of Kreuger; his father, Ernst August; Paul Toll; and "two Kreuger-made men," Major Nils Ahlström and Erik Sjöström. Later testimony indicated that Ahlström had neither the training nor mental capacity to participate in involved financial transactions. But this made little difference, since Ahlström and Sjöström both swore that the directors were never consulted in Kreuger & Toll matters. Later Sjöström pictured an annual meeting of the holding company. "When we had all gathered together," he said, "Kreuger would come walking briskly in and go through a monolog something like this: 'Good morning, gentlemen. Will the secretary please read the minutes? It has been decided to purchase some iron ore mines in Germany and real estate in Paris. It has also been decided to increase the capital of Kreuger & Toll by twelve million kroner by issuing new shares at a rate of two hundred and forty per cent of par. Do I hear any objections? Thank you, gentlemen. Good morning.' " After hearing this testimony a writer commented: "If any one of those present had enough of an idea what was going on to formulate a question, he held his tongue. Kreuger did not like questions."

From the moment of its inception, the great public success of the new Kreuger & Toll was based on its large dividends. But even the original dividend of 20 per cent, future events would indicate, was probably fixed arbitrarily for psychological reasons. Further, it was almost certainly paid out of capital. Kreuger, with his absolute control, was able to use Kreuger & Toll money as a sleight-of-hand artist uses a deck of cards. At the end of 1918 he announced Kreuger & Toll earnings of 4,309,535 kroner and a pleasing dividend of 22½. But what justified such large returns? No one knew. In his plausible annual report Kreuger merely listed over half the profits of Kreuger & Toll as "earnings from various transactions."

Up to the point where he resumed control of Kreuger & Toll, Kreuger had always dealt with tangibles—engineering figures, building materials, the reorganization of match factories, the overwhelming of competition. As such, he had been the businessman-industrialist. But then came another milestone in his career. With Kreuger & Toll, he entered the heady realm of stock-and-bond manipulation. It was also, because of his sound success as head of Swedish Match, a realm of credit, where he could command huge sums of money simply by scrawling his signature.

Thus, the businessman-industrialist had taken a step toward becoming the Financier, but why he wanted to do so is another of the mysterious aspects of a curious personality. At the age of thirty-eight, Kreuger stood forth as the Swedish Match King, absolute ruler of one of the largest and most profitable businesses in the world. It should have satisfied anyone. He was—or shortly would be—a millionaire and over the years his millions inevitably would increase. Further, he would be a millionaire in a country of few rich people, one of the pleasantest countries in the world in which to be rich.

There was more. If the near-arctic climate and long winter nights of his native country grew monotonous, a Swedish millionaire could always, in a few hours, reach the south of France. Swedes understood such winter vacations quite well, for their kings customarily spent long periods on the Riviera, the contemporary one, Gustav Adolph, playing tennis there with the skill of a professional. Nor would the existence of a millionaire Swedish Match King have been only vacations and coupon clipping. With the conclusion of World War I, in November, 1918, there arose new problems to tax the mind of any business genius. Termination of European hostilities brought an export-picture different from any the Swedish match industry had faced in the past.

Before the war, the Swedes had controlled European and other world markets by sheer ability to manufacture better matches. Then the countries of Europe had constituted a sprawling community only too eager to import such commodities. But war changed all that. From 1914 on, European countries of necessity grew more autonomous and, from wartime need, began to manufacture their own matches. These were far inferior to the excellent Swedish product, but they were a domestic product, taxable as such, and therefore a source of much-needed revenue. To ensure the utmost in match revenue, a few countries had made match manufacture a state monopoly. Others in which Sweden once had a flourishing market began protecting domestic factories by erecting prohibitive tariff barriers. Some countries—notably Hungary, Germany and Belgium—had even begun to export matches. These, too, were far inferior to the Swedish product, but low currency rates in countries whose treasuries had been depleted by war made it possible for them to sell at a far lower price than Swedish exporters.

In the Far East, formerly an exclusively Jönköping market, the picture had also changed. In 1913, the Jönköping factory had played host to a group of traveling Japanese technicians. It became an act of international friendliness the Swedes never ceased to regret. Not only did Swedish engineers explain in detail all match-making machinery, but suddenly one of the visitors dropped his hat into a vat full of secret chemical. It seemed like an accident and the hat was retrieved and returned. Later the Swedes realized the hat-dropping had been intentional. In his hotel room the Japanese analyzed the secret mixture. While the war kept Jönköping out of the East, the Japanese had been able to manufacture and sell matches made on the Swedish pattern. To make sure no one missed this point they cannily stamped each box: "Made in Tidaholm, Sweden."

This and other problems would certainly keep a purely Swedish Match King busy. For the Swedish match industry was at a crossroad. It either had to abandon export and resign itself to a ruinously small percentage of its prewar business. Or it could start an aggressive fight for the recovery of former markets.

Yet with this to challenge his abilities there is not the slightest indication that Kreuger ever thought of remaining solely the Swedish Match King. No matter what its rewards and pleasures, such a position in the world promised only millions, where he had begun dreaming in billions. But was it in terms of money that he dreamed? Rather it was in terms of power, which has been defined as "the determination to be among the great ones of the earth." Kreuger's own words bear out the fact that it was lust for power which drove him on. "It is the utilization of money for power that the financier aims at," he later told an interviewer.

Such a man could make only one decision on how to operate with the Swedish match industry. He would start the aggressive fight for recovery of former world markets—and even more. The decision was immediately reflected in his personality. Says a writer: "He resolved himself to the new task with all the energy and ruthless craft in his make-up. Simultaneously, he seemed to withdraw from his old circle of friends, became increasingly mysterious in his movements, and more abrupt in his dealings with underlings."

With ease he obtained from Swedish banks the millions of kroner necessary for Swedish Match to fight for its prewar export profits. He left the actual domestic production of matches to the managers of his Swedish Match factories, who with a generation of match-making already behind them were by now also experienced in carrying out the American innovations Kreuger had introduced.

It all left him free to fulfill his dream of becoming a Match King outside Sweden, and perhaps nothing at this point indicates the grandeur of Kreuger's dreams more than the Match Palace which, shortly after gaining control of Jönköping, he conceived as a world headquarters for Swedish Match, Kreuger & Toll, and such other enterprises as the future might bring. Summoning Ivar Tengböm, Sweden's foremost architect, Kreuger described to him a building the basis of which seemed to extend back to the daydreaming young student who pointed nonchalantly to the Royal Palace, and said, "I'm going to have one like it some day."

Kreuger's conception was a 125-room edifice, complete with board room, executive offices, staff offices and a match museum. For the location of his magnificent new structure he did not choose the business section of Stockholm. Instead, he picked a dignified residential street called Vasträ Trädgardsgaten, just off the Royal Gardens. It was lined with mansions of the *ancien régime* and Kreuger's Match Palace —no other name was possible for the building—did nothing to destroy its atmosphere of old world elegance. The façade of the structure was close to the street, and the American journalist, Isaac F. Marcosson, has described his impressions on entering:

> The moment you passed the finely wrought iron gates you got the atmosphere of some continental palace. Instead of the dusty, tarnished splendour of a departed day, however, it is bright and gleaming. Massive marble columns surround what the French call a court of honour. In the center is a bronze fountain surmounted by a graceful, poised figure of Diana, the work of Carl Milles. . . .

Kreuger's office on the second floor of this noble structure was, of course, impressive. It was soundproofed, and its color scheme of dark brown was carried out in carpet, curtains and woodwork. His severe table-desk, standing beside the first window on the left side of the large room, was decorated by an imposing glass lamp made at the famed Swedish Orrefors factory. The wall on the far side was covered by a Gobelin tapestry in front of which stood a comfortable settee, with two small armchairs and a coffee table.

Here the Match King sat when talking to important visitors. Filling out the handsome room were bookshelves, chairs, and two antique cabinets, while over the door a design showed a torch symbolic of the matches that lighted the world.

At Kreuger's elbow when he worked was a small table on which stood at least three telephones. One of these was a special "Chief's phone," designed after Kreuger's ideas by L. M. Ericsson, president of the Swedish telephone company, which later played such a vital part in Kreuger's life. This unobtrusive telephone possessed extra sensitive mouth- and earpieces. When lifted from its cradle and placed on Kreuger's desk, the Match King, a man who increasingly enjoyed pacing up and down as he talked, could walk around the room while holding phone conversations. Nine of his top executives possessed similar phones, so that Kreuger could hold conferences without summoning his aides to his office. Through the sensitive earpiece he could also hear what they said to him, no matter where he stood in his office. The Chief's phone was also capable of outside calls, and as years passed it became possible for Kreuger to make transatlantic calls through the phone at his desk while sitting at his ease under the Gobelin tapestry.

Under this desk was another gadget which later produced a sensation. This was a button in the floor which, when touched by the Match King's foot, caused one of the telephones to ring. When it suited his purposes, Kreuger could touch the button, then pick up one of the three phones—the number of which later became six. This phone, of course, was a dummy, and if his visitor was an important one, Kreuger could hold impressive conversations with crowned heads and dictators. If his visitor was merely a nuisance, the Match King would claim to be called to another part of the building.

Next to Kreuger's own office, and nearly approximating it in elegance, was that of a man remarkable in that he seemed to be Kreuger's most trusted friend on earth, one of the few for whom the Swedish Match King displayed any personal warmth. This was Krister Littorin, a friend from technical-school days, who also could be addressed as Herr Ingenjör. Littorin, rugged-looking, energetic, radiating simple honesty, displayed a doglike devotion for Kreuger and plainly would accept his employer's word on any matter. To the world Littorin seemed to be Kreuger's second-in-command, and indeed was in charge of the Match Palace when Kreuger was out of Stockholm. But did the worshiping Littorin have any idea what plans were in Kreuger's mind? It was Kreuger's policy to keep his top executives working in a single channel, almost totally unaware of what others might be doing. With the personal warmth he seemed to feel for Krister Littorin, he still did not trust him more than others in a business sense. Beside Littorin's name a future investigator would scribble: "Knows no more than the lift boy at the Match Palace."

When Kreuger and Littorin attended important company meetings in the Match Palace, they repaired to the Board Room on the third floor. This was the most striking room in the entire building, "the last word in imposing elegance." Its outstanding feature was its curve. For as ex-builder Kreuger visualized his Board Room it was too large even for the sizable Match Palace building. Explained architect Ivar Tengböm:

It was somewhat difficult, on account of its size, to fit this room into the rather uniform scheme. In the course of the preliminary work, Mr. Ivar Kreuger evolved the idea that it should be placed in the curved part of the house which encloses the upper arc of the centre courtyard's semicircle, and was not deterred by the fact that the room would in this way be somewhat detached from the directors' rooms. This was the solution. Here it could be extended both in height and in width at the expense of the floor above and the corridor on each side, and the interruption in the corridor system would not cause any inconvenience. From an architectural point of view it was a happy idea, for in this way the courtyard façade gained its special centre of gravity. That the room acquired a curious design on account of its curved form did not appear to suggest any practical drawbacks, but on the other hand could invest the room itself with a particular interest.

No expense was spared in decorating the Board Room. Wall paneling was mahogany inlaid with walnut. The color scheme was "warm red-brown, composed of hues like raw Sienna, terra de Pozzuoli, Venetian red, blended with ochre tones of raw umber, burnt umber, yellow ochre, and gamboge, contrasting slightly with a tone of grayish blue." A painting by the Swedish modern artist, Isaac Grunewald, was a conspicuous feature. The furniture was of citron wood inlaid with ivory. There were also ivory inlays around the edge of the curved directors' table—one ivory design in front of each chair, symbolizing the various countries in which Swedish matches were sold. Covering the long table was a beautiful leather top, decorated with gold. At either end of the curved room stood a large open fireplace of Gropptorp marble. Over each was a mosaic composed of forty-six kinds of wood. One represented Thor's struggle with the giants, the other the Five Continents worshiping fire.

On one mantel stood an antique clock which for a special reason was a Kreuger favorite. On it the hour V was both preceded and followed by IV. The Match King's sharp eye spotted this flaw immediately, and legend has it that he placed the clock conspicuously in the Board Room for a purpose. "No one but me will ever be quick enough to notice the mistake," he stated confidently. And no one, the story goes on, ever was.

But in the Match Palace even the Board Room was in the long run overshadowed in importance by a tiny, hidden room. This was the Silence Room.

For Ivar Kreuger was obsessed by silence. Except when using his powers of persuasion, or on rare social occasions, his conversation was sparse and cryptic. To the press, in answer to probing questions, he was fond of quoting the Swedish proverb, "Great things happen in silence." When Isaac Marcosson asked his three rules of success, Kreuger unhesitatingly replied, "Silence—More Silence—Still More Silence." In every one of his offices and apartments there had to be a small room to which he could retire to perform in total silence the prodigies of concentration of which he was capable.

In Kreuger's Match Palace, the Silence Room was a small hideaway on the third floor. In it were simply a desk and chair, while adjoining it was a dressing room with a couch and a bath, so that Kreuger could spend nights in the Silence Room if he so wished. Of all the rooms in the magnificent Match Palace this bare, tiny one was the most indicative of Kreuger's true personality.

Kreuger had no sooner established himself as the Swedish Match King than he cast around for living quarters in Stockholm suitable to a newly made millionaire. In 1919, he decided on the two top floors of a mansion at 13 Villagatan, and having chosen this mansion, he not only purchased it but all the houses nearby. Then—some inner insecurity apparently assuaged, or his importance having been proved to the immediate neighbors—he commissioned the fashionable Stockholm decorator Hörlin to create a richly furnished bachelor flat.

In time, the Villagatan apartment became something of a show place, with a wide curving staircase, like that in a manor house or palace, leading from the first to second floor. On his first floor—the third floor of the mansion—were a large drawing room and a formal dining room, with valuable but rather stiff furniture. The walls were paneled walnut and the furniture, "oak, in the cabriole-leg Queen Anne tradition." Color was added to the drawing room by etchings by the Swedish artist, Zorn, as well as some Dutch old masters. A grand piano and a massive gramophone cabinet of ebony inlaid with ivory were also prominent.

On the floor above were the intimate rooms where the Match King lived—bedrooms, library, Silence Room, and a smaller dining room where he ate his simple, almost vegetarian meals. From this floor a corkscrew staircase led to what, almost as much as a Silence Room, became an absolute must in any Kreuger apartment. This was a roof garden which, when weather permitted, became a glorious mixture of flowers, some grown on the roof and others delivered by a Stockholm florist to whom Kreuger eventually paid $1,000 a month to keep his apartment and the Match Palace constantly full of fresh flowers. When Kreuger was out of town the Match Palace blooms were delivered as usual, but his personal ones went to his father and mother who had moved from Kalmar to Stockholm to be near their spectacular son.

Yet even as the Villagatan apartment was being readied for him, Kreuger one night appeared mysteriously at the door of a house at 44 Eriksbergsgaten, in an entirely different section of town. Here he rented a whole floor, explaining it was "for my friend Mr. Jordahl, who often visits Stockholm from America." Having rented the apartment, Kreuger expressed dislike of the furniture and ordered it removed. Next day a van brought his own more elegant pieces. But though the apartment was rented for Anders Jordahl, Jordahl never was seen there. Only Kreuger, who would on some occasions arrive bearing a brief case full of papers on which he presumably worked through the night. At other times he seemed to use the hideaway apartment to receive foreign, secretive-looking men. But most often he was observed entering the Eriksbergsgaten flat in the company of young ladies. Inquisitive neighbors noted that his companion was never the same young lady twice. It was also believed that, though invariably young and attractive, the girls accompanying him were girls of the streets. . . .

Equipped with a palatial Stockholm office, a show-place apartment, and a secret hideaway, Kreuger gave still further evidence of an inner need for his own residence wherever he might go. He next bought an island in the Stockholm archipelago, on which he built a small cottage. This, in turn, allowed him to indulge another of his few passions, one for speed. He purchased a speedboat—later he would have many —and sitting behind the wheel would race one of the fastest craft of his time from the island to Stockholm in thirty minutes.

Still, this was not enough. He next bought two hideaway cottages in the deep woods some twenty miles from Stockholm. To one of these, on a hillside overlooking "a forest-girdled lake," he gave a name not only indicative of the inner man, but prophetic of the future as well.

He called it *Skuggan—The Shadow*.

Chapter 9

A New Economic Conception

But once the pleasant city of Stockholm had been turned into what might almost be called a personal domain, perfectly arranged for his labor and comfort, Kreuger proceeded to follow his immense ambition to the point where he practically turned his back on the city and Sweden. By 1920, he was relegating his Swedish activities to second place, leaving them largely to furnish the sound basis of public trust on which he could pyramid future schemes.

For both Swedish Match and Kreuger & Toll were flourishing. In annual reports for 1919, each showed tremendous profits, even though the structure of Kreuger & Toll was becoming increasingly complex. Indeed, from this point on Kreuger operated—if such a comparison can be made— like an orchestra leader with a baton in either hand. As such, he caused the orchestra on his right, which would be Swedish Match, to play excellently, abiding by the score and producing admirable tones. But from the orchestra on the left— Kreuger & Toll—he produced a thunderous dissonance. Musicians dashed in and out, to sound a few blaring notes at raucous random, then disappear. Kreuger, conducting with his skilled left hand, could have made order from this chaos, but did not choose to. Instead, it suited his schemes to play conventional rhapsodies with the Swedish Match orchestra, while keeping Kreuger & Toll in a state of riotous confusion.

In 1920, Kreuger & Toll was well headed toward this

confusion—the players were straggling in and already making their misdirected sounds. In that year the firm expanded again, with capital upped from 16 million kroner to 20 million. Some of these new funds were applied to the purchase of half-interest in a $6 million American Kreuger & Toll operation, which the resourceful Kreuger had formed in November, 1919. The other half of the American Kreuger & Toll capital supposedly was subscribed by "certain American interests," but since Kreuger's transatlantic contacts were then almost nonexistent, it is likely that these assets existed only on paper—or in the Match King's mind. In 1920, Kreuger & Toll also bewilderingly branched into strange fields by buying into the Swedish film industry (Greta Garbo first appeared as an extra in a Kreuger-financed picture) and the Stockholm Mortgage Bank. At the brief 1921 annual meeting, Kreuger brusquely announced he had decided to increase the capital still more—to 28 million kroner and the reserve to 40 million. He would do it simply by issuing 80,000 new Kreuger & Toll shares.

But while he created profound mystification with Kreuger & Toll, Kreuger, as head of Swedish Match and its growing operations, seemed to make eminent sense. Soon Swedish Match Company stocks were listed on foreign exchanges, the first Swedish industrial stocks to be so honored. On behalf of Swedish Match, he was making canny investments in all parts of the world. Factories were being built in British India, to offset the advantage in freight rates enjoyed by the Japanese. Acting through agents, Kreuger had even succeeded in buying half-interest in the main Japanese match company, a fact which indicated a waning of Japanese power in the Far East. With distant markets so well under control, Kreuger himself had turned to face the immediate one in Europe. From Stockholm, he surveyed the "desolate economic battlefield before him. His armies were ready, his plans prepared, his reserves increased by 35 million kroner in new bonds."

What he now planned was to gain control of European match production, perhaps not so much for the Swedish Match Company as for himself—or for the added money and credit such expansion would bring to his hands. But officially he always operated on behalf of Swedish Match, and it is impossible not to be impressed by the manner in which, as he began such operations, his ambitions were assisted by the times in which he lived. At the inception of his plans for European match conquest, it is unlikely that the Swedish Match King had anything beyond a general plan of how to proceed. Yet from the steps he unerringly made, it seems as if Destiny had taken him firmly by the hand to show, by a succession of economic challenges, exactly how his ends could best be achieved.

The first challenge, of course, came with the fact that European countries had erected trade barriers, sometimes monopolies, to protect their matches.

To Kreuger's ceaselessly contriving mind soon came the realization that there was only one possible solution to this. If Swedish matches could not be exported into countries without payment of excessive duties, there was nothing to do but operate *inside* the countries. He must, in short, conquer from within.

This became the initial challenge for the new Kreuger who, leaving Stockholm behind, began tirelessly covering Europe—a preoccupied, inscrutable figure, Homburg-hatted, correctly attired, carrying a brief case and a slim, shiny cane. As such, he sought out in each country the owners of match factories and used all his gifts of persuasion to make them sell out to Swedish Match.

This may seem like a routine operation, requiring little more than initial guile and bargaining nerve, backed by millions in Swedish Match profits. Actually, it was extremely complex, for Kreuger operated in different countries, always facing new and often hostile personalities, which required a mental agility akin to the fancy footwork of a champion boxer. Some of the men he found himself arrayed against simply did not wish to sacrifice a lifetime of effort by selling out, and flatly said so. In such cases, Kreuger used all his powers of inducement. Failing this, he often turned to threats, as when he icily informed a group of Belgian businessmen: "Your assets are worth so much, you make so much profit. I will unhesitatingly pay the price you ask, if you will sell. But if you won't—well, you know how my factories eventually will encircle you. You will be forced out of business. I think you would be well advised to sell."

But with all this, Kreuger's own activities were only the surface of his operations, which were always iceberg-like, concealing far more below than could be seen above.

Thus, while he seemed an earnest, bankerish figure interested in honestly buying up European match factories, he had others assisting him in devious ways. In nearly every country of Europe, Kreuger had important men on his payroll, and it became their job to apply pressures which would dishearten or soften up the owners of match factories before the appearance of the Swedish Match King himself. In this, they were free to use threats or bribery. When hiring his henchmen Kreuger always let it be known that they were paid for results.

Some of these men appeared openly on the Kreuger & Toll payroll as "observers"—in 1920 there was even a Kreuger observer in the United States. Other, more shadowy types, were on Kreuger's hidden personal payroll. One of his favor-

ite psychological tricks with the latter agents was to send
one out ahead of him. Posing as the representative of a domestic business combine, the agent would make an absurdly
low offer for a factory. After the offer had been indignantly
refused, Kreuger would appear on the scene. His offer would
be twice the sum his agent had made, and thus he seemed
like a benefactor in comparison. When such psychological
shrewdness failed to win a factory he coveted, Kreuger would
turn to another agent who might use bribes or political influence to see that necessary materials never arrived at the
factory. Production would grind to a halt and then, again,
a faintly smiling Kreuger would appear at the right moment
to make a fine offer. In Switzerland and Belgium, where local
match manufacturers waited in quaking fear of Kreuger's
skill, he went to the trouble of master-minding the efforts of
an agent named Sven Huldt. An important-looking man,
Huldt suddenly appeared in Belgian match-making circles
to warn manufacturers that Kreuger was coming after their
factories. He suggested that the owners combine their factories
under his management and thus outwit the Swedish menace.
In gratitude the owners did, and as soon as Huldt had secured
enough control, he sold out to Kreuger.

In the final stages of negotiations the inscrutable Kreuger
always took over himself, for he was ever the Solitary One,
trusting only himself. Most of the men who thus faced him
were beaten before the talks began. Already they were aware
of the Match King's rapid rise to towering position in Sweden.
They knew also that awed employes said of him, "I.K. never
fails." But contrary to the popular conception of the ruthless
financial magnate, Kreuger at the beginning of negotiations
was always charming, friendly, sometimes even seeming ill-
at-ease and shy. He never spoke in a loud voice, and seemed
anxious to give the impression of being a slow thinker. "I

can't think as quickly as you do," was a catch phrase of his, a subtle compliment which lulled adversaries into feelings of security. He would ask to have facts and figures repeated, as if not quite sure of his ability to retain them. Then suddenly he would open up, his spectacular mind spewing forth everything he had heard and more. At such moments, says biographer George Soloveytchik, "there seemed to be no complicated issues. Even the most difficult problems became simple and obvious when he depicted them."

Several times, however, the Match King came up against groups of men who would not be frightened or outmaneuvered. Adamantly, they faced the terrifying Swede. And for such cases the Match King reserved a special, especially Kreugerian tactic: he *over*paid. After arguing fruitlessly, he would suddenly whip out his pen and write a check. "Here is five times what your factories are worth," he would snap, holding it out. "You gentlemen will remain members of the board, entitling you to a salary for the rest of your lives. You will have position, money, a life of ease." Few could resist such a dazzling offer. It even caused one rival to say of the Match King, "Kreuger's dirtiest trick was his lavishness."

When he had secured control of enough small factories in a country—say, in Finland, Norway, Denmark, or Belgium, which were the first countries to succumb to him—he closed them all down, "with or without compensation to those left unemployed." Then he built a large, streamlined factory, aimed at destroying all competition. To facilitate this he imported machinery and technicians, and inside the tariff barriers began to produce his excellent Swedish matches. The Swedish Trust, as it was soon called in Europe, knew the superiority of its product and made no effort to undersell its rivals, merely giving better quality for the same price. Generally, the introduction of such matches produced a fall in the profits of other factories, which then became only too eager to sell out to the Swedish Trust. Sometimes, however, the other factories appealed to the government for aid. Then Kreuger lowered prices, or offered special bonuses to retailers. "By one means or another," a contemporary writer stated, "the Swedish Trust always succeeds in gaining its ends."

Kreuger's determination to own every match company in every possible country was widely applauded at the time as a flowering of genuine ambition. But look closely at the man of that moment, moving so swiftly from country to country, negotiating all day, at night sending endless telegrams back to Littorin in Stockholm or scratching out brusque memos signed I.K.

Kreuger's unremitting drive to eliminate all competition seems to transcend mere ambition. This fact was recognized by one reporter, who wrote: "His passion for monopoly surpassed business enterprise. It was mania." There are other indications that the Match King's desire for total control went beyond healthy ambition. He himself once exposed the strain he worked under by complaining to an associate that during negotiations for match factories he was, despite his imperturbable exterior, "keyed-up, upset, nervous." He confessed further that before and after important conferences, he suffered from attacks which today would be called compulsive gagging or vomiting. This raises the possibility that Kreuger, who from childhood seemed so free from fear, was really motivated by it. Climbing steadily to the top in business, he may have begun to find his success frightening. His ambition to control match factories had become an obsession, the basis of which was a terror that someone, somewhere, might rise to threaten his success, which, in turn, proved his superiority. The English journalist Trevor Allen detected this basic fear when he wrote: "One thing he could

never brook was that his plan of the moment fail of ful-
fillment. He concentrated every effort he could muster on
carrying it through. He did not stop short of bribery and he
trusted only one person—himself."

But healthy ambition or unhealthy insecurity, it drove
him ever onward. Partly because of the times, partly because
of his mania for personal control, he ceased to be satisfied
with owning only match factories. In some countries it had
become necessary for him to purchase the factories which
furnished his match works with machinery and other neces-
sities. This fired in him a need to own *every* factory in *every*
country with which his companies did business. In time, he
even bought the forests themselves. Kreuger's Swedish Trust
was now becoming, in every possible country, a Vertical
Trust.

Occasionally, he even found time to stray from matches.
He speculated successfully in German marks and at a Paris
meeting of industrialists felt a sudden hunch which told him
that rich Americans might soon be looking for homes in
European capitals. He sank large amounts of Kreuger & Toll
funds in mansions in Paris and Berlin, offering these properties through the American Kreuger & Toll. The hunch paid
off. Kreuger quickly sold his mansions at a total profit of
more than 100 per cent.

By early 1922, he seemed to have met and surmounted
the challenges that his era had so far placed in his path. But
having done so, he only found himself face to face with the
greatest challenge of all. To surmount it, he shortly conceived the plan which became his lifetime master-stroke.

In 1922, Kreuger had a ring of match monopolies around
the Baltic and was already starting to penetrate Southern
Europe. This represented huge success, but suddenly it became clear to the Match King that by using the methods of

legitimate business—and, in cases of bribery, illegitimate—
he could never really achieve absolute monopoly in all countries. There might always be a few companies strong enough
to hold out against him, and in addition, there were always
the countries—France, Germany, Spain, Poland—in which
match-making was a State Monopoly. Such monopolies left
no possible loophole by which an outsider could penetrate
and gradually gain control. Matches in these countries were
not free enterprise—they were State.

What, then, could a Match King from Sweden do?
Legend has it that Kreuger, with control of some countries
so securely in his pocket, retired to the Silence Room of his
Stockholm Match Palace, where he concentrated for an entire week. On emerging, he had in his mind, as with plans
for Stockholm's first skyscraper, a complete blueprint which
not only gave a solution for the twin problems of eliminating
competition in free-enterprise countries and conquering
State Monopolies, but neatly pointed the way to world conquest of matches as well.

What Kreuger had conceived was something new in economics and finance. In its simplest terms, his plan was this:
*He, an individual, would lend money to the governments of
Europe. They, in turn, would award him match monopolies
in the country. If the country already had a State Monopoly
of matches, so much the better. His loan would simply buy
it outright.*

Only once before in world history had such a thing been
thought of. This was in England in the early 1700's, when
Lord Chief Treasurer Hartley organized what was called the
South Sea Company. This company assumed responsibility
for England's national debt of £150 million, in return for
which it was given a monopoly on the nation's trade with the
South Seas. The South Sea Company functioned success-

fully for a time, but in 1720 its directors became too sure of themselves. They sold so much stock in the novel enterprise that it blew up. Since then, history has called it the South Sea Bubble.

Whether Kreuger ever read about the South Sea Company is something the world will never know. For the close-mouthed man always maintained his famed silence on the background of his great idea, and refused even to admit that it might have come to him in his Silence Room. But what is certain about the State Loan Plan is that Kreuger produced it at precisely the right moment. For in all history there was no better period than the early 1920's for a single individual to function as lender of money to governments. The war had produced a topsy-turvy financial world in which governments had no money, while individuals did. Europe had spent itself in battle, and its countries had been forced into huge indebtedness in order to keep alive through the conflict. To keep alive after, they had resorted to inflation. As a result, European countries in 1922 were impoverished, still suffering the agonies of war and post-war difficulties. Bankers refused to lend them money, for with inflation national currencies had become bits of almost worthless paper. The slight worth such currencies possessed were based on borrowings against the future.

But did Kreuger, the Match King, at this point have sufficient funds to start lending money to governments? Such loans would require hundreds of millions, not once but many times over. Here again we see Kreuger studying every possibility of his plans, peering into every angle of the project before him. Even with the solid profits of Swedish Match and the enormous possibility of paper-credit with the flexible Kreuger & Toll, he would fall far short of being able to advance hundreds of millions to numerous European governments. Still, he was the man who had just performed the impossible by working out a scheme that might crack State Monopoly. He let his deep-set eyes roam over the world of high finance and, says a financial writer on the *Frankfurter Zeitung*, "The study of international capital markets . . . gave him another idea. He saw that for the time being large sums of money were to be raised nowhere but in the United States."

Chapter 10

Conquest of Wall Street

So Kreuger shifted his vision to the United States. In the late fall of 1922—absolutely convinced of the rightness of his claim to control every match in the world, and supremely confident that he could now use the greatest financial market of the time for his own uses—he boarded the *Berengaria* bound for New York.

The America of 1922 was just beginning to sample the intoxicating pleasures of stock-speculation prosperity. The average man had found that he, too, could purchase stocks and, on paper, often seem as rich as his boss. It began a period of national lightheadedness, featuring flag-pole sitters, marathon dancers, mah-jongg, speakeasies, and bathtub gin, with over twenty million cars on American roads and balloon tires the latest advance in speed and comfort. But behind all this mass madness was money madness, with Wall Street leading the way, promising easy market-riches to all. In brochures calculated to encourage more investors the business world called Jesus Christ "the founder of modern business" and Moses "one of the greatest salesmen who ever lived."

It was toward this gaudy, teeming scene that Kreuger headed and even while the *Berengaria* was in mid-ocean he showed that, though in Europe for the past seventeen years, he had kept informed about the United States and still understood it well.

When the liner reached mid-Atlantic on the trip to New York, the Match King performed an act which opened the shrewd publicity campaign which he now began to wage in America. Stepping into the wireless room of the liner, he used his powers of persuasion—backed, no doubt, by powers of cash—to tie up the exclusive services of the facilities and operators for a period of twenty-four hours. "Extreme press of business," he explained suavely.

With this the poker-faced man started his campaign to woo American investors. For it was not in Kreuger's mind to borrow millions from American bankers for his mighty State Loans. Such money would have to be paid back in a short time, and perhaps would have to be meticulously accounted for. Rather, what he wanted from America was millions from the public on which he would need to make no accounting. He planned to obtain this money by getting American bankers to support a flotation of Kreuger stocks on the American Exchange. As a gesture, he might make Kreuger & Toll and Swedish Match stocks available to the American public. But what he really planned was a brand-new American company which would sell straight to the American public, the millions gained immediately being turned over to him.

He had already decided to call this company the International Match Corporation and in the future he would make it appear in the eyes of the world his most important company, as if he had shifted the center of his operations to the wealthy United States. He planned first to inform Wall Street bankers, and later the American public, that all money invested in International Match would be loaned to European countries in return for match monopolies. Then interest paid by the governments and the revenues from the match monopoly would combine to make especially high dividends.

It all made a gilt-edged speculation, to be offered to an American public increasingly willing to invest in any speculations, gilt-edged or not. Since in the end it was the American public which would provide the funds to float his grandiose scheme, he desired to appear before that public in the most confidence-inspiring way, as the sort of intriguing, responsible and dependable figure the public would trust. He already had sketched in his mind the outlines of this figure. It would be a modest, unassuming man to whom finance was paramount. This solitary man would be interested only in making money, not only for himself but for millions of others as well. He would be a totally dedicated individual, a shadow never quite to be defined behind his magnificent financial accomplishments.

In short, he hoped to erect between himself and the American public—and the world public as well—what might be called the Kreuger Legend, and the first-class passengers on the *Berengaria* in the fall of 1922 were the first to be favored with a view of this image. Until he commandeered the radio shack few fellow passengers had paid attention to the sallow, aloof man who appeared infrequently among them. But now those who tried to send messages were turned away with a polite, "Sorry, but Mr. Kreuger has engaged the wires for his exclusive use . . ." It caused a wave of indignation, but indignation turned to fascination as a day-and-night procession of stewards and wireless officers beat a path to Kreuger's cabin. No one could miss the fact that an extremely industrious man was occupied within. But no one saw him, even at meals, and gradually there arose in the minds of other passengers an image of Kreuger as he wished to be seen—the man so immersed in finance that he had no time for pleasure or even for creature comforts.

Few of Kreuger's calculated psychological stunts stopped

with a single impression, and aboard the *Berengaria* his operation with the wireless shack paid off again. When the ship news reporters clambered aboard at Quarantine, the purser immediately told them of the mysterious Swede whose responsibilities were so great that he tied up radio facilities and turned his cabin into an office. The United States was still isolated from Europe, and though Kreuger's name was well known on the Continent, it was not recognized by newsmen here. From the purser, they ascertained that in Europe the man of mystery was known as the Match King. Then they sought him out and here another facet of the canny Kreuger shows through. For the remote, bemused industrialist who worshiped silence now turned his full charm on ship-news reporters and made of them a group of lasting friends.

In the 'twenties, the Match King seemed to cross the Atlantic as often as the average man crossed streets, and through shipboard interviews succeeded in enormously furthering the Kreuger Legend. It was an exceptional accomplishment, for ship-news reporters were constantly on guard against being used, either for the subtle Kreuger type of propaganda or the blatant purposes of returning movie stars. But Kreuger succeeded, and through stories in New York papers presented himself not only as a man inhumanly dedicated to finance, but as having a human side, as well. Among the seventeen-year changes in the United States with which Kreuger had familiarized himself was the fact that John D. Rockefeller, in 1905 the most ruthless of monopolists, was, in 1922, considered a benevolent old man largely because a publicity agent had advised him to pass out shiny new dimes. The shrewd psychologist in Kreuger knew how much the reading public loves to learn of such heart-warming idiosyncrasies in prominent men, and on his initial trip to the United States as a prominent man he pulled off a public relations maneuver which put him practically in the Rockefeller class.

The first questions aimed at him on the *Berengaria* elicited the fact that he was indeed the Swedish Match King, and that he had come to this country to discuss with American bankers the possibility of placing his match stocks before the American public.

Came a pause, and then an irreverent reporter quipped, "Got a match?"

Instinctively Kreuger's slight, almost dainty hand moved toward the pocket where he always kept a wooden box of the matches of which he was so justly proud. But suddenly he paused. How much smarter if the Match King never seemed to have a match! It would be one of the heart-warming touches the public liked to read about. Slowly his hand fell back to his side and his prim lips curled into a rueful half-smile.

"Sorry, gentlemen," he said, "I never seem to have one with me."

The Match King without a match! It was what city editors called a human-interest angle, and this fact—together with the unfailing charm and deference with which he treated them—immediately won ship-news reporters. In later interviews, he supplied other quotable remarks. Asked to name the match companies he controlled, he answered, "It would be simpler for us all if I just name those I *don't* control." As the Kreuger Legend grew, ship-news reporters also tried to pin him down as to whether he was responsible for circulating the world-wide superstition that three lights on a match meant bad luck. According to this story, Kreuger heard a French general tell how Riff marksmen picked off French soldiers in the dark of night when the soldiers let a match flicker long enough to light three cigarettes. Supposedly, the Match King then rushed back to his office and cabled operatives around the world to spread the story that three lights on a match brought bad luck.

Still, with such light give and take there was always a nugget of seriousness in Kreuger shipboard interviews. Usually he stressed in them his great faith in Europe. For, as part of the Legend, he desired to appear before the American public as Spokesman for Europe. In his mild, convincing voice he would plant the idea that, as a European, he naturally understood Europe better than any American could. He well knew that financial and industrial procedures on the Continent might seem backward to such a fast-moving country as the United States, but still, through the medium of men like himself, Europe was learning and growing. There's life in the old European dog yet, his confident manner seemed to say, and through the medium of newsprint his words provided enormous reassurance to public and financiers alike. . . .

. . . But all this came later. On his 1922 arrival, Kreuger was mainly interested in putting over his own message: that his great success in amalgamating match factories abroad would now make it possible for him to offer high-dividend stocks to the American public. He had come here to discuss the pros and cons of this with Wall Street bankers, and he also had in mind a plan which would allow him to float vastly more stocks, paying even higher dividends.

Through contacts in the United States, he had already arranged interviews with top Wall Street bankers and now in plush executive offices, at luncheons at the Bankers Club, and in other citadels of finance, he began applying his shy, deprecatory conference-table manner to a description of his financial achievements abroad. Then he would lead into his new plan for lending money to governments in return for monopoly, and conclude: "Can you imagine, gentlemen, what my extra profits will be if I add only one-half cent to the cost of a match box in every country? Or if, inversely, I remove but one match from every single box I sell. Now, who would ever notice things like that?"

Such talk provoked heady dreams in Wall Street. Says the journalist, Earl Sparling, "For years industrialists in America had been trying to work the same kind of thing in hundreds of shapes and forms on the American public, and were constrained from complete achievement only by the half-effective Sherman Anti-Trust Law." To the listening men-of-money, Kreuger's plan radiated a succulent odor of profit. Bending closer, they asked more details of his electric scheme.

As Kreuger proceeded to explain the details of his plan, it was not so simple as merely lending money to governments in return for monopoly. There were wheels within wheels. As the Great Persuader elucidated, the primary purpose was, of course, the manufacture and sale of more Kreuger matches. But before he got to the point of actual production, Kreuger first planned to create his International Match Corporation. The money raised from sale of stock in this company he would lend to an impoverished government, or perhaps he would buy an issue of a country's bonds. Either the IOU from the government, or the bonds, would be the underlying security behind the International Match securities, so that the foreign country and not International Match would be the party obligated. But, of course, International Match would make a neat profit on such transactions!

Next, as a return for the loan, or purchase of bonds, he would be ready to negotiate two contracts with the borrowing country. The first would be a contract for the sole manufacture of matches in the country. The second would be a sales monopoly in which—a neat Kreuger come-on—International Match and the government would share equally in profits.

But, some bankers asked, what about the security of the loans made to the governments? The countries were impoverished already. If they defaulted later, would not International Match be the obligated party? Kreuger would allow himself a quizzical, tolerant smile. Then patiently, disarmingly he introduced a feature which was to be of the utmost importance to him—and, to Wall Street, a danger—in his future plan. Any possibility of default, he explained, was covered by the fact that each contract would call for *the establishment of a European subsidiary, or holding, company which would administer the monopoly*. Contracts with a country would be drawn in such a way that the subsidiary, and therefore International Match, "would be provided with funds to meet the payments on the loan before the government's share of the profits was paid." Thus there could be no possibility of default. International Match would be covered by the bonds bought from the government, plus the monopoly agreements and the actual physical assets of the subsidiary as well.

Ingenious—certainly! It would allow International Match to make more and more matches, while a government could accept Kreuger's loan, pay it back out of a share of the sales profits, and could even make more by taxation.

Mystifying? A bit—even to the trained financial minds who listened to the plausible Kreuger elucidate it. But as one of his victims—there is no other word—later explained: "He seemed a man of such transparent honesty, his perfect command of the English language, his eloquence and technical knowledge, his inspiring self-confidence, and his ability to translate his thoughts into sound financial and economic arguments—all these brought his listeners completely under his spell."

Another who listened saw him this way: "There was a kind of hypnotism about him. His pale face, with its prim lips, was in repose not particularly attractive, but it seemed to take on an expression of eager innocence when he smiled and looked at a person. Then with the most convincing sincerity he would utter what has since turned out to be an absolute lie."

Today it seems incredible, but it happened. With only one exception, the hardheaded financiers of Wall Street, feared the world over for their astuteness in money matters, seemed willing to take the Match King's easy words and accept them as gospel. Largely this was because he was a financier, already one of them. Still, it was Kreuger's personality, far more than his background, which won Wall Street and his rare ability to make himself believed could even be exercised over those not directly involved in his plans. At one luncheon at the Bankers Club the publicist, Edward L. Bernays, listened to Kreuger. As a nephew of Sigmund Freud, Bernays should have been a highly perceptive man, but he too was carried away. In a state of great enthusiasm, he told his wife that night, "I have just met the New European."

That it was almost childishly easy to win the American bankers to him was a fact not lost on Kreuger. His surface attitude toward the men of Wall Street always remained courteous and deferential, and whenever necessary, he used on them the fawning flattery to which Paul Toll had once objected. But only slightly beneath this outer deference lay a scathing contempt. "You Swedes are blockheads," he once told a friend. "You haggle about giving me money. But when I get off the boat in New York I find men on the pier begging me to take money off their hands." A stronger indication of this contempt may lie in the fact that he began to key his dealings with America to an insultingly low level. In Europe, with his padded profits and sleight-of-hand with Kreuger & Toll, he was on the path to becoming the suave swindler of song and story. Yet now he decided that with Americans he did not even need smoothness. He reserved for them the tricks of the confidence man, the purveyor of Brooklyn Bridge, whose level of operations was geared to the simple sucker—in criminal and carnival lingo, "the mark."

It is likely that his ability to influence the American bankers provided the last step in Kreuger's character development, or lack of it: the final iota of confidence in his own superiority that made the amoral man irredeemably unmoral. For he found himself able to inspire blind trust in the shrewdest financial minds in the world.

Kreuger must have given a particularly sardonic chuckle when in the course of his 1922 visit he was approached by Frederic W. Allen and Donald Durant, respectively president and partner in Lee, Higginson & Company. On the surface, Lee, Higginson seemed just another important Wall Street investment brokerage. Actually, it was probably the most respected house of its kind in the United States. Founded in 1840, it had laid the financial groundwork for such famous stock issues as American Telephone & Telegraph, General Electric, and General Motors. True, Lee, Higginson was a small firm, but its integrity was so monumental that any issues sponsored by it were automatically purchased in large blocks by the most careful investors, among them Harvard College, Yale and Brown Universities, numerous foundations, museums and austere trustees of estates. After which the remaining stocks were offered to the clamoring public.

It has always been believed that Kreuger first contacted

Lee, Higginson, but it is a measure of the effectiveness of the
Match King's propaganda that he did not find this necessary.
A surviving member of the 1923 firm recalls: "It was not he
who approached us, the approach was on our part . . . with
reference to possible operations looking toward our issue of
dollar securities for the benefit of Kreuger companies." In
other words, Lee, Higginson wished to function as his American banker-broker.

By that time a man thoroughly acquainted with the
American financial scene, Kreuger was quite aware of the
sterling reputation of Lee, Higginson, and of the fact that the
brokerage house was perfect for his purposes. Yet he did not
immediately accept their offer to place their enormous prestige behind him. For it is a vital part of the technique of the
confidence man—whether his skill be instinctive, like Kreuger's, or the result of training in the seamy game—first to
snare the interest of the mark, then shrewdly soften him up
further by inexplicably appearing to snatch away the golden
opportunity.

This was the next move on the part of Kreuger. He had
several luncheons with the directors of Lee, Higginson, fascinating them with the story of "how he had begun with
a trio of family match factories and built them up into one
of the world's greatest trusts—he also discussed the possibility of bringing American capital into the still-growing
trust." Then suddenly, Kreuger turned reluctant. It was as
if all at once he had become afraid of the American project.
After buying a Canadian match factory from Percy A. Rockefeller, a director of some sixty corporations and a man whom
Kreuger also promptly charmed, the Match King seemed to
evaporate completely. Almost as rapidly as he had arrived
on these shores he departed for Sweden by way of England.
But still Lee, Higginson might have known in advance that

Kreuger had selected their firm as his American tool. In London, he visited Higginson & Company, an affiliate of the Wall Street firm. Here he told directors that he was going to increase share capitalization of the Swedish Match Company from 45 million kroner to 90 million, and he wished Higginson & Company to sell 40 per cent of the new issue to the English public.

This was a triple-edged maneuver, which not only raised more money for Kreuger, but tightened his ties with Lee, Higginson in New York, and at the same time made Wall Street fear that the Match King might have decided to raise money for his State Loans in England. Lest this last point be missed—as, of course, it was not—Kreuger sent word to friends in New York that he had opened negotiations for a first State Loan with a major European government. Had Kreuger at this point been pushed to a wall and forced to divulge the name of this country, he probably would have said Spain. But whether he had begun such negotiations—or, indeed, ever actually did—will always remain a mystery.

But no one bothered to investigate. Kreuger himself had said he was opening negotiations, and like everything else the Match King ever said to Wall Street or any other financiers, this alone seemed to suffice.

11

Millions from America

To Littorin and other associates at the Match Palace, to which he now returned, Ivar Kreuger seemed every bit the imperturbable Match King who had left Stockholm a few months before. Yet beneath his impassive exterior a final change seems to have taken place. Propelled the ultimate step by the absurd ease with which he had been able to persuade American bankers, a last shift had taken place in his personality.

It was a shift which, at this precise moment in his life, makes Kreuger one of the most baffling human beings who ever lived. There exists a special reason for this. Whether Kreuger himself was fully aware of it, he had, by arousing American interest in his State-Loan idea, added a new dimension to a plan already sufficiently striking to be described by economists "a truly great conception, a new system in modern capitalism."

That could be said of Kreuger's scheme for lending money to governments. But, by going to the rich country that was America for money to give to the poor countries of Europe, he had lifted himself from the realm of private gain to the exalted position of a man whose actions could affect the financial balance of the entire world.

In time, the general public would hail Kreuger's idea of taking money from the big country to the little ones as an act which created a financial Robin Hood—quite forgetting that the Laughing Fellow of Sherwood Forest was still, for all his surface glamour, a robber. On a higher intellectual level, monographs written about the Kreuger State-Loan plan by the German economist, Alfred Marius, and other analysts would say he was

> . . . redistributing wealth in much the way an omnipotent economist might have done. He was borrowing capital in the country that had too much and handing it over to those who were underfed. He was tackling singlehanded the baffling transfer problem which the governments had bungled. He was stabilizing and pacifying Europe. He was administering to an ailing world which no one seemed able to help.

And again

> On one side of the Atlantic was the great creditor nation, declining to accept payment from its debtors in goods, piling up gold and capital that it could not use. On the other side were nations that desperately needed capital and could not get it. Kreuger stepped in and passed the capital around. Stranger than any of Kreuger's fantastic bookkeeping is the fact that so elaborately equipped a civilization had developed no means of performing this vital economic function, and it was left to a man like Kreuger to do.

As a man whose mind was capable of a conception of such earth-shaking dimensions, Kreuger stood on the verge of one of the greatest careers his time offered. He was assured of the power he seemed so desperately to crave, and limitless millions as well. He could move on a level with kings, presidents and prime ministers. The people of the world would be grateful to him, envying and admiring the mighty Match

King. All this he could now attain and keep forever. There was only one price he must pay: he must be honest.

Members of the Kreuger family and Swedish partisans of the Match King have always pictured him as a man who "improved" the assets of his early match companies and of Kreuger & Toll "in the best of faith." That is, these early falsifications were merely expedients of the moment, to achieve his ambitions as rapidly as possible. But once the ambitions were achieved, Kreuger planned—his supporters maintain—to turn honest again. It was a process described thus by the Swedish banker, Oscar Rydbeck: "After he had attained his purpose, everything would go back to its proper place. Everyone would have what he was entitled to, and everyone would feel he had been correctly treated." Thus Kreuger could, after his fling with padded books, return to being the person he really was: ambitious, smart, and—from here on—absolutely honest.

Such is the pro-Kreuger picture—and now, in the early months of 1923, came the moment, if ever, to live up to it. For he was sublimely sure of his eventual ability to get millions from America and absolutely certain of other millions from the flotation of Swedish Match stocks in England. As such a man, Kreuger could slip back the funds he had stealthily claimed for his own companies. From then on, for the rest of time, he could stand forth as one of the great men of the world.

So comes the crux of the Kreuger tragedy. For the Match King did not, *could not*, do this. The complex man who stood on the threshold of such a titanic career was now totally unmoral. His successful voyage to America had completed his personality change, and he could visualize his tremendous future only in criminal terms. The cancer-of-cleverness cited by Max Lerner had spread completely through him, destroying all moral fiber and leaving only a towering belief in himself. Aiding this was the belief in his superiority which had been with him since childhood, the belief that a *difference* from the rest of humanity made him a special being, free to achieve his ends by any means. Joining this were the *Storhetsvansinne*, mind-sickness or megalomania, that made him think *big*, and the psychotic coldness and insensitivity that made him dissatisfied with each accomplishment, drove him always toward the next in the belief it would bring him the peace and inner confidence every man wants. Once he put this last drive into words, saying, "My desires in this world are usually of the moment, and die almost as quickly as they arise. For me possession takes the edge off appreciation. I once bought a diamond for $10,000 because it looked so beautiful at the jeweler's. As soon as I got it home, I put it away and have never set eyes on it since."

All these factors merged to make Kreuger a man incapable of thinking of the world around him, but only of himself and his personal desires. Achievement of these desires, first an abnormal craving, had become a desperate drive. He *had* to achieve things as rapidly as possible so that he could plunge toward the next. With the speed he required, his ends could not be achieved normally, within the give-and-take frame of business and finance dealings. He could not wait that long. The only thing to do was repeat the pattern of the boyhood Sneak—cut corners, which at this stage meant dishonesty on a vast scale. The only way he could see to achieve his ends rapidly enough was the criminal way.

"In him genius and madness had merged imperceptibly," believes the writer Manfred George. So this man, totally confident of his ability to command hundreds of millions from America, began, even in advance of final Wall Street negotiations, a series of shadowy moves which set the stage

124   THE INCREDIBLE IVAR KREUGER

for future manipulation of the sums he got from the United States.

In all Kreuger's future depredations, especially International Match, the key became the subsidiary companies, the idea he introduced with such nonchalance to the American bankers who requested further details of his plan. His hidden scheme with subsidiary companies was this: as rapidly as possible he would move money obtained from the American public to the coffers of a European subsidiary. These subsidiaries—originally it was planned to have only one for each of his major companies, but soon the subsidiaries had subsidiaries—would act as a "leech on the parent company." Each would be small and absolutely Kreuger-dominated. Funds deposited with them could be used instantly by Kreuger, while the money could be left standing on the subsidiary company's books. In time, there came to be 400 of these subsidiaries, though a trusting world was aware of only 250. But in the spring of 1923, Kreuger was merely taking his first steps in this direction. He seemed to be feeling his way as he went. Thus, the first two subsidiaries he ever created did not become very important in the Kreuger structure. But the uses he made of them, even in 1923, are highly important as illustration of how he operated these and subsequently many others like them.

Summoning one of his assistants, Bror Bredberg, to his Match Palace office, Kreuger ordered him to Zurich, Switzerland, there to form an institution to be called *Finanz Gesellschaft fur die Industrie*. Despite its resounding name, this was merely a small bank, "the first of his queer little institutions." Bredberg was joined in Zurich by Walter Ahlström, then Swedish Consul General in Paris, and by Torsten Kreuger, Ivar's younger brother. No sooner had *Finanz Gesellschaft* been properly incorporated and registered under the laws of Switzerland than the trio moved on to Vaduz, in the Duchy of Liechtenstein, a tiny country whose laws governing business were so loose that a company paid taxes by arrangement with the Finance Minister. Kreuger, comments a later writer, "always liked droll little countries with droll little laws."

In Liechtenstein the travelers formed still another company, this one called *Union Industrie Aktiengesellschaft*, capitalized at 5 million francs. Fifty per cent of this was paid by two checks totaling 2.5 million francs drawn on *Finanz Gesellschaft*, which had been formed only two days before. Yet the commercial magistrate in Vaduz was satisfied and registered the new firm with Bredberg as sole director. He turned the two checks over to Bredberg, who immediately transferred them to Torsten Kreuger, who in turned presented Bredberg with 50,000 francs in cash for the *Union Industries* treasury.

Next, Bredberg returned to Kreuger's presence and was instructed to enter on Union Industries books, as an asset, the purchase of 7.5 million francs of real estate in Berlin. He was given no deeds to this property, no opportunity to check the transfer—but then Kreuger never employed men who insisted on such things! Like all Kreuger lieutenants, Bredberg acted as ordered. On July 1, 1923, Kreuger notified Bredberg that he had sold the property to an E. B. Lehmann for 21,200,000 francs. Subsequently, Kreuger forwarded Lehmann's personal note for 18 million francs, with the notation that Lehmann had paid 3,200,000 francs in cash, which should be debited to Kreuger personally. The 18-million franc note supposedly carried interest at 12 per cent annually, and Bredberg asked for Lehmann's address so that he could notify him when the interest came due. Kreuger curtly snapped that he preferred to handle the matter himself. It was all

Bredberg ever learned, while the debt, with interest, mounted to a sum beyond 30 million francs. As such, it was listed as an asset on Kreuger's consolidated books. But no one ever saw the Berlin real estate, or E. B. Lehmann.

This was a beginning operation which as early as 1923 gave Kreuger a bank and a mysterious company to play with. But apparently he was dissatisfied with both, and now himself undertook to set up a similar enterprise, which was to attain top-level importance in the eventual Kreuger edifice.

On a trip to New York in 1922, the Match King had advertised in newspapers for a secretary. Of the several applicants he had picked as suited to his purposes a young Swiss-American named Ernst Hoffman. Hoffman had once been a bank clerk and spoke several languages. Immediately on hiring him, Kreuger informed the young man that he needed a Swiss holding company to escape taxes on profits made in America. Accordingly, he dispatched Hoffman to Zurich, where he was to make a comprehensive study of Swiss financial legislation. He also impressed on his new secretary the importance of doing this work in the greatest secrecy. Under no circumstances was he to tell anyone he was investigating for Ivar Kreuger.

Undoubtedly, the formation of Finanz Gesellschaft in Zurich was a result of information which Hoffman forwarded to Kreuger on the latter's return to the Match Palace. After Bredberg and Torsten Kreuger had established their two firms, Kreuger himself journeyed to Zurich where he was met by Hoffman. Together they proceeded to establish the Continental Investment Corporation, with a capital of 60 million Swiss francs. Actually, this capital consisted of 1 million francs in cash, 9 million in checks, and 50 million in the form of a guarantee from the Swedish Match Company, "executed by Kreuger personally." Like Bror Bredberg with Union Industries, Hoffman was immediately honored by being made sole director of the 60-million Continental. Then the two men left for Stockholm and the story is that they "boarded a fast train carrying a little suitcase in which nestled the entire capital of Continental—cash, checks, guarantee."

Back in Stockholm, Kreuger bethought himself of Liechtenstein and its droll little laws. He instructed Hoffman to go to Vaduz, where the government, ever eager for business, agreed to fix taxes for the multi-million-dollar Continental at 60,000 Swiss francs for the first two years and 30,-000 thereafter, no matter what sums its books might show. Then Hoffman doubled back to Zurich, where he arranged to have Continental moved to Vaduz.

Now Kreuger had a subsidiary—or holding—company for the first millions he would get from International Match. It was a hidden company, for the name of Continental Investment never appeared in any public report of the Kreuger companies. Only those with the most intimate access to the Match King's books knew of its existence. This seemed to make it precisely what the Match King wanted, for in the fall of 1923 he again boarded ship for America. On landing, he wasted no time on psychological subterfuge, but immediately got in touch with Lee, Higginson, hinting again that he had already opened Match-Loan negotiations with a European country, and that the Loan was nearly consummated. He did not identify this as Spain, but persisted in referring to it, in the most intriguing manner, as "X country."

He also informed Lee, Higginson directors that in his absence he had finally become convinced of the necessity of establishing himself in the United States, and that for so doing he could imagine no worthier medium than Lee, Higginson. The directors promptly agreed, making them appear in retrospect as enormously gullible. Yet the entire financial community of the United States must also take blame for Kreuger. Looking back from the vantage point of 1955, a surviving member of the Lee, Higginson of Kreuger's day writes: "We trusted him because of two factors: his record of success in legitimate enterprises and the soundness of his judgment on economic conditions, on public finances, and on the political aspects of business all over the world. He was extraordinarily well read and a man of cultivated tastes. There was nothing of the flashy, aggressive salesman about him. Lee, Higginson, fully realizing the responsibility it had taken on, made it a point to reinforce its judgment of the man by bringing him on contact with the ablest bankers and businessmen in the country, on all of whom he seemed to make a profound impression."

In his first meetings with Lee, Higginson directors, Kreuger had made particular note of a newly created partner named Donald Durant. Affable, personable, in his early forties, Durant became, in American eyes at least, the most tragic figure in the story—except perhaps for the Match King himself. In many ways, Durant was living out the American dream of the Financial Twenties. He had joined Lee, Higginson in 1908 as a stock boy, and by a combination of personality, industry and devotion to Wall Street, had become a general partner of the firm in 1922. This brought particular advantages for in the 'twenties, with the stock market roaring upward, it was almost impossible for a man on the inside not to become rich. Durant was also a popular man on Wall Street. In 1923–34 he was serving a term as president of the Bond Club.

What kindled the Match King's interest in Durant, among Lee, Higginson directors, was not so much his affable personality as the fact that, like Krister Littorin in Stockholm, Durant was so plainly willing to believe. At early meetings it was he who deferred most to Kreuger, he who was most obviously impressed by the Match King's considerable financial success. Again like Littorin, Durant made an excellent front. People liked and trusted him, for he believed implicitly in what he was doing. He was a born worshiper, a man eager to subordinate his personality to one stronger than his own.

Durant became Kreuger's main contact with Lee, Higginson, and early in the fall of 1923 the two men prepared a shiny prospectus for the new company which stated it would "act as an agency for bringing American capital into the Match Trust as a whole." Then they set about filling the Board of Directors chairs of International Match with some of the most reputable men in Wall Street. Among them were Percy A. Rockefeller, Frederic W. Allen, president of Lee, Higginson, and Durant himself.

It is in relations with his International Match directors that the confidence man in Kreuger can be seen at its most ingenious and persuasive. Indeed, his domination of these hardheaded New York bankers and brokers, even before the contract and bylaws of International Match were drawn up, was such a remarkable feat that it might be well to examine the explanations for Kreuger's strange power set forth by American writers who knew the Match King. In his attempt to explain Kreuger's sway over the directors of International Match, Isaac F. Marcosson has this to say:

> Something in the Kreuger make-up, apart from the glamour as Match King, inspired confidence in hardboiled financiers ordinarily highly skeptical. Whether it was this smooth impassiveness, or what seemed the infallibility of his always bulwarked figures and arguments, reinforced by the visible evidence of his industrial achievement, the fact remains that he seemed a per-

son apart. . . . It was the confidence that men had in Kreuger's oftentime unsupported word that led to their undoing.

Earl Sparling, in Kreuger's time a reporter on New York newspapers, sees it this way:

> Secrecy, mystification, those were his means. If any mere banker or business man became too questioning he would become brilliantly devious, shifting from frontier to frontier, until his audience was lost in a maze. Money changed from kroner to pounds to dollars to francs to marks to florin to gulden as he talked. He could name corporations until the ear refused to keep track.

The veteran foreign correspondent of the *Chicago Daily News*, William H. Stoneman, finds extenuating circumstances in favor of the American bankers. He writes:

> There was every indication that Kreuger was honest and there was no indication whatsoever that he was dishonest. His previous success had been ascribed to his personal business genius and to the efficiency of the Swedes whom he had grouped about him in the Swedish Match Company. The Americans were naturally eager to participate in the profits of the Kreuger enterprises and at the same time realized that they knew nothing whatsoever about the match business. The natural thing was to allow Kreuger to "run the show."

But whatever the particular magic Kreuger possessed, he put it to work instantly on the International Match Board. At the first conclave of directors, called to draw up constitution and bylaws of the $28 million corporation, Kreuger, as president of International Match, painted such a beguiling

word-picture of future International Match operations that
his bemused listeners unhesitatingly permitted him exactly
what he asked.

As he visualized it—the purring, electric voice began
from the head of the directors' table—his three companies,
Kreuger & Toll, Swedish Match, and now International
Match would combine to make a kind of financial Three
Musketeers. Their policy would be the classic one of "All For
One and One For All." Each of the three would operate for
the benefit of the others, to make what might be called a
community of financial interest. Of course, it would be possible to administrate each separately, but to do so would
mean a considerable diminishing in profits, and he was sure
all present were primarily interested in profits. Working on
the profitable Three Musketeers principle, his, Kreuger's,
would have to be the sole operating hand, for he alone would
know what was best for each of the three units. Naturally—
he went on deprecatingly—no one could doubt his ability
to administrate this community of finance, since he had
already proved to the world his genius as an administrator.
As to the contracts drawn with all State-Loan countries: "I
am very meticulous about all new contracts. Each is read
by four of my associates and myself, initialed by each, and
locked away for safekeeping."

The magic talk flowed on. All present, the Match King
continued, were aware that the purpose of International
Match was to make American investors more familiar with
Kreuger enterprises and thus allow flotation of securities in
the United States under the most favorable conditions. But
though American capital would pour into International
Match, it could not—on the Three Musketeers basis—be
allowed to remain in this country. International Match
money would have to be Swedish controlled and Swedish

managed. Swedish Match would even own the common stock of International Match, allowing only debentures and participating preferred stock to be sold to the American public. . . . There is no record that any Board member expressed the slightest surprise at having control of the funds of an American firm emanate from Stockholm. Nor did any seem to think it unusual that money from American stock issues should be snatched out of the country, without promise of accounting to International Match about where its money was going, or of direct physical possession of assets—"an unhappy predicament for a company which had collected tens of millions from the public."

But if a Board member had objected, Kreuger no doubt would have reacted as he did on the few later occasions when probing questions were put to him. Then he replied, "I'm glad you asked that," and launched out "convincingly with non-existent facts presented so skilfully both orally and in writing that those listening regarded him with respect amounting to awe and deemed it a privilege to be associated with him."

Indeed, Kreuger's experiences with the International Match Corporation seem to bear out his statement that Americans literally forced money on to him. From its organization in 1923, this American concern received $148,500,-000 as the net return from the sale of securities to American investors. Of this amount $144,000,000 was transferred to Kreuger and to his concerns in Europe, where most of it disappeared into the Kreuger maw.

The Match King's only attempt at reassuring his Board of Directors at this first Board meeting was to state that International Match could keep enough money in this country to pay quarterly dividends. But he did not abide by this. Shortly, in what Kreuger explained as a move to "avoid paying United

States taxes on surplus profits," all monies were sent directly to the Match King. This oft-repeated avoiding-taxes excuse for rushing funds abroad, one commentator says, "gave acts which might have been suspicious an aura of business sagacity." It also created the colossal incongruity of International Match, with eventual assets of $200 million, paying out millions in annual dividends, and seldom, if ever, having as much as $200,000 in the till.

Finally, it was with the International Match dividends that Kreuger performed what was perhaps his most skillful bit of financial legerdemain combined with psychological bluff. He not only paid International Match dividends out of the corporation's own capital, but often sent this money to New York before the quarterly dividend was due. Accompanying this premature payment would be an airy but reassuring message which said, in effect, "We have so much money over here, you might as well have this now." On other occasions he sent a million or so extra and when queried would answer, "Oh, we simply made a mistake. We have so much money here, we just can't keep track of it."

At the first meeting, contract and bylaws of International Match were promptly drawn up, approved, and signed by all present. They were a complete follow-through on the Three Musketeers principle Kreuger had advocated, and seemingly gave the Match King a perfect right to move money from this country to Europe at will. But something about the phrasing bothered the insatiable man, for a few days later he summoned his Board of Directors to a second meeting. At it he guilelessly requested permission to amend Section IX, Article IV of the by-laws. Already, this gave him full power to vote the stock in any or all subsidiary corporations. Now he asked a new by-law, to be called *Special Powers of the President* which would authorize him to

> . . . make and enter into contracts on behalf of the cor-
> poration, to execute any and all instruments of transfer
> of any part of the personal property of the corporation
> . . . provided that the foregoing powers shall not be
> deemed to include the power to enter into any contract
> relating to the organization or capitalization of the cor-
> poration, the transfer or mortgaging of any of its real
> estate or all of its property as an entirety or the issue
> of any of its corporate holdings.

What, exactly, did this mean? Largely, it was a set of contractual clichés erected around the phrase "transfer of any part of the personal property of the corporation." For these words allowed Kreuger, now and forever, to juggle as he pleased the money of International Match or any of its subsidiaries. Which is precisely what he began doing after November, 1923, when International Match offered the American public a $15 million issue of 20-year, 6½ per cent gold debentures. The stocks were gobbled up by a specula- tion-hungry country and shortly International Match sent Kreuger the total sum, minus only New York operating expenses. By this time the Match King was back in Stock- holm, and he quickly transferred $12,244,792 of the Ameri- can funds to the Continental Investment Company of Liechtenstein, whose sole director was Ernst Hoffman and where Kreuger could do with it anything he liked. The re- maining money was dropped into the coffers of other com- panies, while a last $1 million was held to pay interest on American debentures due April 1, 1924.

What Kreuger told International Match about the dis- position of its millions is not on the record. He may have invoked the Three Musketeers. He may have said nothing. But next a block of 450,000 shares was placed on the Ameri- can market at 50, netting International Match $21,824,366.

Kreuger presented $16 million of this to Continental, $3 million to Swedish Match, and kept the usual $1 million for future American dividends.

This time he had the decency to tell his American directors what he had done with the money. "It was used for transactions in Greece, Portugal, Algiers and Manila," he cabled.

12

"Something Dreamed in a High Fever"

In unraveling the Ivar Kreuger story it is important not to lose sight of the numerous really remarkable aspects of the man. For, as one commentator has said, "His power was creative before it became destructive. Here was no common swindler or trickster. We have to consider a man of undoubted genius whose clever technique was used for reckless and dishonest ends. Craft, the ability to outwit the other fellow, these played their part, but only as adjuncts to real organizing ability, foresight, and promptitude in seizing the opportunities of the moment."

Kreuger's true genius becomes the more apparent when one stops to consider the superhuman amount of work he accomplished. First he devoted his energies to building up a Match Trust and was always playing the part of masterhand guiding its glacierlike progress over the entire world. This should have been enough to occupy any man, even a towering genius. Yet on top of it Kreuger placed Kreuger & Toll, an even more complicated and taxing endeavor which might be called a Finance Trust.

Today we know that, astounding as Kreuger may have seemed at the time, he was actually more so. The Match King was a man fond of quoting Napoleon that "One first-class brain is enough for an army," and seemingly he carried through on this dictum by operating two massive and complicated enterprises almost unassisted. But in the shadows behind this already prodigious man lurked another Kreuger. That this shadowy figure was a criminal may in a moral sense detract from his accomplishments. But it in no way diminishes the awesome quality of his mind. Over long periods, it is far more difficult to be criminal than to be honest, and Kreuger, "the all-omniscient ghost, stealing silently among men," was dishonest over a long period. More, he excelled in crime, just as he did in business, industry and finance. He was a man who would not be content to remain just a criminal. He had to be an archcriminal.

So, with the fascination of his financial manipulations and the glimmerings of criminality behind them, it is easy to overlook the steady progress over these same years made by Swedish Match, the least flamboyant of Kreuger enterprises. Yet, eventually, in the words of William Stoneman,

> Swedish Match and its subsidiaries . . . possessed the nearest thing to a world monopoly which had ever been created in an article of universal use. They [eventually] possessed absolute monopolies in 15 countries and *de facto* monopolies in 9 others, while dominating the market in another 10. They operated 250 factories in 16 non-European countries and in every country of Europe except Spain, Russia, and France. *They sold 65% of all the matches used by the population of the world!*

No matter what other affairs engaged his spectacular mind, Kreuger slowly, relentlessly pushed forward with Swedish Match, never losing the dream that was perhaps the one sincere drive of his life. He was determined to be the World Match King, to control every match produced on the face of the earth.

His ambitions with Swedish Match soon led him to another financial innovation which was hailed by economists everywhere. This was the so-called "B" share, which carried only one one-thousandth of a vote and could thus be sold at random without affecting the actual control of the concern. To increase the capital of Swedish Match still further he arranged for the issue of 900,000 such shares, the greater part of which were placed on the British market. In this way the share capital of Swedish Match was increased to 180,-000,000 kroner and its reserve fund to 81,541,081 kroner.

But interesting as such innovations were to economists, the real weapon possessed by the Match King in his dream of world monopoly was the idea of State-Loans. Using funds from International Match and Swedish Match, and negotiating in the name of either or both, he in time got to the point where he had advanced no less than $384 million to 15 different countries, in 19 different transactions. Of these loans, which allowed him to control the 65 per cent of world match production, it has been said:

> There was nothing the least bit fraudulent about most of the monopolies he secured and the money he passed out in such a great golden stream to the nations of the world was extremely real. In a number of cases the monopoly agreements were not executed without crossing the palms of politicians with gold, but these frequent indulgences in bribery were incidental to the whole scheme, which was basically aboveboard and honest.

Yet the man possessing such great power and money still apparently could not achieve his ends without resorting to another of the classic tricks of the confidence man.

This was bluff. For another amazing fact about Kreuger's career is that his two first State-Loans, on which he based his reputation as a solitary banker to governments, and which eventually caused him to be labeled the Savior of Europe, may never have been negotiated at all.

First of these was the loan to Spain. Whether he had actually approached King Alfonso's country when he made his 1923 visit to the United States is not known. But in 1924, after arranging the swift transfer of the International Match millions to his hidden Continental Investment, he began boasting to fellow financiers that he had advanced—or was on the verge of advancing—124 million pesetas (about $25 million) to Spain. In his possession, he said, was a contract signed by Prime Minister Primo de Rivera, dated "January, 1925." Having said this much he would resort to a stratagem which—incredibly—stood him in excellent stead throughout his career as a lender of millions. Holding a warning finger to his prim lips, he would whisper: "Don't breathe a word of this to anyone. If France should learn of it, there might be war."

Perhaps no one did breathe a word—as in a later, far more vital transaction, no one ever did—but Kreuger saw that he whispered to the right persons, and soon the top echelon of the European financial community was under the impression that Kreuger, after conceiving the bold idea of State-Loans, had executed his first one.

But had he? The real answer is swathed in characteristic Kreuger obscurity. In his Match Palace safe, from this moment on, reposed a document and a "receipt" for the loan of the 124 million pesetas at annual interest of 16 per cent. Kreuger informed International Match of the existence of this, for the loan had been made in the name of the American firm, which had so far sent Kreuger nearly $28 millions from sale of its stocks. But he neither sent a copy of the contract to New York, nor did he have any copies made. At several strategic moments in the future, he produced this Spanish contract. Once he showed it to two associates, Anton Wendler and Victor Holm. Telling of this later Wendler recalled that he had been afraid to study the document too carefully, for Kreuger had paced impatiently up and down before him as he held it. Made nervous by Kreuger's actions, Wendler only skimmed the pages hurriedly. It seemed to be a contract between Continental Investment and Spain, signed by Primo de Rivera. Wendler was definitely sure of this last fact. Rivera's sprawling signature covered at least four inches of paper, looking just as a Prime Minister's signature should.

Later, when this contract was studied by experts, details were found to be somewhat different from those Kreuger had leaked. Strangely, it was in English, the supposition being that this language had been used as a help to the directors of International Match, who were putting up the cash. Still, this was odd, and in addition to the fact of the contract being in a language native to neither party, there was the easy nonchalance of the date, "January, 1925." Since when were documents involving such mighty sums and the fate of nations dated so informally? . . . But by the time of this meticulous scrutiny Primo de Rivera was dead and Alfonso a deposed monarch whose denial of the validity of the contract carried even less weight than it would have in the days when he was a playboy King.

Quite possibly the Spanish contract, like so many Kreuger words and actions, was only a half-truth. It is likely that he opened negotiations with Primo de Rivera, and with characteristic impatience immediately had a contract drawn up. Then, if negotiations proceeded slowly, or broke off, the superior, confident man could not face the fact and began speaking as if the loan were settled. Soon he actually believed it—and so did European bankers who from then on proved as gullible as their American counterparts when it came to the bluffs of the Match King. Probably Kreuger added Primo de Rivera's sprawling signature himself, for even at this date the farseeing man was collecting important signatures on letters received and having rubber stamps made of them. And now comes the final Kreuger touch, which may help—or hinder—in understanding the bewildering and unscrupulous manner in which he began to operate. For the Spanish Loan, which probably never went through, was entered on the books of International Match, Continental Investment, and even of Kreuger & Toll, as an asset of $25 million, and there it remained year after year, in the books of each company, rolling up the considerable further asset of interest at 16 per cent.

Equally extraordinary was the loan to Poland, the second State-Loan which Kreuger announced to the world. This was executed on July 22, 1925, and though details were made public, the loan may still be as fraudulent as the one to Spain.

This contract was concluded between Kreuger, acting for International Match, and the Polish Finance Minister, Marjam Glowacki. The sum involved was $6 million, which causes it to rank far behind later loans in importance. But the contract is interesting as an example of the complicated nature of the State-Loan deals. Each involved different factors, and the tireless machine that was Kreuger's mind took care of them all himself. By this contract, the Polish Government undertook to produce and sell for twenty years the matches of a new company consisting of 50 per cent Swedish Match and 50 per cent International Match backing. In return for granting this monopoly, the State was loaned $6 million. In addition, the government was to receive half the profits from sale of these matches, "insofar as it exceeded 12 per cent." After internal requirements had been covered from the products of ten factories amalgamated for the purpose, one third of Poland's match production was to be exported. In twenty years time the factories would revert to the Polish State.

So far the contract was fairly normal. But in the subsidiary clauses and conditions, with special bearing on each country, came the real challenge to Kreuger's skill. In the Polish contract, for instance, there were numerous additional clauses devoted to "conditions of property in the Polish stock of aspen wood, agreements concerning various materials in whose Swedish export Kreuger had an interest . . . the rights to attach the Polish potassium produce against the erection of a potassium-chlorate factory." In each of the nineteen State-Loan deals he finally consummated, these details were different.

Questions about the validity of the Polish Loan arose over whether it had actually been passed by the Polish Diet. Kreuger, of course, proceeded exactly as if it had been passed, and affirmed his confidence by public announcement of the loan. But Glowacki stated later that he had found it impossible to push the loan through the Diet. Yet Poland never bothered to deny receiving the money, perhaps because the poverty-stricken country was not averse to having the world believe it possessed more money than it really had—a fact which may also have motivated Spain in remaining mum despite whispers about a Spanish Loan. So if Kreuger was bluffing, he was using not only men but entire countries as pawns in his game.

Yet perhaps more important in the long run than whether Kreuger advanced $6 million to Poland was that the supposed loan allowed him to create what became one of the most active of all his subsidiary companies. For after establishing the three hidden companies in Liechtenstein, he had discovered that laws in Holland were almost as flexible and inviting as those in Liechtenstein. After Continental Investment, Kreuger had established his future pattern. With each big stock deal, State-Loan, or other transaction calculated to bring him new funds, he promptly created a subsidiary, ostensibly to "hold" the money. Eventually—as has been said—these subsidiaries acquired subsidiaries of their own, until their number reached a staggering 400, while such names as the International Finance Syndicate, Handels Aktiegesellschaft, and Aktiegesellschaft Standard, only added further to the confusion. This made all Kreuger operations, in the words of one investigator, "Take on the quality of something dreamed in a high fever."

But in 1925, after the Polish Loan, the Match King was still occupied with early subsidiaries, and now he announced that because of political conditions in Poland a company must be organized outside the country to take care of Polish Loan profits—though why Kreuger & Toll could not have done this is one of the questions that has never been answered. Accordingly, in sedate Amsterdam, he created the Garanta Company to take care of potential profits from the Polish Loan.

Garanta! In today's world, the name has an Eric Ambler-Alfred Hitchcock ring, and nothing in its operations from 1925 on diminishes this. As director and sole employe of this firm, whose assets would soon be listed as $25 million, Kreuger chose one Karl Lange, an elderly gentleman with a distinguished white beard that fell over a portly chest. Like Ernst Hoffman, Lange had once been a bank clerk, but this employment had ceased when he was unwise enough to grant a loan to himself. In time, the stigmatized man approached Kreuger for a job and was delighted to find that the Match King took a tolerant view of his past offense. "It is the sort of thing that could happen to anyone," Kreuger stated offhandedly. Kreuger gave Lange several confidential missions to carry out and, having tested him, found him satisfactory. His next position was to act as president and sole director of Garanta.

Lange later recalled the formation of Garanta. Before its incorporation in Amsterdam a small office was rented to house the firm. Immediately after the incorporation went through, this office was abandoned, and from that moment the multi-million-dollar Garanta existed as no more than a set of portable books, usually kept in a corner of the living room in Lange's Amsterdam home. Lange never received any of the sums represented in the Garanta books, and never paid out an actual cent. The $25,421,875 assets of Garanta were never more than bookkeeping assets. Kreuger merely instructed Lange to enter such-and-such amounts in the books. When Lange asked how the books could then be balanced, Kreuger gave an invariable answer, "Debit the amount to me."

None of which ever seemed strange to Lange. For the record he later stated, "Ivar Kreuger always seemed to me a very great man, admired by the whole world, whose business genius and honesty were the pride of nations. He is the greatest, noblest man who ever lived."

Yet with all this, Lange did have a few bad moments. One of the strange aspects of the Polish Loan was the fact that, after publicly announcing the sum of $6 million, Kreuger began talking to associates and fellow financiers in terms of $17 million. When queried about the $11 million difference he would enigmatically hold finger to lips and whisper of a "secret" supplementary loan. Again he would drop his mysterious warning about the possibility of war if the total sum should be bruited about. And once more, if Poland heard that Kreuger was dropping hints of a $17 million loan, the country was probably not averse to having the world believe it had received that sum.

One of Lange's first acts as president, board of directors, and sole bookkeeper of Garanta was to establish this amount of $17 million. One night in the fall of 1925 he was summoned to Kreuger's Stockholm apartment. The Match King was just finishing a solitary dinner in his second-floor dining room. During the meal he had been working over his complicated papers, and handing Lange an interim report on the Garanta book balance dated September 27, 1925, he ordered him to sign it then and there.

"But I have not been given a chance to audit the figures," Lange protested.

Kreuger smiled, shrugged and pushed the book at him again. Lange looked closer at it and saw the sum of $17 million. Again he pulled back. "May I know where the money is deposited?" he asked.

Kreuger showed impatience. "It has been used for the Polish monopoly," he snapped. "If you don't trust the statement go to Poland and find out for yourself."

Irritation on the part of the imperturbable Match King always was enough to make his subordinates obey. Lange, of course, was no exception. He signed, and the Garanta books showed that the officeless company had passed $17 million on to the government of Poland.

Lange's further experiences with Garanta show the rapidity with which Kreuger wove a shroud of complexity around his operations. Continental Investment had been formed to facilitate financial matters pertaining to International Match. International Match acted as agent in the Polish Loan, but financial transactions with Poland were not channeled through Continental. They went through Garanta, which thus became another unofficial subsidiary of International Match. But did Garanta deal directly with New York, send back interest or financial statements? Not at all. It worked through Continental, in Liechtenstein, which dealt with New York. Or did it? There was always Finanz Gesellschaft, "helping color the position of International Match and Swedish Match by acting as its debtor." Nor did the public know of the existence of Continental, Garanta, or Finanz Gesellschaft. But now, in Holland, Kreuger established two aboveboard companies, with the impeccable names of Amsterdam Match and Dutch Kreuger & Toll. In charge of the former was an unemployed match jobber named Sven Huldt. Sole director of the high-sounding Dutch Kreuger & Toll was a bookkeeper named Victor Holm. Kreuger paid them both good salaries and they did not bother their heads about matters which he indicated were none of their concern.

Slowly Lange and the other directors of Kreuger subsidiaries learned what was expected of them. Returning to Amsterdam after the dinner-table interview with Kreuger, Lange received on December 31, 1925, a letter from International Match informing him that Garanta had been debited for $17 million with annual interest at 24 per cent from October 1, 1925. In considerable alarm, he rushed to Kreuger to find out how he could now balance his books. Again Kreuger gave his classic answer, "Just debit it to me."

Now the Garanta books showed that Garanta had received $17 million from International Match and had paid $17 million to Kreuger personally. Where, then, was the loan to Poland, the purpose for which International Match had sent the money from New York? By this time Lange neither knew nor cared. Not a cent had actually passed through his hands, and when on July 12, 1927, he received a copy of an

International Match balance sheet showing that Garanta had paid $5,604,288 interest to that date, he was probably much relieved. He decided to "sit tight and keep his books, understanding nothing."

If Karl Lange, elderly bookkeeper with a shady past, decided to shut his eyes to Kreuger's financial sleight-of-hand, the world can see some reason for it. Far more difficult to comprehend are the American bankers who comprised the Board of International Match. Such men should have been surprised by the sudden appearance of Continental, "acting as a leech on International Match." Having been surprised, they should have been alerted further by Garanta, which suddenly appeared as a leech on both International Match and Continental. Yet on the witness stand at future investigations, Ben Tomlinson, treasurer and vice president of International Match, was asked:

Q. What was Garanta . . . ?
A. All I know about Garanta is what Mr. Kreuger told me.

Q. What did he tell you about it?
A. He told me—that was probably about 1925, when the company made the monopoly agreement with Poland and I was told at that time that on account of political consideration it was necessary to have another company somewhere outside of Poland to which most of the profits of the concession would come, and that this Garanta Company was such a company. Therefore, these profits were very high, and we were to charge that interest at the rate of twenty-four per cent per annum, and that after a certain period—I have forgotten just how many years —they would begin to amortize the principal. If I remember correctly, Mr. Kreuger also about that time cabled over a balance sheet of the Garanta

Company showing its assets and liabilities, including its debt to International Match Corporation.

Q. Did you ever see another one?
A. No, I never saw one.

Q. This million dollars a quarter, Mr. Tomlinson, those were just accruals, weren't they—you didn't get the cash from Garanta?
A. The interest was paid by Garanta on January 10 and July 10 every year, I think.

Q. Actually paid?
A. As I recall it, it was generally paid to Continental and then we got it later from Continental.

Q. You don't know whether it was paid to Continental by Garanta?
A. I do not know.

Another matter exposing the complete credulity of Americans was the interest rates established by the Match King. Apparently Kreuger plucked these out of thin air, guided only by his psychological instinct for what, under a given circumstance, was right. He kept the International Match dividends at a straight 11 per cent, which apparently was a figure he decided would satisfy Americans and keep them buying. Swedish Match stock, offered mainly in Stockholm, London, and Paris, was pegged at a provocative 15. The gilt-edged Kreuger & Toll stock, sold around the world, paid off first at a dazzling 25, then a far-more-dazzling 50.

Kreuger had the same instinctive skill at pegging rates to please bankers. International Match investments in Spain, made through Continental, were supposed to earn 16 per cent. The loan to Poland, through Garanta, paid off at 24. There is further Kreuger hocus-pocus in the fact that the 24 per cent was received regularly in America from Garanta, but only enough of Continental's 16 per cent arrived each year to make it possible for International Match to pay the public its 11 per cent.

Yet through all this the New York bankers retained faith. Perhaps this was because they had to, for Kreuger never let them see any of the contracts he made with International funds, in the name of the American corporation. Later, Frederic W. Allen, president of Lee, Higginson, was asked:

Q. Do you recall whether you have seen any of the concessions?

A. I don't think I have ever seen any of them.

And Durant:

Q. Do you recall whether you made it a practice to require photostatic copies of original concession agreements?

A. I don't think we had photostatic copies.

Durant expressed the same ignorance on the subject of the rates of interest when asked:

Q. Do you recall any occasion when there was any discussion in meetings of the Board as to the extraordinary stable character of the earnings?

A. No.

Q. Did the Board of Directors ever discuss whether it was unusual or surprising that earnings every quarter should run with such clock-like regularity? Did it ever strike your mind that there was anything calling for inquiry or study in that regularity in the amount of earnings?

A. It was simply a question of knowing the reason for it.

Q. What was the reason?

A. The reason I understand was not to bring into the parent corporation all the dividends and earnings from the subsidiaries. By not bringing the earnings into the parent corporation each time, but keeping them in the subsidiaries, it was not necessary to pay an income tax on earnings which were not brought into this country.

Q. And it was because of that general scheme that it never aroused any suspicion or wonder?

A. That is right.

So we see Kreuger again using the simplest of evasions —"to escape United States taxes on profits." By its utter simplicity, and inherent appeal to the greed and guile lurking in every man, the phrase was perfect for his con-man purposes. Completely trusting, his Wall Street associates left him free to operate, in the words of William H. Stoneman,

> . . . at his craftiest: the perfect confidence man. Execution (of the International Match swindle) brought into play all those tricks of which the Match King was capable, the use of secret subsidiaries, the payment of dividends, the use of forged documents as assets, and the smooth evasion of inquisitive auditors by confronting them with a mass of interlocking transactions which would have defied the United States income tax authorities. Evasiveness, bluff, and haughty bullying kept the American suckers at bay while Kreuger continued to play with their money as his facile fancy dictated.

Also, it lends credence to a picture of Kreuger which has been passed on by associates. This shows the Match King in his Stockholm office, having just accomplished a particularly satisfying money-making *coup*. Picking up a piece of blank paper from his desk, the ordinarily preoccupied man

The Match King as he appeared, on a train trip, at the peak of his success:
emote, inscrutable, slightly mocking. He usually bought three Pullman
chairs, which allowed him to sit in the middle one, with empty seats on
either side. In part, this was to avoid the prying conversation of strangers,
but equally important was the fact that it added color to the Kreuger Legend.

As a young man only dreaming of worldly success, Kreuger retained the look of eager innocence which allowed him to get away with so much as a boy in Kalmar, Sweden.

As a civil engineer in South Africa, Kreuger (seated, left) piled up vast practical knowledge. This stood him in excellent stead when he decided to return home in 1908.

International

The Match King's Paris apartment at 5 Avenue Victor Emmanuel III was the only one of his apartments which did not possess a roof garden. In this dignified-looking building, he rented the entire next-to-top floor and it was in the bedroom of this apartment that he killed himself.

Kreuger seemed to cross the Atlantic Ocean as often as the average man crossed streets. Seldom, however, did he appear on deck in such sporty attire as this. Usually he was a correct, conservatively clothed figure who walked the deck with a gray Homburg on his head and primly carrying a cane.

Kreuger's New York City penthouse at 791 Park Avenue could have bee
one of the show places of the town, had the Match King desired suc
publicity. His terrace garden, complete with growing tree, flagstones fro
Sweden, and rustic summerhouse, was one of the first and most elabora
penthouse gardens in New York. Yet no one saw it except when Kreug
was there.

One of the Match King's last great moments came in 1930, when Syracuse University—the construction of whose Archbold Stadium he had supervised in 1907—made him a Doctor of Business Administration. Sharing honors that day were Governor Franklin D. Roosevelt and Rabbi Stephen S. Wise. Kreuger arrived alone, carrying a small bag, and promptly departed the same way.

International

Kreuger's funeral (*above*) was a simple affair, with only family and close business associates present. His favorite white lilies of the valley engulfed the coffin, and he was eulogized as a martyr. But six weeks later he was notorious, with crowds (*below*) lining up to parade through his Stockholm apartment. When his possessions were put up for auction, pots, pans and ash trays went for as much as five dollars apiece. His speedboats, however, were sold at enormous loss.

Wide World

waves it aloft and jubilantly cries, "Isn't it wonderful what can be done with a scrap of paper? Why, I can raise millions just by scratching my name on this blank sheet."

After which, according to the story, the exalted man stepped out from behind his desk to execute, before the astounded executives, a small, impromptu jig. And altogether, in the telling, this happy jig bears considerable resemblance to the one Hitler later performed in the forest of Compiègne.

13

The Olympian

This gloating, jigging Kreuger was, of course, a figure the world never saw. Instead, the public was proffered the calm, inscrutable man of the Kreuger Legend: the titan of finance, remote, dedicated only to work, absolutely sure of himself, a Midas who by his very touch seemed able to make money multiply. Above all, the Kreuger of the Legend was a figure reassuring to the millions of other human beings, especially in the United States, who dreamed in the stock-speculation 'twenties of making money rapidly and without effort. For Ivar Kreuger seemed to do just that. He was, in a sense, the living symbol of the immoderate, unrealistic times. Everywhere he went millions astoundingly seemed to appear.

Starting in 1926–27, there was even more money. Most of it was on paper, in terms of credit, but like other investors the world over Kreuger did not seem to mind. Why should he? Bankers and financiers, knowing his solid profits from Swedish Match and the stream of American investment dollars from International Match, stood ready to advance him any possible sums for his name on a piece of paper. Or for his word when he blandly assured them there were millions deposited with subsidiary companies like Continental and Garanta. Once the maniacal man had discovered how easy it was to borrow, he seemingly could not stop his frenzied piling up of credit. Offering as security his "honest" millions from Swedish Match and International Match, and the

slightly dubious millions which were a result of the operations of Kreuger & Toll, he raised hundreds of millions on
paper. No sooner would he acquire a tangible asset than he
would start borrowing on it—not legally once, but illegally
many times over. On the basis of millions in actual profits
and by manipulations of the books of Kreuger & Toll and the
subsidiary companies, he was, in short, creating hundreds of
millions in dubious profit.

What was he doing with it? As in the case with most
swindlers, no one will ever know the precise answer. But in
the eyes of the world in 1926–27, he was using his monumental millions to put the completing touches on one of
the most complex and far-flung organizations the world has
ever known. This was the colossus which, among so many
other things, eventually controlled 65 per cent of world
match production. Composed of financially linked, but administratively isolated units, it was dominated by Kreuger &
Toll, Ltd., which from Stockholm always maintained supreme control.

Extending in one direction from the local Kreuger &
Toll was the Swedish Match Company, soon to comprise
160 match factories in 35 countries. Subordinate to Swedish
Match were two Swedish Match Trusts with 20 factories,
the British Match Corporation with four English firms, and
match factories in Canada, South Africa, Australia, South
America; the American International Match Corporation,
the Chilean Company, and the German Match Monopoly
Company. Associated with these were another Swedish
group, consisting of the German Match Factories Company
and the South German Match Company. In addition, Swedish Match had under its direct control factories in Japan,
China and Belgium.

Extending in the other direction from the central

Kreuger & Toll were the holding companies, finance institutions and bank connections. Most of these were purposely
misleading commercial and financial institutions, affiliated
companies, subordinate firms, associated groups, banks, factories, purchasing companies, and monopoly administrations
which, if described in detail, "would require thick volumes
of classified statistics and formulae, and still hardly contain
everything."

But there was more. The insatiable Kreuger, determined
to buy everything he could set his hands on, also in these
years bought iron-ore concerns, railways, mines, timber and
cellulose interests, not to mention factories, film companies
and general real estate.

It all created in him one of the great figures of the time,
and in some ways the greatness was genuine. No one can
belittle the importance of his State-Loans. For with the
enormous prestige acquired from the dubious loans to Spain
and Poland, he went ahead to consummate *bona fide* deals
with other countries, so that indeed "the money he passed
out in a golden stream to the nations of the world was extremely real." At first these Kreuger loans were made only
to European countries, making him seem to the world the
Banker of Europe. But with loans to Ecuador, Peru and Turkey, he became more the World's Banker. Nor did it stop
there. Much of the nearly $400 million he passed out in his
golden stream was used for humanitarian purposes, which
made him seem less like a banker than a benefactor. To his
own considerable pride, Kreuger was on occasion referred
to as the Savior of Europe, and sometimes as the Savior of
the World.

For example, his loan of $4,866,000 to Greece helped
finance one of the most humane of postwar projects, the
repatriation of Greek refugees from Turkey and Macedonia.

Hungary used his $36 million to compensate landowners who had lost property during the Bolshevik Revolution. Also for putting a vast land-reform plan into operation.

A first loan of $2 million received by Ecuador was used to establish a mortgage bank, a basic step in stabilizing the country's economic system. A second loan was used for a farm-mortgage plan.

Yugoslavia used his $22 million for the establishment of a monopolies administration, the profits of which were used for public works. In Rumania a $30 million loan from Kreuger was used for much the same purpose.

Latvia employed her $6 million for the purchase of seed-grain from abroad, for road building, land reclamation, and loans to municipalities and landowners. Estonia used $2,666,-666 from Kreuger for railroad construction.

So it went, creating in European minds the image of a Kreuger seen by one contemporary writer as a man whose

> . . . ordinary business deals were bizarre, weird. But they were humdrum compared with his pursuit of real or *de-facto* government monopolies. That was a story book thing. The history of industry has no character to compare with this silent, secretive man who slipped from capital to capital, country to country, on his mission of intrigue and profit. Now a midnight meeting with some prime minister in the icy north, next a talk with blackshirt magnificos in sun-soaked Florence, or in Athens with the centuries watching, or in sad Vienna with its memories of waltzes and wine. A conference today and a helping hand; tomorrow a cold, rational statement to the cabinet of a country proud for a thousand years, but now reduced to saving its peasants with match loans.

Such was the Match King Europe saw. But to America he was still the calm, unruffled man who appeared on these shores with a comforting message of faith in the financial stability of Europe. "I can't seem to help making money," his quietly confident manner seemed to say, while out from the veiled eyes shot a quizzical, amused, evaluating look.

It was simple. The American public wanted his stocks, he wanted its money. It could be arranged. The Cagliostro of Finance who was Kreuger knew how easily he could get additional millions from America. The last issue of International Match participating preferred stock, offered at $35 a share, had disappeared as if struck by a tornado. Plainly a public so avid would buy more. Back in this country late in 1926, he submitted to the usual shipboard interview, then proceeded to Wall Street, where he proposed new plans to Donald Durant and the other Lee, Higginson partners. What he visualized this time was a Swedish-American Trading Company, with assets of over $6 million, most of it to be real-estate holdings in Germany and Sweden and stock in banks all over Europe.

In almost no time the Swedish-American Trading Company was in existence, with a Board of Directors rivaling those on the International Match Board in prestige. Among the directors were Edwin S. Webster, president of Stone & Webster; James H. Perkins, president of the Farmers Loan & Trust Company; and, again, Percy A. Rockefeller, who thus became director of sixty-two different corporations.

The assets of Swedish-American were dubious at best: a conglomeration of stocks in sound Swedish banks and legitimate real estate mingled with shares in Kreuger's personally established "banks" and the sort of doubtful real-estate property that Bror Bredberg had been instructed to place on the books of Union Industries. But no sooner had Kreuger completed the formation of Swedish-American than he made the familiar announcement to the directors. In order to avoid taxes on American profits, a foreign subsidiary was needed. Out of his sleeve, as it were, he promptly produced one. This was the Standard Trust Fund, just incorporated in the Duchy of Liechtenstein. Kreuger did not tell his American directors that Standard had no capital stock, or that it had already been registered as owned by Swedish-American. But with the first American money funneled from the parent company the Match King performed a characteristic maneuver with Standard Trust. Having increased the capital of Swedish Match from 90 million kroner to 180 million, he sold one quarter of the new class-B stocks to Swedish-American. Shortly, he was able to resell them at a profit of $1,133,300. But though Standard Trust had been created to "receive" all profits involving Swedish-American, it did not get these. Instead, the money went to Kreuger & Toll—"and this," a later investigator concluded wearily, "only started the tangle."

It was all fiendishly clever, but was the Match King actually getting away with his colossal cleverness?

Not altogether. It was Kreuger's policy to keep his some 150 Match Palace underlings working in a small orbit, so that each had only the vaguest notion of the work of associates. This was a continuation of his summit policy of financially linked but administratively isolated units. Yet inevitably some employes caught a glimmering of Kreuger's financial sleight-of-hand, and it is said that several times in the course of his career the Match King was faced across his desk by employes of Kreuger & Toll or Swedish Match who said to him, "Herr Engineer, there are things going on here that I do not understand."

This announcement was seldom the result of business acumen, for Kreuger made it a policy to hire men of low mental and moral caliber. Rather, those who suspected, or discovered, manipulations in the Kreuger books were men who merely stumbled over evidence. After this they divided in two groups. First, there were those who approached the Match King in all sincerity, confident they had discovered a matter he should be aware of, and seeking an honest explanation of it. Kreuger easily soothed these men with another of his pat phrases. "A mistake has been made," he would say, with a shrug. "Who among us does not make mistakes, but you may rest assured that I will have this one rectified instantly." Then in a few days he might order the transfer of the inquisitive employe to one of the overseas operations of Swedish Match.

In the second group were men more difficult to handle. These were almost as unscrupulous as the Match King himself, and approached him bent on blackmail. "Herr Engineer, I am sure you do not want the world to know about this," they would threaten. With his hidden deep-set eyes Kreuger many times in his life was compared to a reptile in appearance, and it is likely that he resembled one most on hearing these words. Still, he had a tactic prepared for blackmail. As in the days when he was buying European match factories, he overpaid. If the man facing him demanded 100,000 kroner for silence, Kreuger would unhesitatingly write out a check for 200,000. Handing this over, he would say, "You may have this, on condition that you never tell anyone what you know, and that I never see or hear from you again."

It worked. In the years following 1926 there were undoubtedly men on the continent of Europe who knew that the Match King was juggling books, and had accepted money to keep silent about it. And none apparently ever spoke a word. As in so many other respects, the Match King's luck held firm in this.

But in the meantime, America, the country for whose businessmen Kreuger had such supreme contempt, was developing a real nemesis. Or perhaps a better estimate is not one nemesis, but two.

In his early meetings with Wall Street bankers, Kreuger had won much trust by stating that books of any of his American companies must be audited by the accounting firm of Ernst & Ernst. Ernst & Ernst stood as high in its field as Lee, Higginson did in investment banking. Among the companies whose books Ernst & Ernst audited annually were Coca-Cola, Firestone, Timken Roller Bearing, Republic Steel and Chrysler. But when given the International Match books the company's auditors found themselves facing a problem. Almost every entry in the books was based on data or instructions sent from Stockholm by Kreuger, usually by means of transatlantic cable. There were no contracts, no vouchers, no statements, no agreements—only the word of the Match King.

This was a considerable barrier for a firm of integrity to hurdle. But finally Ernst & Ernst decided that if top Wall Street bankers could accept Kreuger on his word alone, they could, too. Accordingly, the auditors began approving International Match books. However, one Ernst & Ernst executive named A. D. Berning found this increasingly hard to do, especially after Kreuger had blithely answered a query about the books of a subsidiary called Atlas by cabling: "In the matter of Atlas, let me say that a personal examination of the books discloses a surplus of $150,000 at the moment."

A later account of Berning's activities states his problem this way: "He found himself confronted by a mass of certificates of deposit and other documents tending to prove the existence of various assets of International Match. To have demanded additional proof would have been to challenge Kreuger's veracity, a thing which he, as an auditor, could scarcely do, particularly when Kreuger enjoyed such implicit confidence among his American associates." Nonetheless, Berning persisted. In 1926 he came across the first reference to Garanta, in connection with its debt of $17 million to International Match. Again his suspicions rose, and he cabled Kreuger for assurance that Garanta could meet its obligations. In Stockholm, the mighty Kreuger must have been irritated indeed at such a request from a mere American accountant. But he had long ago made up his mind that the way to treat all Americans was with deprecating, respectful courtesy, and now he cabled Berning a long statement showing that Garanta's income for 1925 had been 46 million Dutch gulden, where its debt to American called for only 45 million. Thus Garanta could pay with a million to spare.

With word direct from Kreuger himself, Berning could only subside. But he continued to be bothered by Garanta, and also by the Spanish Loan. Apparently his suspicions took him to Europe, for eventually he became one of the few ever privileged to examine the Spanish Loan contract. In Kreuger's Stockholm office, he was handed this detailed document, with its careless date and sprawling Primo de Rivera signature. Again, the last was by far the most convincing item, since it so resembled the scrawl of a Spanish Prime Minister. Further, the thought of forgery connected with Kreuger, a man held in such high esteem in Wall Street, was at this point too much even for Berning. He accepted the validity of the document and contented himself with putting a few sharp questions to the Match King about another of his "little banks," the Netherlandish, which held in account 400 million francs for Continental Investment. This time Kreuger subjected Berning to the secrecy treatment. Lifting a warning finger to his lips, he whispered that Netherlandish existed "to keep certain transactions secret from Swedish and foreign bankers." Of necessity, Berning had to accept this also. But he was still only half convinced on his return to the United States.

Had he known it, however, he was not alone in his suspicions of the Match King. And as an ally, he had one of the most powerful men alive.

For—as stated—there was one Wall Street financier who, on Kreuger's first New York visit, had failed to succumb to the charm of the suave Match King. This was the most formidable financier-banker on Wall Street, or anywhere—none other than J. P. Morgan. Morgan had been informed of the Swede's bold concept of State-Loans in return for match monopolies and had expressed interest in the innovation. Yet he had refrained from meeting Kreuger face to face. Instead, Morgan had unobtrusively joined a group before which Kreuger spoke, and back in his office rumbled out an opinion surprising to his associates. "I don't trust that man," he said, in effect. "I want nothing to do with him."

But with the Match King rising to be Savior of Europe, and in the United States rapidly winning investors and influencing bankers, there was little Morgan could do except mutter indignantly whenever Kreuger's name was mentioned. In time, Kreuger himself learned of Morgan's hostility, and characteristically twisted it to his own uses. With mock-modesty, he would bring Morgan's name into conversations. "I am only a small David, while he is a mighty Goliath," he would say, smiling a rueful half-smile. It made his listeners pity—and admire—him the more.

Then, in 1927, the David who was Kreuger engaged the Morgan Goliath in a way which increased hostility—and perhaps again proves that whom the gods would destroy they first make mad.

When one examines the list of Kreuger Loans up to 1927, it can be seen that most were made to small countries like Greece. This was a fact galling to the Match King, who had his ambitions set on loans to France and Germany, the two titans among Europe's impoverished countries. He had already made overtures to both, and been rebuffed. But in matters concerning Match Loans the eye of the reptilian Kreuger became more like the eye of a hawk, and hawklike he sat back to watch the economies of the titans. In October, 1927, he suddenly saw the French economy waver. He moved in.

Nineteen twenty-seven had been a bad year for the French. The franc had been sliding and at times seemed about to follow the German mark in a final plunge into nothingness. The best Raymond Poincaré, head of the French Cabinet, could do was try to stabilize the franc at one fifth its prewar value. To accomplish this he needed more money from wealthy America, the inexhaustible golden goose which had kept France supplied for ten years. But this time Wall Street flatly refused. The reason was the attitude of J. P. Morgan, to whose banking firm France already owed $70 million. There would be no more money, Morgan stated, until that debt had been paid. Other American bankers in fear of Morgan could only echo his words.

Thus, for a moment in October, 1927, France was defeated. At this point Kreuger stepped forward to offer a loan of $75 million, at the low interest rate of 5 per cent. At first he asked in return a twenty-year match monopoly in France, which a relieved Poincaré and his Cabinet were only too willing to give him. But in the Chamber of Deputies, ever suspicious of foreign interests, there was "turmoil and opposition, bitter debate." Kreuger—eager perhaps for the one time in his career to attain a monopoly for prestige rather than money reasons—quickly modified his demands. He offered to accept the best terms France would give, which turned out to be the exclusive right to furnish the French Monopoly Administration with match sticks, match machinery, and raw materials, together with special "control of imported safety matches."

Now a miracle seemed to take place. It was as if Kreuger's $75 million loan had breathed new life into the French economy. Almost miraculously the country began to recover. Whereas Morgan had been unwilling to gamble on such a recovery, Kreuger did—and won. This alone was annoying to the House of Morgan, and shortly arose a greater annoyance. One of France's first acts with its new prosperity was to pay off the Morgan loan, which had been charged at a rate of 8 per cent. It made everyone happy but J. P. Morgan. His judgment had not only been proved wrong, but he had lost the profitable interest payments—a blow probably more severe than the one to his pride.

Of all the great Kreuger deals, open or hidden, State or otherwise, the 1927 loan to France was by far the most felicitous. From it, France regained confidence and climbed back to her feet. Kreuger and his investors made great profits from it, so that now the Match King was hailed as a man "whose credit in the whole world has asserted itself as supreme."

It did J. P. Morgan no good to mutter against Kreuger, or even to begin a more active hostility. No one would listen. Kreuger had not only outsmarted him, but in a sense outsmarted every banker in the world, and now the world was busy honoring him for it. In recognition of services rendered, Kreuger was awarded by France the Grand Cross of the Legion of Honor. Requested to appear for this ceremony in full decorations, the sallow, immobile man wore only the medal struck to commemorate the Stockholm Olympic

Games of 1912. This was an act of extreme modesty which warmed hearts everywhere, for Kreuger was known to have received many decorations from governments.

Not unexpectedly it was in France, the country bestowing its Grand Cross, that the gesture aroused the most emotion. Said one newspaper editorially, "The French miracle has elevated Ivar Kreuger to the position of superman of finance. From today, he is Olympian."

14

A Kingdom Called Incognito

At the time of his fortunate loan to France, Kreuger was forty-seven and a half years old, a man in whose physical appearance the passage of time seemed only to have made routine changes. As when he returned to Sweden to establish Kreuger & Toll, he still appeared some ten years less than his age. True, his always sparse hair had become nearly non-existent on the top of his head, but the strands remaining there, together with the fuller hair at the sides, contributed to his younger appearance by containing no streaks of gray. He remained big-boned and stoop-shouldered, still favoring the weak heart. But unlike most men of sedentary occupation he had not put on weight or developed an executive-chair paunch. He could never be called slim, but he did seem to be solid, a man whose body carried very little, if any, extra weight.

In all, Kreuger appeared a man of indeterminate middle age, on whom time had only accentuated the facial features. The pursed mouth had grown more sensual than prim, losing some of the sweetness it had retained from childhood. Mounds of flesh over the high cheekbones rose higher, providing greater hiding for the sunken, cryptic eyes. And the forehead, because of the increasing baldness, seemed far higher than before. However, one considerable change had taken place in Kreuger. His sallow skin, always pulpy and large-pored, had over the years become conspicuously clammy.

"His pale skin always seemed moist," said one writer. Another, in a more detailed description, saw

> Above a high forehead, which was not really so high, but appeared so because the hair was receding, lay carefully brushed, sparse locks. Beneath a pointed nose, a rather slack, markedly sensual mouth. Very prominent cheekbones. The skin was not taut. On the contrary it looked curiously loose and porous, and without actually being damp had an unhealthy, greasy appearance.

Because of his moist skin and almost feminine softness in his hands, the act of shaking the Match King's hands could be a strange experience. In A Paris Surgeon's Story, published in 1956, his personal physician, Dr. Charles F. Bove, recalls Kreuger as "stoop-shouldered, his skin loose and porous. . . . His touch was clammy. . . . It was a peculiar sensation to shake hands with him." It may seem almost too pat to be true, but the Match King's dainty, limp hands were remarkable for still another reason. In the traditional gesture of guilt, he always seemed to be washing them. Or, in the words of Dr. Bove, "He had a mannerism of rubbing his hands as if he were washing them with air." The Match King's hands also made a vivid impression on a journalist named Erich Vogeler, who had a long interview with Kreuger on economics. Later he asked in print:

> Why do Kreuger's hands look so repellent when they are lying on the arms of a chair? They make one feel they must be cold and clammy like those of a neurasthenic, although they are not actually at all like that. Every now and then he seemed to be drying them. Then he fidgeted with his fingers and sometimes the movement continued up his arm and then his shoulders

twitched slightly. Otherwise he sat quite still. I cannot say that the general impression made on me by this man was uncanny—although I suddenly and for no reason thought of a drowned man—it was simply unpleasing.

To the majority of those who met him, however, the impression made by the Match King was less one of unpleasantness than of disappointment. "Is this Sweden's great man?" people asked themselves as they shook the damp hand of a sallow, poker-faced man, dressed in dull, correct clothes, who looked at them with an almost total lack of interest. For Kreuger was not only unprepossessing in appearance, but was usually so deep in his thoughts that he made no effort to be pleasant to those he met. This was particularly true at social gatherings, which Kreuger attended as rarely as possible. The Match King's attitude of deprecating shyness in business may have been part of a bland act, but in society the shy Kreuger seems to have been the true one. He was well-read, but he had no taste for the abstract ideas and gossip out of which dinner-table conversation is produced. Nor had he ever taken time out from his relentless upward progress to acquire such social graces as dancing or balancing a demitasse cup gracefully. Isaac Marcosson, who perhaps studied Kreuger more intently than anyone else, says: "Man of the world as he undoubtedly was, I should set him down as unsophisticated on the social side." Marcosson gives an unforgettable picture of Kreuger arriving at a garden party at the Long Island estate of Bradley Martin in "a bowler hat, black sack coat and trousers, and patent leather shoes." To make matters worse, Kreuger was persuaded to play a game of tennis on the indoor court, and promptly began, dressed as he was. But the clue to the Match King's character here is that he did not realize that he looked absurd. For, Marcosson concludes, "It was to his credit that the inappropriateness of his attire did not embarrass him."

Still, Kreuger seemed to realize that lack of social grace, plus intense self-absorption, made him an unrewarding guest. Attending a dinner party, he made it a policy always to present his hostess with an expensive gift, after which he seemed to feel that any obligation had been paid off and he could retire to his thoughts. The novelist-journalist, Countess Waldeck, who in Germany of the 'twenties was Frau Ullstein, gives a hostess-eye view of this Match King:

> He came to dine with us once in Berlin. He was taciturn, unsmiling, courteous, unamusable, distant. He first sent me flowers in a priceless Chinese vase. There was a certain colorless melancholy about him—nothing of the dynamic, adventurous tycoon. His reticence and modesty pleased me. In fact, he pleased me altogether without impressing me too much. He was the sort of man one forgets easily.

It can also be said that those on whom Kreuger made no impression were those who failed to catch his interest —or from whom he needed no favors. For when, in any group or gathering, something was said which caught the Match King's attention, a curious transformation seemed to take place. It was as if a vague, protoplasmic figure suddenly materialized into the very definite personality of a man. Kreuger could be a charmer and he knew it. When his interest was caught, he suddenly seemed to radiate a warm interest in those around him, all of whom immediately responded to the subtle flattery of his interest. "His was a complete abstraction until you said something that attracted him," one associate recalls. "Then he suddenly became alive. There was something almost hypnotic in it. After being indifferent to him, you all at once felt: here is a modest, unpretentious man, whom I truly like."

Once his interest was aroused, Kreuger almost invariably began to talk. For the musical voice seemed to act as the battery which fed the fascination and charm. "His voice was a monotone until he became interested," recalls the New York patent attorney H. R. Van Deventer, who had several business conferences with the Match King. Another man says: "He didn't strike you as much until he began to speak." His voice was soft and vibrant, and when Kreuger spoke English, had "a sort of singsong quality not unlike Chinese articulation," a fact not surprising in one whose basic language was Swedish. But still more conspicuous than any singsong quality was the magic spell Kreuger seemed able to induce with his speech. It brought listeners a feeling of absolute belief in everything he said. One man, attempting to analyze it, concluded: "Ivar Kreuger, when he wanted to, could take the simplest statement and give it an almost statesmanlike ring. You thought—why, everything this man says is important, everything I hear from him must be true."

One group Kreuger especially set out to charm was his employees, for he realized that blind adoration in his subordinates was necessary for his financial manipulations. To executives, secretaries and clerical help, he was always "unobtrusively friendly, all he demanded being unquestioning obedience and unquestioning devotion to the welfare of the business." Indeed, Kreuger may have been one of the first enlightened despots among world tycoons. He had a medical-aid office in the Match Palace, and as he passed employees in the halls he would often nod in a friendly manner and sometimes stop to inquire about health or progeny. Any subordinate could enter his office at any time, which accounts for the ease with which the blackmailers reached him. To his high-echelon executives, Kreuger was something more of a trial, since an inner impatience and determination to get things finished could be sensed in all dealings with him. At meetings in the curved Board Room of the Match Palace he customarily sat with eyes shut, and a hand shielding them, as if concentrating deeply. But when he dropped the hand and exposed the eyes "they seemed to bore through you." It was inevitable that his executives would often be bewildered by the deals he explained with staccato briefness at the beginning of meetings. "But, I.K., you can't do that," one surprised assistant might suddenly burst out. At which Kreuger would swing mocking eyes to the questioner, give his quizzical half-smile and answer softly, "You're quite wrong, my dear fellow, you have no idea how much people will swallow." But once such a protest caught Kreuger with his imperturbability down. Then he rose slowly to his feet, and in a cold, chilling voice demanded, "Are you suggesting that I am falsifying the books?" Dead silence fell over the room, and no one dared answer. After a few pregnant seconds, Kreuger sat down and continued as before.

Few, if any, regular employees of the Match Palace saw Kreuger in such moods, or those of outright irritability with which he reacted to any hesitation on the part of his shadow subordinates like Karl Lange. "A wonderful control and inner coolness ran through everything he did," said one aide. "He never showed himself bad-tempered from overstrain or unstrung from over-fatigue. He was always carefully polite to his secretaries, male and female, and there was only one crime which made him really angry. That was if anyone dared disturb him in the Silence Room."

Actually, however, the Match King had no need to make calculated efforts to win the admiration of employees.

He had already obtained it in the most concrete way possible—by working infinitely harder than anyone else in the organization. Workers in the Match Palace offices, strolling the Stockholm streets at any hour of the night, could see lights burning in I.K.'s office or in the single small window of his under-the-roof Silence Room, and know their phenomenal chief was hard at work. Indeed, the amount of time Kreuger devoted to work was truly superhuman. More so than ever in middle age, he became Napoleonic in his ability to work for days, rest for half an hour, then rise to work again. Sometimes he plunged his fatigued body into ice cold baths to keep his head clear. A clear head was particularly important to him, for the Match King—and the Match King alone—had all the details of his vast financial empire in his own mind. He never kept notes on anything. When an employee brought him a long factual report, Kreuger did not ask for a copy. He had it read to him, while he sat silently absorbing it. Later, he would, from memory, incorporate the figures in another report. The figures were always correct.

On the surface, a day's work consisted largely in dispatching orders like the general of a world-wide army and one contemporary has thus pictured an ordinary moment in an ordinary Kreuger day:

> Sitting in his private office at the Match Palace in remote Stockholm, a red light outside the door announcing that he was busy, he spoke by telephone with the outposts of his financial empire. A Kreuger broker in New York was to buy ten thousand debentures, the manager of a match concession in South America was to buy this or that factory, would Monsieur Blank see the Minister of Finance about that matter, this piece of Berlin real estate was to be sold to So and So at such and such a price. Why hadn't this particular government come through on that deal? So and So in

Zurich was to enter a debit of so and so much on the books of this or that company. Did the Germans mean business or didn't they?

When in New York he ran the Match Palace by cable as deftly as if he were sitting behind his desk. When not dispatching cables, holding conferences, or studying financial statements, he passed his time exactly as he said he did— silently thinking. Asked once to explain his heroic capacity for labor, he stepped to a bookshelf and from one of his favorite volumes on Napoleon, read the Emperor's words to Roederer:

> I am always at work; I think a great deal. If I appeared to be ever ready and equal to any occasion, it is because I have thought over matters for long before I undertake to do the slightest thing. I have foreseen all eventualities. There exists no guardian angel who suddenly and mysteriously whispers in my ear what I have to do or say. Everything is turned over in my mind; again and again, always. . . .

But with all this, not everyone he met could immediately be won over by the Match King—a fact of which he seemed to be aware. Occasionally he bumped up against someone who, like J. P. Morgan, was impervious to his rare powers of fascination. Such individuals, it seemed, could see into him as clearly as if his pasty skin were transparent, like a newly polished windowpane.

On the record is the comment of one man who failed to be seduced by Kreuger's personality. Said he: "Kreuger is a person of colossal gall, whose celebrated feats of persuasion consist only in asserting, asserting, asserting, until people believe in him because of his nerve in so often repeating." But far more dramatic was the remark made at the time Max

Reinhardt, the famed German theatrical impresario, decided
to visit Kreuger in Stockholm. Reinhardt asserted that, having heard so many stories of the Savior of Europe, he must
study the remarkable man at close hand, but unkind souls
have suggested that the producer of spectacles was more interested in Kreuger as a potential financial backer for his
extravagant productions. At any rate, Reinhardt traveled to
Stockholm, where he informed the press that he had come
for the sole purpose of meeting Kreuger. Immediately, obstacles began to appear in his path, as if the Match King
had no desire to be studied by a man of such vaunted perception, so wise in the ways of theatre. But Reinhardt was
an important person and finally the Match King could evade
no longer. He received the impresario in his office, and he
must have decided that his only hope was to charm this man
of the theatre. He promptly did, and Reinhardt, like Edward
Bernays, was swept off his feet by visions of Kreuger as the
New European. Returning to his hotel, he rhapsodized about
Kreuger to all who would listen. That night he went to a
Stockholm theatre with a young German playwright who
had accompanied him to Stockholm. This was also one of
the rare nights when the Match King made a public appearance, sitting aloof and alone in the theatre's center box.
Reinhardt, pointing him out, continued his rhapsody. The
young playwright took a searching look, then exclaimed, "So
that is your great man! I do not even see a human being. I
see a reptile with sunk-in, stinging eyes. I see a devourer of
men. . . ."

No doubt it was fear of meeting such perceptive people
face to face—joined with his childhood conviction that people were determined to destroy superiority—which drove
Kreuger ever deeper into a life in the shadows. Rising higher
in the world, he seemed more than ever determined to cre-

ate a gulf between himself and his fellow man. He even developed an obsessive fear of being recognized when he traveled. On some transatlantic voyages he used an assumed name and when friends expressed surprise at this secrecy, he answered sententiously, "My kingdom is one called Incognito."

Even more, as time passed, the Match King sought to hide behind his accomplishments,—becoming "a shallow Sphinx striving to erect a smokescreen between himself and the eyes of the world." This smokescreen was, of course, the Kreuger Legend, and in order that the world might see him exclusively as the figure of the Legend, he established an organization called the Swedish-American News Agency in Stockholm. In charge he placed a Swedish newspaperman named Böerje Brillioth. Kreuger's orders to him were simple. "Keep me out of the papers, that is your first duty," he exhorted, and Brillioth promptly began a campaign in Germany, France, and the Baltic countries to persuade newspaper editors that Kreuger was not newsworthy. "Believe me," he would state with conviction, "there is nothing at all remarkable about Kreuger, no romance or color. His own development can best be traced in the development of his undertakings."

Brillioth's campaign succeeded best in Sweden, where Kreuger's influence was greatest. "If you want to find out anything about Kreuger," a Swedish member of Parliament lamented to a foreign journalist, "there is no use coming to Sweden. Why? Nobody knows anything about him there. Nobody knows whether he is at home or abroad. Everything he does is kept dark. We are given only three pieces of information—Kreuger is lonely; Kreuger does everything for the good of his native land; Kreuger leads an ascetic life."

Occasionally a foreign journalist did appear in Stockholm with orders to write a feature story on Europe's Savior. Then Brillioth shifted tactics. With bearlike friendliness, he took the journalist under his wing, paid his hotel expenses, showed him the sights, bought copious dinners and drinks, and—if the situation seemed to call for it—provided feminine companionship. Through all this he would repeat endlessly how hard Kreuger worked, that the Match King's dedication to making money for others left him no time for private life, or for such relaxations as interviews with foreign reporters. Home after a highly stimulating sojourn in Sweden, the journalist would sober up to realize that he had not even been allowed to set eyes on the Match King. Still, Brillioth had furnished him with excellent anecdote material for a story. One such—probably true—would tell of Kreuger at a dinner party in Paris where an explorer told of experiences among primitive dwarf tribes in Central Africa. This brought the preoccupied Match King to alert, interested life, asking so many searching questions that the flattered explorer finally said, "You seem particularly interested in the subject, Mr. Kreuger. Is anthropology one of your hobbies?"

"Not at all," Kreuger answered. "I was just thinking it was time those little fellows out there gave up rubbing sticks together and began using Swedish matches."

Like all legends, the one behind which Kreuger sought to obscure himself was a mixture of truth and publicity fabrication. One of the fabrications stated that the Match King bestowed a Rolls Royce limousine on anyone he particularly liked, and that for this generous purpose he kept a standing account of $100,000 in the Paris showroom of the automobile company.

The only basis for this story seems to be that Kreuger himself preferred Rolls Royce limousines and owned several, the one he kept in Stockholm being "bigger than the King's."

But an almost equally improbable-sounding part of the Legend was quite true. This was that Kreuger maintained sumptuous apartments in each of the world cities he visited most. He did, indeed—except for London, where he maintained a year-round suite at the Carleton Hotel. Kreuger had large apartments in Stockholm, Paris and New York. Each was staffed by a housekeeper who kept the place in constant readiness so that Kreuger might appear unannounced at any hour of the day or night and shortly sit down to a well-prepared meal. Further, the apartments contained expensive furnishings, valuable books and works of art. In each was a wardrobe fully stocked with changes of the Match King's conservative clothes, complete to the last cuff link. Thus it was necessary for the traveling Match King to carry a bag only on Atlantic crossings, and then only the smallest of valises.

Of all Kreuger's apartments, his penthouse at 791 Park Avenue in New York was probably his favorite, largely because New York became his favored city. His Paris flat was a third-floor-through at 5 Avenue Victor Emmanuel III, in the exclusive Etoile district. But of necessity he spent most time in the duplex apartment at 13 Villagatan in Stockholm and this, if any of his residences deserved the name, was most like home to him.

With improvements over the years, the Villagatan flat came to contain twenty-three rooms. Kreuger's ingenious engineering mind fixed these so that units could be cut off, to give complete privacy from the rest of the apartment. One part, consisting of six rooms, could be turned into a completely self-sufficient unit. There he sometimes put up important visitors, or when the mood seized him, retired himself. For the most part he lived in bachelor splendor at the Villagatan duplex. His parents now spent part of the year in Kalmar, in a small chateau he had built for them. When they were in their Stockholm house, he appeared to treat his father and mother with great consideration, dining with them once a week and, on his father's birthdays, wearing full decorations, something he failed to do for the French Republic. But on close examination both gestures seem empty. At the weekly dinners he never spoke and his parents, awed by the world-importance of their son, ate in similar silence. The matter of the full decorations seems to have been no more than a clever bit of grist for the mill of the Kreuger Legend. Kreuger's four sisters visited him occasionally, and he seems to have been particularly fond of his sister Britta. Relations with his brother Torsten, who worked for him and had a home and family nearby, were sometimes strained and always of an older-brother-knows-best variety.

In New York, his Park Avenue penthouse was an elaborate ten-room affair, complete with library, Silence Room, silver-tone dining room, and formal drop-step living room, over the fireplace of which hung a Rembrandt, "Man in a Black Hat." But in Kreuger's mind all this elegance was secondary to the fact that in the proper seasons he could, simply by stepping through the French doors of his New York living room, enter a quiet Swedish country garden.

For on renting the penthouse he had cast dissatisfied eyes over the empty flagstone terrace and announced, "I plan to bring up dirt and plant a garden here." Owner and real-estate agent had immediately protested, claiming such a thing could not be done. But Kreuger had not been a civil engineer and builder for nothing. He proved with quick statistics how the job could be managed. Tons of dirt were transported from the street below and then a large tree was planted, some of its branches spreading over the Park Avenue sidewalk below. Under the tree stood a marble fountain on which laughing fauns piped and played. In summer, beds of blooming flowers filled the terrace space, while footpaths with flat stones brought from Sweden rambled in and out.

In one corner of the garden stood a small rustic summerhouse, complete with silver birch benches and wrought-iron love seats. On summer nights, with lights blazing out from the living room inside, Kreuger's garden-in-the-city achieved a truly fairy tale appearance.

Yet with all the beauty and imagination of his roof gardens, and the money lavished on the furnishings of his apartments, Kreuger's various dwelling places only pinpoint the emotional and spiritual emptiness of the man.

It is said that once Kreuger, before departing on a trip, called in his Stockholm decorator to re-do the Villagatan flat in his absence. On his return the Match King examined the new living room and noted a Madonna on one wall. He walked across the room, lifted the painting from its hook, and handed it back to the decorator. "Take this away, I don't like Madonnas," he said.

This, if true, would seem to be the one occasion on which Kreuger even noticed his intimate surroundings. For there is much testimony to the fact that his apartments, lived in though they were, continued to bear the stamp of the interior decorator, so that Kreuger, as he moved among his luxurious possessions, did so with the impersonality of a man who has rented a hotel suite for a few days.

In all, Kreuger's living quarters always seemed perfectly right for a man who lived in the kingdom called Incognito. Dr. Bjerre, who was entertained in Stockholm by the Match King, dwells on this at length, finally summing up: "His dining room looked like a restaurant, his living room like a stage set, his smoking room like a private club. There was no warmth to anything. Everything in the apartment seemed hungry for attention and love, the books to be read, the chairs to be sat on. . . ."

15

The Second Man

So Ivar Kreuger stood before the world, "cosmopolitan financier, sybarite of the world's capitals." He was one of Europe's great men, more important at the moment than the Rothschilds who functioned only as middlemen, impersonal handlers of money. Kreuger was the man of action, rolling back the frontiers of economics, to make himself first a financier, then a super-financier.

But what impulses lay beneath the surface outlines of this mighty man?

At the time of the French Loan, Kreuger was on the verge of becoming, if he had not already become, the most colossal swindler the world has ever known. What psychological forces could create such a gigantic Jekyll-Hyde? What twisted impulses were the forces that molded the real Ivar Kreuger?

Or what lack of impulse? For deep in every human being lurks the desire—on occasion—to kill, steal, rape, or perform other antisocial deeds. Yet no sooner do such desires rise in a normal personality than they are checked by a combination of sanity and self-control. In Kreuger there seemed increasingly to be no such checks. He appeared to live a morally uninhibited existence, feeling free to do anything he felt like doing. In the words of Manfred George, his "overweening egotism had gradually risen to such a pitch that he was incapable of seeing the world apart from his schemes. His

mind was thus in a state of perpetual tension, and this was
doubtless the reason why one part of his nature seemed as if
it were split off from the rest. He lived a true double life,
and in the secondary portion of it all the tendencies that had
to be ruthlessly suppressed in his normal being were given
full play."

But why? This cannot be answered with any degree of
accuracy, for during his triumphant years no one—with the
possible exception of his blackmailers—ever thought of
Kreuger as a criminal. Hence, he was never studied with
thoughts of a twisted personality in mind. As his eminence
in the world increased, it became more difficult—not to say
impossible—to imagine such a man indulging in criminal
acts. "The higher he rose," states George, "the more rarefied
grew the atmosphere." Nor can a world in which an airplane
had yet to fly the Atlantic nonstop be accused of naïveté.
Today it would be equally difficult to suspect a man on whom
the Premier of France emotionally pinned the Legion of
Honor.

Still, in his personality there were signs which might
have struck any observer as wise in the ways of Sigmund Freud
in 1927 as we are now. One thing in particular impressed all
those who knew Kreuger. This was his seeming lack of vanity.

In his *Twelve Against the Gods*, William Bolitho makes
the point that an emotionally unfeeling Napoleon performed
his earth-shaking feats not so much to satisfy himself, as for
the pleasure and satisfaction of his family. "Not only were
his brothers and sisters part of his own body, but they were
the only parts in which he could feel and enjoy. They were
his palate, his eyes, his ears; and his inflamed appetite for
life could only be satisfied through the canals of their enjoyment."

Examination of Kreuger would seem to indicate that

the man of steely self-control and lack of vanity performed his feats of financial skill and criminal deception, not for the sake of his family, but for the approval of a hidden self. Where most men seek power because it brings the admiration and approval of others, Kreuger behaved as though he carried inside himself an ever-watching Cyclopean eye. This was the eye of a secret self and it gave particular appreciation to any examples of the Match King's cleverness, as shown by his ability to outwit others. The gloating approval of the inner eye—or self—seemed to be all the Match King ever wanted or needed.

This, of course, leaves him open to charges of narcissism, which Freud calls the first, and exceedingly immature, stage of emotional development. But Kreuger's was not the accepted enjoyment-of-oneself-in-the-mirror type of narcissism. Kreuger's went far deeper. He seemed to carry his own built-in mirror, and the sight of himself being cleverer than others fed his ego exactly as a glimpse of his own strong profile feeds that of a vain actor. It is a type of narcissism defined by the psychiatrist Dr. Ralph Slater, when he writes:

The term narcissism comes from the Greek legend about Narcissus, a boy who happened one day to see his image in a pool. He fell in love with his beautiful image, couldn't leave it, pined away, and died. . . . Similarly, the narcissist is not in love with his true self but with an image of himself, shimmering in all its glory and magnificence, not in a pool of water, but in his imagination . . . He builds in his imagination a conception of himself in which he glorifies and ennobles himself. In this way he raises himself above other people, and achieves a sense of power, unity, and direction . . . The narcissist, identified with this glorified self, feels himself to be quite wonderful. He has unquestioned belief in his own greatness, omnipotence, and uniqueness. He feels no doubts about himself consciously and disregards or waves away any shortcomings. He gives the impression of boundless self-confidence and buoyancy, and if not frustrated can be extremely charming, gracious, gay, witty, friendly, generous, and self-assured.

Unlike most narcissists on this earth, Kreuger had a genius-mind which enabled him to match his inner image with outer performance. Thus, the inner eye was able to beam constant approval, and when complimented on his vast worldly success, Kreuger was so filled with inner self-satisfaction that he could answer with seeming modesty, "I have only worked hard."

But was he happy this way? Certainly, to the world the Match King appeared to be a man who had found happiness in his work and his splendid achievements, even though they left him a solitary figure on the world scene. If taxed, he would undoubtedly have declared that he was getting the utmost out of his life. When reporters asked why he never took vacations like other successful men, he smiled the deprecating smile and replied, "I couldn't even if I wanted to—something inside me goes on thinking and planning all the time." But according to modern psychiatry Kreuger was that most baffling of all neurotics, a type which comes under the heading of "the mysterious psychopath." This is the man who is unhappy but is not aware of it—or, perhaps better, will not let himself admit it. Dr. Karen Horney has summed this man when describing the basic urges of Kreuger's type as a need "to exploit and outsmart others, and use them." But, she goes on

In understanding the intensity and compulsiveness with which he seeks to fulfill these needs, it is important to keep in mind that these needs are prompted by the necessity of finding relief for the profound, pervasive inner tensions resulting from his basic anxiety.

Or, again to quote Dr. Slater:

> Narcissism is a neurotic—that is, irrational and compulsive—solution to inner conflict. The narcissist, so to speak, has really turned his back on the human being he really is . . . But this self-assurance, beguiling as it was, is only one side of the picture. Hidden behind the overweening pride is hatred and aversion for the real self. The narcissistic individual has no use for what in him is genuine or true. He condemns and rejects it. When occasionally he gets a glimpse of himself he is horrified.

On the Kreuger record is one scene of the Match King waging a fight with what might be called his real self. It begins with a French art dealer deciding to emulate Sir Joseph Duveen by building up a stable of multimillionaires to whom he could readily sell paintings. One of the rich men he picks as a potential patron of art is the Match King, and after much persistent effort the dealer persuades Kreuger to spend a Saturday afternoon touring Paris art galleries. Together the two men start out—the pale, moist-faced Kreuger looking every inch the sedate man of international finance, with gray Homburg, conservative blue serge suit, high, starched Hoover collar, and polished walking stick. In the galleries Kreuger first shows complete indifference to the works of art pointed out to him, but slowly he opens up until, to the dealer's delight, he begins manifesting signs of great interest. Even more remarkable is the fact that the comments he makes are intelligent, showing considerable intuitive feeling for art. But just as the dealer is congratulating himself on a master stroke, Kreuger abruptly turns on his heel and leaves the gallery. The startled dealer follows to the sidewalk, where he holds the

Match King's arm and tries to persuade him to return. Kreuger pulls away, his normally inscrutable face showing unmistakable signs of inner conflict. But suddenly he exerts extra strength to free his arm. "It is not that I cannot afford to become interested in art," he states with great finality, "but I have two interests already. They are matches and Kreuger & Toll. I cannot split my personality further." With that, he strides away.

The Match King had other inner struggles, though not necessarily with his better self. One was against the temptations of drink. Kreuger was in no sense an alcoholic, or even a potential one. Yet, like most Swedes, he did enjoy alcohol and on occasion did drink, so that Dr. Bove recalls, "I knew him as a compulsive gambler and a man who could drink others under the table and keep a clear head." But though his head seemed to remain clear to others, Kreuger himself knew that strong drink put him in a state which, for him, was garrulity. When his capacity and clearheadedness aroused the admiration of others he was usually drinking champagne, for which he seemed to have an unusual tolerance. With whiskeys, the Martinis that were becoming the vogue in America, and aquavit, that notable Swedish favorite, Kreuger was as apt as anyone else to lose his superb mental control, and fear of letting something slip that would alert the world to the peculiarity of his transactions kept him almost totally abstemious. He was also a man of sufficient will power to hold his consumption of cigarettes to a few after dinner. With drink he was equally strong, except on rare occasions, confining himself to "loving the odor of brandies and old wines."

It is revealing that another of the matters in which Kreuger had to watch himself was the writing of personal checks. Some strange compulsion—combined, no doubt, with feelings of guilt—made him prone to misdate, misamount, and generally scramble even the smallest of personal checks, thus further confusing a banking situation already sufficiently confounded. Other of his quirks may or may not expose inner tensions. Those who knew him cannot recall ever having heard him laugh, and he permitted himself the quizzical half-smile only rarely. He was so completely devoid of sentiment that some thought he hated his fellow man. But, says Dr. Bjerre, "to hate one must also be able to love, and he could not love—so he merely looked down on the rest of humanity." Still, he was capable of actions which seemed to indicate human warmth. Like many other high-echelon criminals, he had strong intuitive powers which sometimes seemed to slip over into the mystic. Invalids appeared to get balm from his presence and touch, and the role of healer was one which much appealed to the devourer of men. In Stockholm whenever possible he made visits to the bedside of an elderly lady invalid whose back he gently massaged with his magnetic hands. "Mother always felt better after Mr. Kreuger had been with her," the woman's daughter stated later.

On other occasions Kreuger performed acts which would imply consideration for his fellow man, but probably stemmed more from his deep-rooted fear of having others too near him. Those who phoned the Match King at home were usually surprised when he answered in person, and those who rang his doorbell were equally amazed when Kreuger performed the function of opening the door. His dislike of having things done for him even extended to restaurants, which he avoided because he did not like the ministrations of hovering waiters. Seemingly incapable of embarrassment, the Match King could be embarrassed by one thing. This was praise from someone he liked. With strangers this did not seem to matter, but he flushed and changed the subject when close friends told him he was an honor to Sweden. Dr. Bjerre thinks this was because of the inner knowledge that he was a discredit to his native land and hearing praise from someone close made him truly ashamed. "He was at least that honest," the psychoanalyst concludes.

Practically the only hobby he ever cultivated was his love of speedboats, which he loved to press to top speed, provided he was at the wheel. In a remark about a boat he had bought but never used Kreuger gave further testimony to the terrible emptiness of his life, as well as the insatiability that drove him on. "If I had not got it, I should always be wanting it," he said of the expensive, neglected boat. "Now that I have it, it no longer matters, it has ceased to interest me."

But despite the high phrases of psychoanalysis, Kreuger's life may remain, in essence, no more than a tribute to the power of the guilty conscience. Despite his superiority complex, and his seemingly gigantic self-control, Kreuger lived, in the words of Dr. Bjerre, "like someone afraid of the light. He wanted to hide all the time, and moved constantly from city to city so that people would never get to know him, or understand his operations. This is the reason he traveled around so much, and perhaps why he never married."

Not unnaturally, the perpetually moving Match King came less and less to resemble a Swede. A contemporary article on him recognized this when it said: "He forgot that he was a Swede, severed himself from the roots of his native land, played no part in its distinctive activities. He might equally well have been born in Paris, Berlin, London, or New York."

At the same time, there was something Scandinavian— perhaps as much as neurotic—in his actions. The Swedish proverb "Great things happen in silence" seemed to be the motivating force of his existence. So was his absolute faith in solitude, which Ibsen expressed in *An Enemy of the People* when Dr. Sockmann, having ended his struggle with a disordered world, concludes, "A strong man is strongest alone."

Always Kreuger was a strangely isolated man, split off from the rest of humanity, just as the criminal part of his mind appeared split off from the genius part. Yet he never seemed to mind the isolation. The coldness and remoteness displayed in his youthful letters home continued through life, and indifference remained his attitude toward the rest of the world. His callousness even took physical shape. No one mentioned it when he was an unimportant young engineer, but in the Savior of Europe it was considered interesting that he never seemed to feel heat or cold. In Sweden's coldest weather he wore hat and overcoat only to keep from being conspicuous, and part of the responsibility of his housekeepers and secretaries was to see that the Match King did not make himself ridiculous by showing up for important winter conferences attired in a summer suit, or for a meeting with bankers in the simmering heat of a New York summer in an overcoat. Such things were quite possible with Kreuger. To him the weather, like so much else in reality, failed to exist.

As time went by still another person joined the exclusive company of J. P. Morgan and the young German playwright in seeing through the Match King. This was Mrs. Kate Meyrick, the Texas Guinan of London, who attained fame after notoriety when her beautiful daughters married peers of the English realm. Not unexpectedly, Mrs. Meyrick, as operator of a series of night clubs, became a shrewd judge of human character. "By their leisure shall ye know them," was her maxim, and it helped in understanding Kreuger. However, her perception in his case was not, as with Morgan and the playwright, a swift insight into character, but was based on the fact that the Match King showed up in her clubs in the company of shady characters. "He was always surrounded by yes-men and parasites that a sound man of affairs would never tolerate," Mrs. Meyrick states in her memoirs.

This lights up another cranny of the elusive Kreuger character. Financiers, international bankers, and heads of state seemed to be the one type able to impress the Match King, and he moved contentedly among them as if he were a member of the world's most exclusive club. But if such men represented the height in his ambition, there also appeared to be a bottom. If Kreuger was a top financier himself, he was also an unmoral man and periodically the criminal in him seemed to crave association with others of the type.

These moments seemed to come when the man under killing tension needed to let off steam. Some of his international business associates were vaguely conscious of such emotions, but none ever suspected anything resembling the truth. A few did think that the solitary Match King was a homosexual, but most of his fellow financiers never saw anything odd in Kreuger's behavior. Perhaps his most distinguished associate was Oscar Rydbeck, president of the Skandinaviska Bank. The two men had first met in 1908, when Rydbeck did some work for the new firm of Kreuger & Toll. Their paths parted, until Kreuger, in 1920, began forming distinguished boards of directors for his many companies. Then he thought of Rydbeck, who had risen high in the banking world. He phoned and asked Rydbeck to serve as director of one of his companies. Rydbeck felt curious pricklings of caution and refused. A few days later the Match

King phoned again. "I have justed elected you," he announced in the highest spirits. Rydbeck had to agree.

From then on he served on Kreuger boards and loaned Kreuger millions of kroner through his bank. But when the two traveled together, as business often required them to do, the banker noticed that Kreuger usually disappeared in the evenings, supposedly to work. Later a wiser Rydbeck wrote: "[He] had so many irons in the fire that he generally had to attend other conferences. Yet it now appears that he had acquaintances of whom I knew nothing and that his interest was wrapped up in matters of which we did not have the faintest suspicion. He seems to have found more enjoyable ways of spending his evenings than with inquisitive bankers."

What were these ways? Only one account of Kreuger's hidden hours has ever appeared, and it is printed here not because it is true, but because it could so well be. It is an article sent over the wires by a London news agency. The German source does not identify himself, but his account runs like this:

> At a time when nobody would have expected Kreuger to be in Berlin, a shabbily dressed Scandinavian traveller would appear for a few days, sometimes only for twenty-four hours, in a little hotel beside the Stettiner station. I was informed of Kreuger's arrival by a cipher telegram which usually ran: "Arriving with new samples of stockings, Larsen." And then I used to look him up in his simple lodging at some specified time. For these adventures Kreuger used to wear dark glasses and a badly fitting suit. And in order to allay any possible suspicion, he did not even register himself as a Swede, but passed as a Norwegian.
>
> Kreuger was by nature a gambler, as his business dealings showed. He could not get on without a certain amount of gambling in private life either. Curiously

enough he never played high. What he enjoyed was the excitement. The otherwise quiet, imperturbable man changed before my very eyes. His face varied like an actor's. It grew red, the veins in his forehead swelled, his hands trembled, and his eyes blazed behind the dark glasses. When he lost he was desperate, he actually seemed to identify himself with a little man staking his last penny on the cards. When fortune was not favourable his lips moved unceasingly. Kreuger could spend a whole night at the card table; indeed he often did not sleep for nights on end. When he was in a specially good mood he used to play a game which he called "emptying the tables." The procedure was as follows: Several bottles of different alcoholic drinks were arranged on little tables. Whoever first emptied a whole "table" without losing consciousness was the winner. He had discovered this curious form of amusement when he was travelling in Russia. Kreuger, who had the reputation of never taking alcohol, proved himself to be a hard drinker. In a comparatively short time he learned to empty the bottles on the table without showing any particular signs of intoxication. Long after his boon companions had succumbed Kreuger sat there in the maddest spirits.

This grave individual, who never said a word too much could in certain surroundings be wildly hilarious. Kreuger often used to go and dance in a place that was only frequented by members of the underworld and their ladies. He danced ardently and passionately, and once even favoured the company with a sort of Swedish folk-dance which he executed with tremendous vigour. He twirled around, leapt high into the air, and performed the most extravagant pirouettes, which were greeted with uproarious applause by his delighted audience.

But whether Ivar Kreuger ever kicked his heels high before an audience of the Berlin underworld—which, with its inflation and easy vice, seems to have been his favorite sub-rosa haunt—there remains the peculiar fact that the criminal world of Europe was not unaware of the Match King, and quite possibly also used him as a target for blackmail.

Indeed, one of the shocks to anyone delving into the Kreuger life is that ease with which a story can be unearthed which claims that in Paris during the 'twenties Kreuger shot and killed a young man who was his son!

In all the words written about the Match King there is no real indication of the existence of a son, except the hint of an illegitimate child born in Stockholm during his student years. Yet the tale persists that in a fit of un-Kreuger-like rage, the Match King shot an illegitimate son who had just announced a desire to marry an undesirable girl. After this, some of the Match King's shady associates supposedly hustled the body down in the lift of Kreuger's Avenue Victor Emmanuel flat, stowed it in the back seat of a Kreuger Rolls Royce, and caused it to disappear forever.

Though none of the books on Kreuger dignify this story by using it, the American magazine *True Detective* printed it as fact in its December, 1940, issue. And even now, in the shady regions of London, Paris and Berlin, it is easy to encounter types who, on hearing the name Ivar Kreuger, will probe memories, then reply, "Oh, yes. He's the one who murdered his son."

Chapter 16

Kreuger and Women

But Kreuger's shady associations, surprising though they may be, all but fade into insignificance before another deception in the Match King's hidden life. The English journalist, Trevor Allen, even calls this "the greatest bluff of all." Taking into full consideration the enormous swindles, and the fact that he so completely fooled press and public, Allen still finds it most amazing "that outside Stockholm and even in it, so far as the mass of people was concerned, he was able to maintain the pose of preoccupied man of finance, shy in feminine company, who had no time, no room in his life, for love affairs."

For whatever carefully calculated impression the Kreuger Legend offered to an awed world, behind it lay the fact that the Match King's driving insatiability also included an active sex-urge. Far from being a homosexual, he was, despite the dainty hands and feet and gentle voice, strongly attracted to women. Indeed, the man's amorous activities were so widespread that he was later referred to by a word usually reserved for the Emperors of Rome. This word was "Voluptuary," but in our times a word in much more common use is lecher.

Yet such strong words were largely a shocked world's reaction when, after having accepted the Match King as a dedicated ascetic, it suddenly found out otherwise. Immediately stories began to circulate that Kreuger had subsidized a music hall in Stockholm so that he might have his pick of the chorus girls, and that in other theatres he sat alone in a box—sometimes with empty boxes on either side —solely to impress the girls on the stage. After the final curtain the man who looked so wealthy and intriguing in his aloneness would send a note backstage that he would like a certain girl to join him for midnight supper.

There were also stories of orgies in the country house so aptly called The Shadow, with young girls tossing off diaphanous attire before groups of visiting businessmen, while Kreuger himself reserved the most luscious of damsels for his own use. He also supposedly subsidized careers for many young girls, and the sprightly Mrs. Meyrick observed him in London using a tried-and-true technique for this. She recalls: "I saw him watching a girl dancing once—one of my hostesses—with every mark of pleasure. When the dance was over, he asked me to introduce him. He folded up a £50 note and presented it to her, saying: 'Take it. Thrills of enjoyment are rare now. Whenever one enjoys, one should make offerings. Take it, it was worth much more. Perhaps you have thought of taking up ballet dancing? No? That is a pity. I should have been pleased to arrange it.'"

Stories of Kreuger orgies with girls to whom he gave large sums even popped up in New York. No less a newspaper than *The New York Times* printed a dispatch from Stockholm reporting that the penthouse at 791 Park Avenue had been the scene of parties similar to those at The Shadow. The next day's *Times* carried a retraction. Kreuger's American associates had been able to persuade the newspaper that in New York, at least, the Match King had behaved himself. One of the most convincing corroborations was the word of the night elevator operator at 791 Park Avenue. "I never took anyone up except them finan-ceers," he declared flatly.

But if Kreuger was circumspect in New York, this cannot be said of his actions in other cities. The only thing circumspect was that he got away with it. He may have been a man incapable of love or hate, but he did have a drive to relieve himself erotically, though in exactly what fashion remains for the psychiatrists to figure. "Sexual relationships, like all others, are a battlefield on which he must be the victor," says Dr. Karen Horney, of the Kreuger-type. "He is driven constantly and insatiably to prove that he is a modern Don Juan." She goes on: "Since he is unable to love genuinely he can experience sexual relations only on a physical level." Kreuger followed through on this by adopting toward women the same callous, calculating attitude that he had toward the world—an attitude of which another writer has said, "It is not unfair to assume that such success serves to sap the moral strength and induce a man to think he can do anything, get anything so long as he has the power of money behind him."

It was Kreuger's belief that all women, just like match factories, could be purchased. "Women are for rich men," he stated once, in an unguarded moment, and he acted this out by using on them the same tactic he applied to blackmailers and stubborn rivals in the match business. He overpaid. Says Trevor Allen: "He needed women only for pleasure and beguilement, seldom or never for true companionship. . . . Actresses, opera singers, beautiful women who could not resist the price he was prepared to pay. There was only one condition—they must not talk, they must visit or receive him in secret."

In this there is, of course, further revelation of the emptiness of Kreuger's personality. For, says Dr. Ernest Jones in his biography of Freud:

No man's inner life, the core of his personality, can be comprehended without some knowledge of his attitude toward the basic emotion of love. Nothing reveals the essence of his personality so piercingly and completely as the gross, and subtle, variations of the emotional responses in this sphere, since so few situations in life test so severely his mental harmony.

Kreuger's callousness in sex relations, the closest he could come to love, is seen in every phase of his attitude toward women. "He bought them, and in love one cannot buy," said one of the few associates who ever saw him in an amorous moment. "He lacked the finesse, the tenderness, the sensitivity, the little chivalries of the man who is an artist in love. He had no time for them. They were not in his make-up."

But despite this, the Match King did in time cultivate some skill with women. There was a particular reason for this. In the early years of his career as a Casanova—which apparently began with his world-scale dreams—he was like other middle-aged erotic types in that he preferred the bodies of young, shapely girls. To satisfy such desires, he maintained his hideaway apartment in Stockholm, and, it is said, others in Berlin and Paris. Sometimes in disguise, sometimes not, he would prowl the streets until he saw a particularly attractive young prostitute. Then he would take her to the hideaway.

But nothing is more revealing of the tensions under which the great swindler labored than the fact that in time he came to fear even these encounters. Young girls were scatterbrained, venal. Might not one talk about the well-dressed man who took her to a hideaway which—foolishly, it would seem—was richly furnished? Kreuger, oddly generous in moments of abandon, often pressed extra banknotes on such girls. Would not this make them remember him further? Kreuger was not afraid of blackmail. His unmoral mind seemed to accept this as a necessary hazard in all he did. But he truly feared that some whisper of his secret life might waft upward from the nighttime streets. This would begin to tarnish the Legend. Enough tarnishing would result in his complete unmasking.

So he turned with reluctance from young girls to women of more mature years. These were the actresses, opera singers, and beautiful society women Trevor Allen mentions. They were women of some intelligence, able to realize the sanctity of his position. But contact with them required some finesse, so that necessarily, according to some, his cold, I-can-buy-you attitude toward women turned into a sort of nonchalance which was quite attractive to the softer sex. But his primary weapon remained money. He usually carried several diamond rings with him, for casual encounters. Another of his tactics was to suggest to a beautiful woman that she needed a vacation. Next day, tickets and a hotel reservation in, say, Switzerland would be delivered to her, for "he knew how it pleased a woman to be given a roll of notes and told to go away and thoroughly enjoy herself in some enchanting place where she had not a care in the world." Needless to say, in a day or so Kreuger himself appeared on the scene, and at the end of the period of bliss he would make another payment, the purpose of it, either stated or implicit, being, "Don't say a word about this."

With some women, he subsidized artistic careers or provided a means of livelihood. For one he opened a lingerie shop in Paris, and this lady reigned as his number-one mistress in that city for years. At other times he got jobs, or provided advancement, for husbands, often with the husband well aware of the price being paid. But in one way or another women always cost Kreuger large sums, since there was always the silence-payment at the end. "When I give a woman a large sum of money," he said once, "it is not because I love her, but because I am tired of her and wish to be rid of her." If nothing else, such expenditures provide a slight clue to the eternally tantalizing question—with swindlers—of where-did-the-money-go? In Kreuger's case, a lot went—according to Trevor Allen—in repetitions of the time when

> He cultivated acquaintance with a remarkably attractive girl whom he encountered in one of the banks with which he had dealings. He gave her £10,000. The lovely young girl of the people who was a chorus girl at the Oscar Theatre in Stockholm before she became his protegee and trained for opera. Kreuger traveled by air to be present at her debut at the Royal Opera House; eventually she too went to Paris under the blessings of his patronage. She had sisters, and introduced Kreuger to them. They too were ambitious and wanted to get on. . . .

But no man is an island. Ivar Kreuger's feelings toward women were probably as callous as anyone's can be. He had increased the coldness born in him by cultivating steely will power and a seemingly complete self-sufficiency. His dream was Ibsen's "A strong man is strongest alone." Yet apparently even he needed some love in his life.

In the early 'twenties, shortly after acquiring control of the entire Swedish match industry, he saw at a party a seventeen-year-old Stockholm beauty named Ingeborg Hassler. In her later reminiscences of Kreuger, Ingeborg tells how the Match King's technique operated. "He came over and introduced himself to me," she recalled. "He did not ask me to go to the theatre with him the next night. He *ordered* me to go. It impressed me, and I went." A short time later, the lovely young Ingeborg was established as his Stockholm mistress, sometimes dwelling in the shut-off section of his Villagatan apartment and at other times in a nearby flat.

Ingeborg's life with the enigmatic Match King is revealing. It was, of course, beset with one usual complication, for the young girl could see no reason why she should not become Fru Kreuger. The Match King, determined not to have anyone as close to him as a wife would necessarily be, held her off. "Slowly," Ingeborg writes, "I began to realize that marriage did not suit Ivar. He could not tolerate any ties; he did not like to be under obligation to anyone." Still, the question of marriage continued to be a point of argument between them, and six years later, when she was twenty-three, Ingeborg issued an ultimatum. During one of the periods of living away from Kreuger's apartment, she had met a handsome young engineer named Eberth. "If you will not marry me, I will marry him," she threatened Kreuger. The Match King, as sure of himself as any Menjou-type villain, answered, in effect, "Go ahead, marry him. You will always come back to me." Ingeborg went, married her man —and in a few months came back to Kreuger.

But long before this one special episode between them, there were incidents unusual in a protector-mistress relationship. It did not take Ingeborg long to discover that Kreuger was a truly promiscuous man, who had not the slightest hesitation in bringing other women to his apartment even though she was installed there. Ingeborg recalls often hiding behind the drapes of a window to watch Kreuger alight from his Rolls, then assisting a young lady to step out. Usually, Ingeborg states, she was a young lady of the streets.

At the same time, Kreuger seemed to need Ingeborg

Eberth, for on the occasions when she chose to create scenes over his other women, the seemingly impervious Match King behaved in highly vulnerable fashion. There was one particular night when Kreuger brought a girl home, after phoning ahead to suggest that Ingeborg retire early. Aware that she probably had not done so, he quickly appeared in her quarters to present her with a bouquet of flowers and a Teddy bear as offerings of harmony. Then he kissed her good night and left.

Ingeborg was not mollified. She shrewdly allowed a period of time to pass, then took herself to Kreuger's room where, on opening the door, she found the Match King in the act of seducing the other girl.

Having caught her man in an unforgivable position, Ingeborg proceeded to display a will power worthy of Kreuger's own by returning to her room for a full night's sleep. But in the morning she was angrily packing when a contrite Kreuger appeared to beg forgiveness. Ingeborg had in the past excused his love-adventures as "expressions of the eccentricity of genius," but at last she seemed to be fed up. Coldly she informed Kreuger that she was leaving Stockholm. When she started to go, he banteringly barred the door and refused to let her pass. But when he saw how determined the girl was, he stepped aside and wished her a pleasant journey.

This was only the beginning. At the station Ingeborg found her compartment banked with expensive flowers. The train had hardly been half an hour on its way when the door opened and Kreuger himself entered. He sat down beside her and bestowed on her an affectionate kiss. Ingeborg does not indicate that he apologized further, only reporting that when she reproached him, he "merely smiled." But it was enough to win her back. "Never have I met a man who could

lie as he did," she writes, explaining that already she had
begun to doubt that the events of the night before ever happened. "Even if one had proof of his duplicity, he seemed
able to convince one that he was telling the truth. He had a
remarkable talent for being persuasive."

But if Ingeborg was perhaps too ready to forgive the
Match King, she was not without comprehension of him.
"He could have been the happiest man on earth," she wrote
once, "but I do not think he really wanted to be happy. His
brain had become a machine—a machine constantly striving for new triumphs." Ingeborg also presents a picture of a
domestic Kreuger which would have surprised his business
associates. He was, she says, "nervous and undecided at
home, very high strung and emotional. He was a man of impulses where his personal life was concerned." On one subject the lovely Ingeborg maintains discreet silence, and this
is her paramour's sexual prowess. Instead, she prefers to picture evenings when she tinkled the piano while the weary
Match King, head supported by hand, listened and thought.
But another of Kreuger's amorous conquests was not so discreet. "He was not a very good lover," she later told newsmen, with "a slight curl of the lip." Then she smiled a mischievous smile, and added, "He was what you call a *r-r-rabbit*."

Kreuger's sole intellectual relationship in life seems to
have been with another of his girls, the German-French
daughter of a business associate. Her name was Itta Sandt
and "educated and artistically interesting," she seems to
have been the only person from whom he ever got even the
slightest mental stimulus.

At least Kreuger wrote her letters, which is something
unprecedented in his relations with the world, and one of
these letters is especially revealing. In it he says:

I feel very unhappy when I am obliged to be together
with people and be with them alone for a long time.
I can get along with them only if I can give the orders.
If I can tell them to do this or that. But when they
tell me their troubles I am always bored. They never
even seem to know why they live. . . . One without
stopping talks about his dentist, another about his unhappy marriage, the third about the job he never got.
When I compare these people with the biographies I
read, I clearly see how unimportant and uninteresting
my contemporaries are.

Kreuger was constantly being asked the reason he never
married, and tried just as constantly to provide an answer
which would cleverly turn the question aside. But his supposedly witty replies sound like Oscar Wilde epigrams with
all the sting removed. One was: "The reason I remain a bachelor is that I cannot believe in the faithfulness of a woman."
On another occasion he was franker, saying: "I seek the affection of many women because I cannot find all I need in
one." But to Itta Sandt, if anyone, he may have written the
whole truth when he said: "You asked me once if I could ever
bind myself to a woman. If I must be honest, the answer is
No. I do not care for children. I don't know why I should
have them—they always do the opposite of what you want
them to do. One always gets annoyed with them. Nor do I
wish to be burdened by love. . . ."

Kreuger's unsuspected passion for women leads to another matter for speculation. Many people think he suffered
from syphilis, perhaps contracted when young, dormant for
a period, then returning in the tertiary stages to bring the
delusions of grandeur which caused him to dream of a world
empire of matches.

Such a theory receives support from a strange quarter

—from Kreuger himself! The Match King was obsessed by the subject of syphilis and had a standing order in certain bookstores for any publication, new or old, that could be found on it. One of the few known instances of Kreuger violently losing his temper comes when one bookseller failed to live up to this order. Says a writer:

> Next to biographies and memoirs, the subject that interested him most was that of syphilis. He used to buy and devour every book he could get dealing with this particular disease, which seemed to have a morbid fascination for him.

Dr. Bjerre and others who have studied Kreuger devote much space to the syphilis theory, finally calling it a possibility but not probability. Dr. Bove, his Paris physician, discounts it completely. "The theory that his delusions of power and grandeur rose from the stages of tertiary syphilis is not true," he states. "Ego and pride far surpassed his *folie de grandeur*. He was born a megalomaniac—if not, it stemmed from his early childhood."

More likely than the possibility that he might have actively suffered from syphilis is the possibility that the Match King lived in fear of contracting the disease. In view of the promiscuity of his sex life, and his willingness to consort with prostitutes, this would seem to be plausible. Perhaps the Match King himself was alarmed by the mighty currents that swept through his mind. He may have thought he had syphilis and read medical books in a frantic effort at self-diagnosis. But there is absolutely no record of his ever consulting a doctor about syphilis, or that he was ever listed anywhere as a carrier of the disease.

In the last analysis any consideration of Kreuger and women—and the comfort he may have derived from them—

reduces to the amazing fact that he got away with his active sex life no less than he got away with his financial frauds. Trevor Allen may well be right in calling this the greatest bluff of all. Also, his desire to prowl the streets looking for prostitutes, more than the shady male associates, may have been what the disillusioned Rydbeck meant when he wrote, "He seems to have found more enjoyable ways of spending his evenings than with inquisitive bankers."

Kreuger was able to keep his interest in women such a thoroughgoing secret that his closest associates worried because he was not married. In the United States, Donald Durant and others pushed him whenever possible into the path of wealthy widows, and when he was seen several times in the company of Greta Garbo, rumors immediately began that a romance had started between Sweden's two outstanding exports to the world. But no one seems to have suspected sex-activity under the ascetic surface of the Match King's life. On the surface, all that most of his contemporaries knew about Kreuger and love was that the subject of women was responsible for one of the few clever things the cryptic man ever said.

Whether it came from his own mind, or the sophisticated mind of Brillioth, is not known. But when American ship-news reporters asked Kreuger if he planned to marry an American heiress, he quickly replied, "No, I much prefer a Swedish match."

Chapter 17

"Gentlemen, We Are Fortunate Indeed. ..."

By the unique standards under which the Match King operated, the years 1927, '28, and '29 represented his greatest period of achievement. In those years, accomplishment of his ends seemed increasingly possible to the tirelessly contriving man. "It was all so easy," wrote Harold Callender in a later *New York Times*, "that Kreuger was lured on by the game, fascinated by his own powers." These were also the peak years of the mighty bull market which had roared upward since the beginning of the decade. Stock exchanges of the world were operating at an insane pace, and Kreuger himself stood forth as the most dramatic figure of an increasingly exciting era. His peculations, shady associations, and bizarre love life were all unsuspected, leaving him to resemble only the man who could create gold. On the stock exchanges, his high-dividend stocks were greedily sought after. "People forgot all about the fine points of his business, and poured money into his coffers, then sat back to watch him work his wonders."

It is hardly surprising, then, that Kreuger's faith in his own invincible superiority increased correspondingly. Where in the past he had labored to become the Financier and then the Super-Financier—presumably, because of his temperament, finding each empty on achievement—he now began to picture himself as the Statesman. His mind became more than ever a breeding place, not of plans, but of visions, and the latest of these was that a man who had loaned millions to the French government should be worthy of having a major hand in shaping the affairs of Europe—if not of the world.

Accordingly, he began laying plans for his loan to Germany. In the past, he had broached the subject to Prime Minister Luther and to the canny Dr. Hjalmar Schacht, then president of the Reichsbank. But the Reichsdag had suddenly been dissolved in one of the periodic German crises and Kreuger had to retire to hawklike waiting as he had with France. Still, he was sublimely confident that the German Loan would come to him, as the French had, and this only colored his intoxicating dreams of becoming the Statesman.

And, as always, the astounding thing about Kreuger was that no matter how hard he worked and connived on one level, he was capable of working and conniving equally hard on several others. Indeed, he was now, at his peak, working with what can truly be called diabolical cleverness on three different levels, and perhaps a fourth. On one he was still the world-monopolist, expanding his match empire with the solid profits from Swedish Match and the equally sound profits from foreign match companies controlled by it and International Match. On the second, he was the world-financier, borrowing vast sums on the basis of his match earnings, but doing it so secretly and cleverly that no one knew how much or how often he borrowed—or that his borrowings were astronomically far in excess of the legitimate credit he possessed. On the third level, he was the suave swindler, creating hidden subsidiary companies with profit-packed books which could be used for more borrowing or to cover any emergency, exactly as a stage-magician pulls rabbits out of his hat.

All of which creates what is Kreuger's fourth dimension:

an elusive realm of financial chicanery never before pene-trated by a human being. He was borrowing on his own credit, which was rigged almost from start to finish. It placed him in a financial Never-Never Land in which almost nothing was real except the giant sums that floated back to the Match King whenever he waved the magic wand of his credit power. All in all, nearly a billion and a half dollars was tossed at his feet. His own earnings, enormous as they were, in no way commanded such prodigious credit. But he was ever the man who personified his age. In a world eager to believe in paper profits, where chauffeurs could make as much as employers, a man like Ivar Kreuger seemed perfectly possible.

Again, what did he do with the money? Largely, the facts will always remain a mystery. But Kreuger speculated in stocks himself, and he also lived in the clutches of a mania for buying. Real estate, gold mines, factories, anything that came within the ranging orbit of his own affairs was something to purchase. He even visualized the day when he might finally achieve his dream of a world match monopoly and lest this leave some of his energies unused, he began dreaming of him-self as the Telephone King. Accordingly, in 1927, he started buying up telephone companies, among them, L. M. Ericsson & Company of Sweden, which in a few years would figure im-portantly in his life.

But for all the world could see, Kreuger's fabulous intake of money was almost exclusively devoted to expanding his match monopoly. Turning from his master stroke in France, he found it almost childishly easy to arrange State Loans with Estonia, Latvia, Yugoslavia, Hungary, Rumania, Poland (a second loan), Danzig, Guatemala, Turkey, and Lithuania. Slowly, relentlessly, he was pushing closer to his eventual control of 65 per cent of the world's match production. It all seemed open and aboveboard, but Kreuger was always

Kreuger: the man with the self-approving inner eye, always watching gleefully as he displayed the cleverness which was his real pride. Almost daily, Kreuger did things other tycoons had yet to think of, and such acts provided him his greatest satisfaction. Some of the things he did might have given pause to other men, but Kreuger functioned with the single-mindedness of the egomaniac. Being in his own mind something of a God, he never hesitated for a moment to kindle resentments that a less egocentric person might have been too sensible to arouse.

He had already, for instance, irritated the great J. P. Morgan of Wall Street. Now, in his loan of $6 million to Latvia, he angered the important bankers of Europe and England, as well. A previous loan by European bankers to the city of Riga had never been paid back. The bankers had appealed to the government of Latvia, to be told airily that Riga's loans were the city's own business. Outraged, the bankers had joined in a gentleman's agreement never to lend Latvia money, and American bankers had agreed to go along in blackballing the small country. But such situations were made to order for Kreuger. He stepped forward and advanced Latvia $6 million in return for the usual match monopoly.

There was usually the same amoral twist to be found somewhere in nearly every Kreuger deal, for such crafty outsmarting was the food on which the gloating inner self fed. Lack of conscience was particularly to be found in his South American deals. With world success, the Match King had become increasingly reluctant to leave his orbit of Stockholm, Paris, London and New York, so that his deals in South American countries were usually accomplished through local agents. Nor were all his match monopolies accomplished by the comparatively clean-cut means of the State Loan. Whenever possible, Kreuger saved himself the Loan millions by ruthlessly stamping out competition in any country he was determined to control, as in Brazil, where "the Swedish Match Trust laboured most energetically to destroy the Brazilian match industry." Kreuger always seemed able to find exactly the right man for such ruthlessness, so that such countries came under his control as a result of threats, bribery, political influence, and perhaps a murder or two that his unsavory agents undertook in order to earn his money. Further, Kreuger monopolies, once achieved, were not always the smoothly running, efficient money-making organizations that the Kreuger Legend led the world to believe. In some, there was a distinctly pre-Hitler flavor. The German journalist, Richard Katz, hearing that his country was contemplating a loan from the Match King, filed the following warning dispatch from Lima, Peru:

Germany will be interested in the results of such an agreement with Mr. Kreuger—if only because we Germans are considering one ourselves. And if we are not careful we shall find that it is only the first link in a chain of agreements. A solid, clanking chain. As in Peru.

Thus before a steamer arrives in Peru the captain puts up notices saying: "Passengers are warned that an agreement has been made between the Peruvian Government and the Swedish Match Trust to regulate the production, distribution and sale of matches in the Republic of Peru. In accordance with this agreement, the import of all foreign matches is prohibited by the Peruvian Government. Offenders are liable to a fine of fifty Peruvian pounds. The fine is imposed for the import of even one foreign match."

Fifty Peruvian pounds are, at par, worth about forty pounds sterling—which seems a great deal for one match.

All one's pleasure at arriving in Peru is spoilt. One has no desire to enjoy the glorious Bay of Calla, or to watch the guano birds hovering in great flocks about the ship. Instead, every one searches his luggage for matches. And after having ransacked it half a dozen times he turns out all his pockets—just in case one match might have crept in somewhere—and a match would cost forty pounds. . . .

And once you arrive in the customs house at Callao, the whole business begins all over again. Only this time the search is carried out by officials and spies. Most carefully and systematically. Anyone who discovers a match can claim half the fine—which is always twenty pounds. Customs declaration, inspection of baggage, a stranger's hands all over one's person and in one's pockets—it is offensive, and it goes on for hours. Also it ruins the Peruvian tourist traffic.

It ruins more than that. It ruins character.

Peruvians do not beg much and they hardly ever steal. But the agreement with Mr. Kreuger is gradually training them to be sneaks. The temptation really is too strong—twenty pounds—a fortune to an Indian or mulatto. And so easy to earn.

If anyone who looks at all like a foreigner walks about in Callao, one native after another will ask him for a light—only in order to see what kind of matchbox the stranger will produce. If it is one of the boxes with the llama label on it that the Kreuger Trust produces for Peru—well, the spy has drawn a blank. But if it happens to be of any other manufacture—hurrah! the man wins twenty pounds. He quickly calls up the nearest policeman and claims his share of the fine. It is worth risking for such a prize! The more so, since there are also special prizes to be won in this lottery—petrol lighters which have no Peruvian licence. They carry a double fine. One can set up house on it!

The matchbox or lighter, by the way, are not confiscated after the fine has been paid. Not on your life! There is always the hope that the stranger may be had again. . . .

And what is the point of it all? What do Kreuger

and his Trust get out of it? Mr. Kreuger and his Match Trust have the monopoly in Peru and they make the most of it. They sell boxes with thirty or forty matches in them. Some of these will not light and some break. That does not matter, since they have the monopoly. They charge a penny a box. An average smoker in Peru pays fifty-eight shillings a year for matches. Non-smokers come off more cheaply. But even they need matches. They, too, resent the way Mr. Kreuger and the Government make money out of them. First a production monopoly, then a sale monopoly, then an informers' monopoly. Each monopoly individually brings in money and en masse they corrupt the country.

Kreuger's unremitting drive to be the smartest man alive extended even to his native Sweden, a country which regarded him with a national pride amounting to veneration. In 1927, feeling one of his periodic urges to increase his wealth by seemingly legitimate means, he announced the greatest money-raising campaign of his career. The first step was to raise Kreuger & Toll share capital from 28 million kroner to 50 million, and its reserves from 40,200,000 kroner to 133,700,000. The second step was to issue 900,000 Swedish Match B shares, at the same time increasing share capital from 180 million kroner to 270 million.

It was a gigantic plan, requiring the co-operation of every stock exchange in the world. But for once the mighty Match King seemed to have overlooked something. Clear in the brochure issued to encourage the market was the statement that the securities were subject to heavy taxes by Sweden. In France especially this aroused protest, and the Match King, accustomed to docile acceptance of any stocks he put on the market, was faced by the realization that, before issuing new stocks, steps would have to be taken to prevent what the French were telling the world was "oppression" by the Swedish government.

In this moment of crisis, Kreuger appealed to none other than Eliel Löfgren, the Swedish Minister of Foreign Affairs. Löfgren advised him that the Swedish law could not be changed, but together the two men devoted themselves to the problem and came up with the idea of debentures—certificates of indebtedness—which could be sold instead of shares, thus escaping most of the tax. Kreuger immediately dubbed these "participating debentures," realizing that by this cozy name he had the means to issue still more stocks in all his companies. This he immediately did, through the imposing mediums, in the United States, of Lee, Higginson; the Guaranty Company of New York; the National City Company; Brown & Company; Dillon, Read, & Company; Clark, Dodge & Company; and the Union Trust Company of Pittsburgh. It was another financial master stroke, the savoring of it made all the sweeter by the fact that he had bilked his native Sweden of taxes.

If Kreuger could thus victimize his worshipful native land, he had no hesitation in biting the hand that was doing the most to feed him. This, of course, was the United States, whose stock-buying public was clamoring for any of the high-dividend stocks Kreuger would give them, even participating debentures.

The United States was important to Kreuger in still another way, a fact apparently overlooked by his contemporaries. If the Match King were to attain monopoly of the entire world, as he endlessly schemed to do, he would eventually have to control production in the United States. Yet the laws of his benefactor country strictly forbade anyone acquiring enough power to attain a monopoly. On the record

Kreuger was strictly abiding by this law. His only American match company seemed to be Vulcan Match, a subsidiary of the International Match Corporation, which existed only to distribute Swedish matches in this country.

Yet Kreuger was a man who had not hesitated to use secret agents in Europe and South America. He did not hesitate here. Sometimes using his Kreuger & Toll "observers," at other times elusive, sub-surface henchmen, he put over a series of deals almost as amazing in their secrecy as his secret manipulations and his hidden sex life. By these deals he penetrated far into the American match industry, and at one moment even seems to have controlled it. He did this by having his faceless operatives buy up small blocks of stocks until sizable amounts had been amassed. Using funds of International Match he had, in an unsuspected deal, purchased 350,000 shares in Diamond Match for $13.5 million. The innocent-seeming Vulcan owned 70 per cent of the stock of Federal Match, this having been bought through the agency of Anders Jordahl, Kreuger's engineering friend from South Africa who had become one of his chief agents here. Federal Match, in return, had an agreement to acquire the Union Match Company for $275,000. In addition to these interests, the wily Match King had bought heavily into Ohio Match, North American Match, and Acme Match.

When finally all this was discovered, the American financial community was astounded. But at the same time, in testimony during an investigation of this and his other American activities, the public was given an insight into how the marvelous man worked his financial miracles. Around Wall Street, and equally elsewhere, he had seemed a person of such titanic importance that no one could doubt a thing he said or did. Miss Greta Gluydes, secretary to one of his Kreuger & Toll "observers," expressed this feeling of respect when she described how Kreuger one afternoon came into her office and, pacing up and down for an hour, dictated the annual reports of his world-girdling companies. She was asked:

Q. Did Mr. Kreuger consult any books or memoranda when preparing these statements of the financial position of his companies?
A. No, he seemed to get most of the information out of his mind.

Q. Did you think this strange?
A. Yes, but I accounted for it by the fact that I had often been told Mr. Kreuger was a genius.

Even more effective than the word of a secretary was the testimony of the already quoted Ben Tomlinson, vice-president of International Match. It shows how implicitly his top-echelon associates believed Kreuger. Also, it points up another feature of Kreuger operations. Some of his companies, among them Vulcan, failed to make money. This was galling to the superman. He did not wish any of his enterprises to show a loss before the public, so he calmly informed his executives that he would see to it that the books of all his companies showed an annual profit—"a constant shifting of assets from one company to another to make a favorable showing which earnings did not justify." Concerning Vulcan, the uncomfortable Mr. Tomlinson was asked:

Q. You had a conversation with Mr. Ivar Kreuger . . . of which you made a memorandum, in which he had told you that Vulcan books should be kept so as to show a profit?
A. Well, without seeing the memorandum I cannot be sure. As stated before he had told me that he did not wish Vulcan Match to show a loss, and that it

would be made up by a contribution toward distribution expenses.

Q. Now, the Norden Company, the company was owned by Swedish Match and not by International Match?

A. It was not owned by International Match Corporation, at least, not directly. Who owned it, I do not know.

Q. What is the name of the company, again?
A. Exportaktiebologet Norden; it simply means export.

Q. Norden is what?
A. I do not know.

Q. But it was an existing company that Kreuger controlled; that much you knew?
A. I presume so.

Q. And you knew that nothing in the books or records of International Match gave the slightest indication that International Match owned it or had an interest in that company?
A. Yes.

Q. How could you, even under instructions from Mr. Kreuger, add $325,000 to the income of Vulcan by a gift from a company with which it had nothing to do?
A. There didn't seem anything extraordinary in the idea; it had been done the year before. . . .

While companies like Vulcan were being made to break even, or show profit, by gifts from exotically named companies like Exportakiebologolet Norden, Kreuger's hocus-pocus with other companies was increasing madly. Annual reports to International Match were long on words but short on facts. They seemed to indicate that the American stockholder millions still went to Continental. However, this holding company's assets were now being "deposited" with a whole group of institutions new to the American bankers. Gone was Garanta, while prominent in the new group was the Netherlandish Bank for Scandinavian Trade, about which Berning, the Ernst & Ernst executive, had questioned Kreuger. Netherlandish was never more than a portable set of books, but Wall Street was assured that the bank had turned dollars received from Continental into "a certificate covering 270,-000 shares in Italian *Fabbriche Riunite di Fiammiferi*, 400,-000 francs worth of French *rentes*, and a monopoly contract between Spain and the Continental Investment Corporation worth 144,000,000 Swiss francs." Karl Lange and the other men in the bogus firms solemnly filled out false documents proving that the money had been used as Kreuger said.

Directors of the Swedish-American Trading Corporation were equally bewildered by what happened to their millions. For its holding company, Standard Trust, seemed to have a thriving subsidiary of its own. This was the Erika Holding Company, capitalized for 10 million francs. Kreuger & Toll had put up this sum but immediately after the incorporation had taken it back. Thus Erika was left with coffers bare.

Still, the stock in Erika was turned over to Swedish-American in return for $10,159,295 in Swedish-American assets. Then, by Kreuger's order, Swedish American transferred the Erika stock to Dutch Kreuger & Toll, receiving from the latter 82,008 shares of Swedish-American common stock. Next, Kreuger ordered that these shares be canceled on the Swedish-American books. Thus, according to the books, Swedish-American had called in and retired 82,008 shares of its stock. But as soon as this was accomplished, Dutch Kreuger & Toll returned the stock to Kreuger and received the $10,159,295 in assets. From which labyrinthine tangle this much is plain: Swedish-American was relieved not only of taxation on profits, but of profits as well, and over $10 million in assets.

While engaged in these mystifying operations, Kreuger was also adding to his legitimate holdings. He bought the Grängesberg Company, largest producer of iron ore in Europe; the Swedish Pulp Company, a consolidation of ten established Swedish pulp and lumber firms; Skandinaviska Freditaktiebolaget, one of the largest banks in Sweden; interest in International Telephone & Telegraph amounting to 400,000 shares; and numerous other aboveboard enterprises.

From the vantage point of Wall Street it all added up to such a colossal jumble that at a meeting of the International Match Board of Directors, one member uttered the unthinkable. He turned to Durant and said, "Donald, we really know very little about this man Kreuger and what he's up to. All we ever get is his word for things. Why don't you run over there and see for yourself what's going on?"

The shocked Durant protested that it was never necessary to question anything Kreuger did. Yet he was persuaded to make the trip, and departed equipped with a set of questions to put to the Match King. With the arrival of Durant, Kreuger assumed still another role, that of superb impostor. He entertained the American so lavishly that Durant felt ashamed when the time came to put his questions. But put them he did, and in reply Kreuger spouted reams of such convincing facts that it did not seem necessary to linger long over such business. In conclusion, Kreuger gave a huge party for his American friend at the Villagatan apartment. The guests were distinguished-looking men and beautiful women, and Kreuger whispered to Durant that most of the men were foreign ambassadors. Yet none of them seemed able to speak

English, or to have the slightest interest in meeting the guest of honor. It was the era when simple Americans were dazzled by European titles and pomp. Durant, in a seventh heaven of delight, accepted it all, never for a moment suspecting that the dazzling men and lovely women were movie extras, complete with wardrobe costumes, who had been hired by Kreuger for the night.

Durant returned to Wall Street more pro-Kreuger than ever. However, the replies he brought back to his prepared questions seemed inconclusive and vague as he tried to focus his mind on assembling Kreuger's stupendous facts. The Board listened, but continued curious. It was voted to send Percy A. Rockefeller, its biggest gun, to visit the Match King.

Kreuger cannot have welcomed these inquiring visits from his tame directorate in the United States. Undoubtedly, he knew the real purpose of the announcedly social trips, but the man of colossal gall was more than prepared. Where he had given Durant only superficial treatment, he dug deep for Rockefeller. His foremost weapon was the dummy telephone in his office at the Match Palace. It pealed constantly while Rockefeller sat across the desk, and Kreuger would lift the phone to say, "Certainly, put His Excellency on." Hand cupping the mouthpiece, he would whisper "Mussolini" to the awed Rockefeller. Then, into the phone: "Greetings, Benito, my dear chap. How are you and what can I do for you?" There would follow a long conversation about an Italian match monopoly, and when that call was finished another would come in from Poincaré, Stanley Baldwin, or even—an amazed Rockefeller reported—from Stalin.

Kreuger took Rockefeller for a weekend at his island home, Angsholmen. There was no dummy phone in this island retreat, but the legitimate phone rang constantly with calls from international celebrities, for Kreuger had told his executives at the Match Palace to call him at intervals during the day and not to hang up, no matter what nonsense he talked. "I am playing a practical joke on my American friend," he explained. When finally the calls tapered off, Kreuger put on his most winning manner and said, "Percy, my interests are so manifold, I want you to ask me anything you have in mind." Rockefeller, already partially disarmed, informed Kreuger that Ernst & Ernst needed details about subsidiaries and finances. Kreuger nodded with complete understanding. "I'm glad you brought that up," he said. "Today is Sunday, but even as we talk my accountants are working overtime to assemble all those details. But until they finish, why not just ask me? I have a remarkable memory, you know."

Rockefeller began by asking about a set of figures Kreuger had given International Match three years before. To Rockefeller's amazement, ". . . his host reached back into the recesses of his brilliant mind and reeled off, to the very last dollar, long columns of figures, the same ones that had been written down." Later Rockefeller said that never in his life had he known a person with such an amazing memory. Throughout the rest of the weekend he listened to Kreuger answering questions from memory, and by the time the pair returned to Stockholm he could see no point in waiting for the records which, Kreuger still insisted, were being prepared by busy accountants.

Rockefeller returned to the United States even more impressed than Durant. At the next board meeting he gave a glowing account of his visit and, according to one account, concluded with these words: "That man is the salt of the earth. He is on most intimate terms with the heads of European governments. Gentlemen, we are fortunate indeed to be associated with Ivar Kreuger."

18

The Only Optimist

If economic conditions had continued at the boom-time rate of the frantic 1920's, Ivar Kreuger might still be among us. Today, he might well be an Elder Statesman to whom the advent of old age had brought belated wisdom, leaving him to devote his final years to retrenching and covering up his towering falsifications, as he could have done so easily in 1923.

But this was not to be. The hysterical financial jamboree of the 'twenties could not last. There were many who should have seen the end coming, and almost none who did. In the words of John Kenneth Galbraith in *The Great Crash*, "A roaring boom was in progress and, like all booms, it had to end. . . . When prices stopped rising—when the supply of people who were buying for an increase was exhausted—then ownership on margin would become meaningless and everyone would want to sell. The market wouldn't level out; it would fall. . . ."

The first fall came on October 24, 1929, and it is truly ironic that from the cover of *Time* that week the enigmatic face of Ivar Kreuger peered at the world. Inside the magazine readers could find a sprightly and optimistic recapitulation of the Kreuger Legend.

For the Wall Street Crash of 1929 spelled the end for Kreuger, no less than for the Boom Era he so completely represented. The Match King's financial and industrial em-

pire had been inflated out of all proportion by his vast use
of credit, and the series of financial shocks begun on October
twenty-fourth would inevitably cause credit over the world
first to tighten, then dry up. Kreuger, from October twenty-
fourth, resembled a man standing alone on an island which
at high tide would be completely covered by water. Now it
was low tide, but slowly, inevitably, the waters would
rise. . . .

Kreuger did not seem aware of this. He was in Stockholm when news of the Wall Street Crash came, and he
accepted it with what can only be called aplomb. In fact, at
no time in his career does his superiority complex seem so
close to actual madness as in the period beginning now, with
his seeming conviction that he alone, of all the world, could
still carry on exactly as before. It was the sort of madness,
or at best fanaticism, which allowed him to discount all
reality. The writer George Soloveytchik sees the world-impli-
cations of this when he states: "He never saw the deep inner
associations of a world which was dissolving and reforming.
Hence, Kreuger's economic structures foundered on that
economic world crisis with which a man of Kreuger's calibre
should have reckoned. . . . The clearest head, the most daring schemer of his time, forgot to allow for one thing in his
plans, that where there is no purpose there is no progress.
The same lack of ideas which brought low the capitalist
world with all its madness of power also destroyed Kreuger."

In his set determination to operate in the new world
precisely as he had always operated, Kreuger took several
steps which, if not responsible for, at least hastened his inevitable downfall.

The first was the loan to Germany on which the Match
King had set his mind years before. True, the preliminary
discussions on the loan had been concluded by the first day

of the Crash. According to these discussions Kreuger was to lend the German government the sum of $125 million. Fifty million was to be paid on August 30, 1930, and $75 million on May 29, 1931. The long-suffering International Match was to provide $50 million of this—the American bankers had already agreed—and Swedish Match and Kreuger & Toll would be responsible for the rest.

On October 26, 1929, the day of a second, more serious drop on Wall Street, the contract for the German Loan was signed. Whether or not Kreuger should have—or could have —pulled out of this after the slump of October twenty-fourth is a matter on which no one can speak with any authority. But the fact remains that the German Loan always had a dubious side, and that Kreuger's monumental self-esteem rather than his shrewdness would seem to be the motivating factor behind it. For Kreuger of all people, with his strong psychological intuition, should have sensed that the seemingly stable German people, after a decade of toppling governments, inflation, and starvation, were in a mood to be swept off their feet by a madman like Hitler. But he did not, largely because there were so many factors in the Loan itself which made it seem attractive to him. For one thing, the success with the French Loan had given the gambler in him a feeling for the big loan, a hunch that this one, too, would pay off. Then there was the matter of Kreuger the Statesman. To the world, Germany had pictured herself as a country on the verge of disaster. Actually, conditions in Germany were not that bad, but along with everyone else, Kreuger felt that without his money a country for which he had always felt a fondness might tumble into hopeless chaos. With his money, Germany would have a fighting chance to consolidate her position. This, in turn, could be the cornerstone of Kreuger's dream of becoming the Statesman, perhaps a Statesman mighty enough to wield enough singlehanded power to assure the world international stabilization.

In line with such transcendent dreams there now came an opportunity for Kreuger to attain—if for only a brief, glorious moment—his dreamed-of stature.

At the time of his German Loan negotiations, Kreuger had also persuaded Wall Street bankers to take a more understanding approach to Germany's plight and advance the hard-pressed country another $125 million, in addition to his. Thus he was hailed as "the friend of Germany." France also had considered him a warm friend since 1925, so that when French and German reparation talks at The Hague, in 1930, hit the snags inevitable between two traditional enemies, the Match King was called in by Curtius and Tardieu to lend his services as mediator. He immediately accepted, and "due in no small part to his calm and soothing presence, an agreement was reached."

Having accomplished this much, Kreuger was asked to give more assistance. Flotation of bonds for the Young Plan, which among other things, established the Bank for International Settlements, was not meeting with success in a financially exhausted world. In fact, there seemed a possibility that the bonds would not be fully subscribed. Kreuger again was asked for help and—in a magnificent gesture— agreed to take 110 million kroner of the bonds himself. Kreuger & Toll would be responsible for 56 million kroner of these, while the Swedish public would be given the privilege of buying the other 54 million.

Kreuger also had it within his power, as the man lending $125 million, to insist that a reluctant Germany ratify the Young Plan. He did this by inserting a clause in his Match Loan contract, and as a result Paul Renaud mounted the rostrum of the French Chamber to laud the Match King for the part he had played in making The Hague negotiations successful. It was, perhaps, the moment of moments for Ivar Kreuger.

But while Kreuger the Statesman was the object of flowery encomiums, the other Kreugers—Financier, Super-Financier, Industrialist, Capitalist, Swindler—were being relentlessly pushed in the direction of dire trouble. Ironically, Kreuger's great achievement, his State Loans, were turning into his most besetting problem. As international money grew tighter, some countries began defaulting on loan payments, interest payments, or payment of Kreuger's share of the profits of match sales within the country. But this was only part of the Match King's problem. When one looks at the list of $375 million Kreuger State Loans, each would appear to have been paid in a gigantic lump sum. Actually, the millions were paid in installments over periods of years, so that in 1930 Kreuger was still in the process of paying out loan-money to countries which now suddenly stopped paying him interest on previous installments. Thus Kreuger was trapped by his own scheme. He had to continue making his loan-payments, for "to have slipped a single cog would have thrown a wrench into what was . . . the most perfectly oiled of international and financial machines." Had he, in retribution for non-payment of interest, stopped making his loan payments, the country would have an excuse for pulling out of the arrangement altogether. Kreuger was in the sorry position of the debtor who must keep a creditor going, because that is the only way he may eventually get his money back.

Even this was only part of his over-all problem. Collateral which he had placed with banks as security for loans to Kreuger & Toll was shrinking in value, and new collateral had to be provided to make up for this shrinkage. At the same time it was apparent even to Kreuger that a depression-time public would not absorb any new issues of shares in his companies. For the first time in his life, he found himself unable to raise millions. Instead, he had to turn his fabulous financial skill to shoring up the great edifice his money-raising power had created.

The result was a Kreuger character more ambivalent than ever. On the surface he seemed to retain all his basic optimism in himself and the world he lived in. In this role he even provided balm to a reeling civilization. Other financiers were depressed by the fact that friends were committing suicide and banks were inevitably heading toward the bank-closing period of 1932–33. Realistic men could find no bit of optimism to radiate to a desperate public, but the great Kreuger could. Arriving in the United States in 1930, he informed the public *via* ship-news reporters, "Securities in companies like International Match which operate on a solid foundation will *always* be good." No other tycoons could match even this optimism, a fact which now caused Kreuger to lecture the bankers themselves, saying in a luncheon talk:

> When a foreigner comes to the United States, he is very much impressed with the terrible pessimism here. There is no doubt but that the United States in this respect is far worse than any other place, not excepting Germany. In no other place are quotations so far down as here. . . . The most essential thing today is to get a different spirit in America. If that comes, I am absolutely certain that Europe will react quickly because the troubles in Europe, viewed at closer range, are not as big as they look from a distance. . . . During the next few months things will probably look bad and I think that it is reasonable to expect that particularly the transfer difficulties will become very acute. These difficulties will, however, be of a temporary nature, and nobody in Europe regards them as very serious. At the same time, problems which have long ex-

isted will come to a head. It only means that the solution
of these problems is closer at hand, and I cannot help
but believe that whatever happens will not be of such
a nature that it should worry the people of the United
States. I think that soon we shall see conditions restored
to normalcy.

It is perhaps fitting that the person most convinced by
such soothing, bedside-manner talk was the Match King
himself. For in his increasingly desperate need for funds, he
began speculating on the New York Stock Exchange. Most
of his orders were placed through his trusted associate, Bror
Bredberg, operating out of Zurich under instructions from
Stockholm, using funds funneled into the five companies in
Switzerland and Liechtenstein of which he, Bredberg, was
sole director. Not surprisingly, since the bemused Kreuger
was counting on an upswing in a down-swinging market,
his losses in these transactions were enormous—in fact, so
great that early in 1931 Bredberg journeyed to Stockholm to
reason with his chief.

"Don't you think I'd better stop?" he asked.

"No," the Match King answered. "Keep right on. I expect conditions to turn."

In other ways Kreuger remained Kreuger. His Paris physician, Dr. Bove, tells how in 1931, he treated the Match King
for an ulcer, which no doubt stemmed from his enormous
inner tensions. It was impossible to cure the ulcer, but the
doctor did considerably relieve Kreuger's physical distress.
Apparently overwhelmed with gratitude, the Match King
offered to sell the doctor stocks which in a short time would
triple his money. Dr. Bove was impressed by Kreuger's con-
tagious confidence and consulted his banker, "who enthu-
siastically recommended the investment. He pointed out
that Kreuger was distributing dividends which were the mir-

acle of the investment world." The doctor phoned Kreuger to say that he would buy the stocks, at which Kreuger congratulated him on possessing sound financial sense. Shortly after this conversation, the Match King phoned back to devote his celebrated powers to persuading Dr. Bove to double the amount he wished to invest. The doctor agreed, and in all turned $113,000 over to Kreuger, in return for Kreuger & Toll stocks.

But such matters were small—except, of course, to Dr. Bove. The hidden Kreuger was being subjected to pressure on a mighty scale. Where he had always in the past been hungry for money to push forward and increase his power, he now was desperate for money—or security on which to raise money—which would merely enable him to hold the power he had.

It was a frantic quest, and in it he sank to the tricks of the shadiest of con men. He moved millions in German marks from bank to bank, from each carefully obtaining a receipt. On each receipt he borrowed more millions over and over again. He also performed slick tricks in person, striding —for instance—into the office of the president of a bank in Brussels. Tossing a bundle of currency down on the desk, he said, "Here are four hundred million francs for deposit, let me have a receipt." Flattered at a visit from the Savior of Europe, the bank president immediately wrote one out. After Kreuger had departed the money was counted and the bundle discovered to contain only 5 million francs. When told of this, the Match King apologized profusely, saying a mistake had been made. But he had what he really wanted: a receipt for 400 million francs on a reputable bank. With it he had already raised more hundred millions.

Nor were his psychological tricks confined to Europe. In 1931 Kreuger overpaid the United States Government the

sum of $150,000 on his 1930 taxes. In the world of banking
this was a minor sum, but the fact that the Match King could
seemingly overlook it in a deep-depression year aroused confidence in him on Wall Street. Almost on the basis of this
stratagem alone, he was later able to borrow $4 million from
four Wall Street banks.

But it was Kreuger's tragedy that—with credit ever
tightening throughout a sorely pressed financial world—the
more money he got, the more he needed. As the Depression
continued unabated into 1931, the tides crept high on the
little island the intransigent man had created out of his belief
that the world would inevitably right itself, to fit his rigid
plans. And, as months passed with the world failing to change,
he felt justified in perpetrating an act which—if the French
and German Loans, and his activities at The Hague, represent his peaks in public life—becomes his peak in perfidy.

On March 16, 1931, the Match King dispatched a
message to Captain Akë Wickman, assistant director of the
Bortzell Printing Company in Stockholm. He asked the Captain to bring samples of bond-sheet paper to the Villagatan
apartment.

On appearing there, Wickman was admitted by Kreuger
himself and escorted to one of the second-floor rooms. There
the Match King established himself behind a desk unusually
cluttered for the ordinarily meticulous man. "On Kreuger's
desk," states one account, "were piles of documents, most
of which appeared to be letters from Italian officials, telegrams, cables, together with sheets of paper filled with nota-
tions." While the two men conversed, Kreuger's fingers
nervously ruffled through the piles. Finally, he found what
they searched for. It was a letter from Mussolini, the envelope of which bore the coat of arms of Italy and the Fas-
cist shield.

"I have a job to be done but it must be kept most secret," he said to Wickman. He instructed the printer to find an engraver who would copy both the coat of arms and the shield, and have this engraver make a plate on which one leaned against the other. Next, the two men turned to a discussion of the paper samples Wickman had brought. They settled on one which in size and quality was close to some Italian government bonds Kreuger also had on his desk. Then Kreuger wrote out in longhand some official sounding words which were to be set up in type so that they could be printed on the face of the bonds, under the leaning coat of arms and shield. He wrote in English, since Italian was one language the multi-lingual Kreuger did not know. The only words appearing in Italian were the name of the government and the name under the place for the signature *Direttore Giovanni Boselli.*

When Wickman returned several days later with the blank certificates, the plate containing the emblem, and the type for the English text, Kreuger seemed delighted. "These certificates will be sent to Italy to be signed as soon as political conditions make it possible," he said. "This transaction is one of the most satisfying of my life, for I feel that I have helped create agreement among the powers."

Several nights later Kreuger sat at his desk before the result of Wickman's efforts. Emblem, text and certificate had been combined to create a reasonable facsimile of forty-two Italian treasury bills with a face value of £500,000 each, as well as five certificates of indebtedness from the Italian monopoly administration with a face value of £1,533,700 each. All that these shiny bonds lacked were official signatures and, taking pen in hand, the Match King himself proceeded to provide these, forging the names of both Boselli and Finance Minister Mosconi to the forty-two bonds, and

the name of Boselli alone to the five certificates. In so perpetrating one of the most incredible forgeries of all time,
Kreuger made no special effort to be accurate. He spelled
Boselli's name in five different ways by making mistakes in
the number of s's and ll's. He apparently had no copy of
Mosconi's signature, though he still adhered to the policy
of keeping rubber stamps of important signatures that came
to his office. His forged signature bore only the slightest resemblance to Mosconi's own.

When finished, the Match King had before him $143,-
342,500 in Italian government bonds, supposedly in return
for a loan of that amount to Italy, in return for which he
was also given a match monopoly in the country. As with the
earlier Spanish Loan, Kreuger now locked the new bonds
away and began circulating in banking circles, dropping hints
of a loan to Italy, whispering that it must be kept a secret
because Italy planned to use the money in rebuilding its
navy.

As before, no one breathed a word, while behind this
veil of blessed secrecy Kreuger busily credited his hardest-
pressed companies with "millions" from the Italian Loan. In
New York, Donald Durant, who had been warned in provocative cables that Kreuger was working on a great *coup*, learned
that $14 million had been assigned to the Continental In-
vestment Corporation as International Match's profit from
a great new transaction. What Durant did not know was that
the $50 million in legitimate German bonds, which sup-
posedly also reposed in Continental coffers, had been whipped
away from the holding company long before.

Next, Kreuger himself turned up on Wall Street to
drop further hints of his Italian coup. It is said he brought a
few of the forged bonds with him and that he drew them
from his pocket at an International Match Board meeting.

"Do you realize what these mean, gentlemen?" he supposedly asked grandly. "They mean we are in control of the Italian match industry."

Kreuger's air of high confidence over the Italian bonds was especially comforting to Board members of International Match, since whispers had wafted across the Atlantic that Kreuger had several times been seen in the Crillon bar in Paris, drinking himself into a state of muttering intoxication. In view of the Match King's jubilant air now, such rumors seemed unthinkable.

On this 1931 trip Kreuger also conferred with the President of the United States. This was not the first occasion on which he went to the White House. From 1929 on, he was a frequent visitor there. The roots of these visits seemed to extend back to the trips of Donald Durant and Percy Rockefeller to Stockholm. Speeding his two credulous associates on their homeward way, the Match King apparently decided that Americans were so easily fooled that he could let his guard down completely in that country. Accordingly, when the journalist, Isaac F. Marcosson, wrote asking permission to interview him for *The Saturday Evening Post*, Kreuger cheerfully agreed. Marcosson, known in his profession as "the world's foremost journalist," journeyed to Stockholm where the Match King accorded him every courtesy. "For ten days I saw Kreuger morning, afternoon, and evening," Marcosson recalls. "Except for breakfast I had every meal with him." From the mass of material he collected in these contacts, Marcosson extracted an article-interview called "The Match King." It appeared in *The Saturday Evening Post* of October 12, 1929, and largely was a plea for more and bigger opportunities for monopoly, which were called a boon to mankind. This sentiment was so in tune with the times—for the next two weeks, anyway—that in Marcosson's words, "America became Kreuger-conscious."

One American, in particular, became so. This was Herbert Hoover, President of the United States. Shortly after publication of the interview, Marcosson found himself in the White House, where Hoover said, "That man Kreuger you wrote about seems to be an interesting fellow. We are both engineers. Bring him to see me next time he is in the country." Marcosson did, and the two engineers talked far beyond the time the President's staff allotted for the interview. Later, the President said to Marcosson, "Kreuger gave me the impression of a man of great capacity. I was very glad to meet him."

On Hoover, a harried, pessimistic man, Kreuger during the Depression exerted the same appeal he had for the whole world. He was a man serenely confident of the future when no one else alive seemed capable of the slightest optimism. Thus he had achieved a rarefied atmosphere where he could not only mingle with heads of states as an equal, but soothe them as well. Hoover especially appreciated such soothing, a fact which further boosted Kreuger in the esteem of Wall Street.

But now, as he stepped into the White House again, the Match King had reached the dangerous point in his own affairs when sums like the hundreds of millions he claimed to have received from Italy no longer sufficed. Returning to Stockholm in the early fall of 1931, he asked the Riksbank for a loan of $20 million against the German bonds which he had secured by his first payment to Germany (France had providentially come through with the final payment on *her* loan, making this first installment to Germany possible). The Riksbank had replied that its business was to assist orthodox Swedish banking institutions, not private individuals. Kreuger turned again to the Skandinaviska Kreditaktiebolaget, in which Kreuger & Toll held one ninth of the stock. The bank let him have $30 million, which strained his credit almost to the breaking point. The actual money he applied toward the second payment on the German loan.

In moments of extremity the average man is likely to dream of discovering a gold mine, thus putting an end to all his problems. Kreuger's resources were considerably more than those of the average man, and now he *did* find gold— or so he suddenly claimed. Several years before, in his mad desire to purchase everything possible, he had acquired control of the Boliden Mine, in northern Sweden. Primarily, Boliden was a copper mine. But there was gold there, though the cost and difficulty of smelting it seemed to make the price of mining prohibitive. Kreuger had already persuaded Swedish bankers to finance a $10 million smelter at Boliden. Yet this was only the beginning. A railroad would have to be built through the icy northern wilderness, piers for shipping would have to be constructed, and stout winter homes for the miners—all of which made Boliden highly expensive. Nor were all engineers impressed by Boliden as a source of gold. In response to prodding from Kreuger, the Guggenheims in America had sent a team of engineers to Sweden to report on Boliden. They found the gold content of the mine was insufficient to make Boliden a worth-while investment.

Now Kreuger—who had whispered so successfully about the nonexistent Spanish and Italian match loans—began to drop hints about his Boliden mine and the great gold resources to be found there. This was stimulating talk, especially in Sweden, which country had always dreamed of finding gold in its northern regions. Later in the fall of 1931 Kreuger had the effrontery to visit the Riksbank again, with a request for a loan of $50 million against the new set of German bonds. Again rebuffed, he quickly shifted mental gears to talk about Boliden. He left the Riksbank with a loan of 40 million kroner against his Boliden stock.

Now comes the last of the devious Kreuger stock transactions. For the Match King did not have possession of his Boliden stocks. They reposed in the vaults of the Skandinaviska Kreditaktiebolaget, where the Match King had placed them in return for a loan which made the purchase of the mine possible. Nor, in fact, did the desperate man have any right to either of the batches of the German bonds which he had offered the Riksbank as collateral. These $50 million in bonds rightly belonged to the International Match Company, which had advanced that sum as its part of the German loan. But the bonds had never been delivered to the United States. Instead, after crediting them to the Continental Investment Corporation, Kreuger had first placed them in the Deutsche Union Bank, which he controlled. Shortly they were transferred to his personal account in the Copenhagen Danske Landsmanbank, which, in turn, had been instructed to hold them for the account of Skandinaviska Kreditaktiebolaget. Now, merely by making a phone call to Copenhagen, Kreuger used these bonds—which were not his—to get his Boliden stock out of hock. With the Boliden stock he secured his loan of 40 million kroner from the Riksbank.

It was just enough to carry him for a few months more. . . .

Chapter 19

Collapse

The Match King reappeared suddenly in New York in mid-December, 1931, radiating every bit of the cool self-confidence that so sharply set him aside from the rest of his contemporaries. Questioned on shipboard as to whether he planned to meet once more with President Hoover he became every inch the Statesman, to reply, "I have every expectation of meeting with the President to give him my views on the international situation." Then he elaborated on his favorite theme—that the international situation, really, was not so bad as Americans thought.

On Wall Street he proceeded to lull Durant and others with further talk of the mysterious Italian bonds, continuing the intrigue of the shadowy deal by speaking of it in a conspiratorial whisper and usually referring to Italy as "Y country." But even when conjuring up such mumbo-jumbo his words conveyed the old magic. Says Earl Sparling: "New York bankers clustered around him, had him to luncheons, waited upon him of evenings, anxious for every word from his lips. Of all men, he could tell them the most about international conditions. As usual he was a pillar of stability in a chaotic world. There were world problems, he admitted, but Americans were inclined to take them too seriously. Everything was going to be all right. . . ."

But anyone privileged to observe the Match King's secret actions in Stockholm over the preceding three months might have been inclined to discount his optimism. There, Kreuger had given every indication of a man who—temporarily at least—had come to entertain doubts of his own omniscience. Nor is it any great wonder that doubts were beginning to assail him. World conditions were steadily growing worse. England had abandoned the gold standard and so, two weeks later, had Sweden. Enormous world repercussions followed, causing banks that had promised Kreuger credit to inform him they could not live up to the promises. Worse, the global drying-up of credit proceeded at a faster pace, making other banks call in Kreuger loans, or demand unusually large payments on account. There was all this, and added to it the colossal drain of the payment of monopoly loan millions.

These matters seem to have driven the Match King to take a somewhat more realistic view of his position. What he saw must have truly alarmed him, for the man who usually remained so remote from his family proceeded to take certain safeguards in "the interests of his family and a few friends." In October, he ordered 10,000 shares of the iron-ore Grängesberg Company and 10,000 shares of Swedish SKF removed from the office of Kreuger & Toll. He himself carried these to the Villagatan flat, where he placed them in a secret cupboard near his bedroom, in which already reposed 14,000 shares in Svenska Dagbladet, Sweden's leading newspaper, which he controlled. On the thirteenth and nineteenth of October he gave his brother Torsten two packages of Grängesberg stock, containing 6,000 shares each. Still later he ordered £80,000 of Greek government bonds to be delivered to Torsten.

It is interesting to note that none of these securities, supposedly the safest he owned, were those of the Swedish Match Company or Kreuger & Toll. In his flashes of realism, the Match King must have considered the possibility that his two great companies might be doomed. But if such were his inner fears, they seem shortly to have subsided. When he departed for New York in December, Kreuger seemed his old self. He was even working on a transaction which could bring him another few months of salvation.

The origins of this deal stretched back to the period of high megalomania when Kreuger could look ahead to visualize himself as the entire world's Match King, a man who—with one world empire attained—might turn to devote his driving ambitions to becoming the Telephone King. It was in the toxic glow of this dream that he had purchased the L. M. Ericsson Telephone Company, of Sweden.

L. M. Ericsson, the largest such company in Europe, was an excellent buy, and it had promptly joined Swedish Match and several other big companies to become what might be called the solid citizens of the Kreuger empire. But now, in the fall of 1931, subjected to superhuman pressures from all sides, the Match King may have decided he would have to abandon all dreams of a telephone empire. Or he may merely have realized that Ericsson was his most marketable holding. At any rate, he sent out feelers to the International Telephone & Telegraph Company, in New York. These did not convey the information that Ericsson was for sale—things are never so clean-cut in the heady realm where Kreugers operate. Rather, he suggested an exchange of stock between the two companies. By this, he would give International Telephone & Telegraph 600,000 shares of Ericsson stock. In return, he would receive a lesser block of International Telephone & Telegraph stock, leaving IT&T to make up the remainder—worth $11 million—in convenient cash. Payment of this money would be made only after an audit of the Ericsson books. Pending the audit, Kreuger had deposited his stock and International Telephone & Telegraph deposited its money.

For several reasons this deal was a foolhardy one on Kreuger's part, indicating a dulling-under-pressure of the Match King's greased-lightning mind. For the first time—incredibly—outside accountants would be permitted to examine the books of a Kreuger company. Until this winter of 1931 none but Kreuger's carefully picked, intimidated, largely incompetent accountants had been allowed to work on the books of his holdings. Ernst & Ernst, the American accountants, were still seething with frustration because the International Match directors insisted on acceptance of Kreuger's cabled word for the figures on his books. Even now, that indefatigable nemesis, A. D. Berning, was preparing questions to ask Kreuger about the $50 million in German bonds which rightly belonged to International Match.

But there was another reason why the Ericsson deal can be called foolish on Kreuger's part. International Telephone & Telegraph was a Morgan-dominated corporation whose executives, starting with Sosthenes Behn, its president, had absorbed J. P. Morgan's distrust of Kreuger. For the moment, Ericsson was such a good buy that Morgan officials were willing to overlook this distrust. Yet if anything went wrong there would be this old resentment to contend with: Kreuger had made Morgan look ridiculous and lost him money as well. The Match King was aware of Morgan's continuing dislike, and persisted in his deprecating remarks about a David-Goliath relationship. Even so—it might be said—David did not hesitate to put his head directly into the lion-Goliath's mouth.

So the shadows began to fall. But again Kreuger did not seem to realize it. Spending Christmas of 1931 in New York, he was still the financier "whose confidence was like a climate everywhere he went. His lucid mind reduced economic confusion to a primer-like simplicity. His calm, musical voice made all obstacles seem insignificant. He gave forth, like a personal magnetism, hope and courage and buoyancy. It was like a tonic to talk to him."

He appeared the same throughout January, though he knew that in response to instructions from International Telephone & Telegraph accountants of Price, Waterhouse were journeying from London to Stockholm and by late in the month were at work examining the Ericsson books. Then in early February—after Kreuger had for fourteen years been part of the international scene, "afraid to leave the center of the stage for fear someone would examine the script"— the blow fell. Price, Waterhouse cabled to New York that the L. M. Ericsson Company's cash position was not as represented by Kreuger. Several matters continued to look suspicious, but definitely Kreuger had removed more than $7 million from the company treasury and substituted foreign government bonds of lesser value.

Sosthenes Behn immediately summoned Kreuger to his office. There the Match King was "urbane, unperturbed." The Ericsson money, he explained, was on deposit with Kreuger & Toll, covering a transaction between the two companies by which Kreuger & Toll had purchased two French telephone companies that Ericsson would later acquire. As security for the deposit Kreuger & Toll had given a folio of its match monopoly bonds. The bonds, he pointed out, were worth 125 per cent of the loan.

This was the sort of double-talk that bankers had been accepting from Kreuger for years—a weaving together of elusive facts and figures into a pattern which somehow, as he spoke, made eminent sense.

But Sosthenes Behn, with his Morgan indoctrination, was made of sterner stuff. He found the involved Kreuger explanations as fragile as the smoke from the cigarettes the Match King was now continuously and nervously puffing. Certainly, Behn replied, the bonds Kreuger had deposited with Ericsson were worth 125 per cent on face value. But at market value they were worth only 50 per cent or less. Besides, cash receivable was not cash in the bank. What Behn wanted was $7 million cash in the bank.

This was the first of a series of daily conferences between the two men. For Kreuger was in desperate need of International Telephone & Telegraph's $11 million. In seven days his loan of $4 million from American banks would fall due. In Sweden there was $116,336,000 borrowed from bankers on which he had to pay interest, at least. In the daily conferences with Behn he used every trick of his darting mind and verbal skill, even conjuring up visions of a stream of gold from the Boliden mine, a possibility which left Behn unimpressed. Kreuger did his best to by-pass the missing $7 million and place the deal on a purely personal basis, as he had done so often before. This, too, failed, but he never lost his celebrated imperturbability. "He insisted with quiet assurance that there had been no misrepresentation by him in the Ericsson contract. If there seemed to be, it was because of faulty translation of the balance sheet . . . and a different understanding in America and Sweden as to the meaning of the word cash." Behn merely listened and shook his head. "Just produce the seven million," he said, in effect.

According to one account, Kreuger remained "calm, confident, unworried," until a meeting of the afternoon of Friday, February 19, 1932, at which Behn intimated that the Ericsson deal was off. Then, seated across the polished desk of his unwavering opponent, the Match King suddenly slumped. His head sunk to his hands and he moaned, "*Jag minns inte längre*" (I can't think any more), "*Jag blir galen*" (I am going crazy). Members of Behn's staff were summoned to assist him to his feet. Kreuger's face was twitching convulsively and as he tried to walk, one leg dragged slightly. His speech also seemed thick. Apparently, the Match King was having a slight stroke.

But a second version of the meeting of February nineteenth has him rising calmly to his feet after the turn-down from Behn. "He shrugged, smiled, said something about the stupidity of American bankers." But however he reacted, the seeming collapse of the Ericsson deal was a stunning blow— so much so that on Saturday, the twentieth, he appears to have made plans to kill himself. Arriving at the International Match office on Wall Street in midafternoon he wished the staff a happy Washington's Birthday and dismissed them —this was still the era of the six-day week. Then he devoted the rest of the afternoon to writing farewell letters, after which he turned to business matters and labored through the night. Even when facing death, the Match King found his mind teeming with financial loose ends, and a recapitulation of this Saturday night—taken from later court testimony —is interesting, if for no other reason than indicating the number of loose ends:

> Some of the letters, cables, and trunk-calls of that Saturday night have been traced, and show that Kreuger's main concern was to transfer further securities and cash to his family, and to do it in such a way as to safeguard them against any possible claims. Thus he cables one of his directors, Sjöström, to hand over to his brother, Torsten, two Greek Government bonds, worth £180,000. He phones his secretary, Miss Bökman, instructing her to deliver to Torsten a parcel of shares of the "A. B. Permanens," which controls the *Svenska*

Dagbladet. At 3 A.M. he telephones his broker in Stockholm, telling him to pay his liquid balance of half a million kroner in cash to the very same brother, Torsten. He also sends his brother a cable, informing him of all these measures. Then he writes to Gunnar Eckström, saying that the shares of the *Svenska Dagbladet* previously handed over to his father and to his sister, Britta, constitute their property: they are not a gift, but payment by him for some "Kreuger securities" he has brought from them. Further, he tells his brother-in-law that he should keep one-half of the "Grängesberg" and the "S.K.F." shares in his possession, in settlement of a similar transaction. This letter to Gunnar Eckström is short, precise, and business-like, and its only personal note is the stereotyped form of greeting; altogether a somewhat obvious alibi for the genuineness of these "business transactions" within the family—an attempt to camouflage his gifts. To a certain person in his employ he sends a letter of farewell and thanks, in which he encloses ten thousand dollars. A letter to Torsten, apparently promised him in the telegram, does not seem to have reached Kreuger's brother, according to the latter's evidence. Further, Kreuger writes to the head of one of the subsidiary companies, instructing him to transfer the debit balance of Mr. Sune Scheele, amounting to £100,000, to his own personal account. Thus, in assuming this liability, Kreuger tries to save an old friend and collaborator. To Mr. Krister Littorin he writes a letter describing his hopeless position, but, strangely enough, does nothing to save him from the effects of the coming crash. There were probably other letters to friends and to members of the family.

Yet, after his long night of feverish activity, the Match King—for reasons no one will ever know—decided not to do away with himself. He had mailed some of his farewell letters, and now there were people alive who shortly would learn that Ivar Kreuger was in a morbid state of mind. However, he seems to have made no effort to inform the recipients of these letters of his change of heart. Instead, he returned to the penthouse at 791 Park Avenue, where he went to bed and perhaps slept. From later events it would appear that, if he did not have a stroke in Behn's office, he had one this night in his sleep.

When he awakened the next afternoon, Kreuger may conceivably have wished he had gone through with suicide. For while he slept on Sunday morning, Gordon Rentschler, president of the National City Bank, phoned to George Murnane, a Lee, Higginson partner who lived in Brookville, Long Island. Rentschler told Murnane what Kreuger had kept to himself—that Behn was doubtful of the Ericsson deal. Murnane, like other Lee, Higginson directors, had been informed by Kreuger that the Ericsson deal was settled, and in alarm he called Donald Durant, at Cornwall-on-Hudson. Durant, too, was astounded. "It doesn't seem possible," he told Murnane. "I've known Ivar for years and I'd trust his word anywhere. I suggest we go to see him right away." The two men agreed to meet in New York and proceed to Kreuger's penthouse.

On arrival there, they found the Match King slumped in his living room, wearing yellow silk pajamas and a purple silk dressing gown. His moist face was twitching, his speech incoherent.

"I never had seen anyone in quite that condition," Durant stated later. "He was very nervous, very weak. He didn't pace up and down, which was his normal way of doing. He sat in a chair, slumped down, and it was difficult to talk to him. He was very, very tired. His mind was not at all clear. He kept saying he was very, very tired, and all he could do was sleep. That was the one thing he could do. It was

very pathetic to see him in that condition, a man who had
been so brilliant, so tireless before."

To which Murnane added, "He talked in jumps, with
his hand to his head, and pauses of a few minutes at a time.
He said, 'I'm so tired I just can't seem to get down to anything.' He slumped in his chair, he was anything but normal.
That is what alarmed us so. It was not like him."

After a few attempts to question the stricken man about
the Ericsson transaction, the bankers summoned a doctor,
who, after examining Kreuger, stated that the Match King
was suffering from serious brain fatigue. A long rest free
from financial worries would be necessary, and Durant immediately suggested a vacation to Kreuger. The Match King
waved a vague hand in rejection. Durant studied him for a
few minutes, then went into the library where he sent a
guarded cable to Krister Littorin in Stockholm. It hinted
that I.K. had broken down.

The two Lee, Higginson partners did not dare to leave
the Match King alone for the night, and summoned Alexis
Aminoff, one of the Kreuger & Toll "observers" in New York.
Aminoff, a dapper young man who had been an attaché in
the Swedish Embassy in Washington, stated later that he
found Kreuger in terrible shape. No sooner had the two bankers left than the Match King rose from his chair and began
raging around the room. "I can't remember, I can't think,"
he shouted, striking a clenched fist of one hand into the
open palm of the other.

Aminoff tried to quiet him, and slowly Kreuger's rage
abated. But as he slumped in the chair again, he continued
to mutter, "I can't remember, I tell you. I can't remember."

As night wore on, the atmosphere in the penthouse
high above the city assumed an almost Grand Guignol horror.

Kreuger seemed to be in the grip of a strange insanity, or perhaps stark terror. Out of the tapestries on the walls came nameless things that he stared at, and he listened to voices that had no sound.

Later Aminoff recalled: "He would answer the telephone without anyone calling. He would get up and ask somebody to come in, thinking he had heard someone knocking at the door. He would slump down in his chair and go to sleep for a couple of seconds, then he would jump up again."

The next day Kreuger seemed a bit better. His New York housekeeper, Mrs. Hilda Aberg, took over his care, and he seemed to regain some possession of his thoughts. No sooner did this happen than he began making phone calls: "When he was not slumped in his chair, staring fixedly at nothing, he was at his drawing room desk frantically telephoning to all corners of the world, telephoning for money. And having talked to Paris, to Berlin, to Stockholm, and to other places, he could not remember fifteen minutes after what he had said or whom he had called."

One afternoon late in the week, Durant and Murnane arrived to ask necessary questions about the $4 million owed to the four American Banks. Kreuger became his old self long enough to explain plausibly that $4.7 million was overdue from Spain, and that perhaps he would have to visit Spain personally to attend to it. He instructed Durant to ask for an extension of the American loan. Durant queried the four banks and all agreed, even though one was National City whose president, Gordon Rentschler, was somewhat aware of Kreuger's plight. The Union Trust of Pittsburgh agreed on the condition that the Match King "show cash." The ailing man roused himself, and with difficulty got together $200,000. To it he added some shares in the Diamond

Match Company which few people suspected he possessed. It satisfied the Pittsburgh bank.

With the American crisis thus temporarily averted, Kreuger rallied further. Thereafter, "the phone calls flashed back and forth across the world day and night. Always, night and day, he was making a trans-Atlantic phone call or receiving one. Night after night he sat at his desk waiting tense for some call that never came. Sometimes he would fall asleep sitting there, to awake with a start and begin staring at the telephone again. Then he fell asleep and awakened again, over and over, until the muddy dawn broke over New York's towers of steel."

But despite the phone calls, he seemed unable to raise more money—and now, in his moment of direst extremity— he decided that his native land must save him. In all, he owed some $150 million to Swedish banks, but Sweden was— in his own eyes—a country for which he had done much. Phoning Krister Littorin in Stockholm, he ordered him to go to the Riksbank and demand $2 million. If the demand should be refused, "Tell them if the money is not forthcoming Swedish Match will have to suspend payments, go into bankruptcy." Then he began shouting, "The money must be found! It must be paid by nine-forty-five tonight or we are ruined."

In Stockholm, Littorin, whose world had just tumbled around him, gathered together some Swedish Match directors and the group hastened to the Riksbank. Kreuger already owed this state bank $10,720,000 and to ask for more was all but unthinkable. Yet Littorin's panic, and the anxiety of the others so impressed the chairman of the Riksbank board that after a long conference, he went at 7 P.M. to the home of Prime Minister Ekman. Hauling that dignitary from his dinner, he announced, "We have only until nine-forty-five to save Swedish Match."

Together, the two stunned men returned to the Riksbank for a meeting which eventually was in part responsible for Ekman's loss of his high official post. "It was a difficult meeting," he reported later to the Swedish Riksdag. "I was startled by the utter lack of knowledge shown by the representatives of the Swedish Match Company, especially concerning the coordination of the subsidiary companies and affiliated industries. Others present got the same impression. I therefore told the representatives of the Riksbank that it was my conviction that no further demands for credit should be considered [until] the Riksbank should take the initiative for a thorough investigation of the Kreuger concerns."

But despite this negative opinion, the Riksbank voted to advance Kreuger his $2 million. There were two highly important conditions. The first stated that Swedish government accountants must now have access to the books of all Kreuger companies. Second, Kreuger must return immediately to meet with European bankers and explain the astounding state of his affairs.

In New York, a delighted Match King heard the terms over the telephone and accepted. Perhaps it was wishful thinking, but it was his understanding that the Swedish accountants would not be allowed to examine his books until he himself had got back to Stockholm. He was confident that then he could manage matters so that the Swedes once more would be satisfied. As for the European bankers, he had always been able to handle them. In a cable he set the meeting with them for mid-March, in Berlin.

Altogether, his transatlantic coup acted like a shot of adrenalin to the stricken man in New York. He seemed to be persuaded that his old powers had returned and almost miraculously he seemed to recover. "It had been a week of terror, and now there was a week of recuperation." He was still a nervous, afflicted man, a mere shadow of what he had been, but he managed to attend conferences and even resume his negotiations with International Telephone & Telegraph.

Indeed, for a brief moment there now seemed to be only a single remaining menace. This again was the persistent accountant, Berning. Early in February, he had appeared to question Kreuger about the $50 million in German bonds which had been credited to International Match. Where were they? Why were they not in the United States? Kreuger replied that the bonds could be found in the vaults of the Deutsche Union Bank, in Berlin. Berning requested proof. Kreuger instructed the Match Palace to cable Berning that the bonds were in the Deutsche Union, signing the name of the president of the Kreuger-controlled bank to the cable. The cable arrived, but Berning was still unconvinced. It must have been a sickening shock to Kreuger when he learned late in February that Berning was preparing to embark for Europe on a personal visit to the Deutsche Union Bank.

But two ego-inflating events quickly took his mind off Berning. The first was another summons to the White House, where after a conference with President Hoover, Kreuger told newsmen, "There is no reason why the United States should get hysterical about Europe. Europe can, and will, solve her own problems." Next came a request from Isaac Marcosson for another *Saturday Evening Post* interview. To the surprise of Durant, Murnane, and others, he began "giving more time and care to the interview than to his own tangled and troubled affairs now marching to a desperate climax." In preparing the interview, Marcosson first handed Kreuger a list of questions to be answered in writing. Says Marcosson: "I was struck with the meticulousness with which he did his job. It had required investigation of statistics, surveys of countries, and a broad grasp of the international commercial and financial situation. Obviously he had devoted a great deal of time and thought to the undertaking."

In fact, *The Saturday Evening Post* interview of 1932 stands forth among the last manifestations of the baffling Jekyll-Hyde Kreuger personality. For in it the troubled man gives a remarkably prophetic analysis of world affairs. He predicts the Roosevelt Bank Holiday of 1933 by citing the inadequacies of the American system of bank examination. He foresaw the aftermath of President Hoover's unfortunate moratorium, and forecast the end of deflation. He also put an unerring finger on the part that trade barriers would play in aggravating the international economic derangement. Nor is there any indication of the Kreuger ego in the article. Nowhere is there mention of his own enterprises or stocks. For once, it is truly Kreuger the financier speaking.

Because *The Saturday Evening Post* took five weeks to print, Kreuger's interview would not be due to appear until April 2, 1932. On March fourth, serenely confident that his views would make a sensation in the financial world, and equally certain that the Swedish accountants were doing nothing until his return, the Match King stepped aboard his favorite liner, the *Ile de France*. With him were the ever-admiring Durant and N. Penrose Hallowell, another Lee, Higginson partner. Ostensibly they were accompanying Kreuger to his March bankers' conference, but their presence had a deeper purpose. They were keeping an eye on the Match King's health, for though he seemed to have recuperated remarkably, Kreuger still looked like a man who had survived a serious illness. His pallid face was sallower, his manner listless, and in the puffy cheeks showed a constant, spasmodic twitch.

Fellow passengers on the *Ile de France* remembered Kreuger's shipboard behavior with the sort of bi-focal vision that infuriates police and delights the writers of mystery stories. Some recall him as brooding in his cabin, hardly emerging for meals or turns on deck. Others swear that he was in high, perhaps hysterical spirits, even making a spectacle of himself at the ship's concert where he cavorted in a wild Scandinavian folk dance with a thirteen-year-old Norwegian girl who had just won the skating championship at the Winter Olympic Games at Lake Placid.

Her name was Sonja Henie, and she still recalls Kreuger as a friendly fellow Scandinavian who engaged her in interesting conversations.

20

Death of a Titan

As soon as Kreuger set foot on French soil, he seemed to regain the impenetrable calm that had been foremost among his characteristics before the shattering trip to America.

Gone were all vestiges of the brooding shipboard moods that some claimed to have seen, or the desperate gaiety of his furious Scandinavian dance with Sonja Henie.

He seemed almost the old Kreuger, no more the tense, jumpy man who had made up his mind to kill himself two weeks before, then for reasons unknown suddenly changed it. On the train on which he traveled from Havre to Paris, with Durant and Hallowell, Kreuger was again in the old impassive mold. He had little to say, but then he never did have when important conferences were pending. Sitting with the other two men in the compartment, he opened his dispatch case on his knees, sorted through papers and the cablegrams that had reached him on shipboard, making cryptic notes on each in Swedish.

At the Gare du Nord the three men exchanged brief farewells. In only twenty-four hours—at 11 A.M. on Saturday, March twelfth—they were scheduled to meet again at the Hotel du Rhin at a conference of directors of Kreuger & Toll, Swedish Match, and Higginson's, the London branch of Lee, Higginson.

So there was no need for prolonged farewells. Nor was

Durant uneasy about letting the ailing Kreuger leave his sight. He had cabled ahead to Littorin who already knew from Durant's first cable and from the farewell-dear-Krister letter from New York that the Match King was not in the best of health and would require someone with him most of the time. The conscientious Littorin, Durant knew, could be trusted to carry on from there.

Littorin could. At 11:15, as Kreuger's taxi drew to a stop before the apartment at 5 Avenue Victor Emmanuel, Littorin was waiting on the sidewalk to greet Kreuger with a hearty, "How are you, Ivar?" But if the greeting was hearty, Littorin's anxious eyes carefully scanned the Match King's face. It was sallow, even for the usually sallow Kreuger, and as the men talked going up in the automatic lift Littorin decided that Kreuger's gentle, persuasive voice now stumbled slightly. It was a little furry, blurred, as if the tongue were too heavy to articulate well. Nor did Kreuger move as sure-footedly as before. The impression he gave was of a man from whom an ounce or two of precious energy has been siphoned off, leaving him somewhat weak and vague.

But aside from that, nothing. Kreuger gave his usual warm greeting to his housekeeper, Jeanette Barrault, after which the two men moved into the living room. While Littorin waited Kreuger went through the door to the bedroom, where he deposited the dispatch case. Then he returned. "Tell me how things are," he asked.

This was a moment for which Littorin had no relish. Solely on his own, he had during the ocean-crossing withheld information of the utmost importance from the mighty Kreuger. He had decided to let his beloved Ivar enjoy a few days of comparative peace on the ocean, but such stratagems cannot be prolonged forever. Now he had to give the Match King the unpleasant news that the Swedish Government, in return for the providential $2 million loan, had immediately begun an examination of all Kreuger & Toll books, thus bypassing Kreuger's authority. It was something not even governments had dared do before. While Kreuger had been on the high seas government and Riksbank accountants had moved into the Match Palace, producing warrants to back up demands for the thousands of company ledgers. A nervous Littorin proceeded this far, then paused. "They've found those Italian Bonds, Ivar," he said slowly. "They're asking questions about them."

History will never know how Kreuger reacted to these sudden words, without doubt the most stunning he could have heard. Littorin, in recalling the interview, merely gives the facts, and states he stopped the conversation there in order to give Kreuger time to digest its bulk. We do know, however, that Kreuger did not grow angry or berate Littorin for withholding information. Instead, the two presently sat down to a lunch prepared by the housekeeper, Jeanette. After that they sat back to discuss other matters until 2:30, when three other Kreuger associates, Hennig, Holm and Wendler, made a scheduled appearance.

Littorin was glad, indeed, to see them come. For there were further questions to be put to I.K., and he had no wish to ask them himself. Already, he had found a way out. On the train down from Stockholm, Littorin had made Sigurd Hennig promise to take over in the matter of the more searching questions. Hennig, Kreuger's chief accountant, had agreed reluctantly.

To the three new arrivals, Kreuger seemed nervous and edgy. His mental and physical exhaustion was now apparent, and Hennig realized that any questions would have to be put in the most delicate manner. "He was obviously a sick man," he said later.

Still, the questions had to be asked, and with occasional promptings from the others, Hennig began. They were important questions, but even so, Kreuger's mind seemed detached, far away. When a question was asked, he sat silent and bemused in his gilt Louis chair, until suddenly he appeared to recollect where he was, pull himself together and give an answer. Only when the Italian Bonds were broached did he seem able to give real attention. Then his answer was fast and definite. "They're all in order," he snapped, like the Kreuger of old. "Interest on them has been duly received and credited to the dividend account."

Having said that much, he abruptly rose to his feet, walked stiffly into the bedroom and through it to the bathroom. There he shut the door firmly and after a moment the four men heard the flushing of the toilet. In another instant, Kreuger was back in the room.

Hennig consulted notes on his pad. "But, Ivar, why is it these Bonds were never stamped?" he asked.

To the astonishment of the others, Kreuger again rose stiffly, in an exact duplication of his movements of only a few minutes before. Again he walked through the bedroom door, into the bathroom, closed the door. Hennig spoke into the uneasy silence in the living room. "There is a lot here I don't understand," he said. The others nodded—he had spoken for them all.

Again Kreuger came back to his chair. "But, Ivar," Hennig asked, "where did the 400 million kroner you loaned Italy for these Bonds come from?"

Once more Kreuger was sunk in remoteness. He did not even seem to hear the question, so distant were his thoughts. Then suddenly he jerked upright and muttered something that sounded like, "I knew where to get it, all right."

Under the circumstances, it was a frivolous answer—

and in the mind of Hennig it set off one of those surges of intuition that can occur in tense moments. Almost without knowing what he was saying, he burst out, "I say, Ivar, are these Bonds genuine?"

It was an unthinkable question, and Hennig was immediately filled with confusion. The others were torn between indignation and consternation. Also fear. Each knew that in the past, when his honesty had been questioned, the Match King had risen slowly to his feet, for all the world like a cobra about to strike. From the hooded eyes had shot a look of malevolent hatred that filled his interrogator with terror. But today there was no cobralike hate. Instead, a tortured expression flickered rapidly across the Match King's usually bland face. Quickly he gained control of his features, and for an instant all the old strength and persuasiveness seemed to flood back. "Yes," he stated emphatically—and no one hearing him could possibly doubt that what he stated was so.

Further questions were now impossible. Hennig, Holm and Wendler pushed back chairs, rose, shook hands in embarrassed farewell. Only Littorin remained, to remind Kreuger of a four-o'clock appointment with Oscar Rydbeck at the Hotel Meurice. Shortly the two men had silently donned overcoats and were riding downward in the lift.

To Littorin, Kreuger looked little worse than he had in the morning. Any great shock he had suffered from learning of the Swedish accountants or the Italian Bonds seemed to have been absorbed. So had Hennig's sharp questions. But under the left eye his cheek gave spasmodic jumps. Still, in the taxi some of Kreuger's fundamental optimism appeared to return and he made a few remarks contrasting New York and Paris in winter, coming to the conclusion that in February, as in all other months of the year, he still preferred New York.

The Swedish banker, Oscar Rydbeck, was in Paris to attend a meeting of the Financial Committee of the League of Nations, and also for the conference of Kreuger directors the next day. Like the others he fully expected that tomorrow morning even a sick Kreuger would somehow, "by rattling off figures so fast that not even a trained banker could follow them," explain all problems away. The Match King had performed similar miracles many times in the past, and his associates had full faith in his ability to do it again. But there are indications that Rydbeck was shocked at Kreuger's appearance, for he apparently decided it was best to face brightly the fact that Kreuger & Toll was in a tight spot, and with it Swedish Match. On such a day no responsible Swedish financier could talk to Kreuger without mentioning the Italian Bonds, but Rydbeck did it lightly, referring to the Bonds facetiously as *famous*. "Ivar, can't you raise some money on those famous Italian Bonds?" he inquired during the two-hour meeting. Kreuger hesitated, then replied, "I gave my promise not to pledge them."

Rydbeck had another idea. "Couldn't you make a deal with the Italian Government, so that the Bonds could be sold back to them with a rebate, as an inducement?"

Kreuger, sitting ashen-faced in a comfortable chair, appeared to give this careful consideration. "I suppose I could," he admitted finally. "But I'd have to do it personally. It would mean a trip to Italy, and I want to go first to Stockholm. After that, maybe. . . ."

Rydbeck seemed satisfied. He invited the two men to remain for dinner, but Kreuger said he was worn out from traveling. He also claimed to have important letters to write and phone calls to make. Outside on the sidewalk, Littorin also suggested dinner. Again Kreuger declined, expressing a desire to spend the evening alone. He also said he preferred to go by himself to the Avenue Victor Emmanuel, making this so plain that Littorin, who had expected to remain by his side until bedtime, had no alternative but to say good night. Then Kreuger did an out-of-character thing. Few of his associates had ever seen him walk to a destination. If his Rolls Royce were not waiting, he was a man who on reaching any sidewalk began waving walking stick or dispatch case for a taxi. But now he thanked Littorin for his aid during the day, then unprecedentedly turned and set off on foot for the Avenue Victor Emmanuel.

Before reaching there he made a stop. At the shop of Gastine-Rennette, a small-arms firm that has supplied Frenchmen with dueling pistols and firearms for centuries, he turned in, to be greeted by an elderly clerk who promptly catalogued him as a "tall, calm, prosperous-looking man."

"I want to see some pistols," Kreuger said to him.

"Automatic or plain?" the clerk asked.

Kreuger shrugged his shoulders, an air of vast indifference radiating from him. For once again he was doing what he had done so many times in life—performing an act of the utmost importance as if it were of no importance at all.

The clerk busied himself behind the counter, finally producing several automatics. Kreuger briefly looked them over. "All too small," he decided.

The clerk showed another, and again Kreuger gave a quick, uninterested glance. "Something still larger," he insisted.

Stung to real action, the clerk picked out the largest automatic in the shop, one 9 millimetres in bore. Kreuger took it, hefted it, thumbed the muzzle, nodded approval. "I'll take it," he said. Without handing the revolver back, he shoved it in his overcoat pocket.

French law requires that the name of anyone buying

guns or ammunition be entered in an official register. The clerk asked Kreuger's name, carefully writing down, "To Ivar Kreuger, 5 Avenue Victor Emmanuel, one 9 millimetre automatic repeater, No. 360413." Next he asked if cartridges would be required. Kreuger decided on two boxes and stuck them in his overcoat beside the pistol. After paying for the purchases, he left the store, the heavy pistol making his overcoat swing incongruously as he strode along.

How he spent the remainder of the evening no one knows exactly. According to the concierge and her husband, he departed the apartment once late in the evening, and on reaching the street looked furtively around to see if he was being watched or followed. Other stories say this late-evening foray took him to a telegraph office where he sent four telegrams to cities in Europe. Each carried only one word: SELL.

But in this case neither the words of the concierge or her husband seem completely trustworthy. For on this Friday both had been deeply hurt by their favorite tenant. In the many years he had rented the expensive Victor Emmanuel apartment, the concierge stated later, M. Kreuger had never failed to speak affably to her on going out or coming in. Not only was he the most celebrated of the three tenants of her building, but he was by far the nicest. He invariably asked after her four children, and what was more, knew each by name. When the children were around he paused to speak to them, crouching low on his haunches to reach their level.

Yet on arriving home from the United States that morning—always an occasion for extra geniality—Kreuger had calmly walked by the concierge as she stood with a welcoming smile on her face. That could have been because he was so engrossed in talk with M. Littorin, but on coming downstairs a few hours later with the same monsieur, Kreuger had again passed without nodding. And now, coming in alone, with the strange bulge in his overcoat pocket, he was again too pre-occupied to nod or speak, though the concierge, her husband, and all the children were gathered in the lobby at the time.

But whether the concierge was correct in reporting that the Match King went out during the evening, there is no doubt that the harried man spent most of the time in his favorite manner. The world-famous financier who had told Isaac F. Marcosson that his three rules for success in life were Silence, More Silence, and Still More Silence, passed the evening and night alone—though just what he did re-mains a mystery. One writer has pictured him pacing for hours from living room to bedroom in the apartment. Strid-ing from one room to the other—the writer goes on—Kreuger was seeking frantically in his mind for some way out. The man who so many times had saved his career by brilliant flashes of inspiration now desperately needed the most im-portant flash of all. "But there was too much to remember, too many immensities." Where once his mind had func-tioned like lightning, since his collapse in New York it had become a sluggish instrument, fumbling uncertainly among the million and one details of matches, forests, pulp mills, telephones, banks, real estate, coal mines, copper mines, gold mines, that made up the Kreuger Empire.

Nor was there anyone who could help. He had hun-dreds of directors, managers and subordinates, but through the years he had kept each in the outer darkness of his opera-tions. He had been the one who knew all the details, the one who alone could raise money—"a one-man show, who con-trolled a $1,135,000,000 mammoth of which he alone could make sense." But could he now? At some time during his tireless pacing, the Match King must have faced the fact that he no longer could. "He was a man truly alone that night," a later account said. "Perhaps in those moments the loneliest man on earth."

At some time in the night, he undressed and went to bed. Perhaps the man of steely control even slept. When Littorin arrived at 9:30 the next morning he could see the rumpled, unmade bed through the open bedroom door. Kreuger, who had almost finished dressing and was shaving in the bathroom, called out that he felt rested. Yet when he stepped fully dressed into the living room, Littorin thought he looked like a man who had spent a sleepless night. The two men promptly sat down to a discussion of Kreuger & Toll business, credit problems, and balance sheets to be brought up at the 11-o'clock meeting of directors at the Hotel du Rhin. The day before they had spoken English, today it was Swedish —a sign that Kreuger was again becoming acclimated to Europe. At 10 o'clock Kreuger's Stockholm personal secretary, an attractive girl named Karen Bökman, arrived, her notebooks ready for dictation. Littorin rose to leave, reminding Kreuger again of the 11 o'clock meeting. "I may be a few minutes late," Kreuger said. This seemed to bother Littorin. "They're all good friends of yours, Ivar," he answered. I don't think it would be a good idea to keep them waiting long." Kreuger assured him he would try to be on time. Then he turned and began dictating to Miss Bökman.

Half an hour later Miss Bökman, too, was ready to leave for the Hotel du Rhin. Jeanette, the housekeeper, had already reported that she was leaving to do the shopping. Miss Bökman half expected Kreuger to leave with her, but he explained that he wished to remain behind long enough to write a few personal notes. She had started out the door when suddenly he called her back. Handing her a sealed envelope he said, "You have had so much to do lately, please accept this as a bonus." The startled girl waited until she was downstairs before tearing the envelope open. Inside was a batch of crisp Swedish bills—20,000 kroner.

Upstairs, Kreuger did indeed have personal notes to write. Three of them—one to Littorin; one to his favorite sister, Britta; one to another business associate, Sune Scheele. This done, he carried the notes into the bedroom and placed them carefully on the bedtable. Then he began moving around the room, darkening it by pulling down the shades. From wherever it had been hidden, he took out the revolver, and presumably slipped the ammunition in. After unbuttoning his waistcoat, he stretched himself at full length atop the unmade bed. He turned back the waistcoat so that only shirt and undershirt remained above the skin on the left side of his chest. With his right hand he then lifted the big revolver across his body and pointed it downward at his left chest, pressing it close, so that the muzzle touched the shirt.

Then he pulled the trigger. . . .

Chapter 21

Birth of a Mystery

At the moment Kreuger killed himself, the following group awaited him in a suite at the Hotel Du Rhin: Oscar Rydbeck and Krister Littorin, of Swedish Match and Kreuger & Toll; Donald Durant and N. Penrose Hallowell, of Lee, Higginson; Lt. Col. the Honorable George Akers-Douglas, of Higginson's; Otto Busse, manager of the Paris office of Kreuger & Toll; and Karen Bökman, Kreuger's personal secretary. Because this was a meeting of international bankers whose conversations would involve hundreds of millions of dollars, a staff of secretaries and clerks sat in readiness in the anteroom outside. Some time after the others, Sir Guy Granet, also of Higginson's, arrived. He joined the group inside.

For a time they sat waiting patiently enough, for Littorin had brought along Kreuger's word that he might be a few minutes late. There was little point in commencing any talk of business, for Kreuger alone knew the details of what the business was. He would, of course, talk fast and reassuringly, ask Miss Bökman for papers proving the existence of profits. IT&T would get its $7 million, the Italian Bonds would be explained, and all would depart with the heady knowledge that I.K. once again proved his genius. "A tableau of innocents," one writer later called them.

But as minutes ticked into half hours, the group became restive. Durant afterward recalled trying to ease the tension by saying that in New York Kreuger had recently been two or three hours late for appointments. This was so unlike the punctilious Match King that it must be presumed the men in the room immediately fired questions at Durant and probably drew from him some details of Kreuger's odd behavior in New York. But Durant stopped short of telling the harsh facts of Kreuger's collapse.

At noon, shortly after Sir Guy arrived, Littorin stepped to the phone and called the Avenue Victor Emmanuel flat. There was no answer, the logical supposition being that Kreuger was en route to the meeting and Jeanette was still out shopping. But he had not arrived by 12:30 and again Littorin phoned. Again no answer, and the restless group waited another half hour before trying once more. This time Jeanette lifted the phone, to say that on returning from her shopping only a few minutes before she had decided to straighten Kreuger's bedroom. Opening the door she had been surprised to find her employer on the bed, asleep. She hastily backed out, and now was cleaning another part of the apartment.

From 1 to 1:15, Littorin debated with the others whether to return to the Victor Emmanuel apartment and waken I.K. It was finally decided that he should, and taking Miss Bök-man with him, Littorin started off. At the apartment door they were met by Jeanette, who informed them Kreuger was still asleep. Miss Bökman discreetly remained in the hallway with Jeanette while Littorin walked to the bedroom door and pushed it open. Because of the drawn blinds it was almost dark inside, but the white expanse of Kreuger's shirt told him the Match King was still on the bed, his right arm flung across his body, left hanging down to the floor. Suspecting nothing, Littorin advanced across the bedroom until he stood close to the bed. "Ivar, Ivar," he called. When

Kreuger did not move, he looked closer and noticed the chalky whiteness of the Match King's face and that his half-open eyes were eerily fixed on the ceiling. At the same moment, he caught a glint of the automatic on the floor on the other side of the bed. Suspicion suddenly leaped to his mind, and he bent over Kreuger's body, finding the tiny round role in the shirt above the heart. Around the hole was a brownish, charred ring.

Littorin moved quickly to a window and raised the blind. The light only confirmed his fears that Kreuger was dead, and looking around he now saw the three letters on the bed-table. Finding that one was addressed to him he picked it up to read—in English:

12 March 1932

Dear Krister,

I have made such a mess of things that I believe this to be the most satisfactory solution for everybody concerned. Please take care of these two letters also see that two letters which were sent a couple of days ago by Jordahl to me at 5 Avenue Victor Emmanuel are returned to Jordahl. The letters were sent by Majestic. Goodbye now and thanks.

I.K.

It is a sad commentary on Kreuger's existence that all directly concerned with him thought immediately of money on hearing of his death. Even Littorin, probably the human being closest to him, thought first of Kreuger the financier, not of the man. Quickly leaving the bedroom, he whispered the news to Miss Bökman and the two hastened back to the Rhin, where the bombshell was dropped in the room of waiting bankers. The immediate response of each was that the news must be kept from the world until the New York

Stock Exchange closed at noon. All agreed that to save the
Kreuger empire, and incidentally themselves, this was imperative.

At the same time they realized that Littorin was guilty
of a serious breach of legality in not instantly reporting the
suicide to police. Littorin was apparently acutely conscious
of this himself, and again he set off for the Avenue Victor
Emmanuel, still accompanied by Miss Bökman. It is unlikely that his departure made an impression on the assembled
bankers, each of whom seemed solely preoccupied with his
own responsibilities. Durant, for one, wandered down to the
lobby, where he dispatched a cable to Lee, Higginson, reporting Kreuger's death, but ordering that no announcement
be made of it until an official announcement came through.
Lee, Higginson abided by this, though already, to the surprise
of members of the firm in New York, the Stock Exchange
had opened with a rush of directives from Europe to unload
Kreuger & Toll stock. Shortly after the opening 15,000
Kreuger & Toll certificates were dumped at $5, a down of
37½ from the Friday closing. The sales continued until noon
with a total of 165,000 shares sold, one quarter the total trading of the half-day. If nothing else, this volume of unexpected
sale lends credence to the persistent story of Kreuger's four
SELL telegrams.

In their efforts to keep Kreuger's suicide a secret, the
two Paris groups—Littorin and Miss Bökman constituting
one, the roomful of bankers the other—had a great degree of
co-operation from the gods of chance. March 12, 1932, was
the day of the burial of Aristide Briand, a man beloved by
half of France, hated by the other half. As a result all Paris
gendarmes had been called out on street duty in case of riots
as the cortege passed. Paris officialdom was equally disrupted.

Said a newspaper the next day, "There reigned an incredible chaos in the city, with the police entirely absorbed in the funeral."

Consequently, when the bankers at the Hotel Rhin decided that official pressure must be applied to hide their news, they found a harried Paris police chief only too eager to pass responsibility upward. "You will have to get permission from the Minister of the Interior," he told Rydbeck, who talked to him on the phone. A call was immediately placed to the Minister, to whom Rydbeck pictured world financial dissolution if the Match King's death were to become news in New York before noon. The Minister seemed inclined to agree with this, but what finally carried weight was that Kreuger, because of the loan of $75 million to France in 1927, had the Grand Cross of the Legion of Honor. By French logic, this made him a fine fellow, and the Minister was only too willing to pay last respects to such a great man by covering up his death for a few hours.

Littorin and Miss Bökman, working at a gendarme-on-the-beat level had more varied experiences.

Back at the Kreuger apartment, Littorin left Miss Bökman to take care of Jeanette while he and the concierge's husband set out for a police station. Because of the Briand funeral, the nearest one—at Grand Palais—was shut down. The two men then walked to the Rue Faubourg St. Honore station, where an indifferent *flic* glanced up from official reports to listen to their story. He seemed never to have heard of Ivar Kreuger, or to be particularly concerned about suicides. "You return to the apartment," he said. "We'll be over in fifteen minutes."

Littorin went back. Leaving his companion downstairs, with orders to keep silent, he took the lift up to the apartment, where he placed a call to Stockholm. From this he learned Rydbeck had already phoned from the Rhin, that the Swedish Ministry of Finance and the Riksbank had already been alerted to the sad news, and that a search was on for members of the Kreuger family. So far only a brother-in-law had been located.

Littorin then stepped into the bedroom for a last communion with the body of his friend. When he came out, the gendarmes had arrived, accompanied by a police surgeon named Dr. Grille. The doctor raised all the shades, examined the body and pronounced it dead, at the same time expressing surprise that the region of the neck was still warm. From this and other indications he placed the moment of death at approximately 11 A.M. Kreuger's personal physician, Dr. Bove, who had been summoned from the American Hospital by Karen Bökman, also arrived, to find "the financier stretched out on his bed, fully dressed. His cheeks were a little pastier than usual; his sensuous lips a little thinner than when I had seen him last. I decided that he had died without pain."

Littorin, meanwhile, was endeavoring to impress on the collected police the importance of keeping the suicide a secret. Like the Minister of the Interior, the gendarmes were unimpressed until the Legion of Honor was mentioned. Then one put in a call to the Prefecture, where he received the orders handed down by the Minister. Immediately, a guard was placed downstairs with orders to allow entry to no one except police experts who would determine whether the death was truly a suicide. All of which activity took up so much time that not until 5 P.M. did Kreuger's death become known around Paris, and then it was a rumor so tiny that the Swedish Consul did not hear it. At 6 P.M. this functionary was enjoying a leisurely dinner at home when a newspaper phoned him for comment. He rushed to Kreuger's apartment, where he found the way barred by a stout gendarme. "But I am the Swedish Consul," he protested.

"No one enters," the gendarme growled.

From around the corner, the Consul phoned the apartment, to be informed curtly that no one could view the body or receive confirmation of suicide rumors. "Call again tomorrow," he was told. Again starting to protest, he found himself talking into a dead wire.

Kreuger's suicide made banner headlines all over the world. In London, the *Times* wrote editorially, "The man who was driven on Saturday to this last act was no common adventurer caught up and cornered at last by the self-defeating ingenuity of his devices. Mr. Kreuger seems to have had no weakness of the kind that brings weaker timber to wreck." The *New Statesman* put it more simply, "He was a very Puritan of finance." Around the world headlines and editorials saluted his genius so that, as *Current History* wrote a month later, "The suicide evoked abundant support of the theory that he was one of the world's most influential men. Less concern would have attended the passing of a half-dozen kings or princes."

But in Paris the diligent—or perhaps inept—police activity caused rumors to sweep the city. The muddled situation even gave the London *Times* reason to devote a second editorial to Kreuger, this one stating "The circumstances of Kreuger's death, and especially of the subsequent developments, are certainly not very clear and have created an atmosphere of suspicion."

What suspicion? Over-all, it meant rumors that a different dead body had been placed on Kreuger's bed and that the

Match King, face hidden by a muffler, had dashed across the Victor Emmanuel pavement to leap into a limousine that stood waiting with drawn shades. This had sped him on his first lap into hiding. Several Parisians not occupied with Briand's funeral even claimed to have seen the Match King make this sidewalk dash—or so it was whispered. But they never stepped forward to be identified by police.

More tangible were the curious delays insisted on by the police. After withholding news of the suicide for five hours, police retained the strict guard on the apartment, allowing only Littorin and Bernard Lane, an American undertaker, to enter. Police also refused for three days to certify the death as suicide, claiming this was done in deference to Kreuger's stricken family. The activities of this same family provide another riddle. It was expected that Kreuger's brothers and sisters would immediately fly to Paris. Yet none traveled the short distance from Stockholm until the following Tuesday, four days after the death. Then two sisters arrived. Or did they? It is still believed in some quarters that none of Kreuger's family ever came to Paris which, if true, might lend credence to the story of another body being substituted for the Match King's. Finally, a London cigar-maker literally ignited all the rumors by reporting that a large order of Kreuger's favorite kind of cigar had been received from Sumatra. To the suspicious, this made eminent sense. Kreuger had holdings in Sumatra, and had been there. If he wished to flee, why not pick this familiar, far-off spot . . . ?

At last *Paris Soir* could disregard the stories no longer and delegated experienced reporters to interview everyone who had viewed the body. Those interrogated were M. Maugaud, the Prefect of Police; Dr. Grille, the police surgeon; the Swedish Consul, who had finally been allowed in the apart-

ment; Littorin, Miss Bökman, Jeanette Barrault, numerous
policemen, and finally the concierge and her husband. All
stated that without equivocation the body on the bed was
Kreuger's. Then before doubters could be silenced by this
overwhelming testimony, the American undertaker did something to start new rumors. When the body was finally carried from the Victor Emmanuel apartment, it was taken to
the embalmer's where Lane placed it in a zinc-lined coffin
with a covered top. In the top a small glass aperture left only
Kreuger's face visible. Dead bodies were almost never hidden
this way in Sweden—or anywhere else. So now the rumors
claimed that there was no body in Kreuger's coffin. Only a
wax face modeled to look like his.

As a final contribution to their part of the mystification,
Paris authorities refused to release the body for a full week.
It was Saturday the nineteenth before the coffin was carried
to the Gare du Nord and lifted to a private, flower-filled car.
From there it rode to Hamburg where the funeral car was
coupled to the Stockholm Express. Only on Sunday, March
twentieth, did Kreuger's body finally reach the city that was
his home.

Sorrowing crowds lined the sidewalks as the hearse drove
slowly to the Gustav Vasa Chapel. For now had come still
another of the Match King's many phases, that of Tragic
Insolvent. Following the lead of those English newspapers
which had labeled him the "very Puritan of finance," and
"the man who seemed to have no weakness of the kind that
brings weaker timber to wreck," the world was mourning
Kreuger as an unfortunate figure, caught in a tragic web
that had forced him to expand enterprises while world markets shrank. Naturally, nowhere was this belief more deep-
rooted than in Sweden. To each Swede, the death of the

great Kreuger who had carried their country to world financial eminence was a personal blow, summed up by one Stockholm newspaper which said:

> Had Herr Kreuger taken the country into his confidence
> and admitted his failure to obtain fresh working capital
> and revealed that the constant selling of his stocks was
> proving too much for him to stand, his countrymen
> would have jumped to his assistance.

So it was in real sorrow that Swedes gathered along the
sidewalks to pay last respects to their Match King. The populace was asked by the Kreuger family not to send flowers
to the crematorium chapel, yet every Swedish citizen knew
of Kreuger's love of simple flowers and shortly the chapel was
crammed with azaleas, apple blossoms, roses, and the Match
King's favorite, lilies of the valley. To these were added
ornate floral wreaths from business associates the world over
—one of the largest, ironically, coming from International
Telephone & Telegraph. But before the actual funeral came
one more act which added fuel to mysteries in Kreuger's end.
The family commissioned a photographer to take a last picture of the Match King's face as he lay in the coffin. The
photographer snapped his picture without using the magnesium flash customary at that time. Those eager to find
suspicious circumstances found another here. No flash could
be used, they said, because it would have melted—through
the open glass of the aperture—the wax of the dummy face
in the coffin. The photographer replied that no flash had
been necessary because there was enough light in the chapel.
But the whispers of a wax dummy persisted.

On Tuesday, March twenty-second, Kreuger's family,
together with Littorin, Rydbeck, Durant, and other close business associates, gathered for the funeral in the Gustav Vasa

Chapel. The coffin was covered with lilies of the valley, and over it the minister spoke the 90th Psalm. *"Of him and his work which has covered the world,"* he said, *"we shall not speak here. Quiet and unassuming has been his path in life, so also shall be his last journey."*

Then the body was lifted to the adjacent crematorium, placed in a cylinder, and pushed into the incineration fires. Though they came out no more than a handful of ashes, the remains were put back in the man-sized coffin, driven to the cemetery, and solemnly lowered into the ground.

Thus the world said farewell to the body of the Match King.

Chapter | **22**

How He Duped Mankind

But if Kreuger's mortal remains had disappeared in the earth, his spirit had not. Seldom, if ever, has a ghost walked as tangibly as that of the Match King.

At the Cabinet Meeting hastily called by Crown Prince Gustavus Adolphus, both His Highness and most Cabinet members received another shock. After assimilating the news of the Match King's death, they were told by the Minister of Finance that for two weeks—since the final week of February—there had been in existence a detailed plan for an emergency moratorium in case of trouble for the Kreuger companies. For, the Minister of Finance went on, the uncertain condition of Kreuger & Toll had been known to him and a handful of others for some time. Steps had accordingly been taken, and Kreuger and his companies had been kept under scrutiny. One result was that the man who paced through the night in the Avenue Victor Emmanuel had not been as lonely as he thought. He was being watched.

So at midnight, March twelfth, a moratorium was passed by which all payments by Kreuger & Toll, Swedish Match, and other Kreuger companies, were in Sweden held in abeyance for a month. Said *Current History* later: "Believing the suicide would precipitate a rush of creditors on Swedish companies, the government obtained authority to grant a moratorium on private payments for thirty days. It was hoped that by preventing dealings in Kreuger & Toll and Swedish Match issues for this period that the first feelings of panic could be controlled. The Swedish Stock Exchange would be closed until circumstances permitted, but banking would continue."

Next morning the Crown Prince—and a few hours later his father, the King—appealed over the radio to all citizens of Sweden to remain calm in their hour of crisis. The millions listening to him, though they may have sorrowed, did not panic. On Monday the kroner fell slightly, but on the surface the entire nation continued calm in the face of the Match King's death.

By emergency order, staffs of Kreuger & Toll and Swedish Match were on Sunday summoned from their homes to work day and night preparing statements of the company positions for the government. The government accountants who were studying Kreuger & Toll also redoubled their activity. In charge of all this was placed Ernest Lyberg, a former Minister of Finance, and in a few days Lyberg intimated that a moratorium of more than a month might be needed. "Preliminary results seem to indicate that the position of Kreuger & Toll is not strong," he told the press. Then he conferred privately with King and Cabinet. As a result the Stockholm police were called in and an impartial committee of financiers and industrialists appointed to investigate Kreuger & Toll. The Committee immediately called in more accountants from the London office of Price, Waterhouse.

But to the man in the street all this activity was directed at the affairs of Kreuger the Insolvent. It was still believed that, in the words of *The New York Times*, "Creditors had been closing in on him and he had not been successful in negotiations in the United States. He went to Paris in the hope of getting money there. He evidently failed and his tragic suicide seemed the only way out."

Yet there were many who in the days after Kreuger's

death felt there was more, and following the funeral an electric air of expectancy seemed to fill Stockholm. Many of the important men who attended the funeral stayed on at the Grand Hotel, the only international-type hotel in Stockholm. It was as if some intuition of coming disaster impelled them to remain, and from all over Europe other financiers who had no direct connection with the Match King traveled to Stockholm, as if they too, had been drawn by a knowledge of pending catastrophe.

This created a strange atmosphere in the usually placid city. "Stockholm is tense and feverish," an English correspondent wired home. "The Grand Hotel is full to the bursting with observers." Among those feeling the pull to Stockholm was the French journalist, Jules Sauerwein, who, to *The New York Times*, sent a story which was front-paged under the headline, "FINANCIERS FLOCK TO KREUGER CITADEL —Stockholm Growing Tense as Auditors, Police, Government Push Inquiries." Still another correspondent summed up by writing, "The whole atmosphere is fantastic, as well as tragic."

The city seethed with rumors. Through the Grand Hotel flew inside stories of what the Price, Waterhouse accountants were finding, of what the august Investigating Committee was turning up. Both worked behind closed doors in the Match Palace, where they found plenty to do. Not only were there the hundreds and hundreds of Kreuger & Toll books, but on the day after the Match King's death police had seized 150 sacks of waste paper. In them were found no less than 1900 personal Kreuger telegrams. Had his suicide come a few days later this mass of paper would have been burned. Now it was carried in, load by load, to be studied by the committee of financiers.

Only one light moment was contributed—by the curve-some Ingeborg Eberth. Kreuger's will had been found, its most unusual bequest being $125,000 in Kreuger & Toll stock to Ingeborg, "My friend of seventeen years." Some Stockholmers knew of Ingeborg's existence, but the foreign journalists did not. They tore pell-mell to interview her, finding her living on the top floor of Kreuger's Villagatan flat. It was, thought one reporter, ". . . a luxurious, though somewhat overfurnished apartment, with deep chairs, dark silk hangings and softly shaded lamps." Ingeborg herself he found "full of charm, with smiling but sometimes enigmatic eyes."

"No one knows more about Ivar than I do," she stated promptly. But when asked if she had been the Woman in His Life, she turned cautious. "If I answer *Yes* to that, it will be telegraphed all over the world," she said. "I will only say he left me the most money."

She labeled Kreuger "a fine and noble personality," and unhesitatingly placed herself among those who doubted his actual death. The enigmatic eyes must have flashed fire as she demanded, "Why was Ivar's coffin not opened in Stockholm? What was all that talk about a glass window in the coffin? One does not do such things here. And how about the conflicting stories of the body being embalmed? Why did his brother and sister, Torsten and Greta, announce they were going to Paris and not go?"

But now, with new rumors sweeping Stockholm and the Grand Hotel, questions about Kreuger's death were out of date. Gradually Sweden and the world seemed to be preparing for another blow: financial insolvency. This came on March twenty-sixth when the Investigating Committee released figures showing that most shares of Kreuger & Toll— including Ingeborg's $125,000 worth—were almost worthless because of insufficient funds and heavy indebtedness. The Committee recommended that the Government put 40 million kroner ($7,200,000) at the disposal of Swedish banks which might be further shaken by the new announcement.

But again official statements lagged far behind the unofficial. In the Grand Hotel and elsewhere speculation no longer centered on Kreuger & Toll insolvency. The financiers who had remained after the funeral were now convinced that "other factors" entered the over-all pictures. "Today's papers here stated it had been learned that Kreuger used enormous sums in bribery and was himself a victim of blackmail," said a dispatch from Stockholm to *The New York Times*. It was said that a fictitious item of $140 million had been entered twice in company books, by the Match King himself; that in Kreuger's desk had been found dozens of rubber stamps duplicating important signatures that had come his way on legitimate letters; and that one of the Price, Waterhouse accountants, laboring behind the Match King's own desk, was startled by the pealing of a telephone. Lifting it, he got only silence at the other end. He put it down, moved closer to the desk, and again it rang. He applied himself to the mystery, to find the dummy phone. In New York, where police had been asked to examine Kreuger's penthouse for evidence of blackmail, another dummy phone was found.

Rumors of "other factors" even affected a meeting of the World Bank Board, in Basle, Switzerland, the nerve-center of banking. Ivar Rooth, governor of the Bank of Sweden, was the only Board member not present. "He is detained by the stories that have caused amazement to be felt by these bankers, all of whom knew Mr. Kreuger personally. These men of finance, probably the best judges of character in the world, have always had absolute confidence in the honesty of the Swedish capitalist."

Behind the closed portals of the Match Palace, police, accountants and Investigating Committee were slowly drawing to a conclusion. It was so terrible, so staggering, so vast that one member of the Committee could not keep it to himself. Buttonholing Jules Sauerwein, he led the journalist to a secluded corner of the Grand Hotel lobby, where he burst out:

We are going from one surprise to another. The more definite our investigation becomes, the stranger the personality of Kreuger grows. We all knew him personally, yet we are only discovering him now.

He was a man who actually received more than $1 billion, of which half came from America. He loaned European governments sums which reached, so far as we can now figure, $400 million, of which perhaps a fifth was returned to him. Therefore one can sum up the activities of Kreuger in recent years by saying that he transferred from the United States to Europe $500 million, to which must be added large sums from Swedish, English, French, Dutch, German, and Swiss savings. He saved several countries from a bankruptcy panic, meanwhile building up two essentially healthy industries —those of matches and telephones.

What we keep asking ourselves now is why a man, in controlling these enormous sums, could not reign over his business without recourse to criminal practice?

In the first place, the Depression caused nations owing money to him to default. Second, we now see that Kreuger's genius unbalanced his mind. Power went to his head. In olden days he would have become a great conqueror. In our time he became a giant among businessmen without faith or scruple, playing like a conjurer with the prestige and power he had acquired; diverting himself with his own preposterous combinations, with his madness for diversity.

At the height of his power, when he controlled 260 factories with 75,000 employees, when sovereigns and government officials flattered him, he must have thrown himself lightheartedly into the inextricable complications in which he seems to have lost his reason.

We have reconstructed his inner and outer life in

his last months. The climax was his effort to hoax the Americans. It proved his Waterloo.

From that moment the mainsprings were broken. This man, who had done such really great things, was a walking corpse. On the day after his arrival in Paris, when he committed suicide, he simply completed with a tragic gesture what destiny had already accomplished.

With such criminality known in the Grand Hotel, the world could not long be kept in ignorance of the Match King's financial legerdemain. On April sixth, less than a month after his death, *The New York Times* carried the shocking headline "FIND KREUGER BOOKS ARE GROSSLY WRONG—Some Assets False—Sensation in Stockholm."

What the story went on to describe was a highly dramatic moment just before midnight on April fourth. As the Second Chamber of the Riksdag debated the question of further aid for Kreuger's Skandinavska Credit Bank, the Chairman of the Investigating Committee advanced down the aisle, in his hand the first report of the Price, Waterhouse accountants. On the rostrum, he asked permission to read the report. It was granted, and after the preliminary financial paragraphs, he reached its full impact:

Although the investigation is still but in its preliminary stages, the accountants nevertheless are able to state that in their opinion it is beyond doubt that the balance sheet of Kreuger & Toll of December 31, 1930, as well as the consolidated balance sheets accompanying it, while being in agreement with the balances appearing in the books, nevertheless grossly misrepresent the true financial position of the company.

Under the personal direction of the late Mr. Kreuger, entries were made in the books, which on the one hand eliminated substantial balances showed to be owing to the parent company by him and by subsidiary companies, and on the other hand entirely eliminated liabilities to other subsidiaries purporting to represent assets of substantial sums.

In some instances there is reason to believe that the assets so set up in the books were either greatly in excess of the items they purported to represent, entirely fictitious, or a duplication of amounts belonging or appearing on the books of the associated companies.

Journalists swarmed to the Riksdag on hearing that the report was being read. They reported later that many deputies broke into tears on getting this first confirmation of rumors of Kreuger's criminality. "Now every vestige of the halo around the head of Ivar Kreuger has disappeared," one delegate rose to state bitterly. "He was a cool defrauder who for many years wore the mark of criminal."

Others rose to denounce and a few tried to excuse. Finally Arthur Endberg, editor of *Soziel Demukraten* and a deputy also, got the floor. "We now know that the Kreuger company broke down not because of ill luck or bad conditions, but because of dishonesty," he said quietly. "The report is bound to hurt our reputation abroad. The only way we can retrieve it is by complete honesty. No matter what is yet to be revealed, we cannot allow anyone to have the impression that we are going to hide anything."

To its everlasting credit as a nation, this is exactly what Sweden proceeded to do. . . .

On April fifteenth, acting on orders of the Commission, police arrested Wendler, the accountant who had sat in on the Saturday afternoon conference with Kreuger in Paris. He was accused of failing to detect false entries in the books of Garanta and Ericsson.

A few hours later more arrests were made. They were Karl Lange who, in addition to being in charge of the mys-

terious Garanta, had also become a director of the Gillet
Hotel Company of Amsterdam; Sven Huldt, a director of
the Netherlandska Bank; and Victor Hahn, an ex-postal clerk
who had somehow attracted Kreuger's attention. It was of
these men that a baffled member of the Commission now
said: "Kreuger seems to have created a new company for
every transaction, and to have built up a system so hopelessly
interlocked that he alone could understand it. In addition,
he had a whole retinue of doubtful personages who worked
for him both in Sweden and abroad. He never saw them in
the office, and they were unknown to his regular business associates."

Lange, Huldt, and Hahn were accused of manipulating
balance sheets and/or disregarding falsification of such sheets.
The prosecutor whose job it became to try them and others
who might be arrested said: "This talk about everyone trusting Kreuger blindly is a myth. Investigations early revealed
that Kreuger was not a clever businessman. So far as possible,
he faked and swindled. Investigation also shows that many
persons depended on him, relying not on his business ability,
but on his capacity to dupe mankind."

Such sentiments were now popular. For as new revelations burst nearly every day, the Swedish people, after idoliz-
ing Kreuger for twenty-five years as a man who could do no
wrong, let the cruelty of his deception swing them far to the
other extreme. Newspaper editorials castigated him as a man
who "began to bluff with vast but fictitious profits to maintain the pretense that he was a great financial genius. Yet
it is not as a financier, but as a criminal, that he must be distinguished from other people." The life of the entire Swedish
middle class was profoundly convulsed by shock of the let-
down, and hatred of Kreuger even developed a moral and
social aspect. Suicides in the weeks after his death rose fright-

eningly. An even more peculiar manifestation of the emotional hurt from the Kreuger case was that on April first, thousands of tenants refused to pay rent to their landlords. In some cases, they were affected by loss of Kreuger dividends, but newspapers reasoned that the majority acted because, having been deeply hurt themselves, they had to hurt someone else.

Came mid-April, and two more blows to the reeling country. On the twentieth word came from New York that International Match had gone into bankruptcy, owing $90 million. "Our business is in a chaotic state as a result of the Kreuger suicide," explained Frederic W. Allen, the Lee, Higginson president. It was also pointed out that no member of the Lee, Higginson firm had disposed of personal stock, though partners and their families owned it to the extent of $8 million. Despite this, the average Swede thought America had let them down lamentably in the International Match bankruptcy. The Investigating Committee, still laboring to save Swedish Match and Ericsson Telephone, took a more understanding view. "The American company was so heavily weighted with Kreuger debentures that survival was impossible," its members said.

No sooner was this shock assimilated than another came along—by far the worst of all. Existence of the Italian Bonds, which up to now had only been hinted, was fully admitted and authorities told how Kreuger had forged them. This investigation seemed to indicate that Captain Wickman had not printed up the bonds which were forged. Instead, Kreuger had carried the paper, plates and type provided by Wickman to a small Stockholm printing shop. There the printer, delighted at getting business from so awesome a figure, unhesitatingly agreed to pull fifty proofs of the pseudo Italian Bonds. Kreuger then went home to enjoy a home-cooked meal with Ingeborg Eberth. While she added last minute touches in the kitchen, he sat idly tinkling the piano, seemingly without a care in the world.

A few days later, he again dropped into the printing shop, where with a show of vast nonchalance he made revisions in the fifty proofs. Several days later, he picked up the final Bonds and took them to his apartment.

At the revelation that Kreuger had also forged, Sweden was truly aghast. "One of the greatest forgeries in history," the papers called it, following through on the campaign of brutal honesty. "This shatters the last remnants of romance around the great industrialist."

But there were warnings of worse to come. Said the *Svenska Morgenbladet,* which was in a special position to know since its highly respected editor had been found on Kreuger's private payroll: "This is only the beginning. The months to come will be among the most nerve-wracking ever experienced in Sweden."

23

"The Bankrupt"

The activities of Stockholm police, the Investigating Committee, and Price, Waterhouse auditors continued into the summer of 1932. As they did, the results of their labor became to Sweden less nerve-wracking than an awful realization that deficits in Kreuger companies were rising to a sum larger than the Swedish national debt. Auditors poring over Kreuger & Toll books reported that $237,582,000 seemed to be missing from Kreuger & Toll alone. In Kreuger's personal accounts they found debts and liabilities amounting to another $263,796,000. The Match King's only clear assets seemed to be $100,000 in personal property. This included 178 Rembrandt etchings worth $2,685, and a sumptuous Rolls Royce limousine valued at $3,580.

Then, to breathe vivid life into such astronomical, national-debt figures, came the trials of Huldt, Hennig, Holm —and, lastly, of Torsten Kreuger who, in midsummer, was arrested and charged with falsification of books and balance sheets. From testimony at these trials the world obtained its first idea about how the Match King had operated in his mighty swindles. The most graphic illustration came from the lips of Sigurd Hennig, who had been Kreuger's chief accountant. From the witness stand he told of drawing up the 1930 Kreuger & Toll balance sheet. When completed, this document showed Kreuger personally owing—that is, removing from Kreuger & Toll coffers—the sum of 155,635,345 kroner. Hennig carried it to Kreuger, who complained that his 155 million indebtedness was far too large an amount to remain on the books. He urged Hennig to use all possible ingenuity in crediting the amount to as many Kreuger & Toll subsidiaries as possible. Hennig retired to labor, but the best he could do was reduce the debt to 92,250,319 kroner. Whereupon Kreuger took the job over himself and, using his fabulous skill, caused his indebtedness of 155 million kroner to disappear from the books completely.

He did this largely by utilizing a unique accounting device which, not unnaturally, had aroused early suspicion in the minds of Price, Waterhouse accountants. These experts had found that the books of nearly every Kreuger company contained what was labeled a "Suspens Account"—which, it transpired, was Kreuger's spelling of the English word "suspense." Under the circumstances it was the perfect word, for the millions listed under the various Suspens Account headings had been used for high-stake gambling, the most suspenseful of human activities. Kreuger had conceived the name Suspens Account because some of his great gambles in stock-market speculation excitingly paid off, while others did not. An added beauty of the Suspens Accounts was that the millions listed therein were accountable to no one. If questioned, Kreuger could always shrug and declare he had lost the money in stock-market speculation. So he now made his 155 million kroner indebtedness to disappear by putting 795,000 kroner into a "Spanish Suspens Account," 1,772,305 under "Serius Aktie Suspens Account," and so on, until it was gone.

No doubt in an effort to win sympathy, Huldt, Hennig and Holm, the first Kreuger subordinates brought to trial, claimed to have been dupes of the Match King who had still made efforts to deter him from his mad course. Thus Hennig, from the witness stand, swore that in March, 1931, he had questioned Kreuger about the millions in International Match Corporation dollars which had been snatched away from International's subsidiary, Continental Investment. "I am not the only one surprised at the way Continental assets are deposited," he claimed to have told Kreuger. "Holm and Wendler are surprised, too."

At this, he testified, the Match King flushed red and began to pace the floor angrily. Finally, he stopped directly in front of his chief accountant. "Is this a conspiracy against me?" he shouted. "Have you and Holm and Wendler joined in a conspiracy?"

Hennig's courage had failed him. "Oh, no, I.K.," he answered placatingly. "There is no conspiracy. We want to help you in every way. All we want is to keep you from making any double entries in balancing the books."

Such testimony apparently won sympathy for the three men. Hennig was acquitted altogether, while Huldt was sentenced to a year in prison and Holm was given six months. But Torsten Kreuger, who had been quietly managing several of his brother's enterprises, did not fare so well. He was found guilty and quickly sentenced to three and a half years at hard labor. So the unhappy Kreuger family was again disgraced, and now the dead Match King's eighty-year-old father returned with Fru Kreuger to Kalmar, where in shock and sorrow they lived out their lives.

Still another Swede who suffered greatly from Kreuger's death was the Prime Minister, Ekman.

Following his sensible words in late February, when he advised the Riksbank not to advance the desperate Kreuger a final $2 million, Ekman should have been the strongest man in Sweden when the true nature of the Match King was divulged. He was not. Following the Kreuger revelations of

April and May, whispers began circulating through Stockholm alleging that the Prime Minister had played a two-faced role in opposing the $2 million loan. Ekman could, the rumors charged, take his strong stand against the loan because he knew the Riksbank would extend it anyway. Further, the accusing stories said, the Prime Minister had given private support to the loan, while in public opposing it.

Most of the basis for these rumors came from the fact that in the past Ekman's People's Party was believed to have accepted campaign contributions from the Match King. In mid-May, Ekman stepped forward to admit this, saying that in his Party's name he had taken $10,000 from Kreuger in September, 1931. But, he went on, he had received no other contributions from Kreuger, and certainly had accepted none immediately before the Riksbank loan, as the whispers were now claiming.

This was enough to convince Sweden, and suspicion of Ekman died away. Then, in July, Swedish authorities received a letter from New York. It was from Alexis Aminoff, the young ex-embassy official who had passed the night of Guignol horror in Kreuger's Park Avenue penthouse. Aminoff now stated that at "about the end of January" he had, at Kreuger's order, purchased a banker's check for $10,000. He carried this to Kreuger who had placed it in an envelope addressed to Prime Minister Ekman. The check, Aminoff added, had been payable "to bearer" at the Handelsbank in Stockholm.

Investigators hurried to the Handelsbank, where they discovered that such a check had been cashed on February thirteenth, ten days before the Riksbank credit had been extended to Kreuger. Informed of this, Ekman again denied having received the money. Faced with the canceled check, he branded the endorsement a forgery.

After which, the Prime Minister of Sweden returned home to spend a night with his conscience. In the morning, he summoned the officials who had interrogated him the day before. "I lied to you yesterday," he said, in effect. The reason he advanced for the enormous untruth was, "I gave my word to Herr Kreuger to keep the matter a secret." This failed to find sympathy with the Swedish Cabinet and on August sixth that body convened to accept Ekman's resignation, which was duly proffered. Swedish newspapers opined that the Prime Minister's departure was necessary not so much because he had accepted the money as because he had told a lie.

Thus the suicide of the Match King had toppled the Prime Minister of his native land—but if Sweden was having its quota of shocks following Kreuger's death, so, to a somewhat lesser degree, was the United States.

In America, the scene for the revelations about Kreuger had been set by publication in the April second *Saturday Evening Post* of the Isaac Marcosson interview with the Match King. This had been on the presses on the day Kreuger killed himself, and as a consequence, immediately became the stuff editors' nightmares are made of. On the Monday after Kreuger's death, it was found that 1.5 million copies of the magazine had already been shipped to Europe and western United States. Still, a million remained unprinted and the presses were dramatically stopped while the subtitle "An Interview with Ivar Kreuger" was changed to "A Last Talk with Ivar Kreuger." New plates were also made which changed all references to Kreuger to the past tense.

On the day the magazine went on sale, Kreuger had been buried and for the most part was still mourned by the world as a martyr. But in that week the whispers began to circulate and, recalls Marcosson:

The Kreuger interview was loaded with peculiar incitement for the chronic letter-writers. While many congratulated [*The Saturday Evening Post*] upon an exceptionally timely journalistic stroke the vast majority, particularly after the scandal lifted its ugly head, bitterly upbraided us for giving space to a swindler. The strongest indictment came from holders of Kreuger & Toll securities. It was not until the avalanche of protests that we realized how wide-spread had been the faith and investment in Kreuger. The indignant readers could not understand that when the article was written Kreuger was still the match monarch and the friend of kings, premiers, finance ministers, and the financially great of the earth, all of whom then reposed the utmost confidence in him. So voluminous became the mail protests that it became necessary to print a form letter for replies. This letter stated that no reference was made in the article to any Kreuger securities and therefore embodied no sponsorship of them, and that Kreuger's eminent position as international industrialist and financier qualified him as authoritative spokesman. He had deceived everybody, friend, banker, investor, associate, and interviewer alike.

Against this background, on April thirteenth, the International Match Corporation was declared in bankruptcy. But hearings before the Referee in Bankruptcy were delayed until Donald Durant returned to New York. Durant had gone to Stockholm for Kreuger's funeral and remained to represent International Match and Lee, Higginson, in Stockholm.

Finally, on May second, with the Irving Trust Company acting as Receiver, the hearings opened and what had promised to be routine sessions promptly became "the scene of much confusion and turmoil." One reason for this was that Lee, Higginson still considered itself as representing American investors in Kreuger securities. However, many of the investors felt that the Wall Street firm had failed in its duty

by sponsoring Kreuger securities in the first place. These dis-
gruntled holders of Kreuger stocks formed two angry groups
who retained such distinguished counsel as Samuel Unter-
meyer and Bainbridge Colby to fight for their rights.

On the first day of public hearings recriminations flew
back and forth as the groups struggled for control. But on the
second day the in-fighting ceased while everyone in the court-
room listened in amazement to testimony which for the first
time brought out how little International Match directors
knew about Kreuger's activities. Donald Durant, first to be
interrogated, immediately showed this lack of knowledge
when James N. Rosenberg, attorney for the Irving Trust,
asked him:

Q. Did you or your firm receive a confidential memorandum from Mr. Kreuger personally some time in
   the fall of 1931 as to the whole cash situation?
A. I think it was in the summer. It may have been the
   fall.

Q. I show you what purports to be that confidential
   memorandum and I ask you, do you recognize it?
A. I do.

Q. I refer to page two of that memorandum in which
   Mr. Kreuger writes "The total of $52,685,788 ad-
   vanced for investment in match concessions shown
   in the December 31, 1930 consolidated balance sheet
   of International Match Corporation comprises investments in the match industries of the following
   countries: Poland, $17,538,750." Did it strike you
   that that was a proper investment in a country like
   Poland in one business, of a match concession?
A. Yes.

Q. Then the next item was "X country, $28,979,577."
   Did you know what X meant?

A. We were told in confidence what X meant; it was one of his secret monopolies.

Q. When were you told that?
A. I would have to refresh my memory on that; I don't recall when the contract was made.

Q. Well, it says here that in X, on page 2, "An agreement was entered into between the corporation and the Government on December 16, 1927." Now, you were told in confidence what X country was, is that right?
A. Yes, sir.

Q. And that was an investment of $28,979,577?
A. Yes, sir.

Q. Did any paper come to this country to substantiate the claim that X country investment was for the previous amount?
A. Paper? Statement by Mr. Kreuger?

Q. You have a statement about X country; did you have anything more other than his verbal statement as to what X country was?
A. I don't recall that we did.

Q. Was there ever any piece of paper sent to America, so far as you know, to demonstrate or prove to anyone in America what X—$28,000,000 amounted to?
A. I would have to look that up.

Durant was followed to the stand by an uncomfortable succession of Lee, Higginson partners and International Match directors. Frederic W. Allen, president of Lee, Higginson, embellished Durant's picture of the blind faith the partners had in Kreuger's word; Ben Tomlinson testified to the ignorance of International Match executives in such matters as Garanta and Continental, and told of the bolstering of the Vulcan Match books; George Murnane and Alexis Aminoff described Kreuger's physical breakdown; a representative of Percy Rockefeller testified that Rockefeller personally owned 25,000 shares of Kreuger stocks, and told some details of the financier's visit with Kreuger in Stockholm. It all arrived at a fitting climax with evidence that Kreuger's hysterical actions during his breakdown had failed to shake the faith of his American sponsors. The extent of this abiding faith was brought out in the testimony of Frederic W. Allen, who was asked by Rosenberg:

Q. Am I to understand that Kreuger's illness and his general behavior during December and January in New York were not such as to give you or your partners, or your co-directors in International Match, any alarm as to the financial condition of International Match or the other Kreuger & Troll enterprises?

A. It gave us no alarm as to the financial condition.

Q. Would it be fair to state that so far as you know, you and your partners, and your fellow directors, thought there was nothing rotten in Denmark, or shall we say Sweden?

A. Either. That is what we thought, that is what I thought.

Q. You thought everything was all right?

A. As far as the integrity of the man, as far as the problems he had ahead, there wasn't any doubt that the man was any different from the way we had always regarded him.

Q. Your confidence in the man had not been shaken, but how about your feeling as to the solvency or financial status of International Match and other Kreuger enterprises?

A. We had no question of solvency. I confronted noth-

ing in him beyond the normal problems of business. . . .

And Durant:

Q. Was there any worry on the part of your firm or any
of the other banking houses as to whether [his]
breakdown was symptomatic of possible trouble over
the situation?
A. I did not hear that expressed.

Q. And you felt no fear or suspicion?
A. Not the slightest.

Q. Lee, Higginson had just as much confidence in him
as they always did?
A. Yes.

Q. They were recommending the purchase of securities
of Kreuger & Toll and International Match?
A. That is correct.

Q. Right down to that time?
A. I believe right down to the end. I know when I left
with him for Paris we believed in him absolutely.

In vain did Lee, Higginson try to point out that Kreuger
stocks held by partners and their families amounted to $8
million, and that now these were as worthless as anyone's.
The eminently honorable Wall Street firm, which since 1848
had marketed the most gilt-edged in securities to the American public, had sustained a death blow and now announced
that it was disbanding, to reorganize as a comma-less Lee
Higginson for business on a more limited scale. In Wall
Street, the humbling of this super-reputable concern was as
great a shock as the resignation of Ekman had been in
Sweden.

At the conclusion of bankruptcy hearings, the Irving

Trust Company was confirmed as Trustee in Bankruptcy, and the Trustee immediately established an office in New York which, together with another in Stockholm, would begin the seemingly superhuman task of unraveling the mountainous open and hidden Kreuger dealings. From the activities of this American Trustee and the various Swedish investigations, it should be possible to furnish the final answer to what—in this case—is the $1,000,000,000 question: What did Kreuger do with the colossal amounts he swindled? But this question will probably never be answered, for with his mania to push forward on all financial fronts; to possess everything in sight; to inflate all his legitimate holdings to the utmost; and to keep all his enterprises prosperous in the eyes of the world—with all this, and more, Kreuger's operations achieved a shadow status as elusive as those of the swindlers who toss their millions away on wine, women and song. Final claims on Kreuger's estate totaled $1,168,000,000, and that might be said to be the total amount of his depredations. Of this, $98,000,000 represented losses to American banks and investors. Such sums are more than sufficient to give the Match King the dubious distinction of being far-and-away the greatest swindler who had ever lived. Now, with the tightening international banking and currency laws resulting from his depredations, swindles on such a world scale can no longer take place. The Match King's niche in infamy will forever be secure.

But the two beginning investigations did cast light on a final aspect of Kreuger. This was the frenzy with which he gambled in stocks immediately after the Wall Street Crash. Wildly indiscriminate buying at such a point in his career would seem to indicate that, no matter how optimistic he appeared to those around him, Kreuger knew his empire was doomed. For his pattern became that of the rabid gambler who lives on hope, believing that if he plunges ahead fast enough something, somewhere will turn up to provide the lucky break he needs.

In early 1930, Kreuger was operating secretly through at least twenty Wall Street brokerage houses. Says one account: "He had agents everywhere. Any friend, any employee, might be called on overnight to run some market operation for him in the friend's or employee's name. Sometimes he gave specific instructions. Sometimes he provided money and told the agent to use his own judgment. It was a thoroughly insane business, a madman on the loose with hundreds of millions."

He also speculated in Europe. Driven by his new mania, he not only loaned governments money in return for match monopoly, but bought the country's bonds on a speculative basis. He bought in French francs and German marks. He made a splendid gesture in buying the Young Plan Bonds, but he bought them at 85 and when he died they were 35. For reasons no investigator could ever fathom, he bought $2,224,640 of preferred stock in the Belgian National Railways. At the same time, he told friends he had, in anticipation of a market upswing, sunk $46 million in the stocks of American companies. When the American market continued to go down, he mentioned this potential coup no more. He also bought extravagantly on margin. From Stockholm, he opened an account with the Wall Street firm of H. Hentz & Company. Simultaneously, a European corporation named Mercator opened an account with Hentz. At the International Match hearings it developed that Kreuger and Mercator were the same. Executives of H. Hentz & Company looked at each other in amazement. They had no idea of this, nor did it seem to make any sense.

Ivar Kreuger, who had gone through so many phases in life, went into his final one with the appointment of the Irving Trust Company as Trustee in Bankruptcy for International Match. From then on in the legal papers concerning him, he was referred to simply as "the Bankrupt." It was in an effort to track down the assets left by the Bankrupt, nurture them back to life, and sell them for the slight benefit of stockholders, that the Trustees in Bankruptcy in New York and Stockholm began their labors. In this country the task which *The New York Times* called "the most complex and dramatic bankruptcy in financial history," was finally concluded in October 1945, thirteen years later.

During those years, the Bankrupt became all but a forgotten man to the world. In Sweden, his parents died, and Torsten Kreuger emerged from jail to re-establish himself by becoming the owner of three highly influential Swedish newspapers, among them *Aftonbladet*, published in Stockholm. He is alive today and until recently published the newspapers. Ingeborg Eberth, embittered by the fact that her $125,000 legacy turned out to be worthless, earned money by writing a series of spicy articles about her life with Kreuger. These were published in Sunday supplements the world over. Today, she, too, is in Stockholm. Some of Kreuger's Swedish enterprises also survived him. Swedish Match, always his most substantial holding, was, in five years, back on its feet, "booming with business, still autocrat of the match domain." The Boliden Mine also turned out to be sound, though never the overflowing pot of gold the optimistic Kreuger visualized.

In the United States almost nothing of Kreuger remains. Donald Durant went into business for himself as a broker. He survived Kreuger for ten years, then died of a heart attack suffered on a platform of the Third Avenue El. Many of the Wall Street brokers who knew and trusted Kreuger are still active on Wall Street—the Match King himself would today be seventy-seven—but as source material on Kreuger, these types are uniformly disappointing. Over the years they have rationalized their gullibility where he was concerned. Now anyone who asks an important Wall Streeter questions about Kreuger gets this invariable reply: "Oh, he fooled everyone else around here, but I caught on to him right away."

All factors considered, it is safe to say that the world has seldom labored so hard to forget a man as it has to obliterate the memory of Kreuger. There are good reasons for this. The people who lost money through Kreuger investments were only too anxious to put the unpleasant experience out of mind. The Swedish nation, for which he appeared to do so much but actually did so little, felt he had disgraced Sweden before the world. Finally, the world financiers among whom Kreuger moved as an equal were especially eager to forget him. For, like so many misguided men, Kreuger, in destroying himself, destroyed the thing he most loved. By killing himself, he brought to a sudden end the era of the Financier. He had perpetrated great frauds on the world public, but only because he had succeeded so easily in fooling the great men of money whose period in history his had been. Never again would such men be given the same respect.

So in the years since 1932, Kreuger has been almost forgotten. If nowhere else, he seems to have been remembered in literature—not so much as a man, as a type. A character patterned on Kreuger appears in one of Graham Greene's early novels, *England Made Me*. A similar Kreuger-type figure appears in the background of the classic mystery, *Trent's Last Case*, from which stems this biographer's interest in the Match King. A tycoon-industrialist played an equally shadowy figure in a mystery play-into-movie called *The Night of*

January 16. In both *Trent's Last Case* and *The Night of January 16*, the tycoon, though prominent in the book, is dead. Ironically, most people who hear the name of Ivar Kreuger today associate him with a type of death that was not his. In the recesses of public mind Kreuger jumped from a plane in flight over the English Channel. But this was not Ivar Kreuger. It was the Belgian financier, Lowenstein.

So, when the Match King *is* recalled, he is recalled wrongly—except, of course, in Sweden, which country knows the true facts of his life only too clearly. Or does it? As publisher of three influential newspapers, Torsten Kreuger over the years has waged a shrewd propaganda campaign to clear his brother's name. In this, he is assisted by many Swedes who, willingly or not, have swallowed his propaganda and when traveling eagerly inform those they meet that Ivar Kreuger was a well-meaning but unfortunate business genius brought to his doom only by the tragic economic times. Yet of all men alive today, perhaps those who know Kreuger best are those who for thirteen years conducted the bankruptcy for the Irving Trust. Asked if there can be any doubt of Kreuger's criminality, one of them unhesitatingly replied, "Absolutely none. He was a criminal."

But the spirit of Ivar Kreuger still walks in Sweden. As recently as November, 1955, a book called *Ivar Kreuger Mördad?* (*Was Ivar Kreuger Murdered?*) appeared in Stockholm, where newspapers saluted its appearance by headlines. Apparently sponsored by Torsten Kreuger (it contains a chapter by him which "proves" that the Italian Bonds were not forgeries) the book was written by two journalists named Börje Heed and Sven Stolpe. To Americans its lurid prose and reliance on inference rather than fact bring to mind the *Strange Death of President Harding*, by Gaston B. Means. The purpose of the book, naturally, is to show that Kreuger was murdered in his Paris flat, and as perpetrators of this dark deed the authors pick none other than the Morgan interests. The actual murder, they state, was done by a hired thug who so much resembled Krister Littorin that he could walk by the concierge without being challenged. This the man did, to kill Kreuger, and then calmly departed.

Aside from this premise and its excellent pictures of Kreuger in his coffin, the book is remarkable only for the tacit support it gives to stories of Kreuger's love life. One would expect that a book sponsored by a man whose aim is to clear his brother's name would soft-pedal the brother's amours. But this is not the case. As part of its proof of murder, the book indicates Kreuger's lightheartedness in Paris by claiming that on the night of March eleventh, he enjoyed a night-long rendezvous with a girl from Finland, "long and blonde and cool." In a further revelation of Kreuger's love life, the book implies that Kreuger was also winding up a love affair with his personal secretary, Karen Bökman, who, in the eyes of the world, was the last person ever to see him alive. According to *Was Kreuger Murdered?* Miss Bökman, instead of taking the Match King's dictation immediately before his death, took him to task because he "no longer had time for her." It was directly after her departure, according to the Heed-Stolpe re-creation, that the Littorin-like murderer appeared. At gun point he forced Kreuger to write the three suicide notes. Then he shot the Match King, arranged the body to look like suicide, and left.

But there are still some who do not need re-creations of murders to make them think favorably of Kreuger. His old friend, Anders Jordahl, now a dignified businessman in New York, continues to cherish the memory of Ivar Kreuger. To anyone, Jordahl says: "During my working years, meeting so many different people, I have never met anyone so extraor-

dinarily honest in his relations with other people, or so scrupulous when the interests of others were involved, as was
Ivar Kreuger. In my opinion, the only criticism that can possibly be leveled against Ivar is that he was too optimistic
when it concerned his own ability. . . . When one realizes
how close he came to achieving his goals, one must admit he
was almost right in his optimism."

The ever-cautious psychoanalyst, Dr. Paul Bjerre, sees
him in a somewhat more ambivalent light. He has written:

> I consider Kreuger a good man. It may be a paradox
> but he was good. . . . His life was a logical develop
> ment of certain qualities that can be traced back to his
> childhood. If I were to testify as an alienist I would say
> Kreuger was not insane and did not suffer from syphilis
> as a few have stated. His was a strange genius, and intel
> lectually he could be held responsible for his acts. His
> moral sense is the keynote of my findings, his moral
> outlook. His psychology, when fully understood, will
> make us look at the criminal side of Kreuger from a
> somewhat different viewpoint.

But perhaps the last word in summing up Ivar Kreuger
should be given to Oscar Rydbeck, who in retrospect appears
to be the most understanding and sensitive of all the men
Kreuger knew. Even before the full impact of the Kreuger
revelations had been felt by the world, a saddened Rydbeck
sat down to write:

> He thought he was superhuman and so superior to
> any other intelligence that he could scorn ordinary
> morality. Time and time again, he seemed to lose the
> spiritual faculty of recognizing the connections between
> things. He despised concrete facts and did not consider
> it necessary to regard the world situation as it existed.
> He was convinced that he could master everything by
> himself. . . .

Author's Note

The subject of Ivar Kreuger is still a sensitive one in certain circles, particularly on Wall Street and in Stockholm. Some of my most helpful sources provided information only on the understanding that they would not be mentioned by name.

In the eighteen months immediately after Kreuger's death in March 1932, five books in English were published about him. The two published in America were: *The Life and Death of Ivar Kreuger,* by William F. Stoneman (Bobbs Merrill), and *Kreuger's Million Dollar Bubble,* by Earl Sparling (Greenberg). Three were published in England: *Ivar Kreuger, Match King, Croesus, and Crook,* by Trevor Allen (Long); *The Case of Ivar Kreuger,* by Manfred George (Cape); and *The Financier, A Life of Ivar Kreuger,* by George Soloveytchik (Davies). To round out the books in English, Isaac F. Marcosson's autobiography, *Turbulent Years* (Dodd Mead, 1938), contains a long chapter on the Match King.

The definitive book in Swedish—in which language many others have been written—is still Dr. Poul Bjerre's *Kreuger* (Stockholm: Natur och Kultur, 1932). This important volume was very kindly called to my attention by Dr. Sven Stolpe, co-author of *Ivar Kreuger Mördad?* (Stockholm: Médans, 1955).

I have found valuable material in each of the above volumes, as well as in the files of *The New York Times* and other

You can never take what you love too seriously...

The Periodic Table Series

Periodically, we're all geeks about the things we love and the Periodic Table Series has been created to celebrate this universal fact.

Inspired by The Periodic Table of Chemical Elements*, our experts have applied scientific logic to an eclectic range of subjects that regularly baffle beginners and fire-up fans. The outcome of this experiment is the essential guide you hold in your hand.

Geeky? Absolutely.
Hugely satisfying? Categorically.

*The Periodic Table of Chemical Elements orders all the known matter that makes up our world, from hydrogen to helium, by chemical properties and behaviour to give scientists a handy overview of a rather complex subject.

Molly,
I love you so much
they haven't even invented the maths yet.

Contents

FULL-BODIED WHITE

LIGHTER WHITE

←

The Periodic Table of
WINE

FRUIT & SPICE

FLORAL

GREEN & MINERAL

1 G **C** Chardonnay: oaked			**17 G** **Fu** Furmint		**28 R** **Pp** Picpoul de Pinet	**34 R** **So** Soave	**40 G** **Mt** Müller-Thurgau
2 R **Pl** Pessac-Léognan	**7 G** **Gw** Gewürztraminer	**12 G** **Mu** Muscat	**18 R** **Vy** Vouvray	**23 G** **Mc** Muscadet	**29 G** **Fi** Fiano	**35 G** **Vd** Verdejo	**41 G** **Po** Pinot Grigio
3 G **Sé** Sémillon	**8 R** **Pg** Pinot Gris	**13 G** **Vi** Viognier	**19 G** **Ri** Riesling: Alsace or OZ	**24 R** **Cl** Chablis	**30 R** **Cb** Chenin Blanc	**36 G** **Vm** Vermentino	**42 G** **Al** Albariño
4 G **Mr** Marsanne	**9 G** **To** Torrontés	**14 G** **Sb** Sauvignon Blanc	**20 G** **Ar** Arneis	**25 R** **Sc** Sancerre	**31 G** **Vo** Verdelho	**37 R** **Rs** Riesling: Mosel	**43 G** **Pa** Parellada
5 R **Mn** Mâcon	**10 G** **Ro** Roussanne	**15 G** **Cu** Chardonnay: unoaked	**21 R** **Ga** Gavi	**26 R** **Gd** Greco di Tufo	**32 G** **Fa** Falanghina	**38 R** **Fr** Frascati	**44 G** **Ve** Verdicchio
6 G **Sv** Sauvignon Blanc: NZ	**11 R** **Pb** Pinot Blanc	**16 G** **Ay** Assyrtiko	**22 G** **Co** Cortese	**27 G** **Gv** Grüner Veltliner	**33 R** **Or** Orvieto	**39 G** **Tr** Trebbiano	**45 R** **Vv** Vinho Verde

SPARKLING

105 R **As** Asti	**106 G** **Mo** Moscato	**107 R** **Pe** Prosecco	**108 R** **Cv** Cava	**109 R** **Cr** Crémant

SWEET

		113 R **Iw** Icewine	**114 R** **Vs** Vin Santo	**115 R** **Tk** Tokaji

FORTIFIED

119 R **Fs** Fino Sherry	**120 R** **Ol** Oloroso Sherry	**121 R** **Md** Madeira	**122 R** **Rm** Rutherglen Muscat	**123 G** **Px** Pedro Ximénez

←

LIGHT & FLORAL

FRUITY & RICHER

ROSE   LIGHTER RED   FULL-BODIED
                                                             RED

→

						96 R **Am** Amarone
			64 G **Pz** Pinot Noir: NZ	72 R **Rd** Ribero del Duero	80 R **Pt** Priorat	88 G **Cs** Cabernet Sauvignon	97 G **Cg** Carignan
		57 R **Ct** Chianti	65 R **Ps** Pic St-Loup	73 G **Ma** Malbec	81 R **Bd** Bandol	89 R **Sy** Syrah	98 G **Sh** Shiraz
46 S **Wz** White Zinfandel		58 G **Bb** Barbera	66 G **M** Merlot	74 R **Cô** Côtes du Rhône	82 R **Cp** Châteauneuf-du-Pape	90 R **Ce** Côte-Rôtie	99 G **Zi** Zinfandel
47 G **Gb** Grenache	52 R **Bj** Beaujolais	59 G **Pm** Pinot Meunier	67 R **St** St-Émilion	75 G **Te** Tempranillo	83 G **Ci** Cinsault	91 G **Du** Durif	100 G **Pr** Primitivo
48 R **Nv** Navarra	53 R **Gm** Gamay	60 R **By** Burgundy	68 R **Rj** Rioja	76 R **Bs** Barbaresco	84 G **Gr** Grenache	92 R **Ba** Barolo	101 G **Pv** Petit Verdot
49 R **Ra** Rosé d'Anjou	54 G **Do** Dolcetto	61 G **Pn** Pinot Noir	69 G **Sg** Sangiovese	77 R **Lg** Languedoc	85 R **Ne** Nebbiolo	93 G **Mv** Mourvèdre	102 G **Ag** Aglianico
50 R **Pd** Pays d'Oc	55 R **Va** Valpolicella	62 G **Mp** Montepulciano	70 G **Br** Brunello	78 G **Pi** Pinotage	86 G **Na** Nero d'Avola	94 R **Ca** Cahors	103 G **Ng** Negroamaro
51 R **Pc** Provence	56 R **Bf** Blaufränkisch	63 R **Cn** Chinon	71 G **Cm** Carmenère	79 R **Bx** Bordeaux	87 R **Cf** Cabernet Franc	95 R **Mé** Médoc	104 R **Ta** Tannat

110 R **Ch** Champagne	111 G **La** Lambrusco	112 S **Ss** Sparkling Shiraz
116 R **Sa** Sauternes	117 R **Bu** Banyuls	118 R **My** Maury
124 R **Rp** Ruby Port	125 R **Lp** Late-bottled Vintage Port	126 R **Tp** Tawny Port	127 R **Vp** Vintage Port

ELEMENT KEY
TOP LEFT: ELEMENT NUMBER
TOP RIGHT: TYPE OF WINE
Grape variety (G)
Region/Appellation (R)
Style (S)

→

DARKER,   REDS
DRIED FRUITS

Introduction

Welcome to *The Periodic Table of Wine*. The table has been designed to give a visual overview of how different styles of the world's most popular wines roughly relate to each other. The descriptions later in the book contain more details about the elements of the table.

Dip in and dip out. Use the table practically and get family and friends together to smell and taste wines. Use it as a fun way to gain a deeper understanding of wine attributes, grapes and regions. See if you agree with the relationships. Where does your wine sit? Open more than one wine at a time by asking your friends to bring a different bottle. Use all your senses – eyes, nose and taste, in that order – to notice the differences. Decide which wine you think has the fuller body, or is the fruitiest. Is it spicy or floral, or does it taste 'greener' like herbs, or like minerals such as stones or chalk? Does your wine sit right in the middle of things? Add a rating to indicate how much you liked each wine you tasted and you could find that a pattern emerges, revealing that your favourite style(s) rest in particular areas of the table.

It is not really surprising that there are so many different wines available, but this can make choosing wine confusing. A little like chefs, winemakers all have their own recipes, numerous processes and various techniques they use in production, from the way the grapes are grown and picked to every step of winemaking. Different grapes grow in different countries too. On top of this, the soil, climate, the vintage (the year a wine was made) and the age of the vines all affect how the final wine in the bottle looks, smells and tastes. Sometimes even neighbouring vineyards make wines with varying characteristics, and each commands a different price.

Knowing what is behind the name on a label is a big help in understanding what the wine in a particular bottle will taste like. For this reason, the table represents a bringing together of the most common names found on wine labels and relates them by their general characteristics (body, flavours and aromas): hence the 'style' of the wines. The descriptions contain information to clarify what each name means and should help you know what style of wine to expect. This should remove some of the questions and uncertainty you might have about purchasing an unknown wine while increasing your buying confidence, which should lead you on to some delicious new discoveries. So pop a bottle into your shopping basket and start sipping and discovering.

If you know you already like a certain wine, find it in the table, either directly or via the index. The wines closest to it in the table (above, below, left or right) are similar but have different styles you may also appreciate.

Remember: wine is not an exact science, so additional wines to try are also suggested in each description. Some are way more adventurous than others, and you might enjoy 'researching' those as well.

How the table works

Wine elements, at their most basic, can be divided either into 'grape varieties' or 'appellations'; you'll find that these are the most common way wines are sold around the world. These label names are key pieces of information that point towards what is in the bottle. Thus a label may show the grape variety that was used to make the wine – or varieties, if the bottle contains a 'blend' or mix of more than one grape variety. Look for names like Chardonnay, Cabernet Sauvignon, Sauvignon Blanc and Merlot. Alternatively, the wine might be labelled using a protected name known as an 'appellation', under which wines from a defined region may be sold (see Old World/New World, page 11).

Not all wines are included, but the wines you are most likely to come across are. While they can influence style, brand names, winemakers and vintages have not been included in the table as they cannot always be found locally, plus they represent an additional layer of detail within or behind a single element or building block of the table – but they can be explored further by delving within an element to reveal this deeper layer of diversity. Perhaps you would like to conduct your own research by tasting different wines that fall into one element for yourself. The elements of the table have been designed as a starting point for the enjoyment and understanding of wine, by giving a broad overview of how the main wines made around the world relate. The graphic representation is a simplified bringing together of a diverse subject to provide a good foundation upon which your wine knowledge can build.

The columns broadly illustrate how wines vary by the weight or the feel in the mouth when you taste them. This is called 'body'. 'Full body' is heavier, giving a weightier feeling on the palate in the form of big, bold flavours, textures and tannins (especially in red wines). Full-bodied wines can range from rustic to full of finesse or opulent, if you like. A powerful *and* elegant wine is a sign of quality, especially if it is also described as having 'complexity', meaning lots of layers of lingering flavours. Wines that tend to be full-bodied are placed in the outside columns of the table. They are a good match for flavourful dishes. The wines towards the centre of the table are lighter-bodied and more delicate on the palate – useful when looking for a neutral-tasting, refreshing drink. This subtler style is popular as an apéritif in hotter weather or when sipping on its own, and it pairs well with lighter cuisine because neither overpowers the other.

The rows in the table give an indication of the general types of flavours you might encounter in a wine. With practice (smelling and tasting), especially comparing different wines at the same time, distinguishing these attributes becomes easier. To begin with, focus on identifying whether a wine is young or fruity; only later should you try to start to identify the types of fruit you can taste. The more you practice, the better you'll get at identifying the various characteristics. When you start out, just remember that very few wines actually taste of grapes. Instead, you might spot flowers in your first wine, which places it more in the table's middle rows. Other aromas and flavours, such as herbs or minerals, would put a wine near the bottom of the table. Some wines have many of these traits, so could justifiably find themselves in a different row; however, they have been placed closer to their more usual features.

Always bear in mind that taste and smell are personal. We all taste and smell differently, so there is no 'right' answer. You may find that you prefer one brand or winemaker over another, or that you prefer a particular wine due to the type of food you enjoy or the occasions when wine is drunk. It is OK to have these differences of opinion and create your own table. Some people are more inclined to taste bitter hints and might prefer softer, sweeter wines, whereas others might be better at tasting floral notes instead, so they would find these same wines too sweet. Likewise, wines taste different with and without food, so there is plenty of scope for experimentation here. Usually wines are drunk with food, so why not test out which wine you think is best with what you are eating? With a really good match, both the food and the wine should taste better.

Maybe you've already tasted wines from significant appellations: those defined winemaking regions that are usually controlled by strict local rules concerning the wines made within them. The labels will have names like Bordeaux (aka claret), which is a French wine appellation,

Rioja from Spain, or Chianti, which is from Italy. These popular and well-known places or regions give their names to admired wines that are often blends of more than one grape variety (but not always: Chablis is an appellation that allows only white wines made from 100 per cent Chardonnay grapes to bear its name). The rules in each appellation govern, among other things, the variety of grape(s) that can be used in the wines that carry the appellation name on the label. Although *The Periodic Table of Wine* began with the idea of each entry being a single element, such as a grape variety, the idea of omitting anything on the basis that it wasn't 'pure' – i.e. that it was a blend – seemed wrong and unhelpful. These 'compound wines' are not 'elements' in the strict sense, but they are crucial to include when mapping the world of wine.

Rosés have found a home in the centre of the table, being neither red nor white but a combination of the two colours. However, rosé wines are not normally made from a mixture of red and white wines; instead, their pink colour comes from the skin of red grapes. Typically the fleshy pulp inside the grape contains clear juice, and this juice is turned into wine: fermented by yeasts that eat the fruit's natural sugars, then convert them to alcohol. White wines are, in general, made by fermenting grape juice only. Red winemaking includes a period of time where the skins and clear juice mingle to add colour, resulting in purple, ruby-red or merely pale-garnet wines. Like red wines, rosés are made using red grapes, with the pink colour usually the result of letting the grape juice and skins stay in contact for only a short time – a little like the way colours from a tea bag infuse into the water. The hue, style, weight and texture of still rosés differ depending on the grape variety, as well as details of the infusion method used. Within the Periodic Table, rosés could have been distributed in and among the white and red table wines based on weight (light to full-bodied) and flavour characteristics. However, they would have been lost as an important category of still wines – and so, too, would the appreciation of just how varied pink wines are.

'Rare earth' elements

Three categories have been given separate rows because they are less likely to be drunk regularly and have qualities that make them either taste or feel different to still wines: sparkling, sweet and fortified wines. They are often put into a separate section when you are buying wine too.

Sparkling wines have the extra dimension and texture created by their bubbles, sometimes called 'mousse', as the bubbles in those that exhibit finesse create a smooth, almost creamy sensation. They need not be saved for a special occasion, though, so pop a cork and make any occasion special.

Sparkling wines contain all the elements of still wines and could easily form their own detailed table. They range from young, pale, *pétillant* (lightest of froth) or floral, frivolous, *frizzante* (with a little more fizz) fizzes through to the more edgy, fully effervescent, serious and complex (lots of different layers of flavours and lingering length) bubblies and the richest, most creamily textured, all-honey-and-brioche vintage Champagnes.

Sparkling wines are also made in a variety of colours. They are mainly white wines, although the 'white' can range from pale, almost water-white to a rich, deep, golden colour. There are sparkling rosés, but only a few are the deepest of reds, such as Australia's classic berry and pepper-spiced sparkling Shiraz.

Some bubblies are made in the same way as Champagne via what is called (in the Champagne region only) *méthode champenoise* – i.e. the Champagne method – or, outside the region, *méthode traditionelle,* or the traditional method. These include French *crémant,* Spanish Cava, German Sekt and Italian Franciacorta. Others, like Asti and Prosecco, both made in Italy, have their own methods, because experience has shown that different techniques work better with the grape varieties that grow in their regions, and help to bring out the grapes' fruit and perfumed, floral qualities. All bubble-adding methods take time and skill, however, so sparkling wines tend to cost more than still wines. Wine can be carbonated in the same way that lemonade is: by adding carbon dioxide. While this is a much cheaper, quicker fix, it is not associated with any classic fizz, and creates bursting bubbles that are quickly lost, are not as fine, nor as integrated with the texture and flavour of the wines involved.

Most wines, including sparkling, are dry: that is 'not sweet to the taste' in wine-world speak (rather than 'not wet' in the rest of the world). 'Off-dry' means only a suggestion of sweetness. 'Medium' has a touch more noticeable sweetness, which usually comes from the natural sugars that were in the grapes when they were harvested rather than from added sugar.

Intense and concentrated sweet and fortified wines should not be overlooked, as their layers of flavour can linger on the palate. Discover the pale, bone-dry fino sherries with their flashes of salted almonds and green apples; apricot and stone-fruited dessert wines; and the opaque, inky, powerful dark cherries and chocolate of vintage ports. These are not your everyday wines of choice, but they may be areas to branch into. They are made using different techniques to those used in still wine – hence their diverse characteristics. Many could make a dessert on their own.

Again, even their sweetness is natural. The grape juice may have been concentrated in some way, such as by leaving the grapes on the vine longer so that they start to dry out or 'raisin'. Fermentation – changing the sugar in the grape juice to alcohol – can be stopped partway through the process, leaving some of this natural sweetness remaining in the finished wine. In fortified wines, this is achieved by adding neutral brandy partway through the fermentation to 'fortify' (hence the name) the wine. Note: not all fortified wines are sweet; some have a beguiling concentration wrapped in bone-dry elegance.

To choose your sweet and fortified wines, look for mouth-watering acidity, as that balances intensity and sweetness. As a style, these dessert wines can be refreshing and appreciated even by those who claim not to have a sweet tooth, and they make a heavenly match for cheese or pâté as well as desserts. If pairing wine with a dessert, pick a wine that is at least as sweet as the dessert. A heavier style of sweet wine matches more substantial puddings, while a more delicate, maybe even floral sweet wine works well with lighter fruit desserts. When pairing savoury foods with sweet wines, go by the weight of the food and choose a similarly weighted sweet wine so that salty and fatty flavours from the food are balanced by the sugar and acidity from the wine.

How to use this book

Each element appears in this book following the table order – by column, running left to right across the table – and moves through the types of still wine – from whites to rosés then reds – followed by sparkling, then sweet wines, and finally, fortified wines. Their entries describe the types of flavours, aromas and other attributes you might find in your glass. You'll find food-matching hints here too. There may also be a comment on how they might vary by winemaker or region or how the wines could change with age.

The table is all columns and rows and straight lines, but in practice the boundaries are blurred; in reality you could zoom in further, say, into one grape variety or appellation, and make a new table that shows there is diversity and relationships across countries, regions, and even winemakers. This is something you might like to do in time. Some aspects that create this diversity and depth in wines follow.

The cells here are all the same size, although when it comes down to it, some wine elements are far more important than others, either because of history and/or the volumes consumed. You may have come across some grapes already, as they are the most respected and recognisable grape varieties grown around the world. This is for good reason; historically, these leading international varieties have been valued for their ability to produce quality wines wherever they are grown, and in some regions they are reputed to produce the top wines in the world. They include reds such as cassis-laden Cabernet Sauvignon, softer, plummy Merlot and more delicate Pinot Noir, plus whites such as versatile Chardonnay, aromatic Sauvignon Blanc, and fresh, zippy Riesling. These grapes are behind the labels of some of the most respected wine regions in the world, such as Bordeaux and Burgundy, but because they are used by so many winemakers they are readily found on most wine shelves in numerous places and prices from the most pocket-friendly upwards. Use this table as a springboard to try new wines made from international grape varieties as well as lesser-known grapes, and experiment with all that there is available.

Many wines, but not all, are made in a range of styles, which makes things more confusing. The table is necessarily a simplified representation that gives an overview of how wines relate. Differences could nudge a particular wine in a column one way or another, from middle, lighter-bodied styles to medium-weight, say, or even bump them into the full-bodied arena. This diverseness could be caused by variances in production techniques (such as using oak barrels); the temperature of grape juice at the time of fermentation creates different aromas, which can bring out a more floral side to a grape – or alternatively, a more fruity side. Letting vines grow fewer but more intensely flavoured grapes also affects a wine's concentration and power, and variations in the vineyard express themselves in the final wine. Grapes like Pinot Noir are more likely to convey these aspects of origin. Perhaps you notice qualities in the glass you're tasting that might bump your particular wine into a different position: left or right, up or down. If you like it, make a note to look out for that type of characteristic next time you buy a wine.

Vintage is important for some wines, such as Bordeaux or Port, when wines made in a particular year are thought of as superior to others by taste or longevity potential. They may make the headlines, but they will cost more, and they tend to be less easily available. Zoom in and you are bound to find exceptions, like a particular winemaker who has kicked the general trend. Get an idea of what constitutes a good Bordeaux, for example, then check out vintage differences. For the majority of wines, however, vintage is less important; they are released ready to drink more or less straight away while still relatively young.

Some descriptions include remarks on how layers of flavour are added by using different winemaking techniques, which give a wine 'complexity'. Ageing and other techniques mean that wine production can cost a bit more. There are good reasons for this, such as using better-quality grapes, more steps or extra details in the process, plus the cost of barrels. These all manifest themselves in extra layers of lingering flavours that can make a wine more interesting. The description might comment on this if it could affect the wine.

Experiment. Taste a different wine, a different country of production, a different winemaker, a different grape variety. Be bold. Try a different colour or style. You could find that by swapping one element – say, the winemaker or brand – you like a type of wine you thought you wouldn't. This can happen with all grapes and regions, but a classic example is Chardonnay, because this versatile, juicy, white grape is available in a huge gamut of styles and guises around the globe. Perhaps your first, unhappy experience was with a heavily oaked, super-ripe, full-bodied style of Chardonnay. However, sip a lighter more elegant Chablis or a Chardonnay made without using oak from a similarly cool vineyard elsewhere in the world and you could fall in love with this more refreshing style – made with the same golden grape. Or maybe a delicate, pale gold, *blanc de blanc*s Champagne, with its apple-like notes, is just the Chardonnay for you? Liken it to coffee preferences; some people don't enjoy sugary, creamy coffee but love reviving black coffee. They're both still coffee – just made differently. Tasting wine 'blind' – i.e. covering the labels so you don't know what you're drinking – helps remove preconceptions. Why not arrange a blind tasting with friends? They could each bring a bottle wrapped, and you could compare notes afterwards.

Tasting notes

Wine terms have been kept to a minimum as this is not meant to be a textbook. Some words that are regularly mentioned are worth expanding. If you don't know them, it will not affect what is most important, which is whether or not you like a wine. If you are familiar with them, however, this could help you work out why you like a style of wine and guide you towards what to look out for in future. Some terms have been covered within the text already, but here are a few more:

Old World/
New World: Notice that some wines are named after the region in which it they are made – think of wines like Rioja (in Spain), Chianti (Italy), Chablis and Bordeaux (both in France). These are long-standing, traditional names that define winemaking areas generally occurring in the 'Old World': the more historic winemaking areas found mostly in Europe. The winemaking rules of each region specify the permitted grape varieties, so you would not be allowed to make a Bordeaux wine using Pinotage grapes, for instance, nor make and call it a 'Bordeaux' even if you used permitted varieties but made it outside the region. Having a broad understanding of which grapes are behind an Old World appellation on a label is

a significant step towards knowing what a wine will taste like. The table acts as a foundation here, without going into the detail of the local rules.

Other wines are more simply the name of the grape variety in the bottle: for instance, juicy red Merlot or Malbec. These varietally labelled wines are more likely to have been made in the 'New World' – i.e. outside Europe, in Chile, California or Argentina, for instance. The classification 'New World' doesn't mean there isn't a long history of winemaking in these places; it is a naming convention in wine – another detail that can make wine feel more complex and confusing than it needs to be. Knowing about grape varieties is still the easiest way of knowing what a wine might taste like. Increasingly, Old World wines are helping consumers by including the names of grape varieties on the label.

Acidity: Acidity is regularly mentioned, as it is needed to maintain freshness. When drinking a wine, acidity is what makes your mouth water. It is a key part of the structure of wine, giving it another dimension and bringing out its flavours. Acidity levels vary, depending a great deal on the grape variety, where it was grown and how the wine is handled in the winery. Wines with high levels of acidity are made to accompany food, so if you find a wine style too lip-smacking and lemon-laced on its own, serve it with nibbles or as part of a meal. Acidity is essential, a positive attribute in wine, as in food like tempting dishes making your mouth water in anticipation. Think of fruit that has gone over: it's a bit woolly and flat-tasting compared to a juicy, fresh segment or slice. In wine terms, acidity might be really racy, nervy, or edgy, more middle-of-the-road zesty, fresh, lively, or crisp and then sometimes delicate. An over-the-hill wine is flat, tired, out-of-date, lacking both fruit and good flavours with 'flabby acidity'. We don't wish to be drinking a dull old wine like that as there are far too many bright, fresh, juicy accessible wines to try.

Tannins: Tannin is found in red wines, including fortified ones such as Port. Tannin creates a drying sensation in the mouth, especially around the gums, and creates a feeling like an over-stewed cup of tea, but tannins are important as they are part of a balanced wine's structure. When too high, tannins can feel chewy. Tannic wines soften if drunk with cheese or meat. Decanting tannic wine also helps; this is simply pouring the wine into another bottle or jug to aerate it. If there are any bits, called sediment, at the bottom of the wine bottle, stop pouring before they transfer to the other container. For some wines with plenty of fruit flavours accompanying the tannins, keeping them longer or ageing them before drinking tones down the tannins. Bitter or grippy tannins can be why some people stick with white wines, but not all tannins are unfriendly. Look for tannin-describing words like 'velvety', 'supple', 'soft' and 'silky', with 'firm' being a good halfway house. Not all red wines have high tannins, either. Wines towards the middle of the table are lighter, lower-tannin, easier reds. Try those as a 'starter red' if you usually choose whites. Better styles of reds have tannins that are more at one with the wine, or 'integrated'.

Some white wines also have tannins. They are inclined to be the fuller-bodied styles. As the skins are not usually used when making a white wine, the tannins here come from using oak barrels during the winemaking process and are more subtle than those in most red wines.

Oak: Oak, which is used in both red and white winemaking, adds cream, vanilla and spice notes, especially cloves, and it adds a touch of weightiness to a wine's texture. It can also impart smoky or toasted layers. Coconut nuances are a sign of American oak rather than French oak, and nutty tinges are an indication of long ageing in oak. Newer and smaller barrels add more of these tones. The winemaker decides how much or little is required so as to balance, rather than overpower, the other flavours in the wine. Not every wine would suit the qualities oak brings. It increases the cost of winemaking as well, so expect to pay more for a wine made using oak.

Vieilles vignes (**VV**): The flavour and intensity of a wine can vary with the age of the vine on which the grapes grow. *Vieilles vignes*, 'VV', or old vines bear fewer grapes than younger vines during each autumn harvest. In addition, they are more likely to be hand-picked instead of harvested by machine. The smaller volume of wine that results is more concentrated, and this is reflected in the wine's final characteristics. Expect a deeper, more intense-tasting and often more complex wine with lingering qualities – and anticipate paying more for it.

Now, charged glasses in hand, and your friends close by, go ahead and delight in all the multifaceted elements and compounds the world of wine has to offer.

Whites

Column 1

1 **C** G Chardonnay: oaked	
2 **Pl** R Pessac-Léognan	**7** **Gw** G Gewürztraminer
3 **Sé** G Sémillon	**8** **Pg** G Pinot Gris
4 **Mr** G Marsanne	**9** **To** G Torrontés
5 **Mn** R Mâcon	**10** **Ro** G Roussanne
6 **Sv** G Sauvignon Blanc: NZ	**11** **Pb** G Pinot Blanc

This column represents bold white wines that can have the greatest weight, texture and flavour when you drink them. They might feel more viscous or rounder in the mouth – almost as if they were thicker. They may have more alcohol, so check the level on the label. Sometimes being fuller-bodied is due to the grape variety, or it may be because the grapes used to make the wine have been left to ripen for as long as they can; often it is attributable to the winemaker using methods that add weight to the wine, such as using oak, which adds a creamy texture or dimension.

If you like red wines, you may enjoy this style of white wine more than the lighter styles.

CHARDONNAY: OAKED

A famous, versatile, leading or international white grape variety that makes dry wines in many wine regions across the globe. The fatter, riper style of Chardonnay is often made in hotter regions, where the grapes mature fully. This element of the table represents the full-bodied version of Chardonnay, and these wines may have high alcohol levels. Here winemaking techniques are used that can add a buttery, vanilla, creamy edge and deep colour to the final wine. Once overoaking masked the super-ripe New World fruit bombs of melon, mango and tropical fruits. Now these Chardonnays are more restrained, better balanced and textured with refreshing hints of spice such as ginger and cinnamon as well as toasty notes; the oak and fruit are working together in a more integrated manner. Aspirational white wines of Burgundy are subtly oaked, infusing them with gentle vanilla and cream notes. This fuller-bodied oaked style of Chardonnay is often suitable to keep, and as it ages it becomes more honeyed and nutty. (Another white grape, Pinot Blanc, can be similarly styled.) Full-bodied Chardonnays can pair well with fish pie and dishes with cream sauce, and the finer examples are on restaurant wine lists around the globe. For those who prefer white to red wine, oaked Chardonnays can partner roast dinners, especially Christmas lunch, due to the range of accompaniments.

PESSAC-LÉOGNAN

An esteemed French wine region, or appellation, situated in the northern part of Graves, part of the Bordeaux winemaking region in southwest France. Wines from here are dry, rich and can be mouth-watering whites (and also reds, but see Bordeaux). Whites are usually a blend of the white grapes Sauvignon Blanc and Sémillon plus sometimes a splash of Muscadelle, which adds an extra dimension as a suggestion of musky, floral perfume and a splash of spice. When young, these pale, fresh and lively blended whites are more subtle than a New Zealand Sauvignon Blanc and can have citrus, green apple and fresh nectarine flavours. Premium blends are richer, with a fuller texture, but they are more expensive. They are made using some oak and age well, gradually turning more golden in colour and developing a lusher, smoother texture accompanied by more complex, lingering exotic fruit flavours like mango and clementine, along with notes of honeyed beeswax, nuts, sweet spices and soft leather. Be warned: they can be expensive. Swaps for aged Pessac-Léognans include aged Chardonnays like Burgundy, and you could try riper and more alcoholic blends from the southern Rhône. Pair them with light game, hams, Asian dishes, roast pork and creamy main courses.

SÉMILLON

A leading white grape variety with gold thin skins closely associated with Bordeaux in France, but also with Australia (where it loses the 'é'), especially the Hunter Valley region. It can be used to make both interesting dry and succulent sweet wines with a variety of flavours and textures. It is often blended with Sauvignon Blanc and Muscadelle. Famously it is the majority grape in the luscious, silky-textured, apricot, honey and marmalade sweet wines of Sauternes in Bordeaux (see page 128). Both dry and sweet wines can age. The more affordable wines, as well as those from cooler climates or where the grapes were harvested when less ripe, have fresh flavours of lemon, apple, pear and a touch of waxiness, plus white flowers. This style pairs well with seafood, bass, herbs and pasta. Sauvignon Blancs can be an alternative here. Aged Sémillons and those from warmer regions have richer flavours and aromas, such as mangos, peaches, figs and ginger. They are more likely to be made using oak, and cost more. This maturation adds another layer of flavours like butter, vanilla and a touch of smokiness; there may also be nuts and higher alcohol too. Richer versions are a good match for roast chicken, butternut squash and mushroom risotto. Also try Pinot Gris, Chardonnay and Viognier. Sémillon can be added to Chardonnay to make the wine more zippier, fresher and more affordable, so look for this blend as a midweek sipper.

MARSANNE

A weighty white grape variety found in French wines from the Rhône and further south, and in a few other sun-kissed regions too. Often found blended with Roussanne, which adds heady perfume to the fruit, it is usually dry, with acidity levels that are not too high. It has a full-bodied, smooth texture in the mouth, with plentiful levels of exotic peach and melon fruit, honeysuckle and alcohol. It can be almondy, quince-like and honeyed, especially with age. Famous French wines are called names like St-Joseph, Crozes-Hermitage, and the most expensive, Hermitage. For more affordable Marsanne, try a white Côtes du Rhône or look for one from Languedoc-Roussillon, which might contain other grapes as well. Great with grilled food, butter sauces and mildly spiced

Asian meals. You might also like Chardonnay, Viognier, oaked white Riojas and Pessac-Léognan.

MÂCON

Mâcon is a wine region in the south of Burgundy, France. It makes mostly white wines from Chardonnay grapes, with some red Gamay and Pinot Noir wines. Mâconnais white wines are straw-coloured. (They can have more specific vineyard names, like Pouilly-Fuissé, which typically signifies a better-quality wine than simple Mâcon; Mâcon-Villages is halfway between.) They are dry and fresh with a full (especially in warmer vintages) to medium, rounded, smooth, honeyed texture plus white-flower flavours, citrus fruits and perhaps a touch of crème fraîche. Premium versions are richer, with poise, and offer complexity plus depth of flavours balanced by elegance and minerality from the limestone soil. (Compare with Chablis wines from north of Burgundy which are more acidic and linear in style.) Food-friendly pairings include finger food, dishes in creamy sauces and risottos. They are often better with a touch of age as they soften and are more approachable, developing earthy mushroom notes. Refreshing red Mâcons are light and juicy with red-cherry and soft, red-fruit flavours; perfumed, with light tannins. Try with ham, terrines and pâtés and savoury pastries. The lively, elegant rosés are much harder to come across, though, and being similar to the reds of Mâcon, they pair well with cold cuts, couscous dishes and quiche.

SAUVIGNON BLANC: NEW ZEALAND

Here the white Sauvignon Blanc grape is used in New Zealand to produce an important and popular zesty, pungent but crowd-pleasing style of lively wine. Lots of sunshine, combined with cool climate plus time on the vines, provides vibrant notes of green pepper, gooseberry plus the archetypal 'cat's pee' or asparagus notes together with ripe flavours that sometimes merge into passion fruit and juicy lime zest. These Sauvignons usually have more weight in the mouth than their subtler cousins from Sancerre (France) and elsewhere. Often from New Zealand's Marlborough region, this well-loved wine style has only been around since the 1980s. It's youthful and usually made to drink in the year of production. Its punchiness means it can match stronger fish flavours like mackerel and creamy fish pie. Occasionally, Sauvignon Blancs are made with oak, which mellows and rounds out the wine, adding a creamy flavour and texture. This style is more likely to age. You might also like to try less aromatic Sémillons, Pinot Blancs plus Viogniers and compare it with a more restrained Sancerre.

Column 2

1 C G Chardonnay: oaked		
2 Pl R Pessac-Léognan	**7 Gw** G Gewürztraminer	**12 Mu** G Muscat
3 Sé G Sémillon	**8 Pg** G Pinot Gris	**13 Vi** G Viognier
4 Mr G Marsanne	**9 To** G Torrontés	**14 Sb** G Sauvignon Blanc
5 Mn R Mâcon	**10 Ro** G Roussanne	**15 Cu** G Chardonnay: unoaked
6 Sv G Sauvignon Blanc: NZ	**11 Pb** G Pinot Blanc	**16 Ay** G Assyrtiko

These wines can be rich white wines similar to those in column 1; however, often the weight and texture are lower, plus they may have aromatic characteristics created in the vineyard by leaving the grapes to hang or (less so) by using oak. Richer versions tend to cost more than lighter forms.

GEWÜRZTRAMINER

An aromatic white grape variety that grows best in cooler regions like Alsace in France (where it loses its 'ü'), also in Germany for a slightly lighter style, while Chile makes affordable uncomplicated versions. Prominent notes of lychee, rose petal, citrus to pineapple fruit occur in the ripest styles. Some can have ginger and other spicy hints, as well as a touch of smokiness; they tend to have a higher alcohol content and a weightier texture too. Serve these exotic wines cool to bring out the best of the medium acidity level, balanced with lychee plus floral notes and a touch of residual sugar. German wines can be more subtle and delicate. This makes them a good introduction to this more blousy grape, as are better-value Chilean wines. Look out for *vendange tardive*, or 'late harvest' grapes, which make dessert wines – great with fruit-based puddings. Pair with Thai and Moroccan food, especially spicy cuisine, takeaways, and onion tart. If you want a white wine to match Christmas dinner, an Alsace Gewurztraminer has enough weight to partner the turkey and trimmings; it's good with coriander and coconut too: think of Thai curries. Other fruity, floral wines to try include Muscat/Moscato, Torrentés and, for more acidity and fewer flowers, Riesling.

PINOT GRIS

This is the same white grape as Pinot Grigio. Pinot Gris is the more full-bodied version, found in Alsace, Germany (as Grauburgunder and Ruländer), New Zealand and

Italy. Wines are richer, with a more viscous texture compared to straightforward Pinot Grigio. The grape is versatile so wine styles range from unoaked and light, with fresh pear flesh and a touch of green herbs, to rich and honeyed, with flavours of riper (and even baked) pears. They can also contain stone-fruit flavours such as white peaches, a touch of sweet spice like ginger, hints of flowers and cream from oak. Pinot Gris is also versatile with food; it can accompany a wide range of dishes, including lightly spicy Asian food, pork casserole and hard cheeses (for sweet wines). Some wines, though harder to find, are made to age, like in Washington State, US, where fermenting in oak barrels and adding a splash of Viognier gives creamy and aromatic wines. Pinot Gris is also made in sweet styles called *vendange tardive* (late harvest) wines, and the rare, more concentrated sweet Sélection des Grains Noble (SGN). Both match blue cheeses and fruit desserts. This is a grape to investigate further as it is quite different to its light, neutral, affordable cousin Pinot Grigio. Also try Pinot Blanc, Chardonnay, Sémillon and Riesling.

TORRONTÉS

9   G

To

Torrontés

Argentina's signature perfumed white grape variety is mostly made for early, fresh drinking. These light-yellow, refreshing exotic wines may surprise as they can smell sweet but taste dry. They can be rich with medium body and a pleasant weighty roundness in the mouth. You'll find floral aromas of jasmine and geranium coupled with fruit-salad flavours, green and herb hints like oregano plus citrus acidity (but not overly so) from lemon to more exotic lime. They can also be honeyed with pear and passion fruit. Usually not oaked, the wine shows pure fruit and flower flavours, but be warned: they can be 13%-plus ABV (alcohol by volume), to balance the complexity of flavours. Less-expensive versions have less of the perfume, flavours, weight and complexity, but are nonetheless pleasant to sip. Serve chilled paired with aromatic, lightly spiced Asian and Indian dishes and light fish flavours. This wine slips down easily as an apéritif or patio wine. Try also Gewürztraminer, the peachier Viognier, grapier Muscat and versatile Pinot Gris.

ROUSSANNE

A white grape whose traditional home is on the steep vineyard terraces of the northern Rhône. It is also found in rich, higher-alcohol, more affordable blends in the southern Rhône and other warmer regions in the world. It makes medium- to fuller-bodied, racy, floral, slightly exotic wines with hints of chamomile and herbs and a zesty grapefruit note. It is a versatile wine, so expect to find some versions with more bracing acidity and mineral hints, and others that are much richer and more voluptuous, with nutty notes. It is often blended with Marsanne for a more complete style. Strength tends to be 13%-plus ABV (alcohol by volume) to match its flavours. It is food-friendly so pairs with an assortment of dishes, including exotic cuisine, seafood such as lobster and shrimp, cheeses, nuts and spices. Other blends with Chardonnay and Viognier can yield perfumed, richly-textured wines. If you enjoy this, also try Pinot Gris, Viognier and the less-floral Pinot Blanc.

PINOT BLANC

A white wine grape used mainly for elegant, pale-yellow, slightly creamy dry wines. It can be hard to come across as only small amounts are made in Alsace in northeast France, Italy, Germany, plus Oregon, US. Usually soft and rounded with peach hints, plus a range of apple flavours (green to red). Typically made without oak, which allows mineral notes to come through. Oaked versions are bolder and tend to have hints of nuts (almonds) and more cream or yeasty notes. A good wine for starters and simple main course dishes like omelettes and buffets. (Sometimes it is made into sparkling and sweet wines.) It is even harder to find the northwest Italian version, called Pinot Bianco. This is a lighter, zingier wine so accompanies lemony dishes like chicken, and is a good match for fennel. You could also try easier-to-find Chardonnay and Pinot Gris. Pinot Blanc is not quite so acidic as some wines, hence the softness. This variety can be overlooked but is one to try if you prefer wines that are not too sharp.

Column 3

		17 G **Fu** Furmint
7 G **Gw** Gewürztraminer	12 G **Mu** Muscat	18 R **Vy** Vouvray
8 G **Pg** Pinot Gris	13 G **Vi** Viognier	19 G **Ri** Riesling: Alsace or OZ
9 G **To** Torrontés	14 G **Sb** Sauvignon Blanc	20 G **Ar** Arneis
10 G **Ro** Roussanne	15 G **Cu** Chardonnay: unoaked	21 R **Ga** Gavi
11 G **Pb** Pinot Blanc	16 G **Ay** Assyrtiko	22 G **Co** Cortese

Here the white wines are moving towards medium- to lighter-bodied, forming a large group within white wines. Flavours are less bold.

MUSCAT

The name for a family of grapes found in the world's warmer, sun-blessed regions. Known as Moscato and Zibibbo (a touch lighter) in Italy, and Moscatel in Spain, Muscat is an ancient grape variety; there are many strains of the grape and many styles of wines are made from them, but all have grapiness and exotic floral notes at heart. Muscat wines in all their styles tend to be orange blossom-scented. The grape makes elegant dry white wines, some with a steelier style and touches of herbs, others richer with more texture and roundness in the mouth, but always with the perfumed flowers and fresh-fruit-salad tones. Serve chilled as apéritifs, or with spicy dishes, chicken and cheese on toast. Try Argentinian Torrontes, along with Gewürztraminer wines. See also Moscato and the low-alcohol (5–7.5% ABV) Asti in the sparkling wine section. Sweeter, more viscous dessert wines such as Muscat de Beaumes-de-Venise and Muscat de Lunel – both from France – are tinged with gold. They pair well with fruit salads and warmed peaches. Though fortified, around 15% ABV (alcohol by volume), their flavours are still delicate and floral. They are youthful and should be drunk young and chilled. Richer, darker and more honeyed, with marmalade splashes, Klein Constantia's Vin de Constance, from South Africa, suits fruit cakes and cooked fruits. Australian Rutherglen Muscats, also known as 'stickies', are darker again, with more dried than fresh fruit and spices. Look out for other Muscat sweeties that are similarly styled but more affordable wines made in California and Chile.

VIOGNIER

13 G
Vi
Viognier

A peachy white grape variety whose traditional home is in France's northern Rhône. It is typically bottled on its own, but is also used in blends in some places because of the character it can bring to other, more subtle grape varieties. It is lush, full-bodied, and intensely perfumed, with notes of honeysuckle and apricot. You can find wines made further south in France that include Viognier as part of a blend; it is also found in Australia, New Zealand, South Africa, California and Chile. Not too acidic, it can be softer-styled. Viogniers from Australia can have a touch more texture and zest – lemon and lime hints – and some have sweet spice and pears. Alcohol can be around 14% ABV (alcohol by volume) to balance the exotic flavours. They are best served chilled. Premium versions, meant to be drunk aged, are generous, rich and complex, with exotic tropical and citrus fruits. They can include creamy notes from the dead yeast cells (known as the 'lees') that remain in a wine after fermentation is complete. The more common youthful wines match Asian dishes or delicate curries; others pair well with smoked salmon and lemon chicken. A much more floral wine swap is Gewürztraminer, or Torrontés. You might also like Marsanne and Roussanne wines.

SAUVIGNON BLANC

14 G
Sb
Sauvignon
Blanc

Sauvignon Blanc is a highly aromatic white grape that makes fresh, lively wines throughout the world. It is generally a crowd-pleaser and a good introduction to white wine. See New Zealand for an assertive style, and France (Sancerre) for a subtle, more minerally taste. The grape grows well in a variety of climates and soils, mirrored in the wines. Youthful versions are more readily available, such as the more restrained herby, grassy examples from cooler Bordeaux, with styles from warmer regions offering riper flavours of gooseberry, asparagus, perhaps meadow flowers and even tropical-fruit notes like guava. South Africa, Chile and Argentina make good-value, drinkable Sauvignons typically in a style that is halfway between France and New Zealand, in bottles furnished with a screw cap as these refreshing whites are made to be drunk young and served chilled. In the US, Sauvignon Blanc can be called Fumé Blanc. Great as an apéritif and with green salads, picnics and buffets. Occasionally a Sauvignon has lees (dead yeast cells left over from fermentation) stirred in while it is being made, which adds a cream or crème fraîche layer – think yogurt freshness – as well as more body and roundness. Occasionally Sauvignons are made using oak barrels, which gives them more depth of creamy, vanilla flavours and an ability to age, but always with a higher price tag (these wines tend to have a cork). Pair them with richer food, such as pork or fish in a white sauce.

CHARDONNAY: UNOAKED

Popular and adaptable, this leading, versatile white grape variety makes a leaner, fresher, zippier style when unoaked, moving towards steely acidity. Unoaked Chardonnays tend to be paler, crisper, more minerally and refreshing than their richer, rounder, oaked siblings, with greater elegance. Flavours in this livelier style are more fresh-citrus, even green, with crisp apple and pear tones. The best grapes for unoaked Chardonnays are grown in cooler regions, sometimes near coasts, and at altitude – or at least away from the equator. In these locations grapes take longer to ripen, so the best have extra time to develop a more complex, layered flavour profile. More affordable versions are straightforward or simple, but cheap versions can be a little thin and disappointing. See also Chablis, page 39. Serve chilled with summer foods, seafood and pasta. Other wines to try include Gavi and Cortese from Italy, Sauvignon Blanc for more greenness and aromatics, and for more sharpness try Greece's Assyrtiko. If you moved on from Chardonnay because of the oak, then it's time to revisit this livelier style.

16   G

As

Assyrtiko

ASSYRTIKO

Greece's underappreciated white grape makes a refreshing, medium-bodied, bone-dry wine, with floral and steely notes. It also has ageing potential. Sun imbues this wine with high alcohol. The best, from the volcanic Santorini, give pretty floral/honeysuckle and citrus-filled wines. Those from the oldest vines add more intensity to the racy, zesty, lemony acidity, and include a salty tang, with mineral hints from the volcanic soils. Some are blended with Sauvignon Blanc; others age gently for a short time in oak and have a further soft, creamy note and rounder texture. Serve lightly chilled to accompany meze, plus pasta and other dishes with white sauces; fish, shellfish and white meats. Younger versions are more austere. With age they mellow, and honeyed flavours develop. (There are some sweet versions too.) Try also Sauvignon Blanc, Chablis and Cortese, or for a little more spice, find an older Grüner Veltliner.

Column 4

	17 G **Fu** Furmint	
12 G **Mu** Muscat	18 R **Vy** Vouvray	23 G **Mc** Muscadet
13 G **Vi** Viognier	19 G **Ri** Riesling: Alsace or OZ	24 R **Cl** Chablis
14 G **Sb** Sauvignon Blanc	20 G **Ar** Arneis	25 R **Sc** Sancerre
15 G **Cu** Chardonnay: unoaked	21 R **Ga** Gavi	26 R **Gd** Greco di Tufo
16 G **Ay** Assyrtiko	22 G **Co** Cortese	27 G **Gv** Grüner Veltliner

Wines here are becoming zingier and still have character on top of lemony freshness. Oak is becoming less likely to be used from here on in.

FURMINT

A white grape usually grown in Hungary and used to make the world-famous, complex and long-lived sweet botrytised white wine called Tokaji (made slightly differently to Sauternes in Bordeaux, France). Dry Furmints have fruit, spices and mineral tones like a combination of aromatic Sauvignon Blanc and racy, minerally Riesling, with the ability to be happy if oak is used in production. You should find good weight in this crisp, dry, smooth-textured wine whose depth of flavours include lime rind, ripe pears, light nuts and sometimes sweet spices like ginger, as well as preserved lemons and a touch of smokiness – especially where oak is used. Furmints are becoming easier to find outside Hungary, and it is worthwhile searching for them. Dry Furmints are food-friendly – well worth trying if you come across one on a wine list. A versatile partner, it can match dishes from risotto and pork to lightly spiced food. Sweet Tokaji is delicious on its own, or with light fruit cake, apricot tart and blue cheese salads. If you like dry Furmint, try Gavi, Cortese, aged Chardonnays, racy Chenin Blanc and Roussanne for a riper, fruitier edge. Swaps for sweet Tokaji include Sauternes, Vin de Constance, Montbazillac and late-harvest wines made from Furmint, Sémillon or Sauvignon Blanc.

VOUVRAY

Famous prestigious French region situated in the Loire Valley making white wines mainly from the versatile Chenin Blanc grape. The appellation (and wine) is named after the commune of Vouvray, roughly in the centre of the Loire wine district. Refreshing wines are produced in all styles and levels of sweetness. This can be confusing as Vouvray covers bone-dry, sparkling and sweeter wines, from the medium-sweet *demi-secs* to luscious, mouth-watering, fully sweet, golden dessert wines reflecting the varying weather in this northerly region. It always has high, vibrant, even racy, acidity. Most Vouvrays are drunk young, as they are typically light- to medium-bodied. Expect to find apple, quince and lemon juice flavours, along with blossom notes. The chalk and flint soils along the Loire River can impart a chalky, mineral layer. Premium-priced Vouvrays age well, adding depth and weight to the texture and may be made using some oak. Their flavours become more exotic: apples become baked apricot; blossom notes morph into honeysuckle, and there are honey and classically lanolin/waxy notes too. These wines tend to have more texture, aromatics and balance than lower-costing South African Chenin Blancs. (See Chenin Blanc, page 44.) Sparkling Vouvray, made in the same way as Champagne, is good value and pairs well with sushi and lightly fried food. Try dry styles, chilled, with fish and savoury soufflés, while off-dry wines match pork belly, spicy Indian cuisine, and crab. Tarte tatin is heaven with a sweet Vouvray. Other Chenin Blanc wines you might like are from the nearby Montlouis appellation, or try wines made from Sauvignon Blanc (Touraine, Sancerre) or the less acidic Pinot Gris.

RIESLING: FROM ALSACE OR AUSTRALIA

A perfumed white grape variety with intense, crisp acidity and clean flavours. Wines are dry, medium-bodied and certainly weightier than those from Germany's Mosel region but still retain steely acidity. Made without oak, they demonstrate a purity of style and fruit flavours. In Australia and New Zealand, citrus notes, especially lime, feature heavily. Think lime marmalade, or lime cordial with zest, plus a touch of green apple and blossom.

Some can be sherbetty in their zippiness. Alsace Rieslings feel fatter than Australian versions. Wines are light-yellow to green in colour, but darken with age and develop stone and petrol/mineral notes earlier in life compared to Mosel Rieslings. Premium wines are more generous in all attributes and will age better, although they cost more. Rieslings are food-friendly and pair well with duck, grilled prawns and ceviche, as their acidity is ideal to balance richer foods.

ARNEIS

A white Italian grape variety. It makes dry, herbaceous, pretty wines with gentle floral aromas mingled with hints of orchard fruits. Other flavours include pears and apples, peach stones, and mineral notes like stones, plus a splash of citrus and limes – soft and not too acidic. Arneis wines are usually made to drink young, so look out for recent vintages. Medium-bodied, the best are riper, aromatic and have floral notes similar to those in Viognier or Pinot Gris. They're even rich and viscous in the mouth, and aromas can be more delicate than flavours. More neutral, refreshing styles have herbiness. Arneis is used solely to make the white wines of Italy's Roero Arneis appellation, and it features as the majority grape in some white wines from the Langhe region as well. Great chilled with simple Italian cuisine like spaghetti, garlic and olive oil dishes, and Waldorf salad. If you like this style, you might also enjoy riper versions of Pouilly-Fumé from the Loire, peachier Viogniers, appley Chenin Blancs and more zesty, grapefruity Gavis.

GAVI

A town in Piedmont, northern Italy that also gives its name to crisp, food-friendly, medium-bodied, herby, floral, zesty dry – sometimes bone-dry – white wines made exclusively from Cortese grapes. A range of qualities is made, most of which are best drunk young and usually made without oak influence. Richer versions can have peachy, honeydew melon aromatics, hints of nuts with grapefruit on the finish plus some white-stone mineral qualities. They are the perfect accompaniment to grilled seafood, chicken in white sauce with fresh herbs, and as an apéritif. Try Arneis, also from Italy, or dry Furmint, a more steely Chablis, Fiano, or a white Côtes du Rhône for something riper and more alcoholic.

CORTESE

A white northwest Italian grape, occasionally found as a named variety, although you are more likely to see it as a crisp, zippy, food-friendly, dry Gavi wine. It is also used as part of a blend in other Italian white wines (and a tiny amount is made into wine in Australia) and is similar, but not quite as sharp as breezy Picpouls or steely Chablis, but with more about it than Pinot Grigio. The best are full of citrus/lemon freshness, lime aromatics with a grapefruit finish and perhaps a touch of stone-like minerals. Higher-priced wines have more body, complexity and length of flavour. This is the ideal partner, served chilled, for fish dishes, grilled prawns, salads, lightly poached chicken and pork-based meals. For a less-acidic Italian wine, sip Arneis, or try a more tropical, nutty Fiano from southern Italy. This is a refreshing grape variety to try if you haven't already.

Column 5

17 G **Fu** Furmint		**28** R **Pp** Picpoul de Pinet
18 R **Vy** Vouvray	**23** G **Mc** Muscadet	**29** G **Fi** Fiano
19 G **Ri** Riesling: Alsace or OZ	**24** R **Cl** Chablis	**30** G **Cb** Chenin Blanc
20 G **Ar** Arneis	**25** R **Sc** Sancerre	**31** G **Vo** Verdelho
21 R **Ga** Gavi	**26** R **Gd** Greco di Tufo	**32** G **Fa** Falanghina
22 G **Co** Cortese	**27** G **Gv** Grüner Veltliner	**33** R **Or** Orvieto

White wines are becoming lighter in body and often colour too. These popular styles are suitable for everyday drinking as well as pairing with lighter cuisine, but can come in refreshing, lingering, richer guises with some seriously excellent-quality wines hidden among them. Frequently they are made in a zingy, zesty style.

MUSCADET

Muscadet is the name of a place, a white grape and a light French white wine from around the city of Nantes, found at the western Atlantic end of the Loire Valley. These tangy, citrus wines with a touch of grapefruit, are made from the Melon de Bourgogne, aka Muscadet, grape (which has nothing to do with flowery Muscat and Muscadelle white grapes). Some Muscadet wines are straightforward and fairly neutral so this wine can be underrated, but well-made versions make a refreshing sipper on a hot day to accompany a light snack. Best to look for the more characterful Muscadet-Sèvre-et-Maine *sur lie* wines. These have been left 'on the lees' (dead yeast cells left over from fermentation) over the winter after harvest. This adds a layer of creamy notes, plus provides more texture and depth in the wines. Think of a splash of crème fraîche. These wines should be clean and fresh-tasting, with apple and citrus notes, mineral hints from the chalky soils, creamy if *sur lie*, sometimes with a touch of salinity. Typically no oak is used. Muscadet is made to be drunk young and fresh, and immediately after opening to feel the extra dimension of a tingly spritz on the tongue. A classic to accompany seafood, especially fruits de mer, plus light, herby salads; also makes a great summer sipper. Try instead Pinot Grigio, Frascati, steely Chablis, zippy Picpoul de Pinet and Spanish Parellada wines.

CHABLIS

24	R
Cl	
Chablis	

A white-wine-only appellation in northern Burgundy, France, named after the town of Chablis, making elegant, mouth-watering and steely wines solely from the versatile Chardonnay grape. Chablis wines exist in four quality levels. As we move up the ladder, production volumes drop, prices increase, and the wines become more concentrated, complex and lingering. All should be vibrant, with a steel girder of mouth-watering acidity providing a refreshing linearity in the mouth, rather than a rounded, fatter feeling of some Chardonnays. Look for the most affordable Petit Chablis, but try Chablis (the largest category) if your purse stretches to it, with sharp lemon peel, white blossom and chalk nuances. Next is *premier cru* Chablis and finally the pinnacle and rarest *grand cru* Chablis, a complex wine with long, ripe, peach and baked-lemon flavours and the ability to age; it may also have seen oak in its production. Alcohol is usually around medium levels. Chablis can be found on practically every wine list and is classic served chilled to accompany oysters, shellfish and white fish, other seafood dishes and the likes of mushroom risotto. Try instead unoaked Burgundian Chardonnays, zippy Picpoul de Pinet also with high acidity, Gavi from Italy, and with a touch of spice, Grüner Veltliner from Austria.

SANCERRE

25	R
Sc	
Sancerre	

A celebrated hilly wine district and appellation, named after the small town located in central France overlooking the Loire River, famous for its high-quality, crisp, minerally and aromatic dry white Sauvignon Blanc wines found on many a wine list. (A tiny proportion of Sancerre wines are delicate reds and rosés made from Pinot Noir grapes.) Wines are medium-bodied, with medium alcohol levels. Bracing acidity, although still elegant, accompanies white-blossom perfume, with subtle hints of gooseberries, lemons and leafy nettles plus chalk and a tangy finish. Pair a white Sancerre with goats' milk cheese, also shellfish and asparagus plus onion and other vegetarian tarts. This is a classy summer sipper. New Zealand Sauvignons tend to be fuller-bodied, with more punchy aromatics and riper green flavours. South African Sauvignons are a good halfway house. Pouilly-Fumé, from the opposite side of the Loire river to Sancerre, has more flinty tones due to the different soil. Try also Spanish Albariño, Greek whites and southern Italian whites like Greco di Tufo and, with more apple and pear notes, Fiano.

GRECO DI TUFO

Greco is a widely planted medium-bodied, perfumed and sometimes herbal white grape from southern Italy, grown mostly in Campania and also Puglia. There are several Grecos, the most well-known from Tufo, i.e. Greco di Tufo. It can appear in affordable, light, simple blends from the same region; look for Irpinia and Sannio. Usually dry, some sweet and sparkling examples are made, though these are harder to find. Wines are fresh and typically made to drink young. Flavours include pear, green plum and peach, sometimes with a salty tang or with a touch of bitter almond. A richer alternative to Sauvignon Blanc. A food-friendly and popular wine worth discovering if you haven't already. Serve chilled with pasta, prawns, seafood, especially sea bass, and deep-fried beignets or falafel. Try also other southern Italian whites.

GRÜNER VELTLINER

A versatile white grape that is becoming more readily available. It is the signature white grape of Austria, a country whose wines, in general, are likely to be high quality. Grüner Veltliner has refreshing high acidity, which lingers in the more concentrated wines. Younger, fresher styles to sip are dry, crisp, light and citrussy – think lime, lemon and grapefruit – with notes of green pepper.

As the wines become richer they typically develop more weight and fullness in the mouth, still with steely freshness plus more texture, perfume, mineral hints and characteristic touches of white pepper. This style is harder to find and costs more but tends to be age-worthy. Some are tangy with an aromatic hint of dill. In addition, flavours of nuts, cream and honey also occur when oak is used. Some Grüner Veltliners can age like the best wines of Burgundy, and plantings are expanding around the globe. You may come across Grüner Veltliner wines with higher levels of sweetness, though these are less common. Grüner Veltliner is an alternative to Sauvignon Blanc, but also try Chardonnay, Pinot Gris and Greco di Tufo from Italy. Grüner Veltliner is food-friendly, so makes a good choice for a range of dishes, including lighter meats, spicy meals, creamy cheeses and green vegetables (even artichokes).

Column 6

	28 R **Pp** Picpoul de Pinet	**34** R **So** Soave
23 G **Mc** Muscadet	**29** G **Fi** Fiano	**35** G **Vd** Verdejo
24 R **Cl** Chablis	**30** G **Cb** Chenin Blanc	**36** G **Vm** Vermentino
25 R **Sc** Sancerre	**31** G **Vo** Verdelho	**37** G **Rs** Riesling: Mosel
26 R **Gd** Greco di Tufo	**32** G **Fa** Falanghina	**38** R **Fr** Frascati
27 G **Gv** Grüner Veltliner	**33** R **Or** Orvieto	**39** G **Tr** Trebbiano

Some white wines here have lip-smacking zinginess, although now the table is moving into wines that can be more neutral, easy-drinking and popular, especially when made in large volumes. These middle three columns of white wines are very interchangeable, so this is a part of the table open to lots of experimentation.

PICPOUL DE PINET

A coastal appellation in the far south of France making light, high-acidity, really fresh white wines with a lemony zing from the Picpoul grape that is grown in the region surrounding the small French village of Pinet. Pale lemon-yellow, and usually found in tall, slim, green bottles, Picpoul de Pinet is similar to Muscadet, but with more floral notes, like white blossom, bracing lemon and lime citrus, and a splash of salinity, pear and apple. Some have a touch of peppery spices; others green herbs. A bone-dry, no-oak, breezy white wine that should be drunk young while at its freshest alongside seafood such as mackerel or oysters, and Mediterranean cuisine; it is a surprisingly terrific match for fish-and-chips. A zingy swap for Muscadets, Sauvignon Blancs, Grüner Veltliners and Vinho Verdes.

FIANO

An ancient southern Italian white grape, grown mainly in Campania, especially Fiano d'Avellino, plus Sicily, some other Italian regions and a little is made in Australia. Mainly produced as a varietal wine, though sometimes blended, as in Irpinia wines that are *bianco* (white). It can withstand the southern heat and still yield a vibrant, pure and intensely fruity wine. Alcohol levels can be medium to high. Not as aromatic as Greco di Trufo, Fiano can have minerality if grown on poor, volcanic soils at altitude. Look for label comments about cool-temperature fermentation and expect candied citrus and grapefruit notes, apple, chamomile or white-blossom tones, with perhaps apricot, honey and nut flavours and a waxy texture in the best. Serve chilled with seafood, white meats and cheeses. Try also Greco di Tufo, Sauvignon Blanc or a lighter Frascati.

CHENIN BLANC: FROM THE NEW WORLD

A leading versatile white grape variety known for its high levels of refreshing acidity. It can make dry, sweet and sparkling styles of honey- and quince-flavoured wines, some with the capacity to age. South Africa has the largest plantings of Chenin Blanc in the New World. Its dry wines are more exotically fruit-flavoured (think pineapple, melon and yellow plum), compared to the French wines, which show more of a warm apple tang. Value wines are easy-drinking and made without oak so are 'pure', if perhaps on the neutral side. Terms like 'old-vine', 'bush vine', and 'lees (dead yeast cells) stirring' on the label indicate higher-quality grapes are used. Wines are still pure, though with more concentrated apple, citrus and a touch of lanolin flavour, added texture and weight in the mouth, complexity and length. This style is more likely to be made with oak, which adds a layer of vanilla, though levels vary so explore. Chenin Blanc is food-friendly; match the weight of wine to the weight of the food. The lightest match salads and white fish: try sea bass. Sweeter styles accompany tarte tatin. See also Vouvray for Chenin Blanc wines from France. Zippy wine swaps include pure, fresh Riesling, and lighter Albariños, Chablis for steeliness or oaked Chardonnay for vanilla and tropical flavours as a swap for the richer style of Chenin.

VERDELHO

A white grape variety originally grown in Portugal to make straw-coloured, versatile and light, affordable wines (though full-bodied wines are produced, especially in Australia). Wines can smell and taste of hints of grapes. Blending Verdelho with better-known grapes like Sauvignon Blanc and Sémillon results in a range of styles and weights, and can be a means of making a lighter, more affordable wine. Be guided by the label. Blending with local Portuguese varieties creates an everyday style. European Verdelhos are lighter, more subtle and elegant than New World wines, juicy, with fruit-salad and citrus flavours. Australian versions tend to be more green, with flavours like lime and honeysuckle and can be softened or have vanilla notes, depending on how the wine was made. This quaffable wine is drinkable without food, and pairs well with tapas, appetisers or spicy Asian food. You could also try Godello, Albariño, a lighter style of Chardonnay or more intense Grüner Veltliner. Riesling is generally more acidic and Sancerres have more mineral notes and finesse.

FALANGHINA

32	G
Fa	
Falanghina	

A southern-Italian white grape variety found mainly around Naples in Campania. Its high acidity is useful, yielding fresh, crisp sippers with zesty aromatics. Where grown at altitude Falanghinas can be light-bodied and elegant, with leafy notes plus a touch of honey and tangerine on the finish. The volcanic soil adds a mineral layer of chalk or stone. Enjoy with pasta and pizza, fish, white meats, poultry and as a good apéritif. More flavour than Pinot Grigio, plus an alternative to Sauvignon Blanc, Soave, Chablis and other lighter, crisp wines at the leafy end of the spectrum. Worth discovering if you haven't already.

ORVIETO

33	R
Or	
Orvieto	

A commune in Umbria that gives its name to crisp, youthful, central Italian white wine usually made from a blend of grapes. Usually dry, although sweeter styles are made but mainly drunk locally, and pale. Those labelled *classico* tend to have more character. They are light-bodied, easy-drinking, inexpensive and sometimes neutral. Look for a peachy perfume, citrus notes and hints of crunchy green apples; richer versions include a touch of green pears, fresh peaches and maybe white flowers. Alcohol levels tend not to be high so Orvieto makes a good apéritif and is a crowd-pleaser. Orvietos pair well with simple dishes such as salads, white meats and lighter seafood. Try also Frascati, simple Pinot Grigio and Muscadet, zesty Gavi for something with more weight, and steely Chablis.

Column 7

28 R	34 R	40 G
Pp Picpoul de Pinet	**So** Soave	**Mt** Müller-Thurgau

29 G	35 G	41 G
Fi Fiano	**Vd** Verdejo	**Po** Pinot Grigio

30 G	36 G	42 G
Cb Chenin Blanc	**Vm** Vermentino	**Al** Albariño

31 G	37 G	43 G
Vo Verdelho	**Rs** Riesling: Mosel	**Pa** Parellada

32 G	38 R	44 G
Fa Falanghina	**Fr** Frascati	**Ve** Verdicchio

33 R	39 G	45 R
Or Orvieto	**Tr** Trebbiano	**Vv** Vinho Verde

This column is a mix of lighter grape varieties and wines that are suitable for apéritifs, sipping in the sunshine and for serving alongside lighter cuisine like salads and seafood. If you prefer wines without oak, you are likely to find them here.

SOAVE

More commonly an elegant, easy-drinking, dry, white Italian wine from the Veneto region in northeast Italy made mainly from Garganega grapes, but with Trebbiano and other white varieties added too. (Some sweet Soave is produced, which is a lighter style than Sauternes.) Usually affordable, this is a pale, lemon-green wine with fresh, citrus acidity; it may be fairly neutral, so is popular as a light apéritif. More succulent wines include apricot tones, a stone-like mineral hit from the volcanic soil, green herbal tinges with waxy weight, and a creamy, soft texture, which can be due to using some oak in the production process; these are more expensive. Try it with creamy chicken or chicken Kiev, pasta and gratin dishes, or serve it with a few green olives. You may also like Grechetto, Pinot Grigio and Orvieto.

VERDEJO

A white grape from Rueda in northwest Spain that makes delicate, youthful and fresh wines often blended with some Sauvignon Blanc. Wines are light to medium-bodied, crisp with softness along with refreshing citrus notes like lemon, sometimes grapefruit and lime, also green apple and mineral touches, and they can have light nutty hints too – easy-drinking with suggestions of floral and herbaceous notes. The better wines have more texture, like a touch of cream and richness, and notes of honey. Pairs well with starters and lighter main courses. Alternatively, why not try a Pinot Gris with its similar texture, or a lighter Spanish white, like Airén or Viura?

VERMENTINO

A white grape variety that makes pale, straw-coloured, green-tinged zippy wines in Sardinia. It is the same as Rolle in southern France, and Pigato in northern Italy. Increasingly it is successfully made in Australia. It makes delicious dry, lemon, green-appley and peachy wines that are fresh, zippy and unoaked to retain freshness; these are wines to drink young. Sometimes they include a touch of citrus leaf, basil or white-blossom aromas and a clean mineral note. Pigato styles tend to be more aromatic. This is one to try if you like unoaked light to medium white wines, such as simple Pinot Grigio, the weightier dazzling Gavi and white, peachy, light Orvieto. Delicious with Mediterranean vegetables, salty snacks and seafood. Other wines to sip include Albariño, Verdicchio, and for something even zippier, Picpoul de Pinet.

RIESLING: MOSEL

An aromatic white grape here it is grown on steep slopes by the winding Mosel River in Germany. It is light-bodied, easy-drinking and low in alcohol: around 8% ABV. Flavours are pure and mouth-watering. Usually pale with green hints, with green apples, white peach and piquancy, these clean wines are made without oak influence. Most are designed for early drinking. A range of sweetness levels is available, from off-dry to bone-dry. Drier styles tend to be more alcoholic, but some labels are less helpful than others as far as taste profile is concerned, so persevere. Even *Halbtrocken*, or 'half-dry' wines, where a little unfermented sugar has been left in, appear drier, so are not cloying, because the grape variety contains high levels of acidity. For those that can age, with a much richer, fuller-bodied, premium-priced style, that interesting mineral note described as 'petrol-like' develops later. The light wines are food-friendly and ideal chilled as a summer lunchtime or evening apéritif, their purity pairing well with Japanese and Chinese cuisine. *Halbtrocken* wines are good with Thai dinners. This is an interesting grape to investigate further. Also try, Müller-Thurgau (which is neutral in comparison), Albariño, Chablis, Muscadet and Grüner Veltliner for other refreshing wines. Compare with Riesling from Alsace, Australia and New Zealand.

FRASCATI

A region in Italy near Rome that gives its name to a famous – and ancient – pale-yellow, light, lower-alcohol, dry, easy-drinking and crisp white wine. It is made from a mix of several grapes, including Trebbiano and Malvasia. This popular, affordable crowd-pleaser has delicate apple and lemon flavours and is refreshing, sometimes with hints of wildflowers or grassiness and almonds. Serve young and chilled as a good match for seafood and salads, and simple pasta dishes. If you like Frascati you could try other Italian wines, such as Pinot Grigio, Orvieto, Soave and the more zippy Verdicchio and Vermentino for a tangier style. You could also expand into unoaked Chardonnays and Sauvignon Blancs from Europe (which are more subtle than those from New Zealand).

TREBBIANO

A white grape mainly found in Italy and France that is often not shown on a label as it is blended to make white wines of many names. In France it makes dry, crisp, relatively neutral-tasting, pale, affordable wines for immediate consumption, showing simple citrus and green-apple flavours, a light to medium body and similar alcohol levels. In Italy it may have more colour and zest, but wines are still dry, bright and fruity. Trebbiano d'Abruzzo is a crisp wine with a light floral bouquet. The grape can also form part of Orvieto and Frascati, so you could try these. (See, too, Vin Santo, a sweet Italian wine.) These wines are crowd-pleasers for parties, which also work well with antipasti, simple pasta and seafood meals and light lunches. A good wine swap for Italian Pinot Grigio.

Column 8

34 R **So** Soave	40 G **Mt** Müller-Thurgau	46 S **Wz** White Zinfandel
35 G **Vd** Verdejo	41 G **Po** Pinot Grigio	47 G **Gb** Grenache
36 G **Vm** Vermentino	42 G **Al** Albariño	48 R **Nv** Navarra
37 G **Rs** Riesling: Mosel	43 G **Pa** Parellada	49 R **Ra** Rosé d'Anjou
38 R **Fr** Frascati	44 G **Ve** Verdicchio	50 R **Pd** Pays d'Oc
39 G **Tr** Trebbiano	45 R **Vv** Vinho Verde	51 R **Pc** Provence

This final column of white wines contains quaffable light and neutral styles ideal for beginner white-wine drinkers, with the more mineral styles being the most zesty.

MÜLLER-THURGAU

A white grape variety used chiefly in Germany to make wines which, at their core, are light, drinkable and simple with sweet peach aromas and fruity flavours. Usually these neutral wines are low in acidity and youthful, so buy them for immediate drinking. Often off-dry, they can be part of a lower-alcohol blend of delicate grapes, like Liebfraumilch, found in slim blue bottles, which might also call the grape Rivaner or Riesling-Sylvaner. An easy, uncomplicated drink chilled on its own, or served with nibbles or with light salads and meals. It can be a gentle introduction to white wine. You can also try Mosel Riesling for a more lingering glassful with greater finesse (look for *Kabinett* on the label); Pinot Grigio for a drier, more neutral style; Soave, or the similarly off-dry white Zinfandel from the US and Portuguese rosés.

PINOT GRIGIO

A popular white grape variety that makes value, quaffable, dry wines mainly from Italy that are clean, simple, neutral and ideal as apéritifs. Within this crowd-pleasing style you could find subtle citrus fruits, apple and green pear notes, refreshing acidity and alcohol levels on the lower to medium side. Occasionally made into a rosé, which is similar to the white but with a touch of red fruit such as cranberry and red cherry. For everyday dining, drink chilled with pasta, BBQs, quiche and buffet foods. Also try Soave, Frascati, and for rosé, a dry Provence or off-dry Portuguese or US Zinfandel blush wine. See also Pinot Gris, the same grape variety but made in a richer style.

ALBARIÑO

Dry, white local grape from Galicia, in northwest Spain. Wines are pale-green to lemon-coloured, and light-bodied with lemony acidity. Albariño can be blended with other light grapes. Usually zippy, zesty and refreshing without oak and made to be drunk young. Look for some light, floral aromatics. The best, more jasmine-perfumed, shows hints of white peaches, fresh apricots and almonds, and there is a trend towards this higher-quality style. Great chilled with seafood, light fish, mussels in garlic and herb butter, and salads. In northern Portugal this grape is called Alvarinho; see Vinho Verde (see page 55). Plus look out for Rías Baixas. Try also Muscadet, and mouth-watering Picpoul de Pinet.

PARELLADA

A Spanish white grape used mainly in Cava but also to good effect in still dry wines. Usually delicate, it can sometimes be aromatic. A still wine, it is predominantly available in uncomplicated, fresh, youthful, drinkable, affordable light wines. Look for lemon, lime, white flowers, white nectarine and sometimes herbs in your glass, though often the wine is simple and easy-drinking. Drink immediately, chilled, any time of day. Good for informal lunches with dishes such as rice, fish and shellfish. Its moderate alcohol makes it ideal as an apéritif in the summer. Try also simple Pinot Grigio, herby Orvieto, Muscadet and Frascati.

VERDICCHIO

A white central Italian grape variety that makes dry, bright, lively, citrussy (lemon and lime), fresh, light-styled wines that can have floral, peardrop notes and greenish tinges in the colour – hence the name. Look out for nutty almond hints. The style is usually affordable, uncomplicated and made to consume young, with medium alcohol. A small number of more expensive, complex and age-worthy wines are made, but these are harder to find. Still crisp and fresh, they show more peach and pear fruit with an additional layer of chalk-like mineral complexity; and they can have higher alcohol and body. Punchy enough to pair with pesto-based dishes, risottos, some hard cheeses and Mediterranean cuisine. Other Italian wines to try include Verdejo and Vermentino. Also try Sauvignon Blanc, Albariño and Vinho Verde.

VINHO VERDE

A light, fresh wine made by the coast in northeast Portugal from a blend of local grape varieties. Dry, and usually a pale lemony-green (though there are other styles and colours). This is ideal for summer sipping and as an apéritif. These lively wines are designed to be drunk young. Typically they have low alcohol, a tiny tongue-tingling *petillance*, or spritz, on opening, with fresh, young fruit, light flower hints and an intense crispness. They are ideal for accompanying salads, a wide range of seafood, chicken, sushi and gratins. Other wines to try include Vermentino, the more appley Chenin Blanc, a steely Chablis, more aromatic Sauvignon Blanc, and for something with similar racy acidity, sip a Picpoul de Pinet.

Rosés

The rosé wines appearing in this column are the more common styles obtainable; there are others, as many producers make a rosé alongside their other wines. These showcase the medley of rosé wines to sip, from off-dry and frivolous to serious, dry and savoury, including colours ranging from the palest of pretty pinks to the deepest of cherry-reds. Remember that a pale colour does not always mean dainty flavours. Serve chilled to maintain their refreshing qualities.

Various red wines in the table are also made in a rosé style. These typically reflect the red-grape characteristics but are lighter, usually made without using oak. Frequently they are sold to be consumed while young, fresh and fruity, though not always. If you like red wine, why not seek out the rosé to try and compare? Perhaps do so when the weather is a little too warm for red wine, although increasingly rosés are being drunk whatever the time of year. In the winter look for more warming, higher-alcohol versions, especially if they are well-made, with bold flavours and perhaps a slight texture to balance the alcohol.

Column 9

40 G **Mt** Müller-Thurgau	46 S **Wz** White Zinfandel	
41 G **Po** Pinot Grigio	47 G **Gb** Grenache	52 R **Bj** Beaujolais
42 G **Al** Albariño	48 R **Nv** Navarra	53 G **Gm** Gamay
43 G **Pa** Parellada	49 R **Ra** Rosé d'Anjou	54 G **Do** Dolcetto
44 G **Ve** Verdicchio	50 R **Pd** Pays d'Oc	55 R **Va** Valpolicella
45 R **Vv** Vinho Verde	51 R **Pc** Provence	56 G **Bf** Blaufränkisch

WHITE ZINFANDEL

The name for a popular, soft, easy-drinking style of off-dry California rosé made from the red Zinfandel grape, but confusingly, the 'white' in front of the grape variety means it is a rosé. It is also called 'blush', which is less confusing. Here the Zinfandel grapes are picked early to retain freshness, which balances red-fruit flavours like strawberries, redcurrant and watermelon. This early harvesting also ensures alcohol levels are lower: around 10% ABV. Their pretty pink colour, gained from a short steeping of the grapes in the juice before fermentation begins, and lack of tannins combined with the fruit-juice style, make them popular for midweek drinking, despite the confusing nature of the name. A value fresh and fruity wine made for drinking chilled, while it is still young. Unexpectedly, white Zin is a great match for spicy food such as Thai cuisine and curries, picnics, 'sofa-sipping' and al fresco dining. This style is a good introduction to rosé for young palates as it is not as serious as some rosés. Also try other rosés, famously Mateus Rosé from Portugal, other New World rosés, along with drier styles from the Rhône and Provence.

GRENACHE

Widespread leading red grape variety, used across the globe to make rosé wines in a range of colours, from pale to shocking pink, and styles varying from cheeky and cheerful to sultry and serious. Alcohol levels can sometimes be high, especially where they are made in warmer climates, which allow the grapes to ripen well. Generally this diversity creates a variety of quality levels that is reflected in the price. Leaving the grape skins in contact with the fruity grape juice for different lengths of time affects the colour of the wine. Popular lighter, fruity, less-alcoholic, pocket-friendly US styles are called 'blush' and are similar to white Zinfandels. Also try picnic-friendly, deeper-pink Spanish Garnacha *rosados,* then the more serious, weighty and warming southern French rosés in a range of delightful pinks, from pale blushing-powder (Provence) to the deeper colours of the southern Rhône. As alcohol levels can be high, they are not just summer apéritifs, but can work as autumn warmers as well. Grenache can be blended with other red grapes to bring red berry, cherry and citrus flavours. The best have a touch of white pepper, cinnamon and herbal notes. Serve chilled with salty nibbles, cold meats, prawns and salmon. See Navarra, Provence, and compare with rosés from other areas, Bordeaux, Catalonia and the New World.

NAVARRA

Important wine region in northern Spain, above Rioja along the Ebro River Valley, which is traditionally associated with large volumes of dark-pink *rosado* (rosé) wine from the Garnacha (Grenache) red grape variety. *Rosados* are usually dry, lush and fruity, with flavours of soft strawberries and riper raspberries, sometimes a hint of rose or white spice too. They are easy-drinking, with a fuller body and more alcohol – around 12% ABV – compared to white Zinfandel. Navarras are often pure Grenache, or Grenache blended with other red grapes like Spanish Tempranillo and international plummy Merlot. (As Navarra is located between France and Rioja, look out also for its accessible red and white wines, again from popular grapes like Tempranillo bolstered with other quality leading grape varieties.) Location combined with improvements in winemaking means there are now likeable wines from this region to please all tastes, occasions and pockets. Good with tapas, salmon and picnics. Try also velvety wines from neighbouring Rioja, Rosé d'Anjou or lighter red wines such as Beaujolais, and Pinot Noir and Dolcetto, which are also available as rosés.

49   R
Ra
Rosé d'Anjou

ROSÉ D'ANJOU

A style of rosé wine made in the Anjou region of France's Loire Valley from a blend of red grapes, including the local Grolleau, plus better-known Cabernet Franc and the Gamay grape used in Beaujolais wine. Often pale, peachy and pomegranate-tinged, with a light to medium weight and low alcohol of around 10.5% ABV, these medium-dry, quaffable, salmon-coloured wines are made for early drinking. Expect a fruity bouquet accompanied by classic rosé flavours of red berries, strawberries and redcurrants, a touch of floral rose and confectionery, but with an uplifting freshness from good acidity and hints of mint, herbs or white pepper. Serve chilled with savoury dishes using gentle spices, or salmon or cold meats and light desserts such as fruit salads. Other wines to try are the dry Rosé de Loire, sweet Cabernet d'Anjou and the more serious, rare Sancerre, made from Pinot Noir grapes. Compare with rosés from outside France: white Zinfandel; or with more alcohol, Spanish Riojas and Navarras.

50   R
Pd
Pays d'Oc

PAYS D'OC

Pays d'Oc is a large appellation in southern France that makes all colours of affordable wine across the Languedoc. This classification is now known as *Indication Géographique Protégée*, or IGP – i.e. protected geographical indication – and it can be found on wines from defined large districts across Europe (as well as on foods, such as Cheddar and Parmigiano Reggiano cheeses). The dry rosés made in this Mediterranean location are often crafted from a blend of local red grapes. These can include rich Syrah and Cinsault, which add herbs and spiciness, along with soft, red-fruited, warming Grenache and deeper Mourvèdre. These rosés may have a touch of tannin from the skins that adds texture to balance the juiciness. Ripe, sunny, medium- to full-bodied with medium to high alcohol levels, these are best served chilled as an apéritif or as a partner for light dishes like herby prawns, tuna and Mediterranean cuisine. Compare with *rosados* from Spain, or rosés from Sicily, cheerful northern Italians versions and more specific southern French rosés like bone-dry Bandol.

51   R
Pc
Provence

PROVENCE

A hilly coastal Mediterranean region in the south of France that gives its name to attractive, often very pale pink wines that can have *gris* ('grey') in their names. They are frequently fragrant or perfumed dry rosés made from a variety of different grapes, often as blends. Provence is the world's largest region to specialise in dry rosé, so it is not surprising that this area displays a wide range of colours and textures, with some wines being lighter and others fuller in body and flavours. Experiment in this area of wine. Expect soft red fruits plus herb, floral and green fragrances redolent of the local *garrigue*: the name for the rosemary, lavender and thyme that grow throughout the region. More full-bodied versions include pink-grapefruit notes balanced with a mineral, talc-like backbone and a hint of spice. The better wines can have a long, lingering flavour. Look for the special hourglass-shaped Provence rosé bottle called a skittle. The wines should be crisp, refreshing, food-friendly and versatile: for example, the lower-alcohol (around 12% ABV) examples make ideal apéritifs. They are a good match with seafood, pork, chicken, salads and of course, Mediterranean dishes. Try also dry Tavel rosé for something more serious, and sweeter white Zinfandel for a more frivolous drink. Spanish Navarra rosés are usually darker pinks and, along with rosés from the New World, tend to be full of riper fruits like red plums, and are perhaps less floral in nature.

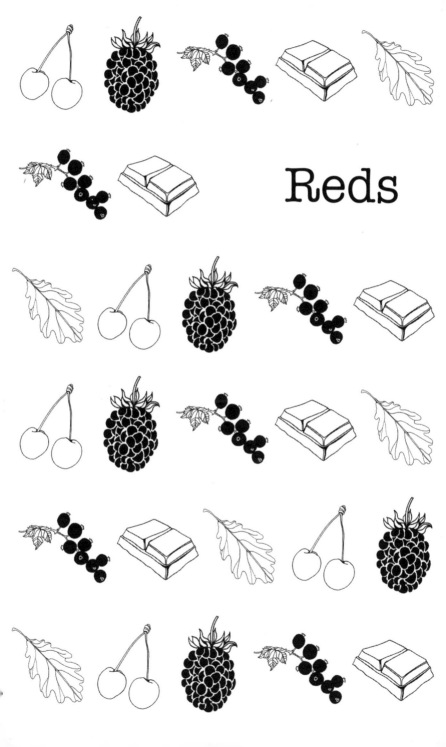

Reds

Column 10

		57 R **Ct** Chianti
46 S **Wz** White Zinfandel		58 G **Bb** Barbera
47 G **Gb** Grenache	52 R **Bj** Beaujolais	59 G **Pm** Pinot Meunier
48 R **Nv** Navarra	53 G **Gm** Gamay	60 R **By** Burgundy
49 R **Ra** Rosé d'Anjou	54 G **Do** Dolcetto	61 G **Pn** Pinot Noir
50 R **Pd** Pays d'Oc	55 R **Va** Valpolicella	62 G **Mp** Montepulciano
51 R **Pc** Provence	56 G **Bf** Blaufränkisch	63 R **Cn** Chinon

Light reds are a good place to start if you are unsure about red wine or you are after a lunchtime red for sipping alongside light meals. Typically made with less tannin, either due to the grape variety or winemaking techniques, they are really quaffable, and some are pleasant served just lightly cooled.

BEAUJOLAIS

Usually a light, fruity, easy-drinking red wine named after the region – south of Burgundy in France – where this juicy wine is made with Gamay grapes. Expect to find red fruits like strawberries, cherries, cranberries and maybe pomegranates in your glass. Beaujolais can be pretty, full of flowery raspberries and violets plus sometimes boiled-sweet notes wrapped up with refreshing acidity. Most (but not all) Beaujolais wine is made to drink young. Historically it used to be about the race to be the first to try Beaujolais Nouveau, the 'new' wine barely out of the barrel. Today, more finesse is found, especially in the better Beaujolais-Villages wines, and those at the best quality level, called *cru*. Their names on the label, like the prettily and aptly named floral Fleurie, or the more powerful and serious Brouilly and Morgan; others have slightly deeper flavours. One for the non-red-wine-drinkers to try, plus it can be served slightly chilled due to low tannin levels. A lovely, elegant wine to accompany informal lunches, pork, light roasts and chicken casseroles or scrambled eggs. Try also Dolcetto or a light Pinot Noir.

GAMAY

This juicy red grape is light in tannins and tends to make typically light-bodied wines that are high in refreshing acidity and boast lively red-fruit flavours. The name of this grape variety might be unfamiliar, but it is the sole basis of the French Beaujolais (see above), plus a little is used in the Loire Valley further west, and Gamay is also blended with the Pinot Noir grape to make the hard-to-find Dole in Switzerland. Gamay is usually made to be drunk young due to the production method that brings out the red-berry flavours and candied elements of tinned strawberries, bubblegum and bananas, so look out for recent vintages. There may also be a leafy green element. A small proportion of wines are being made in more robust styles, so are more like Pinot Noir, a little further north in Burgundy. They have the ability to age. Gamay's light nature means it can be served slightly chilled so it's great with a summer picnic or platter of cold meats. Older – and pricier – wines are more serious and can taste like older wines made from Pinot Noir. This is a good 'transition wine' for those who like white wines and want to try reds.

DOLCETTO

Dolcetto is a juicy red grape from the Piedmont region in northwest Italy. Its name means 'little sweet one', although its wines are nearly always dry. Winemakers tend to use techniques to reduce tannins, happily resulting in easy-drinking, red-fruited wines typically made without oak, so these youthful sippers can be enjoyed soon after production. This grape makes soft-styled (softer than Barbera), less acidic, fruity, often intensely-coloured fragrant wines. Violets and even bitter almonds can accompany red cherry and summer pudding flavours. Occasionally fun strawberry-laced fizzes are produced. Look for the Italian wines called Dogliani, Dolcetto d'Alba and Dolcetto d'Acqui. Also try the firmer, more tannic Barbera from the same region, or Italian Valpolicella – both have a more acidic tang. Further afield, choose French Beaujolais or light Pinot Noirs. Perfect for antipasti, informal lunches and buffets.

55	R
Va	
Valpolicella	

VALPOLICELLA

Valpolicella is a famous northeast Italian district that makes a range of juicy red wines from a blend of local grapes. There is a ladder of quality levels. Most wine is the lightest, affordable, lunchtime-sipper style called Valpolicella *classico*. Next, *superiore* has more concentration and a touch more alcohol: around 12% ABV. *Ripasso* wines are made via a special technique to give a rich, but soft, medium-bodied wine. See Amarone for the full-bodied, big-fruited and high-alcohol style. Valpolicella wines are fresh and elegant, with red-fruit flavours such as cherry and plum, plus herbs like thyme, as well as a slightly bitter finish that adds to the food friendliness. Usually lighter alcohol, but not always, so check the label. Drink with nibbles, pasta and hard cheeses. Try also Beaujolais, Dolcetto and Montepulciano.

56	G
Bf	
Blaufränkisch	

BLAUFRÄNKISCH

A versatile red grape that makes wines ranging from deeply coloured, ripe, earthy reds that can be graceful, light-bodied and fruity, to more intense, heavier-oaked, juicy and denser examples. Mainly Austrian, but also used in Hungary and eastern European countries, although the grape variety there could be labelled Lemberger or Kékfrankos. The versatility of this grape means more affordable, youthful, easy-drinking light styles are produced but still with a lush and velvety texture, blackberries and cherries, and a touch of elderflower and savoury notes. Look for crisp, cherry flavours, sometimes a tannic backbone. The best, with big prices, are made from old vines or *alte Reben*, and so are fuller-bodied, with firm tannins: quite a different style and likely to see a bit of oak, so look on the label for information. Depending on how the wine is made, Blaufränkisch makes a fashionable alternative to many different grapes like Nebbiolo, Syrah and Pinot Noir, therefore it is increasingly appearing on wine lists, together with its Austrian cousin Zweigelt. One to try if you come across it.

Column 11

		64 G **Pz** Pinot Noir: NZ
	57 R **Ct** Chianti	65 R **Ps** Pic St-Loup
	58 G **Bb** Barbera	66 G **M** Merlot
52 R **Bj** Beaujolais	59 G **Pm** Pinot Meunier	67 R **St** St-Émilion
53 G **Gm** Gamay	60 R **By** Burgundy	68 R **Rj** Rioja
54 G **Do** Dolcetto	61 G **Pn** Pinot Noir	69 G **Sg** Sangiovese
55 R **Va** Valpolicella	62 G **Mp** Montepulciano	70 G **Br** Brunello
56 G **Bf** Blaufränkisch	63 R **Cn** Chinon	71 G **Cm** Carmenère

Many red wines fit into the medium-bodied style, which is versatile and can include the most popular and well-known wines of the world – especially as they are frequently neither too tannic or heavy nor too light. This column starts with a large category of reds that continue into the next few columns. Their alcohol levels, as well as flavours and textures, are often mediums, although with such a big category, so many winemakers, and places where they are made around the world, there is still a great deal of variation. Winemakers might make a selection of wines of different quality levels too.

CHIANTI

A widespread region in Tuscany that makes popular Italian juicy, ruby-red dry wines mainly from Sangiovese grapes, which are much improved since the rounded, raffia-clad, mass-produced *fiasco* bottles – although the latter are making a retro comeback. They come in a wide range of prices that generally reflect quality. Smoother, more refined Chiantis have *Classico* (the traditional heartland of Chianti) on the label, plus some other more specific regions, like the more floral Rúfina. *Riserva* wines have been aged for a minimum of two years before sale, which adds body, softness and earthiness, while younger versions are juicy and fruity, with flavours of sour cherries (a classic Chianti tone), damsons and wild herbs, smoke and spice notes. Typical mellow tannins make them easy-drinking and well-liked. Premium-priced *gran selezione* Chiantis are rare, aged for longer and originate from single vineyards, offering more complexity, body and lingering flavours. All usually have zippy acidity, which makes them excellent with a wide range of foods: antipasti (naturally), pasta and pizza, also medium cheeses, tomato-based dishes and slow-cooked meats such as lamb and beef. Also check out Sangiovese, good-value Rosso di Toscana, plus Barbera, Vino Nobile di Montepulciano, Carmignano, Merlot and Rioja.

58   G

Bb

Barbera

BARBERA

The name of an Italian red grape variety that makes succulent, medium- and some light-bodied, vivid, easy-drinking, mostly Italian wines, with fleshy red fruits such as cherries and raspberries, some with a touch of smokiness or vanilla. This grape is local to northwest Italy; think Barbera d'Asti (Barbera from Asti) and Barbera d'Alba (Barbera from Alba), with some plantings in Argentina too. These wines can have light or supple tannins (where a touch of oak is used, as the grape itself is low-tannin) and a silky finish; refreshing Italian acidity makes this a popular plummy wine. More affordable in wines called *vino rosso*, where it could be used as part of a blend. Great with mushroom- or tomato-based pasta dishes like ravioli. Try also Merlot-based wines, or from Italy, softer Dolcetto, Chianti or the lighter, herby Valpolicella. It is interesting to compare with the very differently styled local but much more tannic, serious and pricey Barbaresco and Barolo wines. Further afield, a juicy red-fruited Beaujolais from France is a similarly styled alternative.

59   G

Pm

Pinot
Meunier

PINOT MEUNIER

Important red grape variety most famously used as a partner with red Pinot Noir and white Chardonnay grapes to make Champagne in northern France, and also sparkling wines from other regions, although it is a bit of a forgotten grape in the still-wine sector. *Meunier* means 'miller' in French, so-called as the underside of the grape leaves appear to have a dusting of flour. It can add a touch of *pâtisserie*, apples and sometimes a smoky note to Champagne and her lookalikes. Proudly used by the prestige Krug Champagne house. Krug aside, this grape is often used by more commercial Champagne and sparkling wine houses outside of France, so if you buy a pocket-friendly fizz, you may be drinking Pinot Meunier without knowing it. Lighter in colour and tannins than

Pinot Noir, but with higher acidity, which adds freshness and is helpful when making bubbles.

BURGUNDY

Historic, influential French wine region that gives its name to red Pinot Noir and white Chardonnay dry wines. *Bourgogne* in French, it has variable weather, a patchwork of vineyards and variety of soils; there is therefore a variety of quality in its wines. Confusingly, this is combined with the complicated classification system for wines made in Burgundy; it therefore becomes advisable to find a winemaker whose style you know you like. The classification system here categorises wine quality by vineyard location. Uncomplicated *Bourgogne* (on the label) represents over half of production and grapes can come from anywhere in Burgundy. At the apex of this hierarchy are the exclusive, expensive *grand cru* wines from tiny single vineyards (named on the label in capital letters); these can age for decades. In between are district appellations such as Mâcon through to village names (communes in Burgundy) such as Puligny-Montrachet, up to single-vineyard communes, or *premiers crus*. Red burgundies are pale-coloured, low-tannin and light-bodied with violet hints and red fruits like redcurrants, raspberries and cherries; they are also earth- and herb-scented. Aromas can be beguiling. Flavours can have an inner, graceful strength. They tend to have a chalk-like mineral edge which, along with acidity, gives poise and elegance to these wines over those from outside Burgundy. The best keep developing to evolve savoury, game and mushroom layers with a silky texture, and the use of French oak barrels adds a subtle cream, vanilla and smokiness (to both the red and white wines), but these wines can be high-priced. Pair them with roast chicken, herby pork or sausages, light game, dishes with morel mushrooms and coq au vin. Other reds to try are fruitier Beaujolais, or go for a Pinot Noir from outside Burgundy, which may be riper.

61	G
Pn	
Pinot Noir	

PINOT NOIR

A light-coloured, light-tannin, perfumed, leading red grape variety, usually not blended with other varieties. This fussy red grape is famously the aromatic red wine of the Burgundy region, its homeland. It reflects the different geological aspects, like soil, in which it is grown and is a style to which winemakers worldwide aspire. Pinot Noir can be complex, but is often more costly than other grape varieties, due in part to its small production and because it requires more work than other red grapes. Burgundian wines are dry and elegant, with poise, refreshing acidity, red cherries and brambles with violet perfume. With age, earthy, mushroomy undergrowth and gamey characteristics develop. Oak is used subtly in the winemaking process, adding a hint of cream – perhaps vanilla and smokiness. Pinot Noir is a good match for food like pork, cold cuts, quiche and herby and lightly mushroomed dishes.

From the New World, especially New Zealand and the US, these red wines are much bigger, richer, deeper-coloured and riper, with darker cherries, damsons and perhaps a touch of cooked fruit compote and leather on the palate – not always so aromatic, but perhaps more consistent. Quite a range of styles is produced in New Zealand alone, as experience and spread of the grape in the country grows. From cool-climate coastal Australian vineyards you can find pale-ruby Pinots with fruity flavours of raspberries. Wines from Chile are more straightforward. Pinot Noir from Oregon is a halfway-house style, somewhere between that of Burgundy and New Zealand. Alcohol is medium, body is medium, though both may be on the lighter side in Burgundy and heavier or riper outside the region. Refreshing acidity tends to be a touch more present in Pinot Noirs from Burgundy. Pairs well with baked sea bass, pheasant, herby leg of lamb and vegetarian tarts.

MONTEPULCIANO

Montepulciano d'Abruzzo is a popular, juicy red wine made primarily from plummy Montepulciano grapes grown in the hilly Abruzzo region of central Italy. This is a deep-ruby, generally medium-bodied (some fuller-bodied examples are made), rounded wine, with lots of red-cherries, plums, dried herbs and supple tannins, so a little softer and less acidic than Chianti. It can include savoury notes such as herbs, truffles and pepper. Young wines can be more rustic and lighter, which makes them charming and versatile with food. Though a range of styles and prices is available, most are good-value, lighter, easy-drinking bottles of straightforward delicious dry red wine. *Riservas* are aged so are generally more complex – smoother, with layers of flavours like a touch of spice. Like many Italian wines, high acidity helps Montepulciano pair well with food, including tomato-based dishes, pasta, pizza, pulled pork and hard cheeses. Try lighter, fruitier Valpolicella, Merlot, or go for something much deeper and sunnier like a Sicilian Nero d'Avola.

CHINON

A region in France's Loire Valley, named after its medieval fortress town, which also gives its name to dry red wines made predominantly with herby, aromatic Cabernet Franc grapes. (A tiny proportion of Chinon wines are cherry-fruited rosé and pale, crisp, quince-flavoured whites made from Chenin Blanc grapes.) Here, year of production – the vintage – can be important. Chinons are light- to medium-bodied raspberry, summer pudding, fruity reds. They can have soft tannins or they can be more evident, with darker blueberry fruit, graphite hints of pencil shavings plus vanilla and tobacco-leaf notes as they are more likely to have seen a touch of oak. Cabernet Franc is more herby, with red and black fruits (*fruits de bois*) and fewer tannins and blackcurrant compared with Cabernet Sauvignon. It can be a touch 'green' in a cooler vintage, where the grapes have struggled to ripen. All Chinon wines have good levels of refreshing acidity and a suggestion of chalk minerals from the tuffeau soils, making them suitable to accompany picnic food and white meats, gently braised meats, charcuterie, buffets and informal lunches. Look for names like Bourgueil and Saumur-Champigny made in neighbouring villages. Also try slightly lighter Beaujolais, plummy Merlots and richer Cabernet Francs from further afield, like Chile, which have a sunnier, riper, more viscous texture. Dolcetto, Barbaresco, Chianti and young Rioja are good options for a change.

Column 12

	64 G **Pz** Pinot Noir: NZ	**72 R** **Rd** Ribero del Duero
57 R **Ct** Chianti	**65 R** **Ps** Pic St-Loup	**73 G** **Ma** Malbec
58 G **Bb** Barbera	**66 G** **M** Merlot	**74 R** **Cô** Côtes du Rhône
59 G **Pm** Pinot Meunier	**67 R** **St** St-Émilion	**75 G** **Te** Tempranillo
60 R **By** Burgundy	**68 R** **Rj** Rioja	**76 R** **Bs** Barbaresco
61 G **Pn** Pinot Noir	**69 G** **Sg** Sangiovese	**77 R** **Lg** Languedoc
62 G **Mp** Montepulciano	**70 G** **Br** Brunello	**78 G** **Pi** Pinotage
63 R **Cn** Chinon	**71 G** **Cm** Carmenère	**79 R** **Bx** Bordeaux

This column encompasses some of the world's most well-liked red wines and grape varieties, which makes the wines good for gatherings and everyday drinking. Sometimes they are made to age, which tends to be reflected in a higher price. This is an area of the table where you can experiment, moving up and down and between columns.

PINOT NOIR: NEW ZEALAND

New Zealand has achieved status for its own style of red wine made from Pinot Noir grapes (as it has for white Sauvignon Blanc). These wines are dry, with ripe red and black fruits, sunnier and more concentrated than Old World Pinot Noir, but more elegant than the even riper, heavier Californian versions. A variety of styles is being produced as experience and vineyard locations grow. Typically wines are ripe, with flavours of dark plum and sometimes chocolate, cherry and spicy notes from oak use. Medium-bodied, with soft tannins (higher than Burgundy). Look out for the alcohol level, which can be high, but it is balanced by the intense flavours. Older bottles have savoury, herby and earthy characteristics. New Zealand Pinot Noir is a versatile partner with food served with chutney or sauce trimmings, such as turkey, game birds and duck, roasted fillet of salmon, pork, veal, herby lamb and venison. Compare this with a more subtle Burgundy, a bigger Californian Pinot Noir and those from the New World. You might also like plummy Merlot, Chinon and Rioja.

PIC ST-LOUP

A mountain close to the Mediterranean gives its name to this appellation within the Languedoc region of southern France. The appellation makes perfumed dry red wines from a blend of three main grapes: Syrah, Grenache and Mourvèdre (a little rosé is also made). These wines are ripe, which can give the impression of sweetness, with suggestions of *garrigue*: the rosemary, lavender and thyme that grow across the region. There should be lots of fruit, plums, dark cherries, chocolate and smoke plus spicy notes of pepper from the Syrah, and liquorice. Sometimes there are savoury olive flavours. Tannins can be rustic to silky, and body not less than medium, depending on the blend and the winemaker. Alcohol levels can be high, especially in the bigger, more intense wines, so check the label. Wines with more concentration and fuller body might be labelled *vieilles vignes* (made with grapes from old vines) and sell at a premium. Decanting will soften the wine before drinking. A great pair with BBQs, casseroles, ragoût and herby lamb. Other wines from the area to try include Fitou, Corbières, Minervois and wines from the more affordable Languedoc – the Pays d'Oc name.

MERLOT

A leading soft, plummy red grape variety, which is popular with winemakers and wine-lovers all around the globe, due to its easy-drinking nature and fruitiness. This is one of the main red grapes of Bordeaux wines, along with Cabernet Sauvignon, but Merlot is more velvety, with lower acidity and less tannin, so it can be approachable in youth. Better-value Bordeaux typically has a bigger proportion of Merlot within its blend. It is part of some of the world's most expensive wines and also wines that offer great value for money. Look for New World wines from Chile and Argentina, and less-well-known regions such as Fronsac and Languedoc-Roussillon for best value. This plump, mellow red, with its inclusive style, makes a good choice for a party, with flavours that include cherries, raspberries and plums. Richer wines, often from warmer areas, are riper and more concentrated in style. Graphite, cedar, tobacco, smokiness, vanilla and cloves may also be present, especially when oak is employed in the winemaking process. It can be made as a single-varietal wine – i.e. with only Merlot in the bottle – but just as often as part of a blend. Merlot's broad appeal is due in part to it pairing well with many foods, including stews and roasts, cheeses and pâtés, but take care not to overwhelm it with strong flavours or spices. Other soft sippers include Rioja, Tempranillo, and for a touch more warmth, a red Côtes du Rhône.

ST-ÉMILION

67	R
St	
St-Émilion	

St-Émilion is a pretty town in the Bordeaux region of France, on the right bank of the Gironde Estuary. Its name is associated with easy-drinking red wines. (The main wines of Bordeaux from the left bank of the estuary focus on Cabernet Sauvignon.) Here in this part of the Bordeaux region, these popular St-Émilion wines are based on softer, mellow Merlot, often blended with Cabernet Franc (and sometimes a splash of Cabernet Sauvignon). Wines are rounded, with red fruit – cherry, raspberry, plum – accompanied by a herbal note. Good overall balance and structure come from fresh acidity, and medium tannins, lower than Cabernet Sauvignon, make this red a crowd-pleaser. If oak is used, other layers of flavours such as vanilla, smoke and spice add complexity. Some can be elegant and silky-smooth. A few winemakers are known for their more opulent and rich wine styles, but this comes at a price. Pair with roast meats and casseroles, herby nut cutlets and sausages. Try the smooth, rich, black cherryish, Merlot-based wines from neighbouring Pomerol and the more affordable Lalande-de-Pomerol; also Merlots from around the world; the red grape Carmenère, which has a similar taste to Merlot; soft Rioja; the more sour-cherry-like Chianti, and higher-tannin Bordeaux reds. See Bordeaux and Médoc.

68   R

Rj
Rioja

RIOJA

The most famous Spanish wine region is situated in northern Spain along the river Ebro, and is named after the river Oja, which flows into the Ebro near Haro. Rioja gives its name to mainly dry reds, plus a smaller amount of white and deeply coloured rosé wines. Red wines range from soft and red-fruited, with no or little oak influence, to wines with plums, darker, richer, dried fruits, touches of leather and sweet spices.

Mellow Riojas are released after ageing, mainly in American oak, which adds coconut, vanilla and spicy notes to the fruit and softens the tannins. With longer ageing, like in the rarer *gran reserva* wines, the fruit turns to dried dates, along with earthy, mushroomy, savoury and leather characteristics that linger. Tempranillo, Garnacha and a little Graciano form part of the Rioja grape blend. Garnacha dominates in the juicy, strawberry- and herb-filled dry rosés, called *rosados*, that can have higher alcohol levels than the sweeter and lighter US rosés.

White Riojas vary from modern, clean, fresh, easy-drinking styles to the traditional creamy, soft-fruited kinds that have been fermented in barrels; look for oak use on the label – it rounds out the flavours and texture. Oaked whites are suitable for more robust-styled meals, such as roast chicken and creamy sauces, pastas and risottos, while the lighter styles are refreshing for summer food: salads, fish and buffets.

Reds are food-friendly and crowd-pleasers, pairing well with lots of savoury dishes: classically lamb, but also pies and less-delicate-tasting seafood – think paella. Compare the flavours of Riojas with their different classifications: *crianza*, *reserva* and the premium *gran reserva*. You can also try wines from neighbouring Navarra, Tempranillos, Merlots and Montepulcianos.

SANGIOVESE

This is a widely planted and popular red grape in Italy, traditionally in Tuscany, where it is valued for its zippy acidity, sour cherry and herb tones, hints of tomato leaf, and the savoury and earthy characteristics it gives to the red wines of Chianti. Some Chiantis bring out the floral characteristics of this grape more, like the violet notes in Chiantis from Rúfina. Sangiovese is also the only grape used to make Brunello di Montalcino and it is the majority grape of Vino Nobile di Montepulciano and Carmignano wines. Popular 'Super Tuscan' wines pair Sangiovese effectively with international grape varieties such as Cabernet Sauvignon and Cabernet Franc, Merlot and sometimes Syrah. In Corsica, where it is known as Nielluccio, expect to find more herb-like aromatics and flavours. A wide range of quality is available, so finding a good Sangiovese is confusing, especially as label names may look similar, although price is a good indication. Tannins are firm but not drying. Where the wine spends time in oak, a deeper plummy richness develops, along with earthy notes, plus leather. A natural choice for Italian dishes such as pasta and pizzas, Sangiovese is versatile, so in addition try it with ragu, charcuterie, bread and cheeses, and tomato-sauce based recipes.

BRUNELLO

Brunello is a red grape variety. It is the Sangiovese grape (of Chianti wine fame), but when grown in the region of Montalcino it is called a different name due to its deeper colour. 'Brunello' is often followed by *di Montalcino* – i.e. Brunello from Montalcino. Montalcino is a hilltop town south of Siena in Tuscany where this type of Sangiovese is the sole grape used to make these aged, complex, dry wines with a full range of flavours. The wines are more forthright than Chiantis, and can be succulent, full of generous blackberry fruit, accompanied by herbal and menthol notes. These wines may also include a touch of savoury earthiness, and will age further to give tannins a velvety softness. There is a range of prices, but Brunellos are not usually low-priced, and vintage variations exist. Decanting can help open up a wine before drinking. For a more pocket-friendly version, released after much shorter ageing, try the fruitier, softer and lighter Rosso di Montalcino, which is closer in style to Chianti. Compare with softer Chianti, more tannic Nebbiolo wines like Barolo, and smokier Pinotage. Brunello pairs with flavourful black olives and pine nuts, roasted meats, mushroom risotto and savoury herb dishes.

CARMENÈRE

This red grape variety is grown mainly in Chile as its signature grape. It originated in France in the Médoc region of Bordeaux, but more sun in Chile allows this gently herbaceous grape to shine. As a varietal wine it is fruity, with tones of dark brambles, herbs and spices, and boasts a dark colour. It can have notes of black pepper and even tomato, or chocolate and cassis overtones when riper. Carmenère tends to have more herb and leaf notes compared to Merlot, and cedar where oak is used. With similar smooth, well-rounded tannins to those of Merlot, it is perhaps a touch lighter and more supple than Cabernet Sauvignon wines. It can come blended with these grapes or on its own. These easy-drinking red wines accompany meaty dishes, stews, pizzas, sausages, herby lamb chops and nut cutlets. You might also like Cabernet Franc, Merlot, Cabernet Sauvignon and Bordeaux blends.

Column 13

64 G	72 R	80 R
Pz Pinot Noir: NZ	**Rd** Ribero del Duero	**Pt** Priorat
65 R	73 G	81 R
Ps Pic St-Loup	**Ma** Malbec	**Bd** Bandol
66 G	74 R	82 R
M Merlot	**Cô** Côtes du Rhône	**Cp** Châteauneuf-du-Pape
67 R	75 G	83 G
St St-Émilion	**Te** Tempranillo	**Ci** Cinsault
68 R	76 R	84 G
Rj Rioja	**Bs** Barbaresco	**Gr** Grenache
69 G	77 R	85 G
Sg Sangiovese	**Lg** Languedoc	**Ne** Nebbiolo
70 G	78 G	86 G
Br Brunello	**Pi** Pinotage	**Na** Nero d'Avola
71 G	79 R	87 G
Cm Carmenère	**Bx** Bordeaux	**Cf** Cabernet Franc

Here we are gently moving towards red wines that generally have more weight about them, but are not necessarily full-bodied. Check out the level of alcohol, and also whether or not they are made using oak, which can add spices and texture. Older versions have had time to soften. Those made in warmer places contain riper fruit flavours. Once more, winemakers can make sets of wines from a pocket-friendly, more affordable version to small amounts of premium-quality-level reds, which will have been made using the best grapes and most care. These wines pair well with a wide range of dishes, making them a versatile choice.

RIBERO DEL DUERO

A high-altitude region in Spain that makes deep-flavoured, dark-coloured, fine, dry red wines, mainly using Tempranillo grapes (called Tinto Fino here), with other grapes like Cabernet Sauvignon and Merlot forming part of the blends. Riberos are complex, with cherry fruit, liquorice and spices and supple, velvety to firm tannins plus alcohol, which can be high. They can have a touch of tobacco, be rich and meaty with chocolate tones and a fuller-bodied texture; the more powerful wines have higher prices to match, plus are more likely to have been aged in oak. Both American and French oaks are used, adding coconut, subtle vanilla, cream and cedar layers of aromas and flavours. The oak-ageing classification system here is the same as in Rioja (but without white wines). Decant into a new bottle if you prefer to aerate and soften the wine before serving. This welcoming red wine pairs well with goulash, tagines and warming winter dishes such as cottage pie. Other hearty wines to try include lighter Riojas, plus with more of a blackcurrant edge, Cabernet Sauvignon, ripe southern Rhône and Portuguese reds, and New World wines made from Grenache and Syrah.

MALBEC

A red grape variety grown fairly widely but mainly in Argentina, where it is the country's signature red wine. Historically it originates from Cahors, in southwest France. It makes popular dry wines that are ink-coloured and can at times be full-bodied. It brings juicy fruit flavours ranging from blueberries (a classic note), black cherries, plums and blackberries to the glass. Malbec is available in a range of weights (feeling plump in the mouth), with some wines more full-bodied than others so find your own preferred style, perhaps depending on the occasion. Malbec grapes respond to differences in climate and soils. From Argentina, Malbec wines can have more blueberry than plum flavours, some include a touch of violets, plus they have higher levels of tannins than Merlot. They can be more rustic than Merlots too, and easier-drinking than Cabernet Sauvignons, especially the more affordable, lighter-styled versions, which are good for a party. Argentinian Malbecs are riper and sunnier, with a silky, more velvety texture compared to those from cooler Cahors. For French Malbecs, look for Cahors or Côt. These can be more savoury than Argentinian versions, with firmer tannins – some very tannic, some more rustic – and with a touch of smokiness. Ageing in oak softens tannins on both sides of the Atlantic, making the wines feel rounder in the mouth, and it can add flavours of figs, leather and tobacco, plus spices like cloves and pepper. Sometimes Malbec is blended with other red grapes such as Cabernet Sauvignon or Merlot, reflecting its links with blended Bordeaux wines and adding flavour layers plus colour. If you find it a little tough, decant it to soften and round it out. Try it with calves liver, casseroles, steak, ragu and mature cheeses. Surprisingly, a glass of juicy New World Malbec pairs well with a piece of chocolate cake. Other wines to try include Bordeaux, Côtes du Rhône, heavier and deeper Priorat and Ribero del Duero.

CÔTES DU RHÔNE

A collective name for southern French wines made alongside the river Rhône. Côtes du Rhône covers the majority of wine made across the Rhône region, especially in those appellations close to the southern part of the Rhône River. Côtes du Rhône-Village is one up the quality ladder, so expect to pay a little more and find a touch more complexity of flavours, plus more assurance compared to standard Côtes du Rhône. Usually these popular wines are a blend of Grenache, Syrah and Mourvèdre red grapes, with blending taking place at the bottling stage. Depending on how they are made, these juicy, warming, dry, sunny wines range from easy-drinking, medium-bodied, fruity, lighter tannin-styled reds to more pricey, fuller-bodied wines that bring increased levels of red and black fruits and peppery spiciness, plus tannins that soften with time to yield earthy, smoky, darker tones. (A small amount of usually fuller-bodied and well-rounded white and rosé Côtes du Rhône is made and is certainly worth trying.) This category of wine is recommended, as it is a versatile style for food- and friend-pairing, good for parties and also your pocket. Check the label for alcohol levels, which can be high. Try with pizza, pasta, buffets, shepherd's pie and lasagne. You might also like Chianti, Rioja, and fuller-bodied Châteauneuf-du-Pape, which is also from the Rhône and a step up in quality. For much lighter wines, look towards Beaujolais and Dolcetto.

TEMPRANILLO

A red grape variety used to make medium- to full-bodied wines, especially from Spain: the mainstay of popular Rioja and the touch sharper Ribero del Duero. Also used to good effect in wines from many other areas in Spain. In Portugal, where is it known as Tinta Roriz or Aragonês, it is used for both still, dry table wines and fortified Port. Wines are usually well-coloured with a range of flavours, depending on where the grapes are grown and how the wine is made. Flavours change depending on regional climate and range from red fruits such as strawberries and raspberries, with herby and dusty notes in relatively cooler vineyards, but darker fruits like cherries, blackberries, plums or prunes emerge if the grapes are grown in a hotter area. When Tempranillos are aged, expect earthy, mushroomy and savoury flavours with a pleasant finish. Alcohol levels vary, so look at the label. Tannins tend to be moderate. Except for the fruity, uncomplicated *vin joven* ('young wine') made for immediate drinking, wines are made with oak. A layer of vanilla and coconut aromas and flavours develop from the traditional use of American, rather than French, oak. Modern-styled Tempranillo uses more subtle French oak, which adds cream notes, rounding out the texture. Young, affordable wines are easy-drinking, with red fruits like cherries and plums, plus herbs and medium acidity levels, so these are great for gatherings, pizzas, lamb (a classic combo) and pasta. Leather, clove and savoury notes are found in the pricier, aged bottles, which suit herby, slow-cooked dishes with mushrooms. Location affects the grape and hence the style of wine, so Tempranillo has many synonyms depending on where it is grown, but this can be confusing; look for Tinto Fino in the Ribero del Duero wines, beefy dark Tinto de Toro and Cencibel. Try also Côtes du Rhône, Chianti, Merlot and St-Émilion.

76	R
Bs	
Barbaresco	

BARBARESCO

A province and wine appellation in Piedmont, northwest Italy, which gives its name to dry red wines made using just Nebbiolo grapes. Drinkable earlier, lighter and less tannic compared to its big-brother neighbour, Barolo, these pale-coloured, medium- to full-bodied wines are, like Barolo, fruity and floral when young, turning more savoury when older, and can have high alcohol – the minimum permitted is 12.5% ABV here. With the characteristic Italian zip of fresh acidity, Barbarescos can be more elegant than Barolo, but are still rich and spicy with a suggestion of dried rose perfume combined with red berry- and raspberry-like fruit and perhaps a touch of earthiness – like the aromas released by digging a spade into damp ground. Like many Piedmont wines, this red goes well with mushrooms, especially truffle-infused dishes, stronger cheeses, game and hearty casseroles. A more affordable alternative is Langhe Nebbiolo from the same region, plus try other less tannic Italian wines, including Barbera, Chianti and to contrast, the fruity Valpolicella.

LANGUEDOC

This is a large, ancient, warm winemaking region in the south of France. It borders the Mediterranean, like Roussillon, its neighbour. Often their names are combined. Once known for volume, investment and improvements in all aspects of production have significantly improved quality, especially where vineyards combine sunshine for easy ripening with cooling sea breezes, or when planting occurs on the local mountainsides, which gives freshness to the grapes grown at altitude. A wide range of grapes thrives here, and many styles of wines are produced. Still, the Languedoc is predominantly a red-wine region, producing wines that are rich, ripe, flavoursome and often hearty, making use of blends of grapes like Syrah, Grenache, Carignan and Mourvèdre. Also there is great experimentation with zingy to full-bodied whites. Sparkling wines called *crémants*, like Crémant de Limoux, offer a good-value alternative to Champagne, and importantly, the overlooked red and white fortified wines from this region make a fine accompaniment to the final course of a meal. This area's wines compete on the world stage, not only with other French wines but also with popular wines from the New World. Helpfully this region is permitted to include grape varieties on its wine labels.

Whatever the style of wine, generally there is value for money to be found in the Languedoc, so look here for alternatives to the pricier, more famous wine regions. Naturally, the red wines pair well with cassoulet and other Mediterranean cuisine.

78	G
Pi	
Pinotage	

PINOTAGE

South Africa's trademark versatile red grape is a twentieth-century crossing of Pinot Noir and Cinsault. Recent understanding of how best to treat it has improved the reputation and reliability of the smoky, mainly black fruit-filled wines made from it. Also expect liquorice and sometimes savoury flavours, as well as a suggestion of smoke or tar, not too much acidity and reasonable tannin levels. Pinotage can come in a range of weights, depending on how the winemaker produces it. Youthful versions are lighter, with a touch more red fruit (raspberries); being softer, these wines are designed for early and easy drinking and are also easier on the purse. Jammier forms are available, with riper, cooked-fruit flavours. Some are all coffee and chocolate layers, which will typically be mentioned on the label or hinted at in the name of the wine. Premium versions cost more, show depth, and spend time in oak, which adds sweeter spices to the smoky tones and concentration. With heavier and more serious wines, decanting will lighten and aerate them for serving. This style can be aged (look for 'bush vine' or 'old vines' on the label). Occasionally Pinotage is made into distinctive rosé and sparkling wines. It is often mixed with other red grapes like the Cabernet Sauvignon and Merlot as a 'Cape Blend', and with other varieties such as Shiraz and Cinsault. A go-to BBQ red, and also good with smoked foods, sausages and gammon. Find the style you like and also try Bordeaux 'Cape Blends', or Carmenère, Shiraz and GSM (Grenache, Syrah and Mourvèdre blends).

79   R

Bx

Bordeaux

BORDEAUX

Bordeaux is a vast wine region in southwest France along either side of the Gironde Estuary, and it is also the catch-all appellation of mainly dry red wines, including the most famous wines in the world. (Dry whites are made from Sauvignon Blanc and Sémillon, from young, grassy, light, Entre-deux-Mers wines to rich and creamy, more of an oily-textured, oak-aged whites from the Pessac-Léognan region. Also sweet wines are made in Bordeaux; see Sauternes.) Here is an area where the year the wine is made, the vintage, can be important because variations in the climate each year affect how well the grapes ripen and which variety ripens best. In the UK, Bordeaux reds are also known as clarets, and are generally blends of Merlot and Cabernet Sauvignon, with splashes of Cabernet Franc and Petit Verdot thrown in for seasoning. There are different styles and prices due to the great number of producers and the huge volume of wine made in this large region. The better wines can age well and sell at premium prices. They are made using French oak. Look out for notes of cedar and cigar box. They should have a fine acidity, a mix of red and black fruits, no overripeness, with a classic Bordeaux nose and flavours of herbs, as well as suggestions of graphite and pencil-like mineral notes and sometimes smokiness from the oak. Where Cabernet Sauvignon dominates, more black fruit and tannins accompany the herbs (see Médoc), and these wines are more likely to need decanting to soften them for drinking. Where Merlot leads, the wine is more approachable, with plum and cherry tones and softer in style; see St-Émilion. Bordeaux wines are food wines; there is pretty much a Bordeaux available to accompany most dishes. Wines are made all over the globe with these same grapes, often known as a 'Bordeaux blend' and should be readily available, with Chilean examples offering good value.

Column 14

72 R **Rd** Ribero del Duero	80 R **Pt** Priorat	88 G **Cs** Cabernet Sauvignon
73 G **Ma** Malbec	81 R **Bd** Bandol	89 G **Sy** Syrah
74 R **Cô** Côtes du Rhône	82 R **Cp** Châteauneuf-du-Pape	90 R **Ce** Côte-Rôtie
75 G **Te** Tempranillo	83 G **Ci** Cinsault	91 G **Du** Durif
76 R **Bs** Barbaresco	84 G **Gr** Grenache	92 R **Ba** Barolo
77 R **Lg** Languedoc	85 G **Ne** Nebbiolo	93 G **Mv** Mourvèdre
78 G **Pi** Pinotage	86 G **Na** Nero d'Avola	94 R **Ca** Cahors
79 R **Bx** Bordeaux	87 G **Cf** Cabernet Franc	95 R **Mé** Médoc

Red wines become richer and even more characterful here. This is perhaps not an area in which to start your red-wine drinking. Bold flavours can be accompanied by high alcohol levels, so look at the label; some wines have grippier tannin concentrations too.

80   R

Pt

Priorat

PRIORAT

A region in northeast Spain that gives its name to rich, juicy, intense, full-bodied red wines made from a blend of grapes that gives the wines an extensive range of flavours. Varieties used include earthy Carignan and generous strawberry Grenache augmented with peppery Syrah, Cabernet Sauvignon and plummy, softer Merlot. Look for warm, ripe fruit, summer berries, sweet baking spices and savoury notes of tapenade. These generous, Mediterranean wines are still refreshing and can have significant herbal and mineral notes, depending on the soils in the vineyard, so could readily be at the bottom of the column. A combination of US and French oak is often used for ageing. Wine that spends the least time in oak is most fruity, but long ageing leads to more dried fruit and leather flavours evolving over time. Tannins vary from silky and integrated to firm with grip; here, decanting before drinking can aerate the wine, softening it and bringing out more flavours. Alcohol levels tend to be high, but this is matched by the flavours. Priorat wines pair well with nourishing food like pie and mash, steak-and-kidney pudding and shepherd's pie. Other hearty wines to sip include Châteauneuf-du-Pape, similar blends from Australia, more affordable wines from the Languedoc, as well as lighter Côtes du Rhônes and wines from nearby Monsant.

BANDOL

A small seaside fishing village in Provence, Mediterranean France, famous for the spicy, powerful, dry red wines produced around the region. (Similarly styled rosés are made too, along with a tiny amount of whites.) Reds are robust and juicy, with firm tannins and high alcohol levels. They are made by blending hand-harvested grapes, primarily Mourvèdre, with generous Grenache – which adds a riper, red, fruity touch, and lower tannins – perfumed Cinsault and cinnamon-spiced Syrah. Look for blackcurrant and morello cherry in these sunny wines, along with a flash of Provençal herbs such as rosemary, thyme and lavender. They are fruitier when young and can be kept too, with a few being extremely age-worthy. Sometimes nutty hummus and vanilla hints develop with time. A spicy savouriness and leather tones evolve with age. Bandols make a wonderful accompaniment to herby BBQ sausages, casseroles and lasagne. Try wines from across the region since proximity to the sea and altitude, as well as the blend used, all impact on the flavour and structure of these mouth-filling wines. If you like this style, try more affordable Fitou and Corbières or splash out on a Châteauneuf-du-Pape, or one of its neighbours, Gigondas.

CHÂTEAUNEUF-DU-PAPE

An important village in the southern Rhône that gives its name to probably the most famous dry red wines of the region, which can be ripe, rich, powerful and alcoholic. Châteauneuf can be made from a blend of up to 13 different grape varieties, often with a large amount of fruity Grenache, along with spicy Syrah and more savoury Mourvèdre. (A very small amount of rich, exotic, fruity and creamy white wines are made, but no rosé.) These popular wines are juicy, and can be jammy, with red and black fruit flavours, spiciness and a touch of smokiness. They often show savoury-sweet bouquets, with flowers and cinnamon accompanied by the thyme and rosemary herbs that prevail in the area. Tannins tend to be ripe, due to the sunny Mediterranean climate. With age, they become more savoury, almost brooding and meaty. They can be pricey. Plenty is made; sometimes the cheaper wines do not necessarily live up to this appellation's hearty reputation. For a similar but more affordable style, try better-value wines from neighbouring appellations like Vacqueras, Lirac, Rasteau or Côtes du Rhône-Villages. An Aussie GSM (Grenache, Syrah and Mourvèdre blend) made with comparable grapes can be riper and jammier, with even more cooked fruit compote. You might also like Amarone and Ripasso della Valpolicella. Châteauneuf is a great accompaniment to Christmas dinner, hearty meals in the cooler months and big cheeses.

CINSAULT

An ancient red grape variety that prefers heat, Cinsault is popular in the Mediterranean, where it is sometimes spelled without the 'l'. As a red wine it is usually a small part of a blend, so you are less likely to come across a red varietal Cinsault, but it can be found alone in its elegant and refreshing rosé incarnations, which are full of wild strawberry and juicy raspberry flavours. Cinsault is used a lot in the southern Rhône blends, adding softness (it is low in drying tannins), perfume and more red berry flavours to Grenache, spicy Syrah and/or the more savoury, gamey Mourvèdre. It is permitted in Châteauneuf-du-Pape and neighbouring wines, and is also found in the deeply-coloured, warming, spicy and fruity wines of Languedoc-Roussillon, like Minervois and Corbières. It adds red fruit as part of South African wines, as well as to wines from Morocco, Lebanon, the US and Chile. As a single varietal its low tannins mean it is ideal for light, aromatic and fruity rosés from Provence and surrounding regions. See also Pinotage. And try Grenache. As a red or rosé, Cinsault complements dishes with spicy flavours, such as Moroccan-style lamb dishes, spicy roasted salmon, and aromatic rice.

GRENACHE

A leading red wine grape variety, Grenache, or Grenache Noir, is used for making usually juicy, strawberry-filled, popular high-alcohol wines in a variety of styles and prices. (Less common are white Grenache Blanc grapes.) It is planted widely around the warmer, sunnier areas in the world, so can have high alcohol levels. It is known as Garnacha in Spain and Cannonau in Sardinia. An important component of many ripe, fruity southern French wines which are often blends, most famously Châteauneuf-du-Pape. For value, look to the Languedoc and Roussillon in France. Some of the French Grenache wines have a touch of the perfumed rosemary, thyme and lavender *garrigue* about them, reflecting the greenery in this dry area. It is included in some Spanish Riojas and Navarra wines, where it is usually blended with the Tempranillo grape as it softens the resulting wine. More recently it has become an important element in dry, red, deep Priorat wines, also from Spain. Grenache is often mixed with other grapes, especially Syrah and Mourvèdre. In Australia, a deep, full-bodied, sunny, ripe 'GSM' is a Grenache/Syrah/Mourvèdre blend; the Old Grenache vines make a more bold, concentrated, complex style of wine with lingering flavours, which is reflected in the price. Such a versatile grape (see also the Grenache rosé entry) – look out for sweet *vin doux naturel* wines from Banyuls and Maury in southern France which are delicious with a chocolate dessert.

NEBBIOLO

An old Italian red grape variety from the Piedmont region, Nebbiolo forms the basis of Barolo and Barbaresco wines, and further afield, the more affordable Langhe wines. Named after the *nebbia,* or fogs, of the region, this grape creates pale but intense, full-bodied, dry red wines where fresh acidity combines with flavours of dried cherries, mulberries, spice and roses when young, but with age, savoury layers of tea, tar and earthiness emerge.

Depending on where it is grown, the minimum ageing requirements for Nebbiolo change. Look for words like *riserva*, which means the wines have been aged for longer. This extra time and work is reflected in their higher prices. When young, strong, drying tannins mean this red needs to accompany food. You can try decanting to make it more approachable as well as accentuating its truffle, liquorice and forest-floor aromas. With time, Nebbiolo's pale colour turns brick-orange. It is used in other Italian wines that tend to be more affordable, like Roero, Ghemme and Gattinara. Confusingly, the Nebbiolo grape is also known as Spanna and Chiavennasca. Similar wines to try include (without the tannin) a pale-coloured aged Pinot Noir, or try Greek Xinomavro or older Riojas. This wine suits autumn and winter dining as its big, earthy tones pair with flavoursome food such as thick stews, mushroom dishes and stinky mature cheeses.

NERO D'AVOLA

An iconic and increasingly popular Sicilian red grape, sometimes called Calabrese. It is planted across the island, not only in Avola. In the past, its dark colour meant it was used to bolster other grapes. Today it is much more likely to be the sole grape variety in medium- to full-bodied dry, fruity and sometimes high-alcohol wines. Good winemakers create flavours and scents of violet and herbs, plums, cherries, raspberries and some examples with peppery spices, rather than being too confected. Acidity is medium to refreshing. High, ripe tannins are often velvety, but decanting will soften those that are not so smooth. Those that use oak add toasted almond and vanilla hints. Look for wines from grapes grown on calcareous soil, which have a chalky thread of minerality running through the aromas and flavours. Try also Syrah, softer Merlot and sunny wines from the

Languedoc. Pairs well with lamb couscous, a tomato-beef casserole and of course, Mediterranean cuisine.

CABERNET FRANC

A red grape variety similar to Cabernet Sauvignon, this is its offspring (its other parent was Sauvignon Blanc), although often with less colour and less tannin, making it softer, a little more crisp and more perfumed – a halfway house between Merlot and Cabernet Sauvignon. Found mostly as part of a blend, famously in Bordeaux, it also goes solo in the cooler Loire Valley in appellations like Chinon, Bourgueil and Saumur. Here the greener, herby notes are noticeable, accompanied by a savoury perfume of pencil shavings, plus a graphite-like minerality, tobacco where oak is used, blackberries and blackcurrant including the leaves. Grown widely across the world, but not at the same volumes of Cabernet Sauvignon and Merlot. In warmer locations Cabernet Franc has greater richness, as it is riper, with dark-plum notes, more sweet spices and red liquorice. Pairs well with hams, cassoulet and pork chops. As well as Cabernet Sauvignon and Merlot, you might also like Syrah, Rioja and Carmenère.

Column 15

		96 R **Am** Amarone
80 R **Pt** Priorat	88 G **Cs** Cabernet Sauvignon	97 G **Cg** Carignan
81 R **Bd** Bandol	89 G **Sy** Syrah	98 G **Sh** Shiraz
82 R **Cp** Châteauneuf-du-Pape	90 R **Ce** Côte-Rôtie	99 G **Zi** Zinfandel
83 G **Ci** Cinsault	91 G **Du** Durif	100 G **Pr** Primitivo
84 G **Gr** Grenache	92 R **Ba** Barolo	101 G **Pv** Petit Verdot
85 G **Ne** Nebbiolo	93 G **Mv** Mourvèdre	102 G **Ag** Aglianico
86 G **Na** Nero d'Avola	94 R **Ca** Cahors	103 G **Ng** Negroamaro
87 G **Cf** Cabernet Franc	95 R **Mé** Médoc	104 G **Ta** Tannat

Wines are moving into the full-bodied, bold reds here, with weight and textures in the mouth and often generous levels of tannins, which give these reds greater presence – if the grapes are not ripe enough at harvest, however, the tannins can be drying in the wine. These characteristics come from both the grape and techniques used by the winemaker. These reds are usually darker in colour because of the pigments in the grape skins, although Nebbiolo is famously paler. Expect to find darker, deep, red fruit flavours such as blackberries instead of raspberries. They may need time to soften, or try decanting them before serving. These forthright characteristics make this style of wine a good accompaniment to protein-rich foods like hearty meats and cheeses, as they soften and meld together.

CABERNET SAUVIGNON

'Cab Sauv' is a leading international and popular red grape variety planted all over the globe. Prices range from affordable to investment price tags. It can be made as a single-varietal wine but is versatile enough to blend with many other varieties, which helps to balance the resulting wine. Fruity and savoury, deep red, tannic, often blackcurrant- or cassis-laden, much wine made from this grape is inspired by quality Bordeaux and often produced using French oak, which adds sweet spices, light vanilla tones and softens the texture. Frequently blended with Merlot and Cabernet Franc, or with Sangiovese in Italy's 'Super Tuscans', it is also used as part of a blend in Spanish Priorat wines, as well as being a big wine on its own, superbly in Chile. Cabernet Sauvignon is a big, full-bodied wine. Younger wines and those from cooler regions are more blackberryish, with a herbal earthiness, and notes of green pepper, tobacco and liquorice. You may prefer the wine after decanting softens it. Warmer regions give riper, fruitier wines, still with liquorice and juicy dark cherries, dark plums, vanilla and dark spices, sometimes with a menthol or eucalyptus note. Tannin is a little softer too. Alternatives include the mellower Merlot, Italian Nero d'Avola, Portuguese Touriga Nacional and Malbec, plus for something deep-coloured and more brooding, look to Syrah, Italian Aglianico, tricky-to-find Lagrein, Spanish Monastrell and also Carmenère. Match with hearty winter meals, steaks, burgers, mushroom stroganoff and braised beef.

SYRAH

89	G
Sy	
Syrah	

A leading international and popular red grape variety, called Shiraz where it is grown in warmer regions, which tend to be in the New World (Chile, Argentina, Australia), since the style of the wine changes with climate. See also Shiraz. Syrah is deeply coloured, usually full-bodied, and packed with dark fruit flavours. Age adds black pepper, black olive, herb, liquorice and sometimes savoury bacon notes. Refreshing acidity imparts finesse and can be found in wines made in the cooler regions, plus it benefits the wine by making it more food-friendly. Depending on how the wine is made and its age, tannins can be medium to high. Higher-priced bottles can age. As a single-varietal wine look for Crozes-Hermitage, St-Joseph or Cornas, all from the northern Rhône, where black fruits and spices mingle. Southern Rhône wines include warming Syrah as part of a blend and can be high in alcohol, with the spices being a little softer than black pepper. Look out for Côtes du Rhône, and further south in France for competitively priced early-drinking wines that might mix Syrah with Grenache and Mourvèdre plus other punchy red grapes. These wines show elements of the herby *garrigue* – rosemary, thyme and lavender – from the location. American winemakers called 'Rhône Rangers' use Syrah in their wines that emulate the French versions, most of which are consumed in the US. Try also Cabernet Sauvignon, Primitivo and Durif. Syrah is a good accompaniment to bold dishes, including steaks, blue cheeses and BBQs.

90   R
Ce
Côte-Rôtie

CÔTE-RÔTIE

The name of an ancient region in the north of France's Rhône Valley, after which its premium dry red wines made using spicy Syrah grapes are titled. The grapes are grown on steep slopes in vineyards overlooking the river Rhône. A splash of white Viognier grapes is permitted under the local winemaking rules. This adds a delicate perfume, like floral violet notes, and helps keep the deep colour. A hearty full- to medium-bodied wine with complex flavours of summer, Côte-Rôtie offers black fruits like cherries and brambles, along with sweet and black pepper spices and good levels of fine, silky tannins. Premium versions combine robustness with elegance from the wine's acidity. With age, woodland, leather, tobacco and coffee notes can develop among the herbs. Syrah and Shiraz from Chile and Australia are riper, while Cabernet Sauvignon has more cassis and drier tannins, and Merlot is softer and plummier. Côte-Rôtie is a match for big dishes like beef daube, tapenade, beef ribs and deeply flavoured, spicy, mushroom-based vegetarian dishes.

91   G
Du
Durif

DURIF

A deeply coloured, originally French red wine grape, called Petite Sirah in California, where it prospers today. Durif also makes successful, concentrated, spicy, dark-fruited wines in Australia, often with chocolate, black pepper and blackberry flavours. It is related to the Syrah wine grape and has similarities, although is more straightforward in style. It, too, is full-bodied, inky, rich and has the potential to soften with age. 'Petite' describes the size of the grapes. It has high levels of acidity – useful to keep it fresh, especially where it is grown in hotter regions. High levels of tannin make it a robust wine. Try it blended with Zinfandel and Shiraz, plus other full-bodied reds, including with more blackcurranty Cabernet Sauvignon, and the earthier Carignan,

Mourvèdre and Primitivo. For big foods like beef strips, dark mushroom dishes and richly flavoured curries.

92   R

Ba

Barolo

BAROLO

A hillside village in Piedmont after which the pale, dry, powerful red wines made in the region solely from the local Nebbiolo grape are named. These are not wines for beginner red-wine drinkers because they are tannic and acidic in youth, requiring age to release the truffle plus mushroom notes, as well as always commanding high prices. Don't let their muted colour fool you; they are powerful, full-bodied and can have high alcohol, and are famous for scents of tar or tea and roses. Old and new styles of winemaking collide here in northwest Italy. Modern styles use French oak to soften the tannins at a younger age, making them ready to drink earlier and retaining more of their strawberry fruit. Traditional styles are made by letting the juice and grape skins stay in contact for longer to extract more from the skins, so are less fruity and require more ageing. Both styles benefit from decanting to soften the tannic structure, so allow the wine to spend some time with air in another bottle or decanter before drinking. Find a winemaker whose style you like, as the grape reflects the vineyard soil and general *terroir* as well as winemaking techniques used. The weather during the year, or vintage, affects the quality of Barolo wines, so experiment here too. Due to the characteristics of the Nebbiolo grape, minimum ageing is legally required for the wines produced from it, to allow all the mulberries, violets and spices to gather and transform with truffle and liquorice, sometimes chocolate, complexity; check out older vintages, which might say *riserva* on the label. You could try more affordable neighbouring Barbaresco or simply a Nebbiolo from the Langhe region. Definitely a wine that needs food otherwise the tannins can dry out your mouth. Great with osso buco and with mushroom- and truffle-based dishes.

MOURVÈDRE

A dark-skinned, usually high-alcohol, high-tannin, red grape, similar to Cabernet Sauvignon but more rustic in style. It is called Monastrell in Spain, which has the largest area planted, where you could see Jumilla or Yecla on the label; here it is more gamey. It's also grown in France close to the Mediterranean and in the Rhône, as it likes heat. Often it is part of a blend e.g. with generous Grenache and cinnamon-spiced Syrah in the Rhône, and is key in the red wines from Bandol. Mourvèdre is full of earthy, dark fruits, herbs and spicy black pepper. For alternatives, try Malbec, Rhône blends, Cabernet Sauvignon, heavier Aglianico, spicier Shiraz or Syrah, more tannic Cahors and Tannat, as well as juicy southern French Minervois, Corbières and Fitou. This full-bodied (sometimes smoky if oak has been used) red benefits from decanting and can stand up to big, protein-rich foods, like steak with black pepper sauce, mushrooms with Madeira, and savoury umami dishes with plenty of Parmesan cheese. These rich, dark, earthy flavours soften the tannins. It is also used to great effect in rich, sweet, fortified wines such as Bandol that pair well with rich chocolate and dried fruit desserts, as well as dark fruit cakes.

CAHORS

A small French town east of Bordeaux that is the original home of deeply coloured, full-bodied, dry red wines made mostly from the Malbec grape. These inky wines were traditionally known as the 'black wines from Cahors'. With flavours and aromas of black fruits plus earthy, damp-forest-floor characteristics, they tend to be more savoury, with meat, plum and blackberry notes, firmer tannins and crisper acidity than the riper, more generous, blueberry-laden, creamier Mendoza Malbecs from Argentina. There are different styles made within the Cahors region, ranging from affordable, more straightforward, fruitier 'traditional' wines, to aged, more powerful, complex and concentrated offerings, with prices to match as this style involves using oak, which adds clove, vanilla and mocha notes. Look for the intense and complex *spéciale* wines and consider decanting to soften them and bring out more flavours before drinking. The Malbec grapes can be blended with small amounts of Tannat and plummier Merlot. Match this robust wine with similar food, like a hearty beef stew, game or cassoulet as part of a rustic menu. As well as comparing Cahors with Argentinian Malbecs, other wines to try include cassis-laden Cabernet Sauvignon, softer Merlots and Carmenères, Bordeaux blends and smoky Pinotage.

MÉDOC

95   R
Mé
Médoc

A region within Bordeaux, France, situated on the left bank of the Gironde Estuary. Sometimes wines from here are called Médoc wines but more likely Bordeaux. The Médoc contains the most famous group of appellations, or defined wine regions, in the world in its Haut-Médoc (High-Médoc) district. Though the wines from St-Estèphe, Pauillac, St-Julien as well as Margaux garner much of the publicity, they represent a tiny proportion of Bordeaux wines. See also Bordeaux. Notably, the soil in this maritime region is gravelly, which suits Cabernet Sauvignon better than Merlot vines and is a key reason for the *châteaux* on this side of the Gironde to produce Cabernet Sauvignon-dominated dry red wines, though they are typically a blend of grapes, including Merlot, with perhaps some herbier Cabernet Franc or deeply coloured Petit Verdot. Some of the wines were 'officially classified' in 1855 as top growths, or *crus*, but the less-well-known usually offer better value. Look for red and black fruits, perhaps with some fresh herbs mingling with cigar-box aromas, and maybe a touch of smokiness and vanilla with medium alcohol levels in a medium to full body. Younger wines and Cabernet Sauvignon-strong clarets can have chewier tannins, so serve with meats and cheeses and/

or decant to soften and bring out the flavours, but the tannins will be softer and silky in older wines and where there is more Merlot in the blend. Look for the classic Bordeaux notes of woody herbs, graphite-cum-pencil aromas and minerality. Good to accompany main meals, roasts, casseroles, hard cheeses and heartier vegetarian food. Also check out Cabernet Sauvignon and Merlots from elsewhere, Malbec, darker Cahors, Tannats with higher-tannins and smokier Pinotage.

Column 16

	96 R **Am** Amarone
88 G **Cs** Cabernet Sauvignon	**97** G **Cg** Carignan
89 G **Sy** Syrah	**98** G **Sh** Shiraz
90 R **Ce** Côte-Rôtie	**99** G **Zi** Zinfandel
91 G **Du** Durif	**100** G **Pr** Primitivo
92 R **Ba** Barolo	**101** G **Pv** Petit Verdot
93 G **Mv** Mourvèdre	**102** G **Ag** Aglianico
94 R **Ca** Cahors	**103** G **Ng** Negroamaro
95 R **Mé** Médoc	**104** G **Ta** Tannat

Many of these red wines are known to be bold, powerful and hearty, with deep, brooding colours and flavours. They often benefit from longer ageing, which softens their tannins, so look for older vintages and consider decanting before drinking. They can include dried fruits as well as ripe dark fruits, and these can be accompanied by spicy notes, often from the use of oak in the making and ageing, but some of the grapes here are naturally spicy too. These wines are warming in the winter and make ideal partners for richer cuisine. Note: sometimes winemakers use techniques that do not extract as much from the grapes to make a more approachable style of wine. This can be confusing, but brings in cash for the winemaker and enables him or her to use the best grapes in the bolder wines to age. If this style is made, it is normally less expensive and a good entry point.

AMARONE

Drying red Corvina grapes concentrates their flavours to make this full-bodied Venetian wine taste almost sweet. It is rich and ripe wine with a refreshing acidic tang. Amarones are bold encompassing flavours like chocolate, warm plums, morello cherries, dried fruits, coffee and sweet spices, with a touch of rum and herbs. Alcohol is high – 14%-plus ABV – to match the lingering big flavours, firm but velvety tannins and complex layers. The best are aged in oak, giving complexity plus softness to the power, and they can keep at home. This indulgent style goes well with big cheeses and meaty dishes such as casseroles, and makes a warming winter drink. This is a wine to take your time over. (See Valpolicella for the light, summer-sipping wines from the same region.) You might also like a slightly lighter *ripasso* style of Valpolicella, a fruity, ripe Zinfandel from the US, Shiraz from Australia, or the latter's GSM (Grenache, Syrah and Mourvèdre blend), Châteauneuf-du-Pape and Ports.

CARIGNAN

A deeply coloured red grape variety known as Cariñena in Spain, Carignane in the US and specifically as Mazuelo in Rioja. It has zippy acidity and hard, sometimes chewy, tannins plus is a touch rustic. Usually it is found blended with other grapes like Syrah, Grenache and Mourvèdre, making a more harmonious style of wine. It adds red and blackberry flavours, as well as colour, freshness and tannin and can impart dense, dark fruit – even figs – especially where grapes from old vines (*vieille vignes*) are used; these wines are likely to be juicier and more concentrated. Look for names like the herby and rosemary-scented Corbières, Minervois, Faugères and other wines from the Languedoc. It is also used in Priorat, southern Italy, and some wines from Chile. Its use is declining as there is a trend for more finesse in wine styles. Soften these wines by decanting or by keeping them for a while. A match for a range of strong flavours such as beef, lamb, aged game and BBQs. Try also Durif, Syrah and Shiraz, or for something smoother, a Malbec, Primitivo along with the riper Zinfandel.

SHIRAZ

A leading international deeply coloured red grape variety, aka Syrah, where it is grown in cooler regions, which tend to be in the Old World, since the grape's characteristics and therefore style of the wine changes with climate. See also Syrah. New World Shiraz is riper, fruitier and more full-bodied, with lower acidity, softer tannins and a more viscous texture compared to Old World Syrah. It may have less pepper and more violet, chocolate and coffee in hotter locations. Though less subtle and elegant, it is equally delicious. It has aromas and flavours of dark fruits like blackberries and plums and could have some blackcurrants. This sunnier style of Shiraz is classically found in Australia, on its own and mixed with other varieties, perhaps showing a telltale note of eucalyptus. It has achieved worldwide success in California, South Africa (which makes both 'styles' of the grape), Chile and vineyards across Europe. Alcohol can be high, but it integrates and balances with the bold flavours so check the label. A good match for herby or spicy lamb meals, meatballs, BBQs and hard cheeses. You could also try Amarone, Zinfandel, Ripasso della Valpolicella and wines from the southern Rhône.

99	G
Zi	
Zinfandel	

ZINFANDEL

An old, deep and bold red grape variety, with a large acreage in California (see White Zinfandel, and also Primitivo). Zinfandel is intensely fruity and full of really ripe, dark cherries, sometimes even with dried fruit and chocolate flavours as well as high alcohol – sometimes *very* high, so read the label. Wines are full-bodied, with an unctuous texture, especially where they have been aged in oak, which softens and further rounds out the wine as well as adding vanilla and spicy tones, and is intense where the vines are old (*vieilles*). High alcohol and tannin levels tend to be hidden by the power of the wine. Primitivos from Puglia in the heel of Italy are thought to be the same grape, with more herby, earthy tones plus higher acidity. Surprisingly, this is a good match for Christmas dinner, chiming with all the trimmings, also big BBQs and big cheeses. If you like these rich, juicy Zins, try also Italian Primitivo, Amarone, the slightly lighter Ripasso della Valpolicella, or a spicy Shiraz.

100	G
Pr	
Primitivo	

PRIMITIVO

A southern Italian red wine grape with spicy blackcurrant and raspberry flavours and at times wild berries, mingling with violets and dried figs. It opens out when left in the glass. It can be medium but tends to be full-bodied, with a round, plush texture. Some are more rustic than others, depending on the fineness of the high level of tannins and the age of the vines used. It is known as Zinfandel ot.

in California. Acidity is higher than the more unctuous California Zinfandel, which can make it easier-drinking and helps with flexibility in food pairing. Fuller styles are sunny with ripe, dark, cherry and sometimes chocolate flavours. Alcohol can be high, so check the label. This style of wine needs food, so try a plate of pasta, especially bolognese, generously dusted with savoury Parmesan and black pepper, or match with BBQ ribs. One to taste if you haven't already. See Zinfandel. Other wines to try are Italian Aglianico and Negroamaro, plus Châteauneuf-du-Pape, Shiraz and Durif.

PETIT VERDOT

A deeply coloured, tannic red grape variety that is used predominantly as a minority element of the blend in Bordeaux wines, especially for wines made on the left bank of the Gironde Estuary. It may not even appear on the label as it is added as 'a dash of', like seasoning, rather than as a large dollop. Even so, in this capacity it has the strength to bring colour and tannin as well as spice (pencil shavings and sometimes molasses), floral perfume notes, acidity and alcohol. However, it does not always ripen fully, and when this occurs it can be a touch green (nettles rather than herbs). Due to its Bordeaux connection, Petit Verdot is found around the globe, where it is less likely to struggle to ripen and still plays a role in Cabernet Sauvignon and Merlot blends. In the New World, riper grapes are more likely to be flying solo, but the wines are still tricky to find; these more generous wines will be deeper-coloured, richer and fuller-bodied with darker fruit flavours like black plums accompanied by scents of violets. When mixed with oak, which softens the high tannins, tar, coffee and leather notes emerge. If there is enough information on a label, try Bordeaux blends with differing amounts of Petit Verdot; occasionally it is mixed with the Rhône grape Syrah too.

AGLIANICO

Serious, full-bodied, alcoholic, sun-loving, southern Italian, heavy and deeply coloured red grape. The best grows in volcanic soil, which adds freshness as well as a flash of chalky minerality to its weight. Found in Taurasi in the Campania region and Aglianico del Vulture in neighbouring Basilicata, Aglianico wines are all damson and blackcurrant, with a mineral edge. In youth it has more crunchy fruits, with wisps of violet perfume and vivid purple colours. Usually made with oak, but *rosso*-labelled and unoaked wines can be a lighter and more affordable introduction to the grape variety. Aglianico can be tannic, so let it breathe or decant to soften before tasting. However, along with power, Aglianico wines can offer finesse, and some age well. Older wines, usually made using oak, enjoy finer, not-so-drying tannins as well as a more viscous, generous texture; there are also layers of ashy smokiness, liquorice with vanilla, blackberries and a lingering finish. Vintage, or year of production, can be important. The acidity, flavours and usually high alcohol make this a wine to drink with food like hearty beef dishes, BBQs and warming autumnal and winter fare. Try also big Italian Primitivo or Zinfandel in California.

NEGROAMARO

Negroamaro is a red wine grape and important local variety grown in the Puglia region in the heel of Italy. It is deeply coloured, with medium to high tannins and body, depending on how it is made. It can be varietal wine but is also found blended with Primitivo and Malvasia grapes. Occasionally it is gently pressed to make a lighter-styled (compared to the red wines), summer-fruited, cherry-coloured dry rosé which include flavours of red berries, pomegranates and cherries and can have a mineral note of flint, depending on the vineyard soil, or a yogurt note from lees (dead yeast cells) stirring. Rosés are produced for drinking when young and fruity. Reds are available in a spectrum of styles, from more rustic but approachable, to finer and more serious, reflected in the prices. The Mediterranean sunshine provides vibrant, rich, nutmeg-spiced wines, sometimes with strawberry coulis but more likely robust body with plums, soft blackberries when young, and more intense currants and chocolate flavours plus attractive aromas of liquorice, cloves and rich coffee. Alcohol levels can be high. Look for names like Salice Salentino and others such as Brindisi and Copertino. With good levels of acidity, Negroamaro is delicious served with dishes like meatballs, lamb and grilled tuna. The rosés complement Mediterranean meals garnished with black olives. Also try Cabernet Sauvignon, the more tannic Aglianico, Tannat and Cahors.

TANNAT

A red wine grape that makes deeply coloured, inky, dry and rustic wine with high alcohol levels and mineral aromas of tar along with black fruit flavours such as damson, plum and blackberries. 'Black wines' from Madiran in southwest France are made with a majority of Tannat blended with the Cabernets (Franc and Sauvignon), so have a touch of leafiness about them. It is also successful in Uruguay, where wines can be a touch lower in tannins, but this is all relative. High in natural acidity, with chewy tannins, Tannat is blended too, but with the likes of less-rustic Merlot and Cabernet Sauvignon and even Pinot Noir. Softening winemaking techniques are often employed, or maybe just ageing the wine. These methods, as well as a sensitive use of oak, are bringing about a change to modernise Tannat so that it produces a more harmonious and balanced wine. Decanting can help this process at home. Aged wines cost more and continue the black theme, with aromas of prunes, chocolate and cloves. Pair this wine with sociable rustic fare that boasts dark, concentrated flavours like lamb with a reduced balsamic vinegar sauce, beefy bangers and mash, or mature Cheddar and caramelised onion doorstep sandwiches. Other dark wines to try are Aglianico, Negroamaro, Cahors, Carignan and Durif. Cabernet Sauvignon is fruitier, less tannic and more approachable. Nebbiolo wines, like Barolo, have the tar, with a scattering of roses but a pale colour.

Sparkling

All these sparkling wines have bubbles and are made in regions renowned for the excellence of their fizz. There is diversity within this category, from pale and sweet to deep and lingering. Note how the manner in which the bubbles are created in the wine changes in different regions; simply pumping carbon dioxide into a still wine has no place in any of these quality appellations.

ASTI

105	R
As	
Asti	

Asti is a hilly province in Piedmont, northwest Italy. It gives its name to gentle, sweet, often fun and frivolous pale sparkling wines that used to be known as Asti Spumante. Asti (as it is now known) is made using the floral, orange-blossom and grapey Muscat grape, whose qualities winemakers wish to preserve and highlight. The special Asti production method encapsulates this fruity, flowery, candy-like perfumed freshness while simultaneously adding bubbles and retaining some of the grapes' natural sugars. (The bubbles in some sparkling wines are added to a previously made still wine.) The youthful wine is therefore low in alcohol and sweet, but should be fresh and vibrant, as the hillside location of the vineyards helps keep acidity in the grapes as well as harnessing the sunshine. Astis are slightly less fizzy than Champagne. Drink these lacy wines immediately, otherwise their vivacity and aromas fade and they become sickly. This is not a wine to keep. Serve chilled with meringues, fruit salads, jellies and other fruit-based desserts. Wines labelled 'Moscato d'Asti' are lighter: lower alcohol and sweeter. See also Moscato. In other places in the world, similar Moscato-styled sparklers are available, usually with slightly riper flavours; some are rose-coloured too. These include a layer of red fruits – lovely with strawberry and raspberry desserts. Try also drier, higher-alcohol Prosecco, and if you would like a Champagne or similar from outside that region, choose a wine labelled *demi-sec,* as this will have some sweetness as well as some biscuity layers that result from the different production method.

MOSCATO

Moscato is the Italian name for the perfumed Muscat grape. On the label of a sparkling wine from Piedmont, Italy, it usually refers to Moscato d'Asti (see Asti); however, this entry recognises that there are also similarly styled sparklers (called simply 'Moscato' on the label) made across the globe, including other places in Italy outside the Asti region, as well as further afield in, for example, Australia, California and South Africa. They are often light-bodied, easy-sipping, sweet, but not overly so, wines that are usually pale, almost white, and sometimes candy-floss rose-coloured. These acacia-honeyed wines mix floral orange-blossom and peachy flavours. Rosés involve cherry, strawberry and raspberry layers too.

Confusingly they can be found in a range of sweetness and fizziness levels. The more usual are only lightly sparkling with low-alcohol styles that are ideal as a refreshing summer sipper, well-chilled alongside fruit-based desserts. Weightier wines can complement aromatic, spicy Asian food and light cheeses. The shape of the bottle can hint at the style of the wine: i.e. its levels of sweetness, alcohol and fizziness. Those in Champagne-shaped bottles are fizzy, while those in a 'normal', straight-sided Bordeaux-shaped bottle tend to be less fizzy. If you see lower alcohol on the label, this often means a touch more sweetness. Note that because Muscat is an adaptable grape, some sparkling Moscatos are dry; look for *secco* on the label and higher alcohol levels. See also Muscat which covers the still-wine styles of wine made from the versatile and prolific of grape varieties. Try also Proseccos, which are drier sparkling wines but not as floral nor honeyed and perhaps a little zingier. For a swap to a still-wine style you might also like white Zinfandel, or for more finesse a *Kabinett*

Riesling from Germany for a similar, low-alcohol, off-dry still wine.

PROSECCO

The name of a popular, joyous, lemon-sherbet-tinged sparkling white wine created in Italy near Venice from Glera grapes. Proseccos are produced using a method known as charmat, that retains all the fresh fruit, green apple and melon qualities of the grapes – which is partly why Proseccos are fruitier than Champagnes (the different grape varieties used in both wines also play a big part). Here bubbles are formed in a still wine by a second fermentation in a large tank. The light, refreshing sparkling wine is bottled ready for immediate consumption. The charmat method is also suitable for other aromatic grapes. Proseccos labelled *frizzante* are less fizzy than the customary fully sparkling *spumante* wines; *spumante* does not always appear on the label. Alcohol is usually a touch lower than in Champagne and sweetness levels vary. Unless it specifically states otherwise on the label, any sugar is counterbalanced by the wine's freshness, so Proseccos are not cloying but have a light, refreshing quality. If the label mentions 'DOCG', rather than 'DOC', it indicates a higher quality classification, and the wine will have more layers of flavour, linger longer plus contain finer bubbles, which create a silky sensation in the mouth. Expect to pay a little more for DOCG, although generally this is still a more affordable bubbly than Champagne. If you are planning on making a peachy Bellini cocktail, or adding orange juice for a breakfast treat, plain old DOC Prosecco is all that is required. Similarly styled wines are made around the globe, though they cannot use the Prosecco name on the label. Drink them chilled, young and fresh as an apéritif or for an impromptu midweek celebration.

108	R
Cv	
Cava	

CAVA

Cava is the name of a sparkling wine made using the same traditional method as Champagne but in Spain and usually with different grape varieties. Most is made in the northeast, near Barcelona, although Cava can come from many areas in the country. Cava is typically a non-vintage wine containing a blend of indigenous Spanish grapes, while a few producers draw on grapes like Chardonnay and Pinot Noir that are used in Champagne. *Rosado* (rosé) colouring comes from the skins of Garnacha (Grenache) and Monastrell grapes. Like Champagne, the bubbles in Cava are created naturally during a second fermentation in the bottle, and the wine spends a significant amount of time maturing in the bottle. In this way, layers of biscuit, dough and a touch of cream-like flavours are added to the fruit flavours. Cava typically has a mineral aroma reminiscent of smoke or a rubber balloon. Serve these dry, refreshing, medium-alcohol, more modestly priced fizzes chilled as an apéritif, with smoked salmon canapés, seafood, some Catalonian cuisine and in cocktails. Naturally, also try Champagne and other sparkling wines from around the world made using the *metodo tradicional*, but for something fruitier without the creamy notes, turn to Prosecco.

CRÉMANT

French fizz, from regions other than Champagne, made using the same *méthode champenoise* (aka *méthode traditionelle* outside the Champagne region), *crémants* are usually non-vintage and made with local grapes, which may or may not be the Champagne grapes Chardonnay, Pinot Noir and Pinot Meunier. Typically, the region of production appears in the name: eg Crémant d'Alsace, Crémant de Bourgogne and Crémant de Limoux. Saumur *mousseux* and sparkling Vouvrays are normally better quality than the Crémant de Loire from the same region. Generally produced to be enjoyed young, fruity and fresh, these sparklers are still zippy but with less of the bread, biscuit and dough layers usually found in Champagne. If made using a local grape, a hint of its flavour profile comes through. They are often crafted by famous Champagne houses which bring their skills and backing to the *crémant,* which means these wines can be a good-value alternative to Champagne. Most are, like Champagne, white wines; however, rosés with more red fruits (rarely red) are made. Alcohol is medium. Other countries make sparkling wine using the *méthode traditionelle*; in Germany these are called Deutscher Sekt; in South Africa, Cap Classique; in Italy Franciacorta. In the New World, California, Australia and New Zealand, look for 'Traditional Method' on the label and expect slightly riper fruit flavours.

CHAMPAGNE

A cool region towards the north of France after which its celebratory sparkling wines are named. Three permitted grapes – Chardonnay, Pinot Noir and Pinot Meunier – are used. The latter two are red, but the delicate pressing of the grapes is so gentle that colour is not extracted from their skins, making the vast majority of Champagnes white, with only a few rosés. The *méthode champenoise* dictates that bubbles must be made inside the bottle. Yeast and sugar are added to the bottled still wine, which starts a second fermentation. Here the carbon dioxide is created but is trapped in the sealed bottle, and *voilà*! There is fizz. In the best this is smooth, silky and fine and far removed from the big, short-lived, bursting bubbles of carbonated lemonades and the like. This process takes time, however, so this in part accounts for the premium prices of this special drink. Different Champagne houses – the brands – have their own styles: some young and quite zippy and sharp, others aged, softer and creamier. Find a style you prefer. Alcohol is at the medium level. Sweetness levels range from bone-dry to lusciously sweet *doux* styles. Usually Champagnes are dry to just off-dry *bruts*, which match savoury canapés well. To pair with a dessert and cake choose sweet *demi-sec* wines. There are few other label terms to understand to get the most out of this drink, which is more often than not consumed to mark a special occasion. 'Non-vintage' means the wine is a blend of years, which helps ensure a consistent 'house style'; they are usually released ready to drink, not aged. Vintage Champagnes are made with grapes from a single particularly good harvest. They spend longer ageing – often much more than the minimum. This style of Champagne is richer, more honeyed and lingering and can include both savoury and fruity tones. *Blanc de blancs* Champagne is made solely from white grapes, giving more citrus and green apple hints, becoming buttery if aged. *Blanc de noirs* fizz is made from red grapes only; you may detect a hint of richer red fruits.

LAMBRUSCO

A red wine grape that gives its name to fizzy Italian wines made mostly in the Emilia-Romagna region. The name became synonymous with mass-produced, low-alcohol, simple, sickly, dark-pink fizz. It is worth noting that, although hard to find, the best Lambruscos must be made using a second fermentation to make the bubbles in the bottle – like the method used to make Champagne – so be sure to check the label. A little easier to discover are quality Lambruscos that are created in a similar way to Prosecco. Alcohol and fizz may be a touch lower than in other sparkling wines. These deep-crimson, quality wines are dry, succulent and bursting with red cherries, a hint of violets and refreshing acidity plus herby tannins and a touch of tobacco. Tannins and a touch of bitterness on the finish make them food-friendly. Rosé and white versions are less common, and contain little or no tannins. Delicious when slightly cooled – even the reds – as an accompaniment to flavoursome charcuterie like Parma ham, salami and other rich, savoury delicatessen delights; also a good foil for roast turkey: think vinous cranberry sauce. Be surprised and try one of these.

SPARKLING SHIRAZ

Sparkling Shiraz is a deeply-coloured sparkling Australian red wine made from juicy Shiraz (Syrah) grapes. The best winemakers rein in the potential for it to be big, brash, over-bubbly, oaky and alcoholic, assimilating its best characteristics into a full-bodied and harmonious balance. With a touch of the rebel about them, these wines are weighty and rich, tasting of red berries, blackberries, a touch of violets and peppery spice, with smoke on the finish. Sparkling Shiraz offers redcurrant-like fresh acidity combined with smooth tannins and moussey bubbles. Alcohol can be medium to high. A little bit of oak can soften the wine and if aged, chocolate, meaty, leathery and savoury notes develop, although the price increases. Good with BBQs, roast turkey and cranberry sauce, duck and some game. Those that are off-dry can even pair with a rich chocolate cake.

Sweet

All these sweeties have something in common: a concentration and intensity of flavours that offset the natural sweetness of the grape juice itself. No sugar is added. Drink with food that is equally as sweet to create balance and harmony. High-acidity wines can cut through rich desserts and are refreshing, not cloying, to drink. Dry wines can taste thin or bitter alongside sweet cuisine.

ICEWINE

A type of dessert wine most famously made in Canada and Germany, where it is known as Eiswein, although other countries make it too. Icewine is made from grapes that are left hanging on the vines for a very long time, well into the winter (usually grapes are harvested in early autumn). Grapes destined for Icewine are left until it is so cold that the water inside them freezes, then they are hand-picked, often at night. Pressing these frozen dry grapes (raisins) removes concentrated sugary grape juice that is so rich that after fermentation the wine remains naturally and intensely sweet. The frozen water and ice crystals are not used. These time-consuming practices and the low yields mean Icewine has a premium price tag, and tends to be fuller-bodied compared to wines where grapes are harvested in late autumn. The clean flavours depend on the grape variety used. Typically, Riesling is used in Germany, while in Canada both white grapes, such as Vidal and Riesling, and red grapes, such as Cabernet Franc, are used. Expect especially pure, sharp flavours of tropical fruits, peaches, honey, citrus, melon, and strawberries, with a balanced backbone of acidity. Serve chilled with an ice bucket. Icewine pairs well with flavourful desserts such as chocolate or fruit puddings, and strongly flavoured savouries like pâté and blue cheeses. Try also sweet Riesling from Austria, Tokaji from Hungary, and more affordable late-harvest dessert wines from around the world.

VIN SANTO

A concentrated, Italian sweet 'holy wine' made all over the country and famously associated with Tuscany. The intensity of Vin Santo results partly from drying the grapes, traditionally on straw mats in the sun or winery, for up to six months before gently fermenting the raisined fruit. These variable sweet wines are mainly a blend of white Malvasia and Trebbiano grapes, sometimes with Sangiovese or other varieties. Pale straw to rich amber in colour, these wines are put in small barrels to age untouched in lofts for at least three years. Evaporation through the wood, plus the gentle movement of oxygen into these barrels adds to the intensity as well as layers of flavours and aromas or complexity. Think scents and flavours of apricots, raisins, dried figs and acacia honey. These can evolve into toasted nuts, and caramel or toffee given age, as unopened wines can keep. Vin Santo wines are a touch viscous in texture, with crisp acidity, so the sweetness is not cloying; however, sweetness levels do vary depending on the winemaker; *dolce* is the sweetest. Alcohol is around 16% ABV. Occasionally fortified – look for *liquoroso* on the label – with a touch higher alcohol. Serve cool, classically with biscotti, and desserts like cheesecake and buttery pastries. You could also try Vin Santo from Greece, Madeira, white Port, Muscat de Beaumes-de-Venise for something more floral and less nutty, Sauternes for more marmalade notes, and aged *demi-sec* Champagne for bubbles and lighter alcohol.

TOKAJI

Tokaj is a region in northern Hungary that gives its name, as Tokaji, to golden, refreshing, medium-bodied white dessert wines made predominantly from botrytised (affected by botrytis, a mould otherwise known as 'noble rot'; see Sauternes for more information) Furmint grapes. The winemaking method is similar to that of Sauternes,

with the additional process of steeping nobly rotten, or
aszú, grapes in a still wine. This infusion brings layers of
both freshness and maturity, integrating them in a single
wine. Look for *puttonyos* on the label; this indicates the
grade of sweetness, so the higher the *puttonyos* number,
the sweeter the style. All types of Tokaji should have
balanced, refreshing, citrus acidity; four *puttonyos* is
the most commonly available. A gentle use of oak adds
vanilla and creamy hints to the apricot, spicy citrus and
white-blossom flavours as well as a silky texture. Enjoy
chilled with cakes, peaches, pâté and smoked fish, and
as a treat during celebratory meals. Also sip Sauternes,
dessert Rieslings from Germany and Austria, appley
Vouvrays, and more aromatic Sauvignon Blanc dessert
wines from Chile and Australia.

SAUTERNES

116	R
Sa	
Sauternes	

A village in Bordeaux, southwest France, that gives
its name to honey-coloured, medium-bodied white
dessert wines from that region and appellation. Made
predominantly from white Sémillon grapes that have
been left to hang on the vines to develop more layers
of flavour and become affected by the intensifying
noble rot (botrytis). A touch of Sauvignon Blanc gives
the wine a lift and brightness, and alcohol tends to be
around 14% ABV. Noble rot is a type of friendly mould
that compromises the skin of the grapes, allowing
evaporation. The remaining grape juice inside the berries
becomes more concentrated, complex and luscious.
This adds marmalade notes to flavours of acacia honey
and tropical fruits, and these combine with zesty citrus
flavours and a good level of refreshing acidity, which
balances the sweetness so that the wine is not cloying.
More affordable wines are bottled for drinking soon after
release and in half-sized bottles. The pricier bottles can
age; they deepen in colour, eventually turning almost
amber with time and adding darker honey, dried fruit
and savoury aromas and flavours. Enjoy chilled with

crème brûlée, tarte au citron, rich egg custards, tarte tatin and blue cheeses. From the same region though more affordable, try Barsac, Ste-Croix-du-Mont, and further afield, Montbazillac, Tokaji from Hungary and dessert Sauvignon Blancs from Chile and Australia. More straightforward, floral and youthful, sip Muscat de St-Jean de Minervois. For a more appley style, try sweet Vouvrays and dessert Rieslings from Germany and Austria.

BANYULS

A commune on the Mediterranean coast in the southeast of Roussillon called Banyuls-sur-Mer gives its name to full-bodied, fortified red wines. Similar to ruby and late-bottled vintage ports, Banyuls is made from local Grenache grapes that thrive in this hot, windy region of southern France on the border with Spain. In France, this style is called *vin doux naturel* (or VDN: 'naturally sweet wine'), referring to the adding of grape spirit during fermentation. This stops the yeast fermenting any more of the sugar from the red grapes, resulting in a full-bodied, fruity wine with reasonable tannin levels. Alcohol levels tend to be lower than in ports – about 16% ABV.

Like Port, there is a range of styles from the younger and fruitier to the aged versions, which are more complex and show dried fruits and nuts – more like a tawny Port style. VDNs can also be a touch more herbal, with light floral notes, when a seasoning of Muscat grapes is used. Delicious on its own or paired with chocolate-based desserts and red fruit compotes of morello cherries and poached strawberries, blackberries and raspberries. You might also like Maury, made close by, and Rasteau, plus the lighter, more amber-coloured Rivesaltes – all from France. Commandaria from Cyprus, Mavrodaphne from Greece and some fortified wines from Australia are similar in style too. For a dry red wine with similar full body and alcohol, try neighbouring Collioure and Châteauneuf-du-Pape.

MAURY

A commune in Roussillon that gives its name to full-bodied, fortified wines that are usually red, although rosé and whites are made too. Similar to ruby and late-bottled vintage ports, Maury dessert wines are made from Grenache grapes that thrive in this hot, windy region of southern France. In France, this style is called *vin doux naturel* (VDN: 'naturally sweet wine'), and is made by adding grape spirit during fermentation, leaving a full-bodied, fruity wine with reasonable tannin levels. Alcohol levels tend to be around 15–17% ABV – lower than for ports.

Like Port, there is a range of styles, from younger, tannic, fruitier, plummy wines to aged, complex, savoury examples full of dried fruits and roasted nuts plus a dash of cedar, coffee and chocolate. Maury VDNs are riper and more herbal than Port and are good on their own, but also lovely paired with figs and blue cheese, mince pies and dark, moist fruit or walnut cakes, or with a coffee and chocolate at the end of a meal. If you like this style, you could also try Banyuls, made close by, and Rasteau, also from France; Commandaria from Cyprus and Mavrodaphne from Greece, and some fortified wines from Australia are similar in style too. For a dry red wine with similar full body and alcohol, try the *sec* version of Maury, Châteauneuf-du-Pape, and its neighbouring appellations like Lirac. If you prefer nuts and liquorice flavours, try Pedro Ximénez Sherry.

Fortified

These wines come in a variety of colours ranging from pale-lemon to almost black, with sweetness levels ranging from bone-dry to sweet, and they offer a myriad of flavours, from lasting, fresh and fruity to lingering, deep, dark and viscous. Extra alcohol added during the production process changes the characteristics as well as increasing the alcohol in the final wine.

Sherry can only come from Jerez in southern Spain, and is made using mainly white Palomino grapes. Port can only come from the Douro Valley region of Portugal and is made using a blend of highly coloured red grapes local to the region. Similarly, Madeira can only come from the island after which it is named. A variety of styles is available in all these fortified wines because of the long history of winemaking in these regions. To help highlight and clarify the diversity of these wines, Sherry and Port in particular occupy more than one cell. Find out more for yourself by trying the diverse styles of fortified wines.

FINO SHERRY

Fino sherries are the pale-coloured, bone-dry, generally tangy and lip-smacking varieties, bursting with citrus notes like lemon juice and zest, pithy grapefruit and fresh, nutty almonds. Finos are made using a *solera*, a maturation system that creates complex blends of wines from different years. A special native Spanish yeast called *flor* helps imbue these zippy apéritifs with yeasty dough notes too. Typically alcohol is around 15% ABV. These light wines are fresh, designed to be consumed chilled soon after release, plus within a few days of opening; otherwise they become tired-tasting and dull. Winemakers also produce other styles of fino-based sherries. Fino sherries are sometimes salty, a good example being Manzanillas, which are finos that are produced closer to the Spanish coast. Manzanillas are the palest of the finos, and very tangy and saline in flavour because of their proximity to the sea. 'Pale cream' sherries are fino sherries that have been sweetened using concentrated grape juice. All of these lighter-styled sherries make a perfect accompaniment for salted almonds and tapas dishes and can stand up to really savoury, flavoursome meals with plenty of umami notes like fish and chips, as the tanginess of the wine makes taste buds water.

OLOROSO SHERRY

A deep, amber-coloured, walnutty, dry, dark-style of Sherry, olorosos are produced from the same white Palomino grapes that are used to make light styles such as fino. They start life as light still wines, which are fortified to around 17% ABV – a higher strength than for a fino Sherry. This kills the special protective blanket of Spanish Sherry yeast (*flor*). The wine is then left to mature in partially-full old barrels. This means oxygen works with the wine, gradually deepening the colour and creating flavours such as leather, toffee, spices and nuts; the wine becomes richer, quite full-bodied and weightier in the mouth. The longer the ageing, the more intense dried-fruit flavours that develop (think dates and figs), and alcohol levels increase to around 20% ABV or more. Winemakers also produce other styles of darker sherries. Amontillado sherries are a halfway mix between fino and oloroso. They have a touch more alcohol than finos and in flavour profile are halfway between pale fino and nutty oloroso with an amber hue. If sweetened, they are called 'medium Sherry'. Cream sherries are typically oloroso sherries sweetened with concentrated grape juice. These sweeter styles accompany fruit and walnut cakes, plus caramel and nut-based desserts such as pecan pie. Dry olorosos pair well with more meaty and savoury tapas and even pork stews and sausages and mash with rich onion gravy.

MADEIRA

This Portuguese island in the Atlantic Ocean gives its name to fortified wines that range in sweetness levels from dry, refreshing and nutty apéritifs to sweet, dried-fruit types that pair well with desserts such as Christmas cake and pudding – and all styles in between. So note that not all Madeiras are sweet. These often fragrant and nutty wines start life as a still wine that has Portuguese grape spirit added to it to bring the alcohol level to around 20% ABV. Next, and unusually, the wine is exposed to gentle heat for a long period (this would ruin most wine). Because the wines are stored in barrels, air enters, which oxidises the contents. Colours darken and flavours intensify to dried fruit, nuts, orange zest and coffee notes. This heating means a Madeira wine will keep for a reasonably long time without spoiling once opened (unlike most wines, which need to be consumed soon after opening) – handy for an intermittent tipple. Madeira styles vary from the sweeter, richer **Malmsey** and slightly less rich **Bual** to the drier **Sercial** and **Verdelho** for off-dry. These are also the names of the white grapes used to make each style of Madeira, so look for them on Madeira wine labels. The range of styles and their mouth-watering acidity makes Madeiras pair well with a variety of dishes. Added to gravy, they make a roast dinner taste extra-special. These wines work well with mushroom-based sauces, with sweeter styles complementing dark chocolate puddings, brownies, nutty flans and ice cream.

RUTHERGLEN MUSCAT

Rutherglen is a hot region in Victoria, Australia after which this sweet, amber-hued, fortified dessert wine is named. Muscat grapes are partially dried, or raisined, by leaving them hanging on the vines in the heat. Their pure, concentrated juice starts fermenting. Spirit is added during the fermentation process, which halts it, so natural sweetness remains. These 'stickies', as they are known, taste of raisins and ripe grapes, with floral flavours like rose petal, as well as fruit cake, Christmas pudding, citrus zest and sweet baking spice notes combined with a luscious, viscous texture. Alcohol is around 17% ABV. The youngest wines are most readily available and simplest in flavour. Other longer-aged styles are made by maturing in wood, usually under hot tin roofs, and also using a *solera* system (which blends wines of different ages, like in Sherry production). These are more intense and nuttier, with treacle tones and higher levels of alcohol. Serve chilled with mince pies, dark fruit cakes and matured cheeses. Try other sweet wines like Madeira, Tokaji or Vin Santo and maybe a tawny Port.

PEDRO XIMÉNEZ

The name of a white grape grown across Spain and used in Andalucia as 'the second' Sherry grape. It is used both to name and make this dark, rich, viscous, sweet Sherry, which is a complete contrast to other styles – hence it gets its own listing here. Pedro Ximénez, or PX, Sherry is made from sun-dried bunches of grapes left until they raisin. The concentrated remaining juice is partially fermented, then neutral high-alcohol spirit is added, which stops the process. The wine is matured in the *solera* system of barrels, which allows complex blending across years to create a consistent quality product with layers of flavours. Alcohol level is about 16% ABV. The result is an unctuously sweet, dark-brown wine, bursting with flavours of figs, dried fruits, molasses, citrus zest, marmalade, liquorice and prunes that evolve in the mouth as it is sipped. Deliciously intense when savoured on its own, drop by drop, or, classically, poured over vanilla ice cream.

RUBY PORT

A full-bodied, fruity, youthful, fortified, deep-red wine made in the Douro region of Portugal from a blend of robust, deeply coloured local grapes. It is aged for a relatively short time: two to three years in large oak vats. Rubies are straightforward, sweet, rich, red wines with flavours of concentrated, ripe, crunchy red plums and other berries, sometimes with a hint of flowers. Alcohol is around 20% ABV and can be more fiery than in tawny Port. Similarly tannins tend to be more noticeable. Reserve ports are comparable but are higher quality as they are aged for slightly longer. Fine rubies are more affordable and less complex. This Port style is released to be consumed rather than age further, and does not need to be decanted before drinking as the Port is filtered before bottling. See also Late-Bottled Vintage Ports. Good with nuts and chocolate puddings, plus the sweetness enhances salty food, including the classic Stilton cheese.

LATE-BOTTLED VINTAGE PORT

A full-bodied, tannic and complex sweet, fortified, deep-red wine made in Portugal. The deeply coloured red grapes are indigenous to the Douro River region. Late-bottled vintage (LBV) ports use a blend of grapes from a single declared vintage (year) only. This occurs only once every few years. Similar to the more prestigious vintage Port, LBVs spend much more time in large casks before being bottled; this makes them approachable to drink earlier, as the tannins soften and flavours integrate during this time. They are more affordable too. The sweetness comes from the grapes, which do not totally ferment due to the addition, or 'fortification', of the wine with high-strength neutral grape spirit. LBVs are richer, well-rounded and with more layers of flavour compared to ruby ports; they are also fruitier but less complex than vintage ports and without the nutty and savoury hints of a tawny Port. Alcohol, like other ports, is around 20% ABV. 'Traditional' on the label means it will need decanting before drinking; otherwise LBVs are ready to drink. Tannins can be high, but drink with hard cheeses or meat platters to round them out in the mouth, plus try with hot chocolate puddings. Sample also Banyuls and Maury.

TAWNY PORT

A rich, mellow style of medium to full-bodied sweet, fortified red wine that has been aged in large casks in the Douro region of Portugal, before being bottled ready to drink. Named after its classic reddish-tawny hue that fades further in older wines. The cask-ageing allows oxygen to permeate the wine: hence the faded colour and more nutty, dried-fruit, 'oxidative' flavours and aroma profile. Unlike vintage ports, tawnies do not need to be decanted, nor will they improve with keeping. They can be served cool – i.e. at 'cellar temperature' – with more flavours evolving as they warm in the mouth. Sweetness and alcohol are balanced by a soft, red fruitiness, nuts and fruit-cake spices and lingering flavours. Older tawnies are more about nuts, dried fruits, butterscotch and softer tannins but come with higher prices. Younger ones show fresher red fruits and are more affordable. A ten-year-old tawny is a mix of the two flavour profiles that please most. Alcohol is usually around 20% ABV. A good match for hard, nutty cheeses like manchego, salty nuts, and desserts made with chocolate, figs, baked oranges and crème brûlée, though the rarer, more expensive old categories are best savoured, sip by sip, on their own.

VINTAGE PORT

A full-bodied, tannic and complex fortified, deeply coloured, sweet, big red wine made in Portugal. Like all ports, the red grapes are indigenous to the Douro River region. For these vintage ports, grapes come from a single vintage (year) that is of an 'officially declared' high quality. This only occurs once every few years; for some years no vintage Port at all is made. The superior grapes are rapidly turned into a deeply coloured still red wine, but, before the fermentation is complete, a neutral brandy spirit is added to 'fortify' the wine. This halts the fermentation, resulting in a high-alcohol red wine that is naturally sweet, as some of the sugar from the grapes remains in the wine.

Vintage is the most concentrated of all ports. It spends only a couple of years in large casks before being bottled and left to mature, integrating and softening as it does so. It is this full-bodied style of Port that should age for years, even decades, before layers of red and dried fruits, chocolate and zesty, sweet spice all meld together and the tannins become velvety. The Port is only then ready to drink, and not until after decanting into another vessel without transferring the sediment that has built up during the maturation process. This decanting softens the wine further. Alcohol, like other ports, is around 20% ABV. Tannins can be high, especially when drunk too young. Traditionally drunk after dinner, this special-occasion beverage should not be rushed so as to appreciate its many layers, texture and length of flavour.

Further reading

Sources of sipping information are readily accessible. There is plenty on the Internet, as well as apps to help you find out about individual wines, plus sections in most newspapers and magazines, often with topical recommendations or good offers to try. The more you combine tasting with reference, the deeper your interest and knowledge will become. Many of the references mentioned have helped with this book; some are included as further signposts for additional places to look.

Books

These are brilliant for beginners as they recommend specific bottles of wine to try from particular areas of the world:

500 White Wines by Natasha Hughes and Patricia Langton
500 Red Wines by Christine Austin
Wine & Spirit Education Trust books, from beginners to advanced levels. Plus the Trust runs all sorts of courses, from tastings for beginners to serious wine enthusiasts.
Wine Grapes by Jancis Robinson, Julia Harding and José Vouillamoz. This is a superb book, geeky and bursting with detail about 1,368 individual wine varieties, their history and characteristics. More grapes than you'll ever need to know about! One for the real enthusiasts.

Websites

Many retailers, like supermarkets and specialist independents, have a really informative website. Some include large amounts of free helpful information over and above a snappy description of the wine. A number offer courses or tastings, and if you are passing, they all have helpful staff that will be only too glad to talk to you about wine.

bbr.com – London-based Berry Bros. & Rudd, wine merchant and fine wine specialists,

tanners-wines.co.uk – Tanners Wine Merchants, mainly borders and Wales-based outlets.

waitrosecellar.com – Features a wider selection of wine to order than available in the stores.

tesco.com – Buy wine as a grocery item or see the wine-by-the-case section. Tesco also has a wine magazine and runs tasting fairs.

majestic.co.uk – Wine merchant, plus sign up to the magazine blog or visit for free tastings and courses.

sainsburys.co.uk – Go to the drinks section.

Other supermarkets, like Asda, The Cooperative and Morrisons, all have information about wine too; look at one with a store near you.

wine-searcher.com – Provides the latest wine news and prices plus information about regions and grape varieties.

winefolly.com – A good way to learn about wine supported by fabulous clear pictures.

decanter.com – Dedicated to wine, includes a magazine, fairs, tastings and trips.

thewinesociety.com – You can join The Wine Society to have access to good wine at good prices; viewing the informative website is free.

jancisrobinson.com – Offers a wealth of information about wine, grapes, regions and tasting notes. Some is free; paying to join gives you access to a long history of articles and comment. Robinson has collaborated with Hugh Johnson to write *The World Atlas of Wine*, which can be viewed via the site too.

Many wine regions have their own websites to guide you through the grapes, history and characteristics of the area:

bordeaux.com
bourgogne-wines.com

vinsvaldeloire.fr
vinhoverde.pt/en/vinhoverde
winesfromspainuk.com
winesofportugal.info
discovercaliforniawines.co.uk
languedoc-wines.com
rhone-wines.com
wineaustralia.com
austrianwine.com

Look for logos indicating that a wine has been judged an International Wine & Spirit Competition (IWSC) and/or an International Wine Challenge (IWC) medal-winner.

Index

Acknowledgements

I would like to thank the following people who have inspired me along the way: The Wine & Spirit Education Trust (WSET), Michelle Cherutti-Kowal, Anne McHale, Nina Cerullo, Godfrey Spence, Christopher Donaldson, Andrew Jefford, Michael Walpole and Emma Symington. With special thanks to Rosie Reynolds and Laura Higginson, plus the team at Ebury, without whom this project would not have come to fruition.

A toast to you all.